THE CAMBRIDGE HANDBOOK OF FACIAL RECOGNITION IN THE MODERN STATE

In situations ranging from border control to policing and welfare, governments are using automated facial recognition technology (FRT) to collect taxes, prevent crime, police cities, and control immigration. FRT involves the processing of a person's facial image, usually for identification, categorisation, or counting. This ambitious handbook brings together a diverse group of legal, computer, communications, and social and political science scholars to shed light on how FRT has been developed, used by public authorities, and regulated in different jurisdictions across five continents. Informed by their experiences working on FRT across the globe, chapter authors analyse the increasing deployment of FRT in public and private life. The collection argues for the passage of new laws, rules, frameworks, and approaches to prevent harms of FRT in the modern state and advances the debate on scrutiny of power and accountability of public authorities which use FRT. This book is also available as Open Access on Cambridge Core.

Rita Matulionyte is an associate professor at Macquarie University Law School and a senior fellow at the Lithuanian Centre for Social Sciences. An international expert in intellectual property and technology law, she has published over sixty papers in the field and co-authored commissioned reports to the European Patent Office and the governments of South Korea and Australia.

Monika Zalnieriute is a senior lecturer (associate professor) at the University of New South Wales, Sydney; and a senior fellow at the Lithuanian Centre for Social Sciences. Her research on law and technology has been translated to German, Russian and Mandarin, and is widely drawn upon by scholars and organisations such as the Council of Europe, the World Bank, the European Parliament, and WHO. She is the co-editor of *Money, Power and AI* (Cambridge, 2023).

The Cambridge Handbook of Facial Recognition in the Modern State

Edited by

RITA MATULIONYTE

Macquarie University and the Lithuanian Centre for Social Sciences

MONIKA ZALNIERIUTE

The University of New South Wales and the
Lithuanian Centre for Social Sciences

Shaftesbury Road, Cambridge CB2 8EA, United Kingdom

One Liberty Plaza, 20th Floor, New York, NY 10006, USA

477 Williamstown Road, Port Melbourne, VIC 3207, Australia

314–321, 3rd Floor, Plot 3, Splendor Forum, Jasola District Centre, New Delhi – 110025, India

103 Penang Road, #05–06/07, Visioncrest Commercial, Singapore 238467

Cambridge University Press is part of Cambridge University Press & Assessment, a department of the University of Cambridge.

We share the University's mission to contribute to society through the pursuit of education, learning and research at the highest international levels of excellence.

www.cambridge.org
Information on this title: www.cambridge.org/9781009321198

DOI: 10.1017/9781009321211

© Cambridge University Press & Assessment 2024

This work is in copyright. It is subject to statutory exceptions and to the provisions of relevant licensing agreements; with the exception of the Creative Commons version the link for which is provided below, no reproduction of any part of this work may take place without the written permission of Cambridge University Press.

An online version of this work is published at doi.org/10.1017/9781009321211 under a Creative Commons Open Access license CC-BY-NC-ND 4.0 which permits re-use, distribution and reproduction in any medium for non-commercial purposes providing appropriate credit to the original work is given. You may not distribute derivative works without permission. To view a copy of this license, visit https://creativecommons.org/licenses/by-nc-nd/4.0

All versions of this work may contain content reproduced under license from third parties. Permission to reproduce this third-party content must be obtained from these third-parties directly.

When citing this work, please include a reference to the DOI 10.1017/9781009321211

First published 2024

A catalogue record for this publication is available from the British Library

A Cataloging-in-Publication data record for this book is available from the Library of Congress

ISBN 978-1-009-32119-8 Hardback

Cambridge University Press & Assessment has no responsibility for the persistence or accuracy of URLs for external or third-party internet websites referred to in this publication and does not guarantee that any content on such websites is, or will remain, accurate or appropriate.

Contents

List of Figures	*page* ix	
List of Contributors	xi	
Acknowledgements	xix	

Introduction: Facial Recognition in the Modern State   1
Rita Matulionyte and Monika Zalnieriute

PART I FACIAL RECOGNITION TECHNOLOGY IN CONTEXT: TECHNICAL AND LEGAL CHALLENGES

1   **Facial Recognition Technology: Key Issues and Emerging Concerns**   11
Neil Selwyn, Mark Andrejevic, Chris O'Neill, Xin Gu, and Gavin Smith

2   **Facial Recognition Technologies 101: Technical Insights**   29
Ali Akbari

3   **FRT in 'Bloom': Beyond Single Origin Narratives**   44
Simon Michael Taylor

4   **Transparency of Facial Recognition Technology and Trade Secrets**   60
Rita Matulionyte

5   **Privacy's Loose Grip on Facial Recognition: Law and the Operational Image**   74
Jake Goldenfein

6   **Facial Recognition Technology and Potential for Bias and Discrimination**   87
Marcus Smith and Monique Mann

vi   *Contents*

7   Power and Protest: Facial Recognition and Public Space Surveillance   96
Monika Zalnieriute

8   Faces of War: Russia's Invasion of Ukraine and Military Use of Facial Recognition Technology   112
Agne Limante

PART II FACIAL RECOGNITION TECHNOLOGY ACROSS THE GLOBE: JURISDICTIONAL PERSPECTIVES

9   Government Use of Facial Recognition Technologies under European Law   127
Simone Kuhlmann

10   European Biometric Surveillance, Concrete Rules, and Uniform Enforcement: Beyond Regulatory Abstraction and Local Enforcement   139
Paul De Hert and Georgios Bouchagiar

11   Lawfulness and Police Use of Facial Recognition in the United Kingdom: Article 8 ECHR and *Bridges v. South Wales Police*   155
Nora Ni Loideain

12   Does Big Brother Exist? Facial Recognition Technology in the United Kingdom   173
Giulia Gentile

13   Facial Recognition Technologies in the Public Sector: Observations from Germany   186
Andreas Engel

14   A Central-Eastern Europe Perspective on FRT Regulation: A Case Study of Lithuania   198
Eglė Kavoliūnaitė-Ragauskienė

15   An Overview of Facial Recognition Technology Regulation in the United States   214
Mailyn Fidler and Justin (Gus) Hurwitz

16   Regulating Facial Recognition in Brazil: Legal and Policy Perspectives   228
Luca Belli, Walter Britto Gaspar, and Nicolo Zingales

Contents   vii

17 **FRT Regulation in China**   242
Jyh-An Lee and Peng Zhou

18 **Principled Regulation of Facial Recognition Technology: A View from Australia and New Zealand**   253
Nessa Lynch and Liz Campbell

19 **Morocco's Governance of Cities and Borders: AI-Enhanced Surveillance, Facial Recognition, and Human Rights**   267
Sylvia I. Bergh, Issam Cherrat, Francesco Colin, Katharina Natter, and Ben Wagner

Figures

2.1	AI system life cycle	*page*	32
2.2	AI system key components		35
2.3	AI versus ML		37
2.4	Symbolic AI versus ML		38

Contributors

Ali Akbari is a leading industry expert with a PhD from Tokyo Institute of Technology, specialising in computer vision and NLP. He has 20 years of experience in various industries delivering successful AI solutions for market leaders such as KPMG, Australian Dep. of Home Affairs, Kansai Airport, Commonwealth Bank, and many East Asian semiconductor manufacturers. Actively advocating safe and ethical AI, currently Ali is director of AI practice at Gradient Institute and represents Australian Institute of Company Directors on the National AI Committee of Standards Australia.

Mark Andrejevic is Professor of Media and Communication at Monash University and a chief investigator at the Australian Research Council Centre of Excellence for Automated Decision-Making and Society. Andrejevic is particularly interested in social forms of sorting and automated decision-making associated with the online economy. He writes about digital technologies from a socio-cultural perspective, and his current research interests encompass digital media, surveillance, and data mining. With Neil Selwyn, Andrejevic is co-author of *Facial Recognition* (Polity, 2022).

Luca Belli is Professor of Digital Governance and Regulation at the Getulio Vargas Foundation Law School, Rio de Janeiro, where he directs the Center for Technology and Society and the CyberBRICS project. Luca is also Editor of the *International Data Privacy Law Journal*, published by Oxford University Press, a board member of the Alliance for Affordable Internet and Director of the Latin-American Computers, Privacy and Data Protection conference. He is the author of more than fifty publications, which have been quoted by numerous media outlets, including *The Economist*, the *Financial Times*, *Forbes*, *Le Monde*, the BBC, *China Today*, the *Beijing Review*, *The Hill*, *O Globo*, and *Folha*.

Sylvia I. Bergh is a senior researcher at the Research Group Multilevel Regulation and the Centre of Expertise on Global and Inclusive Learning at The Hague University of Applied Sciences. She also holds the position of Associate Professor in Development Management and Governance at the International Institute of Social Studies, Erasmus University Rotterdam. She completed a MPhil in modern Middle Eastern studies and a DPhil in development studies, both at the University of Oxford. Sylvia has published widely on state–society relations in the Middle East and North Africa.

Georgios Bouchagiar is a doctoral researcher in criminal law and technology at the University of Luxembourg and the Free University of Brussels. He holds a law degree (Athens Law School, 2011), a Master of Science degree in information technology (High Honours, Ionian School of Informatics and Information Science, 2018) and a Master of Laws degree in law and technology (with Distinction, Tilburg Institute for Law, Technology, and Society 2019). Since 2018, his professional experience has included tutoring and lecturing on information law and general principles of law, and research on information law, distributed ledger technology, and face recognition and spying technologies.

Liz Campbell is the inaugural Francine McNiff Chair of Criminal Jurisprudence at Monash University Law School, having previously been Professor of Criminal Law at Durham University. She is Adjunct Professor at Queensland University of Technology School of Justice and University College Cork. Professor Campbell is an expert in corporate crime, organised crime, corruption, and biometric evidence, and an appointed member of the UK Home Office Biometrics and Forensics Ethics Group. Previously she chaired Durham Constabulary's Ethics Committee and served on the National Health Service Research Ethics Committee (Scotland).

Issam Cherrat is an Emerging Research Affiliate at the Center for Applied Research in Conflict Transformation (CARiCT), and an independent consultant. Issam worked extensively on local development, governance, community mobilization, youth engagement and empowerment with local and international NGOs. Issam holds a Master's degree in International Politics and Security Studies from Bradford University, United Kingdom, and a Certificate in Peace from the Hiroshima University, Japan.

Francesco Colin is a PhD researcher at the International Institute of Social Studies and an associate fellow at the Moroccan Institute for Policy Analysis in Rabat. His doctoral research focuses on civic engagement and active citizenship through local petitions in Morocco. He collaborates with different research projects on political participation, social accountability, decentralisation, and the impact of technology on local governance. Prior to his research activities, Francesco graduated from the Erasmus Mundus Joint Master Degree 'Crossing the Mediterranean: Towards Investment and Integration' and worked for the Heinrich Böll Foundation in Rabat as a junior expert in the democratisation component.

List of Contributors

Andreas Engel (Dr iur, LLM. (Yale)) is a lecturer at Heidelberg University. He is interested in the law's reaction to digitalisation and in this context has recently been working on data protection law, intellectual property, AI, and cyber-security. A second focus of his research is the field of private international law, on which he wrote his doctoral dissertation at the Max Planck Institute for Comparative and International Private Law in Hamburg. Dr Engel has studied law at Ludwig Maximilian University of Munich, New College, Oxford, and Yale Law School and clerked at the German Constitutional Court.

Mailyn Fidler is an assistant professor at the University of New Hampshire Franklin Pierce School of Law. Her research focuses on the intersection of criminal law, technology, and speech. Her current projects look at changing technology and the Fourth Amendment, speech at 'non-standard' moments of the criminal process, and the regulation of cyber-security. She teaches criminal law, criminal procedure, cyber-security, and copyright. Previously, she clerked on the Tenth Circuit Court of Appeals, served as the Tech & First Amendment Fellow at the Reporters Committee for Freedom of the Press, and was a fellow at the Berkman Klein Center for Internet & Society at Harvard University.

Walter Britto Gaspar is a researcher at the Centre for Technology and Society at Fundação Getulio Vargas Law School. He is a PhD student in the Public Policies, Economy and Development programme at the Federal University of Rio de Janeiro and holds a Master's degree in public health from the Social Medicine Institute at the Rio de Janeiro State University. He has been the National Coordinator of Universities Allied for Essential Medicines in Brazil, worked in research projects with Fiocruz and the Shuttleworth Foundation, among others, and published books and book chapters on the overlap between science, technology, and innovation in society.

Giulia Gentile is Fellow in Law at the London School of Economics (LSE). Her research interests lie in European Union (EU) constitutional law, the protection of EU citizens' rights in the post-Brexit era, and the promotion of human rights within the digital environment. Dr Gentile joined LSE Law School in 2021, having previously worked as Lecturer and Postdoctoral Researcher at Maastricht University and as Visiting Lecturer at King's College London. She holds a PhD and LLM from King's College London and an LLB/MA from the University of Naples Federico II.

Jake Goldenfein is a senior lecturer at Melbourne Law School and a chief investigator in the Australian Research Council Centre of Excellence for Automated Decision-Making and Society. Jake writes about how law constructs the data economy, platform regulation, digital surveillance and facial recognition, and the governance of automated decision-making. Prior to his appointment at Melbourne Law School, he was a postdoctoral researcher at the Digital Life Initiative at Cornell Tech. He is the author of *Monitoring Laws: Profiling and Identity in the World State* (Cambridge University Press, 2019).

Xin Gu is Senior Lecturer in the School of Media, Film and Journalism at Monash University. She is an expert appointed under the United Nations Educational, Scientific and Cultural Organization 2005 Convention on the Protection and Promotion of the Expression of Cultural Diversity. She has published widely on urban creative clusters and agglomerations, cultural work, creative entrepreneurship, cultural and creative industries policy, media cities, maker culture, and cyber-culture. Her recent publications include *Red Creatives* (Intellect, 2020), *Re-imagining Creative Cities in Twenty-First Century Asia* (Palgrave Macmillan 2020) and 'Media Capital and Digital Media Cities in Asia' (in *Media in Asia*, Routledge, 2022).

Paul De Hert is a professor of law at the Free University of Brussels and associated professor at Tilburg University. His work addresses problems in privacy and technology, human rights, and criminal law. Professor De Hert is Vice-Dean of the Faculty, Director of the Research Group on Human Rights, and former Director of the Research Group on Law, Science, Technology & Society, and of the Department of Interdisciplinary Studies of Law. He is a board member of several Belgian, Dutch, and other international scientific journals, such as the *Computer Law & Security Review*, the *New Journal of European Criminal Law*, and *Criminal Law & Philosophy*.

Justin (Gus) Hurwitz is Senior Fellow and Academic Director of the Center for Technology, Innovation, and Competition at the University of Pennsylvania. He is also the Director of Law & Economics Programs at the International Center for Law & Economics and was previously Professor of Law and Founding Director of the Governance & Technology Center at the University of Nebraska. His work draws on his background in law, economics, and computer science to study the relationship between technology and society.

Eglė Kavoliūnaitė-Ragauskienė is a researcher at the Lithuanian Centre for Social Sciences. Since 2002 she has authored over thirty research papers and has worked on a wide range of issues in legal regulation, public administration, and policy making, including the Public Accountability Mechanisms Initiative (World Bank, 2010); the Global Integrity Report 2008 (Global Integrity, 2008); as EU Profiler (Roman Schuman Centre for Advanced Studies, European University Institute, 2009); and EUandI (European University Institute, 2014). Dr Kavoliūnaitė-Ragauskienė provided training to law enforcement officials under the Rising of the Anticorruption System project (Warsaw, Poland, 2013–2014).

Simone Kuhlmann is a postdoctoral researcher at the Centre of Law in Digital Transformation at the Law Faculty of the University of Hamburg. After she graduated from the University of Göttingen, Dr Kuhlmann worked as a research assistant to the Chair of Public Law, Media and Telecommunication Law at the Law Faculty of the University of Hamburg, as well as at the law firm Taylor Wessing in the technology, media, and telecoms practice area. Her research focuses on knowledge

List of Contributors

generation based on data, in particular in the context of health care and security concerns, as well as on media law and public law.

Jyh-An Lee is Professor and Executive Director of the Centre for Legal Innovation and Digital Society at the Chinese University of Hong Kong Faculty of Law. He is an expert in intellectual property law and information law. Professor Lee has been appeared on ABC News, BBC News, and Bloomberg News, and been featured in the *Financial Times*, *Fortune*, the *South China Morning Post*, and the *Wall Street Journal* as an expert on intellectual property and internet law. His work on intellectual property has been cited by the US Court of Appeals for the Fifth Circuit and the UK High Court of Justice.

Agne Limante is a chief researcher at the Law Institute of the Lithuanian Centre for Social Sciences. She received an MA in EU law from King's College London (awarded with the Prize for Best MA Dissertation in EU Law) and a PhD from Vilnius University. Dr Limante is an expert in human rights and has authored several publications in this area. Since receiving her PhD, Dr Limante has published over forty papers, including articles in national and international journals and book chapters. Dr Limante also has extensive experience working in international teams and conducting comparative research.

Nora Ni Loideain holds BA, LLB, and LLM degrees from the National University of Ireland (Galway) and a PhD from the University of Cambridge. She is Director and Senior Lecturer in Law at the Information Law & Policy Centre, Institute of Advanced Legal Studies, University of London. Her research focuses on European human rights law, EU law, and data protection. In 2019, she was appointed to the UK Home Office Biometrics and Forensics Ethics Group. She is an editor of the journal *International Data Privacy Law* and author of the forthcoming monograph *EU Data Privacy Law and Serious Crime* (Oxford University Press).

Nessa Lynch is an associate professor in the Faculty of Law, Te Herenga Waka–Victoria University of Wellington. Her expertise is in youth justice, sentencing, and biometrics and state surveillance, particularly FRT. In 2019/2020, she led a Law Foundation-funded team which produced a report, *Facial Recognition Technology – Towards a Legal and Ethical Framework*, which has directly influenced government policy and public awareness of the risks and benefits of the technology in New Zealand. Recently she carried out an independent review of the use and potential use of FRT by New Zealand Police.

Monique Mann is a senior lecturer in criminology and a member of the Alfred Deakin Institute for Citizenship and Globalisation at Deakin University, and an adjunct researcher with the Law, Science, Technology and Society Research Centre at the Free University of Brussels. Dr Mann's research focuses on new technology for policing and surveillance, human rights and social justice, and governance and regulation. She is the author of *Politicising and Policing Organised Crime* (Routledge, 2020) and *Biometrics, Crime and Security* (Routledge, 2018) and the editor of *Good Data* (Institute of Network Cultures, 2019). She is Vice Chair of the Australian Privacy Foundation and Vice President of Liberty Victoria.

Rita Matulionyte is an associate professor at Macquarie University Law School, a senior fellow at the Lithuanian Centre for Social Science, and an affiliate at the Australian Research Council Centre of Excellence for Automated Decision-Making and Society. She is an international expert in intellectual property and technology law, with her most recent research focusing on legal and governance issues surrounding AI technologies. Rita has had over fifty research papers published by leading international publishers and has co-authored commissioned reports for the European Patent Office and the governments of South Korea and Australia.

Katharina Natter is an assistant professor at the Institute of Political Science at Leiden University. She researches migration politics from a comparative perspective, with a particular focus on the role of democratisation and autocratisation in immigration policy-making and has worked on European migration policies and on the link between migration and development. Assistant Professor Natter received her PhD in political sociology from the University of Amsterdam in 2019. Prior to that, she worked at the International Migration Institute (University of Oxford) and studied comparative politics at Sciences Po.

Chris O'Neill is a research fellow in the School of Media and Communication at Monash University and a postdoctoral research fellow in the Australian Research Council Centre of Excellence for Automated Decision-Making and Society. Chris completed his PhD at the University of Melbourne in 2020. His doctoral research examined the analysis of body-sensing technologies, such as heart rate monitors and productivity sensors. Chris's current research involves analysing the social and operational issues arising from the deployment of automated decision-making systems, including biometric technologies such as facial recognition cameras.

Neil Selwyn is a professor at the School of Education, Culture & Society, Monash University, having previously worked in the University College London Institute of Education and the Cardiff School of Social Sciences. His research and teaching focuses on the place of digital media in everyday life and the sociology of technology (non-)use in educational settings. He is currently working on nationally funded projects examining the roll-out of educational data and learning analytics, AI technologies, and the changing nature of teachers' digital work. With Mark Andrejevic, Selwyn is co-author of *Facial Recognition* (Polity, 2022).

Gavin Smith is an associate professor in the School of Sociology at the Australian National University, having previously worked at the University of Sydney and City University London. Much of Gavin's research focuses on the social impacts of digital technologies, data practices, and dataveillance – with a particular interest in the social impacts of surveillance, specifically looking at the intersubjective meanings ascribed to everyday practices of watching and being watched, be that through CCTV camera surveillance systems or social media cultures. Gavin is the author of *Opening the Black Box: The Work of Watching* (Routledge, 2014).

Marcus Smith is an associate professor of law at Charles Sturt University in Canberra. His qualifications include an MPhil from the University of Cambridge and LLM and PhD degrees from the Australian National University. Prior to entering academia, he worked in a range of Australian government research and policy agencies. He currently undertakes research and teaching across the field of technology law and regulation but has a particular interest in law and policy associated with biometrics. His publications include thirty academic articles and five books, most recently, *Technology Law* (Cambridge University Press, 2021) and *Biometric Identification, Law and Ethics* (Springer, 2021).

Simon Michael Taylor is a 2023–24 Visiting Fellow at the School of Regulation and Global Governance, the Australian National University. As a Science & Technology Studies scholar he interrogates infrastructural and genealogical dimensions that constitute autonomous decision systems. This includes data and digital elements from biometrics, machine learning, operational sensing, and autonomous drones. As a committee member of Standards Australia he has contributed to working groups on Artificial Intelligence and to policy on Cyber-Security, the Internet of Things, Privacy, and digital identity fields. Publications include articles for a special law issue of AI & Society (2020), for Science, Technology & Human Values (2022), and in a collection edited by members of the Mellon Sawyer Seminar Histories of AI: A Genealogy of Power for Cambridge University.

Ben Wagner is Assistant Professor at the Faculty of Technology, Policy and Management at Delft University of Technology, as well as Professor of Media, Technology and Society and Director of the Sustainable Media Lab at Inholland University of Applied Sciences. His research focuses on the governance of socio-legal systems, in particular human rights in digital technologies, and designing more accountable decision-support systems. He is a visiting researcher at the Human Centred Computing Group at Oxford University, an advisory board member of the data science journal *Patterns*, and is on the International Scientific Committee of the UK Research and Innovation Trustworthy Autonomous Systems Hub.

Monika Zalnieriute is a Senior Lecturer (Associate Professor) at the University of New South Wales, Sydney; and a Senior Fellow at the Lithuanian Centre for Social Sciences. Monika is also an Australian Research Council DECRA Fellow and Associate Investigator at the Australian Research Council Centre of Excellence for Automated Decision-Making and Society. Her research on law and technology has been translated to German, Russian and Mandarin, and is widely drawn upon by scholars and organisations such as the Council of Europe, the

World Bank, the European Parliament, and WHO. She is the co-editor of Money, Power and AI (CUP 2023).

Peng Zhou is a PhD student at the Faculty of Law of the Chinese University of Hong Kong (CUHK). Dr Zhou holds a PhD in Art History from CUHK. He also has a Master of Music from Yale University and a Bachelor of Music from Oberlin College, USA. Before joining the CUHK Faculty of Law, Zhou had practiced law in the People's Republic of China. His current research includes a comparative analysis of data protection and AI governance laws, focusing on machine ethics and China's digital governance.

Nicolo Zingales is Professor of Information Law and Regulation at the Getulio Vargas Foundation in Rio de Janeiro, where he heads the e-commerce research group. His work on digital rights spans data governance, fundamental rights, and platform regulation. He is a founding member of the MyData Global Network, a director of the Computers Privacy and Data Protection Conference (Latin-American edition), and a member of the Medialaws Steering Committee. He is also an affiliate scholar at the Stanford Center for Internet and Society, the Tilburg Institute for Law, Technology and Society, and the Tilburg Law and Economics Center.

Acknowledgements

This book is the outcome of the project 'Government Use of Facial Recognition Technologies: Legal Issues and Possible Solutions', funded by the Lithuanian Research Council (2021–2023, agreement number S-MIP-21-38). We sincerely thank our co-investigators in this project, Dr Agnė Limantė and Dr Eglė Kavoliūnaitė-Ragauskienė, for their invaluable co-operation and collaboration in working towards the objectives of this project.

The papers published in this book were first presented at the Facial Recognition in the Modern State international conference, which took place on 15 September 2022 (online); this was organised by the Law Institute of the Lithuanian Centre for Social Sciences and co-hosted by Macquarie University Law School, the University of New South Wales, the Australian Research Council's Centre for Automated Decision-Making and Society, the LSE Law School, the Internet Governance Project at George Tech, the Centre for Law in the Digital Transformation at the University of Hamburg, and the University of New South Wales Allens Hub. We sincerely thank the organisers and the co-hosts of this conference for contributing to the success of this event, as well as all presenters at the conference for their insightful and highly engaging presentations.

Most of all we express our gratitude to all the thirty-two contributors who wrote chapters for this book. We are grateful for them sharing their knowledge and insights on this topic and appreciate the hard work involved in writing the chapters. We thank you for your patience and co-operation in finalising the manuscript of this book.

We hope the book will contribute to the important international discussion on the challenges posed by automatic facial recognition technologies, how they have been managed so far in different national and regional jurisdictions around the world, and how the regulation of these controversial technologies could look like in the future.

Introduction

Facial Recognition in the Modern State

Rita Matulionyte and Monika Zalnieriute

I.1 FACIAL RECOGNITION AND ITS CHALLENGES

From border control to policing and welfare, governments are using automated facial recognition technology (FRT) to collect taxes, prevent crime, police cities, and control immigration. 70 per cent of police forces have access to some form of the technology and 60 per cent of countries have facial recognition in some airports.[1] In Australia, France, the United Kingdom, Germany, the Netherlands and the United States, it has been employed by border security at the arrival gates.[2] It has been used or trialled in national policing efforts to detect suspects or missing people in various countries.[3] FRT is increasingly used by governments for identity verification and identification, as well as categorisation or counting.

Concerns around an increased use of automated FRT, especially in public spaces such as airports, train stations, and city streets, have been expressed across the globe. Privacy and data protection, bias and discrimination, the lack of transparency, explainability, public oversight, and accountability are among the most popular concerns associated with FRT. Freedom of expression, peaceful association, and assembly are other examples of the fundamental rights that can be impacted and undermined by

---

[1] Paul Bischoff, 'Facial recognition technology (FRT): 100 countries analyzed' (8 June 2021), Comparitech, www.comparitech.com/blog/vpn-privacy/facial-recognition-statistics/#:~:text=Five%20countries.

[2] Ibid.

[3] Australia: E. Gillespie, 'Are you being scanned? How facial recognition technology follows you, even as you shop' (4 March 2019), *The Guardian*, www.theguardian.com/technology/2019/feb/24/are-you-being-scanned-how-facial-recognition-technology-follows-you-even-as-you-shop; Canada: Office of the Privacy Commissioner of Canada (OPC), 'Police use of facial recognition technology in Canada and the way forward' (10 June 2021), www.priv.gc.ca/en/opc-actions-and-decisions/ar_index/202021/sr_rcmp/; Italy: European Digital Rights (EDRi), 'Italy introduces a moratorium on video surveillance systems that use facial recognition' (15 December 2021), https://edri.org/our-work/italy-introduces-a-moratorium-on-video-surveillance-systems-that-use-facial-recognition/; France: Statewatch, 'Legal action against police facial recognition technology' (22 September 2020), www.statewatch.org/news/2020/september/france-legal-action-against-police-facial-recognition-technology/; United Kingdom: Rhiannon Williams, 'UK police forces testing new retrospective facial recognition that could identify criminals' (31 July 2021), *i news*, https://inews.co.uk/news/technology/uk-police-testing-retrospective-facial-recognition-identify-criminals-1128711.

FRT. These risks have been recognised both by courts and policymakers alike. For instance, the UK police use of automated FRT was successfully challenged in 2020 in the *Bridges* case, where the Court of Appeal of England and Wales held that police use of automated FRT was unlawful because it was not 'in accordance with law' under Article 8 of the European Convention of Human Rights.[4]

Ethical and legal risks of FRT have led many non-governmental organisations (NGOs), professional organizations, local municipalities, and legislators around the globe to call for regulation or even outright bans on FRT use. In the United States, FRT use was initially suspended in a number of the states, with some of the temporary bans being recently lifted.[5] In the EU, the draft EU Artificial Intelligence Act suggests that law enforcement could be allowed to use live FRT in certain exceptional scenarios,[6] while the European Parliament has called for an outright ban of certain FRT uses.[7] Recent cases in China to a certain extent limited FRT uses by the private sector,[8] while an extensive employment of FRT by government remains intact. Regional and international organizations, such as the European Data Protection Authority, World Economic Forum, and Interpol developed specific guidelines on how FRT should be used in law enforcement context.[9]

However, regulatory solutions are lagging behind. Owing to the controversy of the technology and multiple competing interests, there is yet no country that has a comprehensive legal framework regulating the use of FRT by states. Policymakers around the world are struggling to find the most suitable regulatory solutions to both enable the beneficial uses of facial recognition and manage threats posed by these technologies.

Academic literature on FRT is expanding, with legal literature mostly focussing on privacy and data protection implications of FRT.[10] Previous books on AI and law in general touch upon some of the issues this book covers, such as transparency, discrimination and privacy issues of AI, however, they lack a specific focus

---

[4] *R (Bridges)* v. *South Wales Police* [2019] EWHC 2341, High Court; [2020] EWCA Civ 1058, Court of Appeal.

[5] P. Dave, 'U.S. cities are backing off banning facial recognition as crime rises' (13 May 2022), *Reuters*, www.reuters.com/world/us/us-cities-are-backing-off-banning-facial-recognition-crime-rises-2022-05-12/.

[6] European Commission, 'Proposal for a Regulation of the European Parliament and of the Council laying down harmonised rules on artificial intelligence (Artificial Intelligence Act) and amending certain Union legislative Acts' (2021), COM, 206 Final.

[7] European Parliament, 'Report on artificial intelligence in criminal law and its use by the police and judicial authorities in criminal matters' (2021) (Report-A9-0232/2021).

[8] See *Guo Bing v. Hangzhou Safari Park Co.*, Ltd., Hangzhou Fuyang District People's Court Case No. (2019) Zhe 0111 Minchu 6971, 20 November 2020.

[9] World Economic Forum, UNICRI, INTERPOL, Netherlands Police, 'A policy framework for responsible limits on facial recognition' (2022); European Data Protection Board (EDPB), 'Guidelines 05/2022 on the use of facial recognition technology in the area of law enforcement', version 1 (12 May 2022), https://edpb.europa.eu/system/files/2022-05/edpb-guidelines_202205_frtlawenforcement_en_1.pdf.

[10] See, e.g., M. N. Harnois, *Facial Recognition Technology: Best Practices, Future Uses and Privacy Concerns* (Nova Science, 2013); E. J. Kindt, *Privacy and Data Protection Issues of Biometric Application* (Springer, 2013).

Introduction 3

on FRT.[11] Books dealing specifically with FRT examine isolated legal issues related to FRT such as privacy and data protection,[12] or legal challenges posed by FRT in specific jurisdictions.[13] Authors in disciplines other than law track technological progress in FRT and detail its uses globally,[14] analyse the technological limitations of these technologies,[15] or its challenges in specific government sectors, such as the criminal justice system.[16] However, there is currently no book in law that offers an international comparative examination of legal challenges and regulatory initiatives targeting FRT in jurisdictions around the globe. FRT raises similar legal and ethical challenges around the world, and thus a global discussion and exchange of lessons learned and best practices are needed to inform national and regional policy discussions and regulation of FRT. Moreover, there is still a lack of interdisciplinary discussions where law, technology, and social and political science academics share and exchange their insights on how to approach challenges posed by facial recognition technologies.

I.2 THE AIM AND ORIGIN OF THIS BOOK

This book aims to provide the first in-depth socio-legal analysis and international comparison of government use of FRT across domestic and regional jurisdictions in five regions of the globe (Europe, North America, South America, Asia-Pacific, and Africa). Building on comparative legal methods, qualitative interviews, political theory, and case studies, the book examines how FRT is increasingly used by different governments, what legal and ethical challenges different FRT uses raise, and whether legal and governance frameworks that have been implemented or proposed by various stakeholders to address these challenges in diverse jurisdictions are adequate and appropriate.

---

[11] See, e.g., W. Barfield (ed.), *Cambridge Handbook on the Law of Algorithms* (Cambridge University Press, 2021); S. Chesterman, *We, the Robots? Regulating Artificial Intelligence and the Limits of the Law* (Cambridge University Press, 2021); R. Abbott, *The Reasonable Robot: Artificial Intelligence and the Law* (Cambridge University Press, 2020); M. Ebers and S. Navas (eds.), *Algorithms and Law* (Cambridge University Press, 2020); J. De Bruyne and C. Vanleenhove (eds.), *Artificial Intelligence and the Law* (Intersentia, 2021); D. E. Harasimiuk and T. Braun, *Regulating Artificial Intelligence: Binary Ethics and the Law* (Routledge, 2021); J. Turner, *Robot Rules; Regulating Artificial Intelligence* (Springer, 2019).

[12] See Harnois, *Facial Recognition Technology*; Kindt, *Privacy and Data Protection Issues*.

[13] For example, N. Lynch, L. Campbell, J. Purshouse, and M. Betkier, *Facial Recognition Technology in New Zealand: Towards a Legal and Ethical Framework* (Law Foundation New Zealand, 2020); J. Lynch, *Face Off: Law Enforcement Use of Facial Recognition Technology* (published independently, 2019), with a focus on the United States.

[14] K. A. Gates, *Our Biometric Future: Facial Recognition Technology and the Culture of Surveillance* (New York University Press, 2011).

[15] S. A. Magnet, *When Biometrics Fail: Gender, Race, and the Technology of Identity* (Duke University Press, 2011).

[16] M. Smith, Monique Mann, and Gregor Urbas, *Biometrics, Crime and Security* (Routledge, 2018). A. G. Ferguson *The Rise of Big Data Policing: Surveillance, Race, and the Future of Law Enforcement* (New York University Press, 2017).

The book focusses on FRT use *by government*, which has raised most significant concerns around the globe. Governments are able to use FRT to exert power with coercion, which is not possible for private sector companies. The role of private technology companies and their collaboration with governments when deploying FRT is, however, touched on in many chapters of this collection (e.g., Chapter 7 on protests, Chapter 17 on China), as are legal tools corporations and governments use to shield their collaboration from public eye (Chapter 4 on transparency and trade secrets).

The chapters for this collection are based on the presentations made at an international conference, *Facial Recognition in the Modern State*, held online in September 2022. The conference and this book were a part of the project on *Government Use of Facial Regulation Technologies: Legal Challenges and Possible Solutions (FaceAI)*, funded by the Lithuanian Research Council (2021–2023) and conducted by Rita Matulionyte, Monika Zalnieriute, Agne Limante, and Egle Kavoliunaite-Ragauskiene.

I.3 STRUCTURE OF THE BOOK

The book is structured in two main sections.

Part I, 'Facial Recognition Technology in Context: Technical and Legal Challenges', written by experts in technology, law, and sociology, explores the main legal, social, ethical, and technological challenges related to FRT. Five chapters introduce technical FRT aspects and explore socio-legal challenges posed by FRT, especially to the rule of law and to fundamental rights such as a right of information, privacy, non-discrimination, freedom of information, and political freedoms.

Chapter 1, written by a team of researchers in social science – Neil Selwyn, Mark Andrejevic, Chris O'Neil, Xin Gu, and Gavin Smith – provides an introductory overview of the recent emergence of FRTs into everyday societal contexts and settings. It provides valuable social, political, and economic context to the legal, ethical, and regulatory issues that surround this fast-growing area of technology development. The authors argue that despite the seemingly steady acceptance and practical take-up of FRT throughout everyday life, FRT technology still poses significant risks and requires continued critical attention from scholars working in the social, cultural, and legal domains.

Chapter 2, written by a computer scientist and an industry expert in computer vision, Ali Akbari, introduces legal audiences to FRT from a technical perspective. This chapter explains the fundamentals of AI and FRT, their common development life cycle, essential building blocks, and some of the crucial challenges that computer and data scientists currently face in ensuring the accuracy, effectiveness, and trustworthiness of these technologies. This technical introduction will serve as a foundation to the examination of legal and ethical challenges surrounding FRT technologies, which are frequently connected to technical characteristics of the technology.

Chapter 3, by Simon Michael Taylor, introduces the reader to FRT history and development of FRT from the perspective of science and technologies studies. Grounded in the history of science and technology, the chapter demonstrates how critical aspects of FRT infrastructure are aided by scientific and cultural innovations from different times and locations: mugshots in eighteenth-century France; mathematical analysis of caste in nineteenth-century British India; innovations by Chinese closed-circuit television companies; and computer vision start-ups conducting bio-security experiments on farm animals.

Building on this social, technical, and historical introduction to FRT, Rita Matulionyte focusses in Chapter 4 on a paramount ethical and legal challenge related to the use of FRT: the lack of transparency around the use and implementation of these technologies by government institutions. By focussing on trade secrets, the chapter examines in which situations these have an ability to inhibit transparency around FRT and whether current limitations to trade secret law, such as a 'public interest' exception, is able to address an emerging conflict between the interests of AI developers who own trade secrets over FRT algorithms and public and experts who demand more transparency around these technologies.

Chapter 5, by Jake Goldenfein, focusses on privacy that has long been central to understanding and addressing the impacts of facial recognition and related technologies. This chapter criticizes the 'representational' understanding of images embedded in current privacy and data protection, which leads to confusion and diversity in the juridical treatment of facial recognition, and the declining coherence of legal concepts. The author suggests that online images are better understood as 'operational' and demonstrates how privacy law's failure to accommodate this theorisation of images leads to confusion and diversity in the juridical treatment of facial recognition and declining coherence of legal concepts.

The book then moves to another core problem of FRT, its potential bias and discrimination. Written by Marcus Smith and Monique Mann, Chapter 6 rejects the implied objectivity of technology and argues that FRT might result in discrimination both owing to data on which it is trained and as a result of a social context in which it is applied. The authors argue that FRT will continue to advance the established power relations in the criminal justice system, unless both data-based and societal-based reasons for inequality and discrimination are remedied.

In Chapter 7, Monika Zalnieriute examines FRT use in public spaces and demonstrates how FRT can interfere with political freedoms of individuals. She argues for a prohibition on the use of FRT in public spaces owing to their disproportionate interference with fundamental rights; especially rights to peaceful protest and freedom of assembly.

Chapter 8, the final chapter in Part I, written by Agne Limante, examines the emerging use of FRT in a war context. It focusses on Russia's invasion of Ukraine, the first major military conflict in which FRT has been used openly. The chapter identifies available information about current FRT use by both Russian and Ukrainian militaries and governments and examines the potential and risks of the use of FRT in a war situation. Together, the chapters in Part I demonstrate that, despite legitimate intentions to achieve security and other public policy goals, governments' use of FRT poses significant ethical and legal risks that require urgent attention.

Part II, 'Facial Recognition Technology across the Globe: Jurisdictional Perspectives', explores how increasing deployment of FRT in public spaces is perceived in different jurisdictions over five regions. It also investigates what regulatory initiatives are in place to address the challenges posed by FRT to fundamental rights and the rule of law, and what approaches could be adopted in the future. Part II consists of eleven chapters and examines FRT use and regulation in Europe (the EU as a separate jurisdiction, United Kingdom, Germany, and Lithuania), North America (United States), South America (Brazil), the Asia-Pacific (China, Australia, and New Zealand), and Africa (Morocco). Its broad geographical reach enables readers to understand how experts around the world – in democratic and authoritarian regimes, in developed and developing jurisdictions – perceive challenges caused by FRTs, and how they judge the actions different governments take to address FRT challenges that have been identified and discussed in Part I.

Part II opens with two chapters analysing legal challenges raised by FRT in the context of EU law. In Chapter 9, Simone Kuhlmann identifies different uses of FRT by governments around Europe, highlights the legal challenges around such uses, and then examines whether and to what extent government use of FRT can be accepted under current EU law. Chapter 10, by Paul de Hert and Georgios Bouchagiar, goes one step further, calling for concrete rules to ban, halt, sanction, or frame specific FRT uses that interfere with fundamental human rights, including the right to privacy and personal data protection. The contribution emphasizes the global reach, risks, and possible global harms of facial recognition technologies, and calls for concrete law-making and uniform enforcement in the field.

The book then moves to specific European jurisdictions, with two chapters focussing on FRT in the UK. Chapter 11, by Nora Ni Loideain, focusses on *Bridges* v. *South Wales Police*, the world's first case examining the legality of a facial recognition system deployed by police, and examines the adequacy of judicial interpretation adopted in the case. In Chapter 12, Giulia Gentile provides an overview of sociological and regulatory attitudes towards FRT in the UK, discusses the *Bridges* saga and its implications, and offers reflections on the future of FRT regulation in the UK.

From the UK we travel to continental Europe. In Chapter 13, Andreas Engel explores the legal framework for the use of FRT in the public sector in Germany, with a particular emphasis on the pertinent German data protection and police laws. The chapter examines German constitutional framework for FRT and whether the

Introduction

current laws in Germany provide a sufficient 'legal basis' that is required for FRT use to avoid the infringement of fundamental rights. The European discussion is concluded with Chapter 14 on FRT regulation in a Central-Eastern European country: Lithuania. Eglė Kavoliūnaitė-Ragauskienė's contribution analyses the lack of specific regulation of FRT use under Lithuanian laws, and draws attention to a minimal public discussion and NGO involvement on this topic. The chapter emphasizes the need for more public awareness around the challenges associated with FRT, which is necessary to push for adequate regulation in the field and its effective implementation.

The next two chapters focus on FRT regulation in selected jurisdictions in North America (United States) and South America (Brazil). In Chapter 15, Mailyn Fidler and Justin (Gus) Hurwitz discuss the current state of laws regulating FRT in the United States. They analyse general laws there, such as those that regulate the use of biometrics, and those that more specifically target FRT, for example, laws that prohibit the use of such technologies by law enforcement and state governments. Particular attention is given to the different regulatory institutions in the United States, including the federal and state governments and federal regulatory agencies, as well as different treatment of governmental and private users of FRT. In Chapter 16, Luca Belli, Walter Britto Gaspar, and Nicolo Zingales provide an overview of the current status of FRT regulation in Brazil, where numerous cities are using FRT in a bid to automatise the public safety, transportation, and border control sectors. It discusses the minimal and incomplete guidance for FRT use found in general frameworks or sectoral legislation in Brazil, and examines whether current rules allowing FRT use for public safety, national defence, state security, investigative activities, and the repression of criminal activities are reasonable and justified.

The last three chapters of the book focus on the Asia-Pacific region and Africa. In Chapter 17, Jyh-An Lee and Peng Zhou overview government use of FRT in China and analyse laws regulating FRT use by private entities. They argue that a recent decision in *Guo Bing v. Hang Zhou Safari Park* that restricts the use of FRT in the private sector does not sufficiently limit surveillance as it does not apply to public authorities. Chapter 18, on FRT in Australia and New Zealand, by Nessa Lynch and Liz Campbell, acknowledges the potentially detrimental and discriminatory impacts that FRT use by the state might have and advance discussion on what principled regulation of FRT might look like. The authors argue that it should be possible to prohibit or regulate unacceptable usage while retaining less hazardous uses of FRT, and propose approaches to how such regulation could be achieved.

Chapter 19, by Sylvia I. Bergh, Isaam Cherat, Francesco Colin, Katharina Natter, and Ben Wagner, examines FRT use and regulation in Africa, with a focus on Morocco. The authors argue that Morocco serves as an example of how technologies such as FRT are becoming key tools of governance in authoritarian contexts.

Based on qualitative fieldwork, including semi-structured interviews, observation, and extensive desk reviews, this chapter focusses on the role played by AI-enhanced technology in urban surveillance and the control of migration between the Moroccan-Spanish borders. The authors highlight the lack of transparency, institutional oversight, and public debate on FRT, and demonstrate how AI-enhanced surveillance is a matter where private interests of economic gain and public interests of national security collide with citizens' human rights.

Overall, this timely and innovative interdisciplinary book encourages a global dialogue on FRT among leading scholars from around the world, with the purpose to inform policy and regulatory debate on these challenging technologies.

PART I

Facial Recognition Technology in Context:
Technical and Legal Challenges

1

Facial Recognition Technology

Key Issues and Emerging Concerns

Neil Selwyn, Mark Andrejevic, Chris O'Neill,
Xin Gu, and Gavin Smith

1.1 INTRODUCTION

Facial recognition technology (FRT) is fast becoming a defining technology of our times. The prospect of widespread automated facial recognition is currently provoking a range of polarised responses – from fears over the rise of authoritarian control through to enthusiasm over the individual conveniences that might arise from being instantly recognised by machines. In this sense, FRT is a much talked about, but poorly understood, topic of contemporary social, political, and legal importance. As such, we need to think carefully about exactly what 'facial recognition' is, what facial recognition does, and, most importantly, what we as a society want facial recognition to become.

Before this chapter progresses further into the claims and controversies surrounding FRT, a few basic definitions and distinctions are required. While various forms of technology fall under the broad aegis of 'facial recognition', we are essentially talking about technology that can detect and extract a human face from a digital image and then match this face against a database of pre-identified faces. Beyond this, it is useful to distinguish three distinct forms of facial technologies that are currently being developed and implemented. First, and most widespread to date, are relatively constrained forms of FRT that work to match a human face extracted from a digital image against one pre-identified face. This 'one-to-one' matching will be familiar to the many smartphone users who have opted for the 'Face-ID' feature. The goal of one-to-one matching (sometimes termed 'verification' or 'authentication') is to verify that someone is who they purport to be. A smartphone, for example, is programmed to ascertain if a face in front of the camera belongs to its registered user (or not) and then unlock itself accordingly (or not).

In this manner, one-to-one facial recognition makes no further judgements beyond these repeated one-off acts of attempted identification. Crucially, the software is not capable of identifying who *else* might be attempting to unlock the device. In contrast, a second 'one-to-many' form of FRT is capable of picking a face out of a crowd and matching it to an identity by comparing the captured face to a database containing thousands (or even millions) of faces. This form of isolating any face from a crowd and making an identification has more scope for mass surveillance and tracking. Alongside these forms of facial recognition technologies designed to either verify or ascertain *who* someone is, is a third form of 'facial processing' technologies, ones that seek to infer *what* someone is like, or even *how* someone is feeling. This is technology that extracts faces from digital images and looks for matches against databases of facial expressions and specific characteristics associated with gender, race, and age, or in some cases even emotional state, personality type, and behavioural intention. This form of facial scanning has prompted much interest of late, leading to all manner of applications. During the height of the COVID-19 pandemic, for example, we saw the development of facial processing technology designed to recognise high body temperature and thus infer symptoms of virality through the medium of the face.

All told, considerable time, investment, and effort is now being directed towards these different areas of facial research and development. For computer scientists and software developers working in the fields of computer vision and pattern matching, developing a system that can scan and map the contours and landmarks of a human face is seen as a significant computational challenge. From this technical perspective, facial recognition is conceived as a complex exercise in object recognition, with the face just one of many different real-life objects that computer systems are being trained to identify (such as stop signs on freeways and boxes in warehouses). However, from a broader point of view, the capacity to remotely identify faces en masse is obviously of considerable social significance. For example, from a personal standpoint, most people would consider the process of being seen and scrutinised by another to be a deeply intimate act. Similarly, the promise of knowing who *anyone* is at any time has an understandable appeal to a large number of social actors and authorities for a range of different reasons. A society where one is always recognised might be seen as a convenience by some, but as a threat by others. While some people might welcome the end of obscurity, others might rightfully bemoan the death of privacy. In all these ways, then, the social, cultural, and political questions that surround FRT should be seen as even more complex and contestable than the algorithms, geometric models, and image enhancement techniques that drive them.

1.2 THE INCREASING CAPABILITIES AND CONTROVERSIES OF FACIAL RECOGNITION TECHNOLOGY

Facial recognition has come a long way since the initial breakthroughs made by Woody Bledsoe's Panoramic Research lab in Palo Alto nearly sixty years ago. By 1967 Bledsoe's team had already developed advanced pointillistic methods that could assign scores to faces and make matches with a mugshot database of what was described as 400 'adult male Caucasians'. Despite steady subsequent technical advances throughout the 1970s and onwards, FRT became practicable on a genuinely large scale only during the 2010s, with official testing by the US National Institute of Standards and Technology, reporting accuracy rates for mass-installed systems in excess of 99 per cent by 2018.

As with all forms of AI and automated decision-making, FRT development over the past ten years has benefited from general advances in computational processing power, especially deep learning techniques, and the data storage capabilities required to develop and train large-scale machine learning models. However, more specifically, the forms of FRT that we are now seeing in the 2020s have also benefited from advances in cheap and powerful camera hardware throughout the 2010s (with high-definition cameras installed in public places, objects, and personal devices), alongside the collation of massive sets of pre-labelled photographed faces harvested from publicly accessible social media accounts.

Thus, while the technical 'proof of concept' for FRT has been long established, the society-wide acceleration of this technology during the 2020s has been spurred primarily by recent 'visual turns' in consumer digital electronics *and* popular culture towards video and photo content creation, and the rising popularity of self-documenting everyday life. But, equally, it has been stimulated by the desire of organisations to find automated solutions for managing the problem of distancing and anonymity that networked digital technologies have effected, as well as by vendors who market the virtues of the technology as a means to improve security, convenience, and efficiency, while eliminating the perceived fallibilities of human-mediated recognition systems. Thus, a combination of cultural factors, alongside exceptional societal events such as the COVID-19 pandemic, and the wider political economic will to propose and embrace techno-solutions for redressing social issues and to increasingly automate access to various spaces and services, has fashioned receptive conditions for an expansion in FRT and its concurrent normalisation.

And yet the recent rise to prominence of FRT has also led to a fast-growing and forceful counter-commentary around the possible social harms of this technology being further developed and implemented. Growing numbers of critics contend that this is technology that is profoundly discriminatory and biased, and is something that inevitably will be used to reinforce power asymmetries and leverage unfair ends. Such push-back is grounded in a litany of controversies and misuses of FRT over the past few years. For example, the United States has seen regular instances of FRT-driven racialised discrimination by law enforcement and security agencies – not least repeated instances of US police using facial recognition to initiate unwarranted arrests, false imprisonment, and other miscarriages of justice towards minoritised social groups. Similar concerns have been raised over FRT eroding civil liberties and human rights – constituting what Knutson describes as conditions of 'suspicionless surveillance', with state authorities emboldened to embark on delimited 'fishing expeditions' for all kinds of information about individuals.[1]

---

[1] A. Knutson, 'Saving face' (2021) 10(1) *IP Theory*, www.repository.law.indiana.edu/ipt/vol10/iss1/2/.

Elsewhere, FRT has proven a key element of Chinese authorities' suppression of Muslim Uyghur populations, as well as in illegal targeting of political protesters by authorities in Myanmar and Russia. Moreover, for others, FRT represents a further stage in the body's progressive colonisation by capital, as the technology has enabled the capture of increasingly detailed information about individuals' activities as they move through public and shared spaces. This data can be used to sort and manipulate consumers according to commercial imperatives, tailoring the provision of products and services so that consumption behaviours are maximised. All told, many commentators contend that there have already been sufficient examples of egregious, discriminatory, and harmful uses of FRT in everyday contexts to warrant the cessation of its future development.

Indeed, as far as many critics are concerned, there is already ample justification for the outright banning of facial recognition technologies. According to Hartzog and Selinger, 'the future of human flourishing depends on facial recognition technology being banned before the systems become too entrenched in our lives'.[2] Similarly, Luke Stark's thesis that 'facial recognition is the plutonium of AI' advocates the shutdown of FRT applications in all but the most controlled circumstances.[3] In Stark's view, the potential harms of using FRT for any purpose in public settings are sufficient reason to render its use too risky – akin to using a nuclear weapon to demolish a building. Such calls for the total suppression of FRTs have been growing in prominence. As noted scholar-activist Albert Fox Cahn recently put it: 'Facial recognition is biased, broken, and antithetical to democracy. … Banning facial recognition won't just protect civil rights: it's a matter of life and death.'[4]

1.3 JUSTIFICATIONS FOR FACIAL RECOGNITION AS PART OF EVERYDAY LIFE

While some readers might well feel sympathetic to such arguments, there are also many practical reasons to raise doubts that such bans could ever be practically feasible, even with sufficient political and public support. Proponents of FRT counter that it is not possible to simply 'dis-invent' this technology. They argue that FRTs are now deeply woven throughout the fabric of our digital ecosystems and that commercial imperatives for the information technology and surveillance industries to continue developing FRT products remain too lucrative to give up. Indeed, the technology is already becoming a standard option for closed-circuit television

---

[2] W. Hartzog and E. Selinger, 'Facial recognition is the perfect tool for oppression' (2 August 2018), *Medium*, https://medium.com/s/story/facial-recognition-is-the-perfect-tool-for-oppression-bc2a08f0fe66.
[3] L. Stark, 'Facial recognition is the plutonium of AI' (2019) 25 (3) *XRDS – Crossroads, The ACM Magazine for Students* 50–55, https://doi.org/10.1145/3313129.
[4] Cited in A. Hern, 'Human rights group urges New York to ban police use of facial recognition' (25 January 2021), *The Guardian*, www.theguardian.com/technology/2021/jan/25/new-york-facial-recognition-technology-police.

(CCTV) equipment and is regularly used by police even in jurisdictions without any formal rules governing its deployment. The industry-led and practitioner-backed promissory discourse that propagates the various virtues of FRT is already so deeply entrenched in organisational thinking and practice that it would seem highly unlikely for systems and applications to be withdrawn in the various social contexts where they now operate. In this sense, we perhaps need to look beyond polarised discussions over the fundamental need (or not) for the existence of such technology and instead pay closer attention to the everyday implications of FRT as it gets increasingly rolled out across various domains of everyday life to transform how people, things, and processes are governed.

Proponents of FRT – especially those with a commercial interest in encouraging public and political acceptance of the technology – will often point to a number of compelling 'use cases' that even the staunchest opponents of FRT will find difficult to refute. One common example is the use of FRT to reunite kidnapped, lost, or otherwise missing children with their families. The controversial face recognition company Clearview AI, which has scraped billions of face images from online sources, has highlighted the use of the app to identify victims and perpetrators of child sexual abuse.[5] Other pro-social use cases include the use of face recognition to identify people whose documentation has been lost or destroyed during natural disasters, as well as the development of specialised facial recognition software to identify the victims of war and disaster, providing some sense of closure to loved ones and avoiding the time and cost of alternative methods (such as DNA analysis or dental records). Even critics such as Luke Stark concede that FRT might have merit as a specialised accessibility tool for visually impaired people. Indeed, given the fundamental human need to know who other people are, it is always possible to think of potential applications of this technology that seemingly make intuitive or empathetic sense.

Of course, were FRT to remain restricted to such exceptional 'potential limited use cases',[6] then most people would rarely – if ever – come into contact with the technology, and therefore the concerns raised earlier over society-wide discrimination, biases, and harms would be of little significance. Nevertheless, we already live in times where a much wider range of actual applications of FRT have proven to be largely ignored or presumed uncontentious by a majority of the general public. These 'everyday' uses of FRT, we would argue, already mark the normalisation of a technology that is elsewhere perceived as controversial when in the hands of police, security services, the military, and other authorities.

These 'pro-social' uses span a diverse range of everyday contexts and settings. Perhaps one of the most established installations of facial recognition can be found at airports. FRT is a key component of 'paperless boarding' procedures, allowing

---

[5] K. Hill and G. Dance, 'Clearview's facial recognition app is identifying child victims of abuse' (7 February 2020), *New York Times*.
[6] Stark, 'Facial recognition', p. 55.

airline travellers to use this one-to-one biometric matching capacity between their e-passport photo and their physical face to check in, register their bag-drop, and then proceed through the departure and arrival gates. A major rationale for this automated infrastructure is that it makes travel processes more seamless, lessening queues and cutting costs, while also enhancing the recognition capacities (and thus organisational efficiency) of the airport authority. For instance, various studies on recognition have illustrated that the technology outperforms human recognisers, in this case, the security officials and airline clerks stationed at passport control or check-in counters. Another public setting with a long history of FRT is the casino industry. Most large casinos now operate some form of FRT. For example, the technology is strategically used to enforce blocklists of banned patrons, to enforce 'responsible gaming' by identifying under-age and 'impaired' players, and to support the exclusion of self-identified problem gamblers, as well as for recognising VIP guests and other high spending customers at the door who can then be quickly escorted to private areas and given preferential treatment.

Various forms of facial recognition and facial processing technology are also being deployed in retail settings. The most obvious application is to augment retail stores' use of CCTV to identify known shoplifters or troublemakers before they gain entry to the premises. Yet, as is the case with casinos, a range of other retail uses have also come to the fore – such as using FRT to recognise repeat customers; target screen-based advertising to particular demographics; collect information on how different customers use retail space and engage with particular arrangements of goods; and gauge satisfaction levels by monitoring the facial expressions of shoppers waiting in checkout lines or engaging with particular advertisements. Another major retail development is the use of 'facial authentication' technology to facilitate payment for goods – replacing the need to present a card and then tap in a four-digit PIN with so-called 'Pay By Face' systems, and thus lessening the 'friction' that stems from a customer forgetting or wrongly entering their code on the EFTPOS terminal, while also reducing opportunities for fraudulent activity to occur.

Alongside these cases, there are other instances of FRT being used in the realms of work, education, and healthcare. For example, the growth of FRT in schools, universities, and other educational settings encompasses a growing range of activities, including students using 'face ID' to pay for canteen meals and to check out library books; the detection of unauthorised campus incursions; the automated proctoring of online exams; and even gauging students' emotions, moods, and levels of concentration as they engage with content from the curriculum and different modes of teaching delivery. Similarly, FRT is finding a place in various work settings – often for 'facial access control' into buildings and for governing the floors and areas that employees and contractors can (and cannot) enter, as well as for registering who is in the building and where people are in the case of emergency. Other facial recognition applications also allow factory and construction employees to clock in for work via contactless 'facial time attendance' applications, and – in a more disciplinary sense – can be utilised to monitor the productivity and activities of office staff who are working from home. Similarly, in healthcare contexts, FRT is being used for multiple purposes, from more efficient recognition of patients' identities as they enter clinical facilities so that the need for documentation is reduced (a handy administrative feature in the case of a medical emergency or to support those suffering from mental conditions such as dementia or psychosis), to improving knowledge on wait times and thus better targeting resources and services. FRT is also used to enhance facility security by controlling access to clinical facilities and identifying visitors who have previously caused trouble, as well as for patient monitoring and diagnosis, even to the point of purportedly being able to 'detect pain, monitor patients' health status, or even identify symptoms of some illnesses'.[7]

These workplace technologies are complemented by the rise of domestic forms of FRT – with various products now being sold to homeowners and landlords. One growing market is home security, with various manufacturers producing low-cost security systems with facial recognition capabilities. For example, homeowners are now using Wi-Fi-enabled, high-definition camera systems that can send 'familiar face alerts' when a person arrives on their doorstep. Anyone with an inclination towards low-cost total surveillance can run up to a dozen separate facial recognition cameras inside a house and its surrounding outside spaces. Facial recognition capabilities are also being enrolled into other 'smart living' products, such as the rise of in-car facial processing. Here, some high-end models are beginning to feature in-car cameras and facial analysis technology to infer driver fatigue and trigger 'drowsiness alerts'. Some systems also promise to recognise the faces of different drivers and adjust seating, mirror, lighting, and in-car temperatures to fit the personal preferences of whoever is sitting behind the wheel.

1.4 THE LIMITS OF FACIAL RECOGNITION 'FOR GOOD': EMERGING CONCERNS

Each of these 'everyday' forms of FRT might appear innocuous enough, but taken as a whole, they mark a societal turn towards facial technologies underpinned by a growing ecosystem of FRT, perhaps even biometric consciousness, that is becoming woven into the infrastructural fabric of our urban environments, our social relations, and our everyday lives. Most importantly, it could be argued that these growing everyday uses of FRT distract from the various latent and more overt harms that many people consider this technology to perpetuate, specifically in a landscape where the technology and its diverse applications remain either under-regulated or not regulated at all. Thus, in contrast to the seemingly steady acceptance and practical take-up of FRT throughout our public spaces, public institutions, and private

---

[7] M. Johnson, 'Face recognition in healthcare: Key use cases' (21 January 2022), Visage Technologies, https://visagetechnologies.com/face-recognition-in-healthcare/.

lives, there is a pressing need to pay renewed attention to the everyday implications of these technologies in situ, especially to temper some of the political rhetoric and industry hyperbole being pushed by various proponents of these systems.

1.4.1 *Function Creep*

A first point of contention is the tendency of FRT to be adopted for an ever-expanding range of purposes in any of these settings – in what might be described as processes of 'function creep'. The argument here is that even ostensibly benign implementations of FRT introduce logics of automated monitoring, tracking, sorting, and blocking into everyday public and private spaces that can then lead quickly onto further (and initially unanticipated) applications – what Andrejevic describes as a cascading logic of automation.[8] For example, scanning the faces of casino guests to identify self-excluded problem gamblers in real time may seem like a virtuous use of the technology. Yet the introduction of the technology fits with other uses that casino-owners and marketers might also welcome. As noted earlier, facial recognition can be a discreet way of recognising VIP guests and other lucrative 'high rollers' at the door who can quickly be whisked away from the general melee and then provided with personalised services to capture, or manipulate, their loyalty to (and thus expenditure in) the venue. This logic can then easily be extended into recognising and deterring repeat customers who spend only small amounts of money or whose appearance is not in keeping with the desired aesthetic of the premise, or to identify croupiers whose tables are not particularly profitable.

This cascading logic soon extends to various other applications. To continue the casino example, face recognition could be used to identify and prey on excessive gamblers, using incentives to entice them to spend beyond their means – thereby contributing to the ongoing toll the industry takes on those with gambling addictions. What if every vending machine in a casino could recognise customers through the medium of their faces before displaying prices? A vending machine that could adjust the prices based on information about customers' casino spending patterns and winnings might be programmed to serve as Robin Hood and to charge the wealthy more to subsidise the less fortunate. The more likely impulse and outcome, however, would be for casino operators to attempt to extract from every consumer as much as they would be willing to pay over the standardised price at any given moment. It is easy to envision systems that gauge the motivation of a purchaser at a particular moment, subject to environmental conditions ('how thirsty do they appear to be?', 'what kind of mood do they seem to express?', 'with whom are they associating?', and so on).

This tendency for function creep is already evident in the implementation of facial recognition by governments and state authorities. For example, the development

---

[8]   M. Andrejevic, *Automated Media* (Routledge, 2020).

Key Issues and Emerging Concerns

of facial recognition 'check-in' systems during the pandemic lockdowns to monitor COVID-19 cases undergoing home quarantine have since been repurposed by police forces in regions of India to enforce periods of house arrest. Similarly, in 2022 the UK government contracted a tech company specialising in monitoring devices for vulnerable older adults to produce facial recognition watches capable of tracking the location of migrants who have been charged with criminal offences. This technology is now being used to require migrants to scan their faces and log their geolocation on a smartwatch device up to five times a day.[9] Similarly, Moscow authorities' use of the city's network of over 175,000 facial recognition-enabled cameras to identify anti-war protesters also drew criticism from commentators upset at the re-appropriation of a system that was previously introduced under the guise of ensuring visitor safety for the 2018 FIFA World Cup and then expanded to help track COVID-19 quarantine regulations. All these examples illustrate the concern that the logics of monitoring, recording, tracking, and profiling – and the intensified forms of surveillance that result – are likely to exacerbate (and certainly not mitigate) the manipulative, controlling, or authoritarian tendencies of the places within which they are implemented.

1.4.2 *The Many Breakdowns, Errors, and Technical Failures of FRT*

A second category of harms are those of error and misrecognition – whether this is misrecognition of people's presumed identities and/or misrecognition of their inferred characteristics and attributes. In this sense, one fundamental problem is the fact that many implementations of FRT simply do not work in the ways promised. In terms of simple bald numbers, while reported levels of 'false positives' and 'false negatives' remain encouraging in statistical terms, they still involve large numbers of people being erroneously 'recognised' by these systems in real life. Even implementations of FRT to quicken the process of airport boarding only report success rates 'well in excess' of 99 per cent (i.e., wrongly preventing one in every few hundred passengers boarding the plane). Airports boast the ideal conditions for FRT in terms of well-lit settings, high-quality passport photographs, high-spec cameras, and compliant passengers wanting to be recognised by the camera to authenticate their identity and thus mobility. Unsurprisingly, error rates are considerably higher for FRT systems that are not located within similar ideal conditions. More egregious still is the actual capacity of facial processing systems to infer personal characteristics and affective states. As Crawford and many others have pointed out,[10] the idea of automated facial analysis and inference is highly flawed – in short, it is simply not possible to accurately infer someone's gender, race, or age through a face, let alone

---

[9] N. Kelly, 'Facial recognition smartwatches to be used to monitor foreign offenders in UK' (5 August 2022), *The Guardian*, www.theguardian.com/politics/2022/aug/05/facial-recognition-smartwatches-to-be-used-to-monitor-foreign-offenders-in-uk.

[10] K. Crawford, *Atlas of AI* (Yale University Press, 2021).

anticipate and thus modulate their emotions or future behaviours. As a consequence of technological limitations, as well as flaws regarding the knowability of human cognition and controllability of futures, this imaginary remains better off situated in the science fiction genre than as a plausible part of current policy and practice.

Whether or not one is perturbed by not being allowed on a plane at the first attempt or correctly recognised as feeling happy (or sad) probably depends on how often this inconvenience occurs – and what its consequences are. An erroneous emotion inference might simply result in a misdirected advertising appeal. However, in another instance it could jeopardise one's job prospects, or might even lead to someone being placed under police suspicion. System failures can have more alarming consequences – as reflected in the false arrests of innocent misrecognised individuals, people being denied access to social welfare benefits or Uber drivers being refused access to their work-shift and thereby their income. When a face recognition system fails or makes erroneous decisions, it can be onerous and time-consuming to prove that the machine (and its complex coding script) is wrong. Moreover, trial programs and test-cases continue to show the propensity of FRT to misrecognise certain groups of people more frequently than others. In particular, trials of FRT continue to show racial bias and a particular propensity to mis-recognise women of colour.[11] Similarly, these systems continue to work less successfully with people wearing head-coverings and veils, and those with facial tattoos – in other words, people who do not conform to the 'majority' appearance in many parts of the world.[12]

Of course, not being immediately recognised as a frequent flyer or a regular casino customer is unlikely to lead to serious inconvenience or long-term harm in the same way that being the victim of false arrest can generate trauma and distrust – or even ruin someone's life. Yet even these 'minor' misrecognitions and denials might well constitute further micro-aggressions in a day already replete with them. In celebrating the conveniences of contactless payments and skipping queues, we need to remember that FRTs are not experienced by every 'user' as making everyday life smoother, frictionless, and more convenient. These systems are layered on long histories of oppression and inequity, and often add further technological weight or a superficial technological veneer to already existing processes of social division and differentiation.

1.4.3 The Circumstantial Nature of Facial Recognition 'Benefits'

As these previous points suggest, it is important to recognise how the nature and extent of these harms is experienced disproportionately – with already minoritised populations bearing the worst effects. Indeed, the diverging personal

---

[11] See J. Buolamwini and T. Gebru, 'Gender shades', Conference on Fairness, Accountability and Transparency (January 2018), *Proceedings of Machine Learning Research*, pp. 77–91.

[12] See S. Magnet, *When Biometrics Fail* (Duke University Press, 2011).

experiences of technology (what Ruha Benjamin describes as 'vertical realities' of how different groups encounter the same technology) go some way to explaining why FRT is still being welcomed and embraced by many people.[13] While many groups experience facial recognition as a technology of surveillance and control, the same technologies are experienced as sources of convenience and security by others. As Benjamin reminds us, 'power is, if anything, relational. If someone is experiencing the underside of an unjust system, others, then, are experiencing its upside'.[14]

In this sense, much of what might appear as seemingly innocuous examples of FRT are apt examples of what Chris Gilliard and David Golumbia term 'luxury surveillance' – the willingness of middle-class consumers to pay a premium for tracking and monitoring technologies (such as personal GPS devices and home smart camera systems) that get imposed unwillingly in alternative guises on marginalised groups. This asymmetry highlights the complicated nature of debates over the benefits and harms of the insertion of FRT into public spaces and into the weave of everyday social relations. Indeed, 'smart door-bells', sentient cars, and 'Pay By Face' kiosks are all examples of how seemingly innocuous facial recognition features are being quietly added to some of the most familiar and intimate settings of middle-class lives, *at the same time* as major push-back occurs against the broader use of this technology in public spaces and by police and security forces, where the stakes are perceived to be higher or much less certain. At the moment, many middle-class people seem willing to accept two different modes of the same technology. On the one hand is the 'smart' convenience of being able to use one's face to unlock a smartphone, pay for a coffee, open a bank account, or drive to work in comfort. On the other hand is the general unease at the 'intrusive' and largely unregulated use of FRT in their child's school, in their local shopping centre, or by their local police force.

Yet this ambiguity could be seen as a slippery slope – weakening protections for how the same technology might be used on less privileged populations in more constrained circumstances. The more that FRT is integrated into everyday objects such as cars, phones, watches, and doorbells, the more difficult it is to argue for the complete banning of the technology on grounds of human rights or racial discrimination. Even requesting limitations on application gets harder the more diversified, hard-wired, and normalised the technology becomes. Thus the downside of middle-class consumers continuing to engage with forms of facial recognition that they personally feel 'work for them' is the decreased opportunities to initiate meaningful conversations about whether this is technology that we collectively want to have in our societies and, if so, under what kinds of conditions. As Gilliard and Golumbia conclude:

---

[13] R. Benjamin, *Race after Technology* (Polity, 2019).
[14] Ibid., p. 65.

We need to develop a much deeper way of talking about surveillance technology and a much richer set of measures with which to regulate their use. Just as much, we need to recognize that voluntarily adopting surveillance isn't an isolated choice we make only for ourselves but one that impacts others in a variety of ways we may not recognize. We need always to be asking what exactly it is that we are enthusiastically paying for, who 'we' are and who is 'them' on the outside, and what all of us are being made subject to when we allow (and even demand) surveillance technology to proliferate as wildly as it does today.[15]

1.4.4 *The Harms of FRT Cannot Be 'Fixed'*

A fourth point of contention are the ways in which discussion of the harms of FRT in political, industry, and academic circles continues to be limited by a fundamental mismatch between computational and societal understandings around issues of 'bias'. The idea that FRT can be 'fixed' by better data practices and technical rigour conveys a particular mindset – that algorithms and AI models are not biased in and of themselves. Instead, algorithms and AI models simply amplify bias that might have crept into the datasets that they are trained in and by, and/or through the data that they are fed. As such, it might appear that any data-driven bias is ultimately correctable with better data. Nevertheless, as Deb Raji describes, this is not the case.[16] Of course, it is right to acknowledge that the initial generation of data can reflect historical bias and that the datasets used to develop algorithmic models will often contain representation and measurement bias. However, every aspect of an algorithmic system is a result of programming and design decisions and can therefore contain additional biases. These include decisions about how tasks are conceived and codified, as well as how choices are modelled. In particular, algorithmic models are also subject to what are termed aggregation and evaluation biases. All told, any outcome of an algorithmic model is shaped by subjective human judgements, interpretations, and discretionary decisions along the way, and these are reflected in how the algorithm then autonomously performs its work and acts on the world. In this sense, many critics argue that FRT developers are best advised to focus on increasing the diversity of their research and development teams, rather than merely the diversity of their training datasets.

Yet increasing the diversity of AI development teams will do little to improve how the algorithmic outputs and predictions of FRTs are then used in practice – by, for example, racist police officers, profit-seeking casino owners, and suspicious employers. Ultimately, concerns over the bias and discriminatory dimensions of FRT relate to the harms that an FRT system can do. As many of the examples outlined in previous sections of this chapter suggest, there are a lot of harms that are initiated and amplified through the use of FRT. While many of these are existing harms, the bottom line

---

[15] C. Gilliard and D. Golumbia, 'Luxury surveillance' (6 July 2021), Real Life, https://reallifemag.com/luxury-surveillance/.

[16] D. Raji, Post, Twitter (24 April 2021), https://twitter.com/rajiinio/status/1385935151981420557.

remains that FRT used in a biased and divided society will result in biased outcomes, which will then result in the exacerbation of harm already being disproportionally experienced by socially marginalised groups. Thus, as Alex Allbright puts it, rather than focussing on the biases of predictive tools in isolation, we also need to consider how they are used in different contexts – not least social settings and institutional systems that are 'chock-full' of human judgements, human discretions, and human biases.[17]

In this sense, all of the harms of FRT discussed so far in this chapter need to be seen in terms of biased datasets, biased models, *and* the biased contexts and uneven social relations within which any algorithmic system is situated and used. To the extent that it concentrates new forms of monitoring and surveillance power in the hands of commercial and state entities, the deployment of facial recognition contributes to these asymmetries. This means that algorithmic 'bias' is not simply a technical data problem, but a sociotechnical problem constituted both by human relations and the ensuing human–data relations that seek to represent and organise the former (and therefore not something that can ever be 'fixed'). Humans will always act in subjective ways, our societies will always be unequal and discriminatory. As such, our data-driven tools will inevitably be at least as flawed as the worldviews of the people who make and use them. Moreover, our data-driven tools are most likely to amplify existing differences and unfairness, and to do so in opaque ways, unless they are deliberately designed to be biased towards more inclusive outcomes and 'positive' discrimination.

All told, there cannot be a completely objective, neutral, and value-free facial recognition system – our societies and our technologies simply do not and cannot work along such lines. The danger, of course, is not that FRT will reproduce existing biases and inequalities but that, as an efficient and powerful tool, it will exacerbate them – and create new ones. As such, the development of a more 'effective' or 'accurate' means of oppression is not one to be welcomed. Instead, many applications of FRT can be accused of bolstering what Ruha Benjamin terms 'engineered inequality' by entrenching injustices and disadvantage but in ways that may superficially appear as more objective and scientific, especially given their design and implementation 'in a society structured by interlocking forms of domination'.[18] Thus, as far as Benjamin is concerned, more inclusive datasets 'is not a straightforward good but is often a form of unwanted exposure'.[19]

1.5 FUTURE DIRECTIONS AND CONCERNS

The development of FRT to date clearly raises a host of important and challenging issues for regulators and legislators to address. Before we consider the prospects for what this handbook describes as 'possible future directions in regulating

---

[17] A. Albright, 'If you give a judge a risk score' (29 May 2019), www.law.harvard.edu/programs/olin_center/Prizes/2019-1.pdf.
[18] Benjamin, *Race after Technology*.
[19] Ibid., p. 125.

governments' use of FRT at national, regional and international levels', it is also worth considering the broader logics and emerging forms of FRT and facial processing that have been put into train by the development of FRT to date, and the further issues, concerns, and imperatives that this raises.

One obvious emerging application of concern is the growing use of facial processing to attempt to discern internal mental states. Thus, for example, face recognition has been used by job screeners to evaluate the stress levels and even the veracity of interviewees. While these inferences are without scientific basis, this does not necessarily stop them from being put to use in ways that affect people's life chances. This raises the human rights issue of protecting the so-called forum internum – that is, control over the disclosure of one's thoughts, attitudes, and beliefs. Inferential technologies seek to bypass the ability of individuals to control the disclosure of the innermost sentiments and thoughts by reading these directly from visible external signs. We are familiar with the attempt to 'read' sentiment through non-verbal cues during the course of interpersonal interactions, but automated systems provide these hunches with the patina of (false) scientific accuracy and machinic neutrality in potentially dangerous and misleading ways. The inferential use of this type of automated inference for any type of decision making that affects people's life chances should be strictly limited.

Second is the prospect of the remote, continuous, passive collection of facial biometric data at scale, and across all public, semi-public and private spaces. At stake is not simply the diminishment of individual privacy, but also the space for democratic participation and deliberation. Unleashed on the world, such technology has a very high potential for a host of new forms of social sorting and stalking. Marketers would like to be able to identify individuals in order to target and manipulate them more effectively, and to implement customised offers and pricing. Employers, health insurers, and security officials would be interested in using it for the purposes of background checking and forensic investigations. With such technology in hand, a range of entities could create their own proprietary databases of big spenders, poor tippers, potential troublemakers, and a proliferating array of more and less desirable customers, patients, employees, tenants, clients, students, and more.

Indeed, the continued integration of facial processing capabilities into urban CCTV systems with automated facial recognition also marks a fundamental shift in how surveillance in public space operates. Standard 'dumb' forms of CCTV see the same thing and record what people already see in public and shared space – but do not add extra information. The ability to add face detection and recognition enables new strategies of surveillance and control that are familiar from the online world. For example, with facial recognition, the target of CCTV surveillance can shift from particular individuals or groups to overall patterns. Cameras that track all the individuals within their reach enable so-called pattern of life analysis, looking for different patterns of activity that facilitate social sorting and predictive analytics. For example, the system might learn that particular patterns of movement or interaction with others correlate with the likelihood of an individual making a purchase, getting into a fight, or committing a crime. This type of analysis does not necessarily require identifying individuals, merely recognising and tracking them over time and across space.

Finally, then, there are concerns over how FRT is part of an increasing turn towards surveillance as a replacement of trust. As the philosopher Byung-Chul Han puts it, 'Whenever information is very easy to obtain, as is the case today, the social system switches from trust to control.'[20] No amount of surveillance can ever fully replace trust, but it can undermine it, leading to an unfillable gap that serves as an alibi for ever more comprehensive and ubiquitous data collection. Han describes a resulting imperative to collect data about everything, all the time, in terms of the rise of 'the society of transparency'. It is not hard to trace the symptoms of this society across the realms of social practice: the collection of increasingly comprehensive data in the workplace, the home, the marketing realm, and public spaces. As sensors and network connections along with data storage and processing become cheaper and more powerful, more data can be collected with respect to everything and anything. Face recognition makes it possible to link data collected about our activities in shared and public spaces to our specific identities – and thus to link it with all the other data troves that have been accumulating both online and offline. All told, the concern here is that the technology addresses broader tendencies towards the automated forms of control that characterise social acceleration and the crisis of social trust associated with the changing information environment.[21]

1.6 THE NEED FOR (AND PROSPECTS OF) REGULATION AND OVERSIGHT

With all these issues in mind, it seems reasonable to conclude that FRT requires to be subject to heightened scrutiny and accountability. For many commentators, this scrutiny should involve increased regulatory control, government oversight, and increased public understanding of the issues arising from what is set to be a defining technology of the next decade and beyond. That said, as this chapter's brief overview of the sociotechnical complexity of the technology suggests, any efforts to regulate and hold FRT to account will not be easy. We therefore conclude by briefly considering a number of important concerns regarding the philosophical and regulatory implications of FRT, issues that will be developed and refined further in the remainder of the book.

As with most discussions of technology and society, many of the main concerns over FRT relate to issues of power. Of course, it is possible to imagine uses of FRT

---

[20] B. Han, *The Transparency Society* (Stanford University Press, 2015), p. vii.
[21] R. Garland, 'Trust in democratic government in a post-truth age' in R. Garland (ed.), *Government Communications and the Crisis of Trust* (Palgrave Macmillan, 2021), pp. 155–169.

that redress existing power imbalances, and provide otherwise marginalised and disempowered populations with a means of resisting authoritarian control and to hold power accountable. For example, during the 2020 Black Lives Matter protests, activists in Portland developed FRT to allow street protesters to identify and expose violent police officers. Nevertheless, while it can be used for sousveillance, the mainstream roll-out of FRT across society looks set to deepen asymmetry of power in favour of institutions. Indeed, there is an inherent asymmetry in both power and knowledge associated with these processes of datafication. Only those with access to the databases and the processing power can collect, store, and put this information to use. In practice, therefore, face recognition is likely to become one more tool used primarily by well-resourced organisations and agencies that can afford the necessary processing power and monitoring infrastructure.

As such, any efforts to regulate FRT need to focus on issues of civil rights and democracy, the potential misuse of institutional power, and resulting harms to marginalised and minoritised groups. In this sense, one of the profound shifts envisioned by the widespread use of automated facial recognition is the loss of the ability to opt-out. When public spaces we need to access for the conduct of our daily lives – such as the shops where we get our food, or the sidewalks and streets we travel – become equipped with face recognition, we do not have a meaningful choice of whether to consent to the use of the technology. In many cases we may have no idea that the technology is in place, since it can operate passively at a distance. The prevalence of existing CCTV networks makes it possible to implement facial recognition in many spaces without significantly transforming the visible physical infrastructure.

Following this logic, then, it is likely that automated face recognition in the near future will become a standard feature of existing CCTV surveillance systems. Regulatory regimes that rely on public notification are ineffective if they do not offer genuine opt-out provisions – and such provisions are all but impossible in shared and public spaces that people need to access. When face recognition is installed in public parks or squares – or in commercial locations such as shopping centres, the only choice will be to submit to their monitoring gaze or avoid those spaces. Under such conditions, their decision to use those spaces cannot be construed as a meaningful form of consent. In many cities CCTV has become so ubiquitous that its use passes without public notification. Without specific restrictions on its use, facial recognition is likely to follow the same trajectory. Seen in this light, there are many reasons why regulation and other attempts to hold FRT to account faces an uphill battle (if not the prospect of being thwarted altogether). This is not to say that regulation is not possible. For example, more than two dozen municipalities in the United States banned government use of one-to-many face recognition during the first few years of the 2020s, and the European Union continues to moot strict regulation of its use in public spaces. Nevertheless, the use of the technology by private entities for security and marketing and by government agencies for policing continues apace.

All our future discussions of possible FRT regulation and legislation therefore need to remain mindful of the strong factors driving continued demand for FRT and its uptake. For example, the promise of convenience and security combined with increasing accuracy and lower cost all serve as strong drivers for the uptake of the technology. There are also sustained commercial imperatives to continue this technology – not least the emergence of a $5 billion FRT industry that is estimated to grow to $50 billion by 2030. At the same time, we are living in a world where there are a number of powerful authoritarian drivers to continue the uptake of FRT regardless of pushback from civil society. As discussed earlier in this chapter, universal automated access comes at the expense of perpetual tracking and identification. In addition to the pathologies of bias and the danger of data breaches and hacking, there is also the threat of authoritarian levels of control. Widespread facial recognition creates the prospect of a tool that could, in the wrong hands, be used to stifle political opposition and chill speech and legitimate forms of protest. It can also be used to extract detailed information about people's private lives, further shifting control over personal information into the hands of those who own and control the monitoring infrastructure.

Regardless of such impediments and adversaries, many people contend that the time to develop clear regulations in keeping with commitments to democracy and human rights is now. Building support for such regulation will require concerted public education programmes that focus on the capabilities and potential harms of the technology. At the moment, its potential uses and capabilities are not understood widely and are often framed in terms of personal privacy invasion rather than its potentially deleterious effects on democracy and civic life. Developing appropriate regulation will also require negotiating the tension between the commercial pressures of the data-driven surveillance economy, the security imperatives of law enforcement, and civic values of freedom of expression, movement, and personal autonomy. The outcome we need to avoid is the one towards which we seem to be headed: a situation in which the widespread deployment of the technology takes place in a regulatory vacuum without public scrutiny or accountability.

The legal challenge of FRT lies in the fact that the consent scheme is not the best approach to protect individual rights as discussed earlier. And in some contexts, preventing its uses based on individual rights' argument may not be in the interest of the general public. In this complex situation, we should not be forced into making a choice between protecting the individuals and protecting the society at large (an argument that Chinese lawmakers are now working on through the introduction of a revised data protection law effective in 2021). Instead, we need to develop laws that will not obscure self-governance (individual rights protection) in relation to the promotion of the application of FRT as public interests. The boundaries of legal application of FRT need to be established. In it, the liability of those who are collecting, collating, and analysing facial data should be a key consideration. For example, if the use of FRT is permitted, the re-use of such information without individual authorisation should be prohibited. The emphasis should also be about how to prevent harms resulting from public interest exceptions.

1.7 CONCLUSIONS

These are just a few opening observations and points in what needs to be a prolonged society-wide discussion over the next decade and beyond. While it is unlikely that a consensus will ever be reached, it is possible to develop a clear sense of the boundaries that we want to see established around this fast-changing set of technologies. That said, such is the pace of change within biometrics and AI, it might well be that *facial* recognition technology is only a passing phase – researchers and developers are already getting enthused over the potential scanning of various other bodily features as a route to individual identification and inference. Yet many of the logics highlighted in this chapter apply to whatever other part of the human body this technology's gaze is next trained on – be it gait, voice, heartbeat, or other.

Of course, many of the issues raised in this chapter are not unique to FRT per se – as McQuillan reminds us, every instance of 'socially applied AI has a tendency to punch down: that is, the collateral damage that comes from its statistical fragility ends up hurting the less privileged'.[22] Nevertheless, it is worth spending time unpacking what is peculiar about the computational processing of one's face as the focal point for this punching down and cascading harm. This chapter has therefore presented a selection of issues that we identify from the perspective of sociology as well as culture, media, and surveillance studies. There are many other disciplines also scrutinising these issues from across the humanities and social sciences – all of which are worth engaging with as bringing a valuable context to legal discussions of FRT. Yet we hope that the law and legal disciplines can bring an important and distinctive set of insights in taking these issues and conversations forward. Legal discussions of technology bring a valuable pragmatism to the otherwise ambiguous social science portrayals of problematic technologies such as FRT – striving to develop 'a legitimate and pragmatic agenda for channelling technology in the public interest'.[23] We look forward to these conversations continuing across the rest of this handbook and beyond.

---

[22] D. McQuillan, *Resisting AI* (University of Bristol Press, 2022), p. 35.
[23] R. Calo, 'The scale and the reactor' (9 April 2022), SSRN, https://papers.ssrn.com/sol3/papers.cfm?abstract_id=4079851, p. 3.

2

Facial Recognition Technologies 101

Technical Insights

Ali Akbari

2.1 INTRODUCTION

The best way to anticipate the risks and concerns about the trustworthiness of facial recognition technologies (FRT) is to understand the way they operate and how such decision-making algorithms differ from other conventional information technology (IT) systems. This chapter presents a gentle introduction to characteristics, building blocks, and some of the techniques used in artificial intelligence (AI) and FRT solutions that are enabled by AI. Owing to simplification and limitation, this is by no means a complete or precise representation of such technologies. However, it is enough to better understand some of the available choices, the implications that might come with them, and considerations to help minimise some of the unwanted impacts.

When talking about facial recognition technologies, usually the first thing that comes to mind is identifying a person from their photo. However, when analysing an image that includes a face, quite a few processes can be done. Apart from the initial general image preparation and enhancement steps, everything starts with a face detection process. This is the process to find the location of all of the faces within an image, which usually follows by extracting that part of the image and applying some alignments to prepare it for the next steps.

Face recognition that follows the detection step deals with assessing the identity of the person in the extracted face image and can be either an identification or a verification process. Face identification is when a 1:N, or one-to-many, search happens and the target face image is compared with a database of many known facial images. If the search is successful, the identity of the person in the image is found. For example, when doing a police check, a newly taken photo of the person might be checked against a database of criminal mugshots to find if that person had any past records. In the verification process, by performing a 1:1, or one-to-one check, we are actually trying to confirm an assumed identity by comparing a new facial image with a previously confirmed photo. A good example for this can be when a newly taken photo at a border checkpoint is compared with the photo on the passport to confirm it is the same person.

Although it is not always categorised under the facial recognition topic, another form of facial image processing is face categorisation or analysis. Here, rather than the identity of the person in the image, other characteristics and specifications are important. Detecting some demographic information such as gender, age, or ethnicity, facial expression detection, and emotion recognition are a few examples with applications such as sentiment analysis, targeted advertisement, attention detection, or driver fatigue identification. However, this sub-category is not the focus in this text.

All of the above-mentioned processes on facial images fall under the computer vision field of research, which is about techniques and methods that enable computers to understand images and extract various information from them. This closely relates to image processing, which can, for example, modify and enhance medical images but not necessarily extract information or automatically make decisions based on them. Eventually, if we go one step further, along with computer vision and image processing, any other unstructured data processing such as speech processing or natural language processing falls under the umbrella of AI. The importance of this recognition is that facial recognition technologies inherit a lot of their characteristics from AI, and in the next section we take a closer look at some of these specifications to better understand some of the underlying complexities and challenges of FRT.

2.2 WHAT IS AI?

Although there have been many debates around the definition of AI, we do not yet have one universally accepted version. The definition by the Organisation for Economic Co-operation and Development (OECD) is among one of the more commonly referenced ones: 'Artificial Intelligence (AI) refers to computer systems that can perform tasks or make predictions, recommendations or decisions that usually require human intelligence. AI systems can perform these tasks and make these decisions based on objectives set by humans but without explicit human instructions.'[1]

2.2.1 *AI versus Conventional IT*

While the OECD has provided a good definition, in order to better understand AI systems and their characteristics it would be beneficial to compare them with conventional IT systems. This can be considered across the following three dimensions:

---

[1] OECD, *Artificial Intelligence in Society* (OECD Publishing, 2019), https://doi.org/10.1787/eedfee77-en.

- *Instructions* – In order to achieve a goal, in conventional IT systems, explicit and step by step instructions are provided. However, AI systems are given *objectives* and the system comes up with the best solution to achieve it. This is one of the most important factors that makes the behaviour of AI systems not necessarily predictable because the exact solution is not dictated by the developers of the system.
- *Code* – The core of a conventional IT system is the codebase in one of the programming languages that carries the above-mentioned instructions. Although AI systems also contain codes that define the algorithms, the critical component that enables them to act intelligently is a *knowledge* base. The algorithms apply this knowledge on the inputs to the system to make decisions and perform tasks (so called outputs).
- *Maintenance* – It is very common to have periodic maintenance on conventional IT systems to fix any bugs that are found or add/improve features. Moreover, an AI system that is completely free of bugs and performing perfectly might gradually drift and start behaving poorly. This can be because of changes in the environment or the internal parameters of the models in the case of continuous learning capability (this is discussed further in Section 2.3.4). Owing to this characteristic, apart from maintenance, AI systems need *continuous monitoring* to make sure they perform as expected along their life cycle.

2.2.2 *Contributors in AI Systems*

A common challenge with FRT and more broadly AI systems is to understand their behaviour, explain how the system works or a decision was made, or define the scope of responsibilities and accountability. Looking from this angle, it is also worth reminding ourselves of another characteristic of AI systems, which is the possibility of many players contributing to building and applying such solutions.

For example, let us consider a face recognition solution being used for police checks. The algorithm might be from one of the latest breakthroughs developed by a research centre or university and publicly published in a paper. Then a technology provider may implement this algorithm in their commercial tools to create an excellent face matching engine. However, in order to properly train the models in this engine, they leverage the data being collected and prepared by a third company that may or may not have commercial interest in it. This face matching engine by itself only accepts two input images and outputs a similarity score that cannot be used directly by police. Hence a fourth company comes into play by integrating this face matching engine in a larger biometrics management solution in which all required databases, functionalities, and user interfaces exactly match the police check requirements. Before putting this solution into operation, the fifth player is the police department, which, in collaboration with the fourth company, runs tests and decides the suitable parameters and configuration that this solution should use when implemented. Finally, the end users who will take a photo during operation of the system may affect success as the sixth player by providing the image with the best conditions.

In such a complex scenario, with so many contributors to the success or failure of an FRT solution, investigating the behaviour of the system or one specific decision is not as easy as in the case of other simpler software solutions.

2.3 AI LIFE CYCLE AND SUCCESS FACTOR CONSIDERATIONS

Considering the foregoing, the life cycle of AI systems also differs slightly from the common software development life cycle. Figure 2.1 is a simple view of these life cycle steps.

2.3.1 *Design*

Following the inception of an idea or identification of a need, it all starts with the design. Many critical decisions are made at this stage that can be based on various hypotheses and potentially reviewed and corrected in the later steps. Such decisions may include but are not limited to the operations requirements, relevant data to be collected, expected data characteristics, availability of training data or approaches

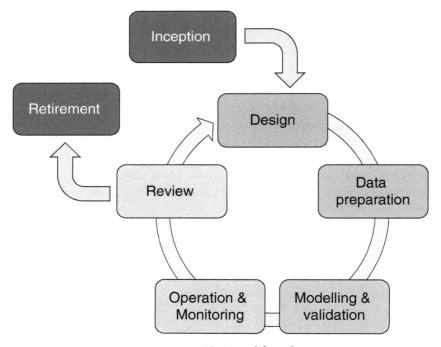

FIGURE 2.1 AI system life cycle

to create them, suitable algorithms and techniques, and acceptance criteria before going into operation. For example, an FRT-based access control system developer might assume that their solution is going to be always used indoors and in a controlled imaging environment, and decide only simple preprocesses are required based on this consideration. A system developed based on this design may perform very poorly if used for outdoor access control and in a crowded environment with varying light and shade conditions.

2.3.2 *Data Preparation*

The data preparation can be one of the most time-consuming and critical steps of the work. As discussed in Sections 2.3.3 and 2.6, this can also be an important factor in success, failure, or unwanted behaviour of the system. This stage covers all the data collection or creation, quality assessment, cleaning, feature engineering, and labelling steps. When it comes to the data for building and training AI models, especially in a complex and sensitive problem such as face recognition, there is always the difficult trade-off between volume, quality, and cost. More data helps to build stronger models, but curating lots of high-quality data is very costly. Owing to the time costs and other limitations in the creation of such datasets, sometimes the developers are forced to rely on lower quality publicly available or crowd-sourced datasets, or pay professional data curation companies to help them with this step. For a few examples of the datasets commonly used in FRT development, you can refer to Labeled Face in the Wild,[2] Megaface,[3] or Ms-celeb-1m.[4] However, developers should note that not only it is a very difficult task to have a thorough quality check on such huge datasets, but also each has its own characteristics and limitations that are not necessarily beneficial for any type of FRT development activity. Inadequate use of such datasets might lead to unwanted bias in FRT solutions that only gets noticed after repeatedly causing problems.

2.3.3 *Modelling and Validation*

When the data is prepared, actual development of the system can get started. The core of this stage, which is one of the most iterative steps in the AI life

---

[2] G. B. Huang, M. Ramesh, T. Berg, and E. Learned-Miller, 'Labeled faces in the wild: A database for studying face recognition in unconstrained environments' (2007), Technical Report 07–49, University of Massachusetts, Amherst.

[3] I. Kemelmacher-Shlizerman, S. M. Seitz, D. Miller, and E. Brossard, 'The megaface benchmark: 1 million faces for recognition at scale', *Proceedings of the IEEE Conference on Computer Vision and Pattern Recognition (CVPR)*, Las Vegas, USA (27–30 June 2016), pp. 4873–4882, doi: 10.1109/CVPR.2016.527.

[4] Y. Guo, L. Zhang, Y. Hu, X. He, and J. Gao, 'Ms-celeb-1m: A dataset and benchmark for large-scale face recognition' in B. Leibe, J. Matas, and M. Welling (eds.), *European Conference on Computer Vision* (Springer, 2016), pp. 87–102.

cycle, is to find the most suitable algorithms and configurations, and train some models by applying the algorithms to previously prepared training data. This is followed with running enough test and validation processes to become confident of the suitability of the models for the intended application. Usually, many iterations are required to get to the desirable performance levels and to confidently sign off a model to operate in the production environment. Incorrect selection of the algorithms or performance metrics and validation criteria can easily cause misleading results. For example, when checking a suspect's photo against a database of previous criminal records, we may want to consider different acceptance levels for false positive versus false negative rates; hence, a straight accuracy measure is not enough to pass or fail a model. Similarly, for a sensitive application, we might want to check such measures separately for various cohorts across demographic dimensions such as gender and ethnicity, to minimise any chances of bias. An accurate technical understanding of performance measurement metrics and meaning is critical in the correct selection and application of FRT. Unfortunately, a lack of adequate AI literacy among some of the business operators of FRT technologies can cause the choice of solutions that are not suitable for their application. For example, a technology that works well for a 1:1 verification and access control to a digital device does not necessarily perform as well as 1:N search within a criminal database.

2.3.4 *Operation and Monitoring*

Following the build and passing all readiness tests successfully, the AI system is deployed and put into operation. AI systems, as any other software, need considerations such as infrastructure and architecture to address the required security, availability, speed performance, and so on. Additionally, as briefly discussed earlier, operators should make sure that the conditions of the application are suitable and match what the models were intended and built for. What should not be forgotten is that AI systems, especially in high-risk applications, are not 'set and forget' technologies. If an AI system performs very well when initially implemented, that does not necessarily mean it will continue to keep performing at the same level. If continuous learning is used, the models keep dynamically changing and adapting themselves, which of course means the new behaviour needs to be monitored and confirmed. However, even if the models are static and not changing, a drift can still happen, which changes the performance of the models. This can be due to changes in the concept and the environment in which the model is performing. For example, specific facial expressions in different cultures might appear differently. Hence, an FRT system that is built successfully to detect various facial expressions in a specific country might start behaving poorly when too many people from a different cultural background start interacting with it. A monitoring process alongside the main solution makes sure such unexpected changes are detected in time to be addressed properly. For instance, a very simple monitoring process for the scenario described here can be to observe the ratio of various expressions that are detected on a regular basis. If a persistent shift in detecting some specific expressions happens, it can be a signal to start an investigation. A good approach is to build the pairing monitoring processes in parallel with the design and development of the main models.

2.3.5 Review

Review can happen periodically, similar to with conventional software, or based on triggers coming from the monitoring process. It can be considered as a combination of simplified evaluation and design steps that identifies the gaps between the existing circumstances of the AI system and the most recent requirements. As a result of such an assessment, the AI models may go through another round of redesign and retraining or be completely retired because of changes in circumstances.

2.4 UNDER THE HOOD OF AI

At a very simplistic level and in a classic view, an AI system consists of a form of representation of knowledge, an inference engine, and an optional learn or retrain mechanism, as illustrated in the Figure 2.2.

Knowledge in an AI system may be encoded and represented in different forms including and not limited to rules, graphs, statistical distributions, mathematical equations and their parameters, or a combination of these. The knowledge base represents facts, information, skills or experiences from human knowledge or existing relationships, associations, or other relevant information in the environment that can help in achieving the main objective of the AI system. For example, in an FRT system the knowledge might define what shapes, colours, or patterns can indicate the location of a human face in the input image. Or it can suggest what areas and measurements on

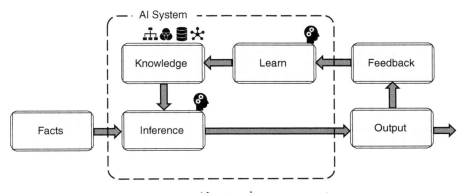

FIGURE 2.2 AI system key components

the face would be the most discriminating factors between two different human faces. However, it is not always as explicit and explainable as these examples.

Inference engine consists of the algorithms, mechanisms, and processes that allow the AI system to apply knowledge to the input facts and observations and to come up with the solutions for achieving its objective, making a prediction or a decision. The type of inference engine depends on the knowledge representation model to be able to apply that specific type of model, and usually they come as a pair. However, these two components are not always necessarily separable. For example, in AI systems based on artificial neural networks (ANNs), the knowledge is stored as the trained parameters and weights of the network. In such cases we can consider that the inference engine and knowledge base are combined as an ANN algorithm together with its parameters after training.

Learn or retrain, as already mentioned, is an optional component of the AI system. Many AI systems after being fully trained and put into operation remain static and do not receive any feedback from the environment. However, when the 'learn' component exists, after making a decision or prediction, the AI system receives feedback that indicates the correct output. The learning mechanism compares the predicted output with the feedback and, in case of any deviation or error, it tries to readjust the knowledge to gradually minimise the overall error rate of the system. For example, every time that your mobile phone Face ID fails to identify your face and you immediately unlock the phone using your passcode, it can be used as a feedback signal to improve your face model on the phone by using the most recently captured image. While this is a great feature for improving AI models, it also has the risk of changing their behaviour in an unexpected or unwanted manner. In the example just given, if with each failure your mobile phone keeps expanding the scope of acceptable facial features that unlock your phone, it may end up accepting other people whose faces are only similar to yours.

2.4.1 *The Source of Knowledge*

We have just mentioned how the knowledge base might be updated and improved based on the feedback received during the operation. But what is the source of the knowledge and how that knowledge base is created in the first place? Generally speaking, during the initial build of an AI system the knowledge base can be created either manually by the experts or automatically using suitable data. You might have previously seen illustrations similar to Figure 2.3, which tries to explain the relation between AI and machine learning (ML). However, before getting to the details of ML, it might be good to consider what is AI outside the ML subset.

The AI techniques outside the ML subset are called *Symbolic AI* or sometimes referred to as Good Old-Fashioned AI. This is mostly based on the human expert knowledge in that specific domain, and the knowledge base here is being manually

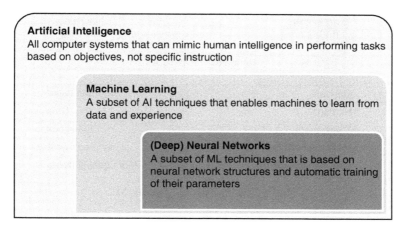

FIGURE 2.3 AI versus ML

curated and encoded by the AI developers. As a result of that, it is mostly human readable (hence symbolic) and usually separable from the inference part of the system as described in the building blocks of AI earlier. Expert Systems are one of the well-known and more successful examples of symbolic AI, where their knowledge is mainly stored as 'if-then' rules.[5]

Symbolic AI systems are relatively reliable, predictable, and more explainable owing to their transparency and the readability of their knowledge base. However, the manual curation of the knowledge base makes it less generalisable and more importantly converts the knowledge acquisition or updating step into a bottleneck owing to the limited availability of the domain experts to collaborate with the developers. Symbolic AI solutions have therefore had limited success, and we have not heard much about them recently.

To obtain knowledge without experts dictating it, another approach is to observe and automatically learn from the relevant examples, which is the basis of computational learning theory and ML techniques. There is a wide range of ML techniques starting from statistical models and mathematical regression analysis to more algorithmic methods such as decision trees, support vector machines, and ANNs, which are one of the most well-known subsets of ML in the past couple of years, thanks to the huge success stories of deep neural networks.[6] When enough sample data is provided, these algorithms are capable of training models with automatically encoded knowledge that is required to achieve their objectives when put into operation. The table in Figure 2.4 summarises some of the key differences between these two groups of AI techniques.

---

[5] P. Jackson, *Introduction to Expert Systems* (3rd ed., Addison, Wesley, 1998), p. 2.
[6] Stuart J. Russell and Peter Norvig, *Artificial Intelligence: A Modern Approach* (4th ed., Pearson, 2021); T. Hastie, R. Tibshirani, and J. Friedman, *The Elements of Statistical Learning* (Springer, 2009).

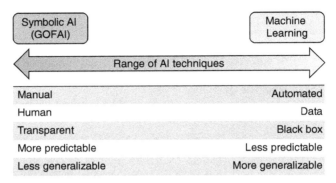

FIGURE 2.4 Symbolic AI versus ML

2.4.2 *Different Methods of Learning*

Depending on the type and specifications of the data available to learn from, there are several different methods of learning in ML algorithms. Each one of these options has strengths and weaknesses. In an application such as FRT where we might not easily access any type of dataset that we want, it is important to be aware of the potentials and limitations of different methods. Below are a few examples among many of these methods; it is an increasing list.

Supervised learning is one of the most common and broadly applied methods. It can be utilised when at the time of creating and training ML models there are enough samples of input data along with their expected output (labels). In an identity verification example under FRT domain, the trained model would normally be expected to receive two face images and give a similarity score. In such a case, the training dataset includes many pairs of facial images along with a manually allocated label, which is 1 when those are photos of the same person and 0 otherwise. In FRT applications, preparing large enough labelled datasets for supervised learning purposes is time consuming, expensive, and subject to human errors such as bias.

Unsupervised learning applies when only samples of the input data are available for the training period and the answers are unknown or unavailable. As you can imagine, this method is only useful for some specific use cases. Clustering and association models are common examples of this learning method. For example, in a facial expression categorisation application, during the training phase a model can be given lots of facial images and learns how to group them together based on similarity of the facial expression, without necessarily having a specific name for those groups. For such FRT, it might be easier to source unlabelled sample data in larger volumes, for example through web scraping. However, this is subject to privacy implications and hidden quality issues, and thus works for limited applications only.

Reinforcement learning is used when neither the samples nor the answers are available as a batch in the beginning. Rather, a reward function is maximised through trial and error while the model gradually learns in operation. For example, you can imagine an AI system that wants to display the most attractive faces from a database to its user. There is no prior dataset to train the model for each new user, however, assuming the amount of time the viewer spends before swiping to the next photo is a sign of attractiveness, the model gradually learns which facial features can maximise this target. In such situations, the learning mechanism should also balance between exploring new territories and exploiting current knowledge to avoid possibilities of local maxima traps. It is easy to imagine that only very few FRT applications can rely on such trial and error methods to learn.

Semi-supervised learning can be considered as the combination of supervised and unsupervised learning. This can be applied when there is a larger amount of training samples, but only a smaller subset of them is labelled. In such scenarios, in order to make the unlabelled subset useful in a supervised manner, some assumptions such as continuity or clustering are made to relate them to the labelled subset of the samples. Let us imagine a large set of personal photos with only a few of them labelled with names for training a facial identification model. If we know which subsets are taken from the same family albums, we may be able to associate a lot more of those unnamed photos and label them with the correct names to be used for better training of the models. Although this can help with the data labelling challenge for FRT applications, the assumptions necessarily made during this process can introduce the risk of unwanted error in the training process.

Self-supervised learning helps in another way with the challenge of labelled data availability, especially when a very large volume of training data is required, such as deep learning. Instead of a manual preparation of the training signals, this approach uses some automated processes to convert input data to meaningful relations that can be used to train the models. For example, to build and train some of the largest language models, training data is scraped from any possible source on the internet. Then, an AI developer could use, for example, a process to remove parts of the sentences, and the main model is trained to predict and fill in the blanks. In this way the answer (training signal) is automatically created, and the language model learns all meaningful structures and word relationships in human language. In the FRT domain you can think of other processes, including distortions to a face image such as shadows or rotation, or taking different frames of the same face from a video. This produces a set of different facial images that are already known to be of the same person and can be used directly for training of the models without additional manual labelling.

2.5 FACIAL RECOGNITION APPROACHES

Similar to the AI techniques, facial recognition approaches were initially more similar to Symbolic AI. They were naturally more inclined towards the way humans might approach the problem and were inspired by anthropometry.[7] Owing to the difficulty of extracting all important facial features and accurate measurements that could be easily impacted by small variation in the images, there was limited success in such works until more data driven approaches were introduced; these were based on mathematical and statistical methods and had a holistic approach to face recognition, an example being Eigenfaces,[8] which is basically the eigenvectors of the training grayscale face images (An eigenvector of a matrix is a non-zero vector that, when multiplied by the matrix, results in a scaled version of itself.). This shift towards ML techniques got more mature and successful by combining the two approaches through other ideas such as neural networks in DeepFace,[9] and many other similar works. More in-depth review of the history of FRT is discussed in Chapter 3, so here we just look at technical characteristics and differences of these approaches.

Feature analysis approaches rely on the detection of facial features and their measurements. Here, each face image is converted to a numeric vector in a multidimensional space and the face recognition challenge is simplified to more common classification or regression problems. Similar to symbolic AI, the majority of the knowledge, if not all, is manually encoded in the form of rules that instruct how to detect the face within an image and identify each of its components to be measured accurately. These rules may rely on basic image and signal processing techniques such as edge detection and segmentation. This makes the implementation easier and, as mentioned earlier when discussing symbolic AI, the process and its decision-making is more transparent and explainable. However, intrinsic to these approaches is the limited generalisability challenge of symbolic AI. In ideal and controlled conditions these methods can be quite accurate, but changes in the imaging condition can dramatically impact the performance. This is because in the new conditions, including different angles, resolution, or shadows and partial coverage, the prescribed rules might not apply any more, and it would not be practical to manually find all these variations and customise new rules for them.

Holistic approaches became popular after the introduction of Eigenfaces in the early 1990s.[10] Rather than trying to detect facial features based on human definition of a face, these approaches consider the image in its pixel form as a vector in a high dimensional space and apply dimensionality reduction techniques combined with other mathematical and statistical approaches that do not rely on what is inside the image. This largely simplifies the problem by avoiding the facial feature extraction

---

[7] A. J. Goldstein, L. D. Harmon, and A. B. Lesk, 'Identification of human faces' (1971) 59(5) *Proceedings of the IEEE* 748–760, https://doi.org/10.1109/PROC.1971.8254.

[8] M. Turk and A. Pentland, 'Eigenfaces for recognition' (1991) 3(1) *Journal of Cognitive Neuroscience* 71–86.

[9] Y. Taigman, M. Yang, M. Ranzato, and L. Wolf, 'Deepface: Closing the gap to human-level performance in face verification' (2014), *Proceedings of the IEEE Conference on Computer Vision and Pattern Recognition*, pp. 1701–1708.

[10] Turk and Pentland, 'Eigenfaces for recognition'.

and measurement step, together with its sensitivities. This shifts the face recognition approach towards the classic ML techniques and changes the training to a data-driven problem rather than manual rule development. Unfortunately, purely holistic approaches still suffer from a few challenges, including statistical distribution assumptions behind the method that do not always apply, and any deviation from the controlled imaging condition makes it worse.

Deep neural networks made a leap in the advancement and success of face recognition approaches. After Eigenfaces and its variations, there were many other small improvements made to the holistic approaches by adding some generic feature extraction steps such as Gabor prior to the main classifier,[11] followed by some neural network-based ML approaches. However, it was not as successful until the introduction of deep learning for image processing,[12] and applying it for face recognition.[13] Convolutional neural networks convert the feature extraction and selection from the images to an unsupervised process, so it is not as challenging as manually defined facial features and not too generic like the Gabor filters used prior to some of the holistic approaches. The increasingly complex and important features that are automatically selected are used in a supervised learning layer to deliver the classification or recognition function.[14] This is the key in the success of object and face recognition of deep neural networks.

2.6 THE GIFT AND THE CURSE OF COMPLEXITY

Many variations of ANNs have been used in ML applications including face recognition. However, the so called shallow neural networks were not as successful owing to their limited learning capacity. Advancements in hardware, use of graphical processing units, and cloud computing to increase processing power along with access to more training data (big data) made the introduction of deep learning possible. In addition to novel network structures and the use of more sophisticated nodes such as convolutional functions, another important factor in the increased capacity of learning of DNNs is the overall complexity and scale of the network parameters to train. For example, the first experimental DNN used in FaceNet includes a total of 140 million parameters to train.

While the complexity of DNNs increases their success in learning to solve challenging problems such as face recognition, these new algorithms become

---

[11] C. Liu and H. Wechsler, 'Gabor feature based classification using the enhanced fisher linear discriminant model for face recognition' (2002) 11(4) *IEEE Transactions on Image Processing* 467–476.

[12] A. Krizhevsky, I. Sutskever, and G. E. Hinton, 'Imagenet classification with deep convolutional neural network' in NIPS'12: *Proceedings of the 25th International Conference on Neural Information Processing Systems*, vol. 1 (Curran Associates Inc., 2012), pp. 1097–1105.

[13] Y. Taigman, M. Yang, M. Ranzato, and L. Wolf (2014). Deepface: Closing the gap to human-level performance in face verification. Proceedings of the IEEE conference on computer vision and pattern recognition, pp. 1701–1708.

[14] Hannes Schulz and Sven Behnke, 'Deep learning' (2012) 26 *KI – Künstliche Intelligenz* 357–363, https://doi.org/10.1007/s13218-012-0198-z.

increasingly data hungry. Without going into too much detail, if the number of training samples are too small compared with the number of parameters of the model, rather than learning a generalised solution for solving the problem it overfits the model and memorises the answer only for that specific subset. This causes the model to perform very well for the training samples, as it has memorised the correct answers for the training set, but fail when it comes to test and unseen samples, owing to a lack of generalisation and fitting the model only to the previously seen examples. Therefore, such successful face recognition systems based on DNNs or a variation of them are actually trained on large training facial datasets, which can be the source of new risks and concerns.

Privacy and security concerns are one of the first to pay attention to. It is difficult and expensive to create new and large face datasets with all appropriate consents in place. Many of these large datasets are collected from the web and from a few different sources where copyright and privacy statements raise problems from both legal and ethics perspectives. Additionally, after collection, such datasets could be potentially a good target for cyber-attacks, especially if the images can be correlated to other information that may be publicly available about the same person.

Data labelling is the next challenge after collection of the suitable dataset. It is labour intensive to manually label such large datasets to be used as a supervised learning signal for the models. As discussed earlier, self-supervised learning is one of the next best choices for data-heavy algorithms such as DNNs. However, this introduces the risk of incorrect assumptions in the self-supervised logic and the missing of some problems in the training process even when performance measures seem to be adequate.

Hidden data quality issues might be the key to most of the well-known face recognition failures. Usually, a lot of automation or crowdsourcing is involved in the preparation of such large face datasets. This can prevent thorough quality checks across the samples and labels, which can lead to flawed models and cause unexpected behaviour in special cases despite high performance results during the test and evaluation. Bias and discrimination are among the most common misbehaviours of FRT models, which can be either due to such hidden data quality issues or simply the difficulty of obtaining a well-balanced large sample across all cohorts.

2.7 CONCLUSION

Face recognition is one of the complex applications of AI and inherits many of its limitations and challenges. We have made a quick review of some of the important considerations, choices, and potential pitfalls of AI techniques and more specifically FRT systems. Given this is a relatively new technology being used in our daily lives, it is crucial to increase the awareness and literacy of such technologies and their potential implications from a multi-disciplinary angle for all its stakeholders, from its developers and providers to the operators, regulators, and the end users.

Now that with DNNs the reported performance of FR models is reaching or surpassing human performance,[15] a critical question is why we still hear so many examples of failure and find FR models insufficiently reliable in practice. Among many reasons, such as data quality discussed earlier, the difference between development and operation conditions can be one of the common factors. The dataset that the model is trained and tested on may not be a good representation of what the model will receive when put into operation. Such differences can be due to imaging conditions, demographic distribution, or other factors. Additionally, we should not forget that the performance tests are usually done directly on the FRT model. However, an FRT-based solution has a lot of other software components and configurable decision-making logic that will be applied to the facial image similarity scores. For example, such surrounding configurable logic can easily introduce human bias to a FRT solution with a good performing model at core. Finally, it is worth reminding that like many other software and digital solutions, FRT systems can be subject to adversarial attacks. It might be a lot easier to fool a DNN-based FR model using adversarial samples or patches compared with the human potential for identifying such attempts.[16]

Hence, considering all such intentional and unintentional risks, are the benefits of FRT worth it? Rather than giving a blanket yes/no answer, it should be concluded that this depends on the application and impact levels. However, making a conscious decision based on a realistic understanding of potentials and limitations of technology, along with having humans in the loop, can significantly help to minimise these risks.

---

[15] P. J. Phillips, A. N. Yates, Y. Hu, C. A. Hahn, E. Noyes, K. Jackson, J. G. Cavazos, G. Jeckeln, R. Ranjan, S. Sankaranarayanan, J-C. Chen, C. D. Castillo, R. Chellappa, D. White, and A. J. O'Toole, 'Face recognition accuracy of forensic examiners, superrecognizers, and face recognition algorithms' (2018) 115(24) *Proceedings of the National Academy of Sciences* 6171–6176, https://doi.org/10.1073/pnas.1721355115

[16] Yaoyao Zhong and Weihong Deng, 'Towards transferable adversarial attack against deep face recognition' (2020) 16 *IEEE Transactions on Information Forensics and Security* 1452–1466, doi: 10.1109/TIFS.2020.3036801.

3

FRT in 'Bloom'

Beyond Single Origin Narratives

Simon Michael Taylor

3.1 INTRODUCTION

On 10 September 2020, Pace Gallery in London held an exhibition by the artist Trevor Paglen examining the visual products from artificial intelligence and digital data systems.[1] Titled 'Bloom', the exhibition featured an over-sized sculpture of a human head. Bald, white, and possibly male, this eerily symmetrical 'standard head' had been modelled on measurements from canonical experiments in facial recognition history by Woody Wilson Bledsoe, Charles Bisson, and Helen Chan Wolf occuring at Panoramic Research Laboratory in 1964.[2]

Centring this 'standard head' in the space, Paglen surrounded it with photographic prints of leaves and flowers re-composed from RAW camera files by computer vision algorithms. These machine visualisations of nature encircled the 'standard head' illustrating how digital imaging using autonomous toolsets can achieve significantly different graphical outcomes. The exhibit foregrounded face recognition technology yet provoked viewers to consider the cross-practice connections between computing and data classification, humans and nature, and how image-making is becoming technically autonomous.[3] Another take-away is how these systems require

---

The author would like to acknowledge Stephanie Dick, Ausma Bernotaite, and Kalervo Gulson for their generous insight on different case-studies that comprise this chapter. Thanks also to Monika Zalneirute and Rita Matulionyte for their editorial guidance, and finally, Kathryn Henne at Australian National University, School of Regulation and Global Governance for her continued support.

[1] Trevor Paglen, 'Bloom', Pace Gallery (10 September–4 November 2020).

[2] Paglen obtained the dataset and visual materials on Bledsoe's experiments from correspondence with Harvard trained historian of technology Stephanie Dick and her research at the Briscoe Center for American History, University of Texas. See Bledsoe, Woodrow Wilson, and Helen Chan. "A man-machine facial recognition system—some preliminary results." Panoramic Research, Inc, Technical Report PRI A 19 (1965), Palo Alto, California.

[3] Paglen states that 'sophisticated machine learning algorithms that classify and categorise people are incentivized by assumptions of a stable relationship between the image and its measurement – but there are usually bad politics attached [and a misapprehension that these are human ways of seeing and of comprehending]'; Camille Sojit Pejcha, 'Trevor Paglen wants you to stop seeing like a human' (15 September 2020), *Document*, www.documentjournal.com/2020/09/trevor-paglen-wants-you-to-stop-seeing-like-a-human/.

multi-faceted elements to work and the 'mushrooming and blossoming from all kinds of datasets'.[4]

As a form of networked visual surveillance, facial recognition technology (FRT) works from the extent to which it operates in larger information infrastructures, FRT 'is not a single technology but an umbrella term for a set of technologies'.[5] These digitally networked systems allow imaging data to transform from one state to another, and transfer from one site to another. Recent improvements in FRT, as a remote identification system, has reached a point to be technically possible to capture biometric images and data from subjects in public, private, and personal spaces, or interactions online, without their consent or awareness, or adequate regulatory oversight. This includes a distribution of sensitive and personal user information between state and private-sector organisations, while contributing to training machine learning tools using honeypots of data, and enabling 'ever more sophisticated and effective forms of social control'.[6]

Unlike the suggestion of Paglen's exhibition, the origins of FRT cannot be reduced to the experiments in 1964. We need to widen the lens as the technical operations Stakeholders inside these systems are globally distributed and as Chair of Electronic Frontiers Australia's Policy Committee, Angus Murray iterated require 'bargains of trust'.[7] For example, Domestic and federal police agencies use systems that rely on huge amounts of data aggregation in private cloud servers and proprietary hardware that store and transmit data from online platforms, smart devices, foreign owned closed-circuit television (CCTV) companies and creators of wearable body cameras.[8] In Australia, retail outlets such as Bunnings use FRT and identity data to extract information from social media, where most people have images of themselves uploaded. They perform analysis based on the specific visits and transactions for certain shoppers.[9] Similarly images captured in public spaces, of crowds or of protesters, can be matched to social media posts or online forums managed by global technology firms, such as Facebook and Google, or transnational intelligence agencies such as

---

[4] David Gershgorn, 'The data that transformed AI research – And possibly the world' (26 July 2017), Quartz, https://qz.com/1034972/the-data-that-changed-the-direction-of-ai-research-and-possibly-the-world. Noted by Fei-Fei Li (the creator of the machine learning database Image-Net). For use of machine learning systems on Image Net, see E. Denton, A. Hanna, R. Amironesei, A. Smart, and H. Nicole, 'On the genealogy of machine learning datasets: A critical history of ImageNet' (2021) 8(2) *Big Data & Society*, https://doi.org/10.1177/20539517211035955.

[5] Nikki Stevens and Os Keyes, 'Seeing infrastructure: Race, facial recognition and the politics of data' (2021) 35(4–5) *Cultural Studies* 833–853, at 833.

[6] Kelly A. Gates, 'Introduction: Experimenting with the face' in *Our Biometric Future: Facial Recognition Technology and the Culture of Surveillance* (New York University Press, 2011), p. 5.

[7] 'Expert Panel: AI, Facial Recognition Terchnology and Law Enforcement' hosted by AUSCL Australasian Society for Computers + Law, May 5th 2022.

[8] Katelyn Ringrose, 'Law enforcement's pairing of facial recognition technology with body-worn cameras escalates privacy concerns' (2019) 105 *Virginia Law Review Online* 57–66.

[9] Dennis Desmond, 'Bunnings, Kmart and The Good Guys say they use facial recognition for "loss prevention". An expert explains what it might mean for you' (15 June 2022), *The Conversation*, https://theconversation.com/bunnings-kmart-and-the-good-guys-say-they-use-facial-recognition-for-loss-prevention-an-expert-explains-what-it-might-mean-for-you-185126.

the NSA and GCHQ. In the United Kingdom, Daragh Murray witnessed FRT software draw rectangles around the faces of people in public streets from a live CCTV feed. The system then extracted key features and compared these with stored features of criminal suspects in a watch list.[10] Matching an image to a watchlist is not the only function to consider here, but a need to query the distribution and ownership of data in the system being collectively assembled by the Tokyo-based technology giant NEC, in the example provided above.[11] Other examples of this diffuse and operational data flow include how China's Zhejiang Dahua Technology Co. Ltd sold thermal imaging cameras, armed with facial recognition software, to scan workers entering Amazon factories during COVID-19, that is despite them being black-trade listed in the United States.[12]

FRT and its computer procedures are therefore systems and 'technologies in the making', not artefacts with singularly defined origins and easy to regulate outcomes.[13] While an abundance of research looks at the use of FRT in border security and biometric surveillance,[14] retail shopping or school aged education,[15] and the gendering and racial divide between datasets with calls to ban these systems,[16] other elements also require scholarly, legislative, and regulatory attention.

---

[10] Pete Fussey and Daragh Murray, 'Independent report on the London Metropolitan Police service's trial of live facial recognition technology' (July 2019), University of Essex Repository, https://repository.essex .ac.uk/24946/1/London-Met-Police-Trial-of-Facial-Recognition-Tech-Report-2.pdf; see also Davide Castelvecchi, 'Is facial recognition too biased to be let loose?' (2020) Nature 587 347–349.

[11] NEC, 'A brief history of facial recognition' (12 May 2020), NEC Publications and Media, www.nec.co.nz/ market-leadership/publications-media/a-brief-history-of-facial-recognition/.

[12] China's Zhejiang Dahua Technology Co Ltd shipped 1,500 cameras to Amazon in a deal valued at close to $10 million – see Krystal Hu and Jeffrey Dastin, 'Exclusive: Amazon turns to Chinese firm on U.S. blacklist to meet thermal camera needs' (4 April 2020), Reuters, www.reuters.com/article/ ushealth-coronavirus-amazon-com-cameras/exclusive-amazon-turns-to-chinese-firm-on-u-s-blacklist-tomeet-thermal-camera-needs-idUSKBN22B1AL?il=o. For the black-listing of Dahua, see US Department of Commerce, 'U.S. Department of Commerce adds 28 Chinese organisations to its entity list', Office of Public Affairs, Press Release (7 October 2019), https://2017-2021.commerce .gov/news/press-releases/2019/10/us-department-commerce-adds-28-chinese-organizations-its-entity-list.html

[13] This is needed as a corrective to those who focus uncritically on such things as 'the computer and its social impacts but then fail to look behind technical things to notice the social circumstances of their development, deployment, and use'. Langdon Winner, 'Do artifacts have politics?' (1908) 109(1) Daedalus 121–136, at 112.

[14] Lucas D. Introna and David Wood, 'Picturing algorithmic surveillance: The politics of facial recognition systems' (2004) 2(2/3) Surveillance & Society 177–198; Lucas D. Introna, 'Disclosive ethics and information technology: Disclosing facial recognition systems' (2005) 7(2) Ethics and Information Technology 75–86; Lucas D. Introna and Helen Nissenbaum, Facial Recognition Technology: A Survey of Policy and Implementation Issues (Center for Catastrophe Preparedness and Response, New York University, 2010), pp. 1–60.

[15] Mark Andrejevic and Neil Selwyn, Facial Recognition (John Wiley & Sons, 2022).

[16] Luke Stark, 'Facial recognition is the plutonium of AI' (2019) 25(3)XRDS: Crossroads, The ACM Magazine for Students 50–55; Richard Van Noorden, 'The ethical questions that haunt facial-recognition research' (2020) 587 Nature 354–358. Joy Buolamwini and Timnit Gebru, 'Gender shades: Intersectional accuracy disparities in commercial gender classification' (2018) 81 Proceedings of the 1st Conference on Fairness, Accountability and Transparency, in Proceedings

This chapter considers how large-scale technical systems such as FRT have *bloomed* yet build on the echnical roots of multiple systems and the provenance of data sources that remain under considered. Tracing the genealogical origins and provenance of such datasets and statistical toolsets plays an important role in framing current uses for regulatory challenges. In this regard, this chapter presents empirical findings from research on early Indian statistical measures, the convergence of Chinese and Western technology companies, and the increase in computer vision experiments including those conducted on animals for bio security identification purposes. This chapter argues these diverse material innovations and information domains not only act as testbeds for FRT systems, but encompass some of the globalised products contained in FRT infrastructure.[17]

3.2 FRT DOES NOT HAVE A SINGULAR ORIGIN, THEY ARE 'SYSTEMS IN MOTION'

Bledsoe's 'standard head' algorithm didn't remain at the University of Texas nor in the domain of artificial intelligence history. Owing to funding by the RAND Corporation, the algorithm worked its way into informational models for law enforcement purposes. In the development of the New York State Intelligence and Identification System (NYSIIS), Bledsoe was recruited to develop his algorithm to computationally solve 'the mug-file problem'.[18] By contributing to the world's first computerised criminal-justice information-sharing system,[19] as Stephanie Dick posits, Bledsoe's algorithm and its ideas *travelled* with his over-simplifications and data assumptions in tow.[20] This

---

of Machine Learning Research 77–91; Jacqueline Cavazos, Jonathon Phillips, Carlos Castillo, and Alice O'Toole, 'Accuracy comparison across face recognition algorithms: Where are we on measuring race bias?' (2019) 3(1) *IEEE Transactions on Biometrics, Behavior, and Identity Science* 101–111; Morgan Scheuerman, Kandrea Wade, Caitlin Lustig, and Jed R. Brubaker, 'How we've taught algorithms to see identity: Constructing race and gender in image databases for facial analysis' (2020) 4(CSCW1) *Proceedings of the ACM on Human-Computer Interaction* 1–35.

[17] A main debate is whether this process should be considered a 'diffusion' from an established centre, such as Beldsoe's laboratory, or a more globalised network of exchanges. This changes the way these systems can be understood, explained, and regulated. Decentred histories give attention to members of other classes, such as the experiences of women, exploitation of Indigenous groups, and non-humans including animals. They include histories from parts of the world outside the United States and Europe. See Eden Medina, 'Forensic identification in the aftermath of human rights crimes in Chile: A decentered computer history' (2018) 59(4) *Technology and Culture* S100–S133; Erik Van der Vleuten, 'Toward a transnational history of technology: Meanings, promises, pitfalls' (2008) 49(4) *Technology and Culture* 974–994.

[18] Ben Rhodes, Kenneth Laughery, James Bargainer, James Townes, and George Batten, Jr, 'Final report on phase one of the Project "A man-computer system for solution of the mug file problem"' (26 August 1976), Prepared for the Department of Justice, Law Enforcement Assistance Administration, National Institute of Law Enforcement, and Criminal Justice, under Grate 74-NI-99-0023 G.

[19] Jeffrey Silbert, 'The world's first computerized criminal-justice information-sharing system, the New York State Identification and Intelligence System (NYSIIS)' (1970) 8(2) *Criminology* 107–128.

[20] Stephanie Dick, 'The standard head' in Gerardo Con Diaz and Jeffrey Yost (eds.), *Just Code!* (Johns Hopkins University Press, 2024).

influenced not only law enforcement databases and decisions on criminal targets in the United States, but also FRT developments that followed.[21] In its final state the algorithm was not used to automatically detect faces – as FRT does now – but contributed to a standardisation of 'mug shot' photos for computer filing systems. Bledsoe, who was later the president of the Association for the Advancement of Artificial Intelligence, used 2,000 images of police mug shots as his 'database' for making comparisons with a new set of photographs to detect any similarity. This American National Standards Institute Database, whose archives of mug shots featured convicted criminals (and those just accused), was the predominant source of visual information for Bledsoe's facial-recognition technology (a role now filled by social media).[22] To this end, Bledsoe and his Panoramic Research collaborators manually drew over human facial features with a device that resembled an iPad called a GRAFACON or RAND tablet. By using a stylus, images were rotated and re-drawn onto the tablet and recorded as coordinates on a grid. This produced a relatively high-resolution computer readable image. A list of distances were calculated and recorded as a *person's identification code* for locations such as the mouth, nose, or eyes.[23] Facial recognition (at this time) was a mathematical code of distances between features, drastically reducing individual and social nuances between them, and largely informed by Bayesian decision theory to use '22 measurements to make an educated guess about the whole'.[24]

In essence, Bledsoe had computerised the mug shot into a 'fully automated Bertillon system for the face'.[25] This system, invented by French criminologists Cesare Lombroso and Alphonse Bertillon in 1879, gained wide acceptance as a reliable and scientific method for criminal investigation, despite problematic eighteenth-century anthropometric experiments. The mug shot was invented to

[21] See A. Jay Goldstein, Leon D. Harmon, and Ann B. Lesk, 'Identification of human faces' (1971) 59(5) *Proceedings of the IEEE* 748–760; also Takeo Kanade, 'Picture processing by computer complex and recognition of human faces' (1973), PhD thesis, Kyoto University; and finally, the development of Principle Component Analysis – a compression of facial data that allowed for faster computer comparisons to be made (crucial to automation). Lawrence Sirovich and Michael Kirby, 'Low-dimensional procedure for the characterization of human faces' (1987) 4(3) *Josa a* 519–524.

[22] In other words, original facial-recognition software was built from images of prisoners repurposed by the US government without their consent. Trevor Paglen produced another artistic work on this - 'They Took the Faces from the Accused and the Dead …(SD18)', 2020, the artist and Altman Siegel, San Francisco. For how these databases are constructed and configured see Craig Watson and Patricia Flanagan, 'NIST special database 18: Mugshot identification database' (April 2016), Information Technology Laboratory, National Institute of Standards and Technology, www.nist.gov/system/files/documents/2021/12/06/readme_sd18.pdf.

[23] By producing a tape that could be fed to another, more powerful computer, the distance between specific points on the face then became a 'coded definition of that face'. Dick, 'The standard head'.

[24] For a biographical narrative of Bledsoe's efforts with Panoramic Research see Shaun Raviv, 'The secret history of facial recognition' (21 January 2020), *Wired*, www.wired.com/story/secret-history-facial-recognition/.

[25] As Aradau and Blanke argue, controlling error in these systems requires repeated measurements and often converge towards' the average'. This becomes the 'standard' benchmark with which to measure and render individuals uniquely identifiable. Claudia Aradau and Tobias Blanke, 'Algorithmic surveillance and the political life of error' (2021) 2(1) *Journal for the History of Knowledge* 1–13, at 5.

FRT in 'Bloom'

recognise criminal suspects who were repeatedly arrested: portraits were drawn and statistically labelled on common morphological characteristics.[26] The resulted 'mug shots' were standardised and collected by police departments and accepted as evidence in courts. Photo IDs modelled on the mug shot not only became an official format for policing, but have become standard issue in nation-state passports presented at airports and for driver's licence photographs. The first ever US photo driver's licence, issued in 1958, was created by French security company IDEMIA – a world leader in biometric security. Founded in 1922 as the defence contractor SAGEM, it then became SAGEM-Morpho in the 1980s, and parts of IDEMIA go back even further, and they have effectively led to every shift in the photo identity issuance and credentialling in the US since.[27]

Bledsoe's 1960s laboratory experiments thus relied on two separate building blocks invented in France. Hampered by the technology of his era, Bledsoe's ideas for FRT were not truly operationalised until the 1990s – driven by a technological wave of mobile phone and personal computer sales, online networked wireless video systems, and digital cameras.[28] Yet the experimental use of FRT is still being conducted in a way largely never done before.[29] Clare Garvie contends that forms of automated imaging for policing actions remain unregulated and represent a 'forensic science without rules':

> [T]here are no rules when it comes to what images police can submit to facial recognition [databases] and algorithms to help generate investigative leads. As a consequence, agencies across the country can, and do, submit all manner of probe photos – low-quality surveillance camera stills, social media photos with filtering, and scanned photo album pictures. Records from police departments show they may also include computer-generated 3D facial features, or composite and artistic sketches.[30]

---

[26] From vast literature on Bertillon, refer to Jonathan Finn, *Capturing the Criminal Image: From Mug Shot to Surveillance Society* (University of Minnesota Press, 2009); Keith Breckenridge, *Biometric State: The Global Politics of Identification and Surveillance in South Africa, 1850 to the Present* (Cambridge University Press, 2014).

[27] This also included the first automated fingerprint system for the FBI, building contactless scanners, and the launch of electronic ID (eID) in the United States in 2017. See IDEMIA, 'Innovation wall: A history of expertise' (2022), www.idemia.com/wp-content/uploads/2021/01/idemia-history-of-expertise .pdf; and see FindBiometrics, 'IDEMIA's Matt Thompson on the reality of mobile ID and "Identity on the Edge"'(4 May 2021), Interview at Find Biometrics: Global Identity Management, https:// findbiometrics.com/interview-idemia-matt-thompson-mobile-id-identity-on-the-edge-705059/.

[28] For an analysis of 'smart photography' and facial recognition see Sarah Kember, 'Face recognition and the emergence of smart photography' (2014) 13(2) *Journal of Visual Culture* 182–199. The use of digital photography also challenges 'how can the photographic image continue to "guarantee" the existence of reality in what it shows when pixel by pixel manipulation allows a seamless modification?' Scott McQuire, 'Digital photography and the operational archive' in Sean Cubitt, Daniel Palmer, and Nathaniel Tkacz (eds.), *Digital Light* (Open Humanities Press, 2015), chapter 6 (pp. 122–143), at p. 142.

[29] Clare Garvie, 'Garbage in, garbage out: Face recognition on flawed data' (16 May 2019), Georgetown Law, Center on Privacy & Technology, www.flawedfacedata.com/.

[30] Clare Garvie, Alvaro Bedoya, and Jonathan Frankle, 'The perpetual line-up: Unregulated police face recognition in America' (18 October 2016), Georgetown Law, Center on Privacy & Technology, www.perpetuallineup.org.

50   *Simon Michael Taylor*

In the next section, I explore how the automation of FRT relies not only on a diverse manufacturing of 'images' – products of reduction, appropriation, transformation, or digital manipulation – and situated instances of exploitation conducted in South America, the United States, France, Russia, Japan, and China to name a few different jurisdictions, but also how modern FRT resurrects a century old vision of 'statistical surveillance'.[31] To do so, I consider how a 100 year old mathematical experiment in British India has aided the probabilistic functionality of autonomous FRT systems.

3.3 THE 'MIND BOGGLING SYSTEMS' WHERE EVERYONE ONLY EVER HAS ONE ID

In 1991 Turk and Pentland produced the first real-time automated face recognition.[32] Famously, this was deployed at the crowded USA Super Bowl in 2001. This experimental trial was called 'Facefinder'. The system captured surveillance images of the crowd and compared them with a database of digital mug shots held by Tampa police, the Florida Department of Law Enforcement and the FBI.[33] The experiment not only demonstrated the potential for remote surveillance of crowds, but also led to the National Institute of Standards creating a Face Recognition Vendor Test (FRVT) to evaluate this emerging FRT market.

A quick look at the ongoing FRVT of 1: N facial algorithms reveals a globalised picture: 'The report lists accuracy results alongside developer names as a useful comparison of facial recognition algorithms and assessment of absolute capability. The developer totals constitute a substantial majority of the face recognition industry.'[34] This includes performance figures for 203 prototype algorithms from the research laboratories of over fifty commercial developers and one university. Similar to Beldsoe's 1960s experiments for NYSIIS, this evaluative test scenario also uses

---

[31] Oscar H. Gandy, 'Statistical surveillance: Remote sensing in the digital age' in Kevin Haggerty, Kirstie Ball, and David Lyon (eds.), *Routledge Handbook of Surveillance Studies* (Taylor & Francis, 2012), pp. 125–132.

[32] The approach used a process to break down human faces into principle components via statistical means and these became 'standardised ingredients' known as eigenfaces. The experiment was constrained by environmental factors, but created significant interest in automated face recognition. M. Turk and A. Pentland, 'Eigenfaces for recognition' (1991) 3(1) *Journal of Cognitive Neuroscience* 71–86.

[33] At the Super Bowl signs advised fans that they were under video surveillance. The system identified nineteen people – all petty criminals. No one was detained or questioned because Facefinder was an experiment. See Vicky Chachere, 'Biometrics used to detect criminals at Super Bowl' (13 February 2001), *ABC News*, https://abcnews.go.com/Technology/story?id=98871&page=1.

[34] Patrick J. Grother, Mei L. Ngan, and Kayee K. Hanaoka, 'Ongoing Face Recognition Vendor Test (FRVT) Part 2: Identification' (November 2018), NIST Interagency/Internal Report (NISTIR), National Institute of Standards and Technology, Gaithersburg, MD, https://doi.org/10.6028/NIST .IR.8238. The primary dataset is comprised of 26.6 million reasonably well-controlled live portrait photos of 12.3 million individuals. Three smaller datasets contain more unconstrained photos: 3.2 million webcam images, 200,000 side-view images, and 2.5 million photojournalism and amateur photographer photos. These datasets are sequestered at NIST, meaning that developers do not have access to them for training or testing.

FRT in 'Bloom'

frontal mug shots and profile view mug shots alongside desktop webcam photos, visa application photos, immigration lane photos, and traveller kiosk photos.

A brief survey of this report illustrates the scale and scope of a global FRT market. To name a few vendors, the developers and their places of origin include NEC (Tokyo); Microsoft (United States); Veritas (Spain); Herta Security (Spain); AnyVision (Israel); IDEMIA (France), utilised in Kenya and in Turkey; Daon (Ireland); Dahua (China); Moonwalk (China); Sensetime (China); Hyperverge (California); Cognitec (Germany); QNAP (Taiwan); Tevian (Russia); VisionLabs (Russia/Netherlands); Clearview AI (United States); DeepGlint (China) and finally Neurotechnology (Lithuania), which is a provider of deep-learning-based solutions for high-precision biometric identification and object recognition technology.

Importantly, the Lithuania based Neurotechnology recently partnered with Tata Consultancy Services as one of three biometric service providers for the largest biometric ID system in the world, Aadhaar.[35] Co-ordinated by The Unique Identification Authority of India, the system registers people and compares their facial biometric with the existing records of 1.3 billion people to verify applicants have not registered under a different name. Aadhaar is 'a mind-boggling system', says Anil Jain, a computer scientist who consulted on the scheme, 'and the beauty is that it ensures one person has only one ID'.[36]

India has a rich history of producing material and statistical innovations to identify individuals based on their physical characteristics.[37] In 2020, Google posted an online tribute to Professor Prasanta Chandra Mahalanobis (1893–1972) as part of its 'Arts and Culture' series.[38] Mahalanobis is famous for creating new statistical and biometric functions as key technologies he advocated to the world through his Indian Statistical Institute.[39] The global celebration of his work was recognised in part after his creation of a similarity distance metric in 1936. This was produced from his specific interest in

---

[35] Neurotechnology, 'Neurotechnology and TCS selected by UIDAI to provide biometric de-duplication and authentication for India's Aadhaar ID program', Neurotechnology Press Release (22 March 2021), www.neurotechnology.com/press_release_india_uidai_aadhaar_id.html.

[36] For references on Aadhaar, see Bidisha Chaudhuri and Lion König, 'The Aadhaar scheme: A cornerstone of a new citizenship regime in India?' (2018) 26(2) *Contemporary South Asia* 127–142; Amiya Bhatia and Jacqueline Bhabha, 'India's Aadhaar scheme and the promise of inclusive social protection' (2017) 45(1) *Oxford Development Studies* 64–79; Kalyani Menon Sen, 'Aadhaar: Wrong number, or Big Brother calling' (2015) 11(1) *Socio-Legal Review* 85–108.

[37] See Keith Breckenridge, *Biometric State: The Global Politics of Identification and Surveillance in South Africa, 1850 to the Present* (Cambridge University Press, 2014). Chapter 3 (pp. 90–114), titled 'Gandhi's biometric entanglement: Fingerprints, satyagraha and the global politics of Hind Swaraj', perfectly captures the complexity when dealing with the question of biometrics, and a mobility in their use.

[38] Indian Statistical Institute, 'Father of Indian statistics: Prof. Prasanta Chandra Mahalanobis' (2020), Google Arts and Culture, https://artsandculture.google.com/exhibit/father-of-indian-statistics-prof-prasanta-chandra-mahalanobis%C2%A0/oAISK23-669lLA.

[39] Prasanta Chandra Mahalanobis, 'Statistics as a key technology' (1965) 19(2) *The American Statistician* 43–46; and refer to Paidipaty Poornima, 'Testing measures: Decolonization and economic power in 1960s India' (2020) 52(3) *History of Political Economy* 473–497.

racial classification.[40] He developed a biometric function to analyse and identify people based on physical and racial similarity. To do so he compared data collected from the Chittagong Hill Tract area (modern Bangladesh) with international race data sets collected from Swedish and Chinese records.[41] He then set about learning how to create an identification of race based on statistical measurements of facial features and their similarity, which he could apply in India. The aim was to help identify exotic and ethnic caste groups to be classified in the British colonial administration.[42]

Significantly, he also innovated by using facial photographs of living subjects to compare the accuracy of his biometric measurements, compared with analysing skulls in the era's practice of phrenology.[43] By testing his distance function with the invention of an experimental imaging device in 1937, Mahalanobis was a central figure in pushing 'part of a biometric nationalism in which the face provided a form of data'.[44] His metric, commonly known as a Mahalanobis Distance Function, despite being created eighty-six years ago, is consistently used in modern FRT.

Even the most sophisticated and large-scale FRT systems necessitate this basic approach of comparing images on facial features by using scores that compare a match of the similarity.[45]

In technical terms, the selection of a decision metric – such as the Mahalanobis Distance Function – '[h]elps to measure distances between specific facial features and generate a unique representation (as a 'facial signature') for each human face.[46] Similar to Bledsoe's code, this is then compared with a database of stored images in order to match a face to similar images.

In this regard, similarity measure functions operationalise the matching process as a critical decision-making module. Selection of the proper similarity measure is thus

[40] Dasgupta Somesh, 'The evolution of the D statistic of Mahalanobis' (1993) 55(3) *Sankhyā: The Indian Journal of Statistics, Series A (1961–2002)* 442–459; Prasanta Chandra Mahalanobis, 'On the generalized distance in statistics' (1936) 12 *Proceedings of the National Institute of Science India* 49–55.

[41] Simon Michael Taylor, Kalervo N. Gulson, and Duncan McDuie-Ra, 'Artificial intelligence from colonial India: Race, statistics, and facial recognition in the Global South' (2021) 48(3) *Science, Technology, & Human Values*, https://doi.org/10.1177/01622439211060839.

[42] Somesh, 'The evolution of the D statistic', p. 448.

[43] Mahalanobis Prasanta Chandra, 'A new photographic apparatus for recording profiles of living persons' (1933) 20 *Proceedings of the Twentieth Indian Science Congress. Patna Secondary Anthropology* 413.

[44] Mukharji Projit Bihari, 'Profiling the profiloscope: Facialization of race technologies and the rise of biometric nationalism in inter-war British India' (2015) 31(4) *History and Technology* 376–396, at 392.

[45] This applies whether for connectionist approaches such as using neural networks or deep learning; or statistical based approaches using hidden Markov models; or biometric probes with template feature matching; or geometric approaches to frontal face recognition such as eigenface images or geometrical feature matching.

[46] Ada Lovelace Institute, 'Beyond face value: Public attitudes to facial recognition technology' (September 2019), Nuffield Foundation, Ada Lovelace Institute, London, p. 5, www.adalovelaceinstitute.org/wp-content/uploads/2019/09/Public-attitudes-to-facial-recognition-technology_v.FINAL_.pdf.

FRT in 'Bloom' 53

an important determination for the accuracy of the matching result. Such measures include Minkowski distances, Mahalanobis distances, Hansdorff distances, Euclidean, and cosine-based distances.[47] Yet the Mahalanobis distance is the best at structuring data for unknown targets. This is critical to criminal subject investigations for matching suspects from surveillance images in supermarkets, stadiums, or of protest crowds. The similarity measure enables high-speed cluster analysis – critical to a speed of decision-making – especially for faces with a high-number of variables and in relation to fitting an unknown person into a known database. FRT can then determine if an unknown image (taken from a web profile or a surveillance camera) matches a person in the database (compared with drivers' licences or mug shots). This approach is also suitable for machine learning and is a prominent approach for training systems on person re-identification by 'improving classification through exploiting structures in the data'.[48]

As Adriana Dongus suggests, '[t]he large datasets produced by science and law enforcement at the turn of the nineteenth century continue to form the material backbone and precedent to current machine learning.'[49] By examining the critical and ubiquitous distribution and embedment of early decision classifiers, we establish the importance of selecting certain rule functions in 'a statistical layer' of FRT systems.

When applied to machine learning, this includes assigning weights to autonomously identify the importance in probable matches. This is used in image-labelled data sets,[50] to estimating facial position poses from video,[51] to automatically locating an unproductive worker on a factory floor,[52] or identifying ethnic minority faces in a crowd, as is occurring in China with the Uyghur (Uighur) population. While much important work on facial recognition is salient to the United States,[53] there is a need to examine

---

[47] Enrico Vezzetti and Federica Marcolin, *Similarity Measures for Face Recognition* (Bentham Science, 2015).

[48] The Mahalanobis distance function is ubiquitous owing to its algorithmic and biometric efficacy for structuring unknown datasets, its acceptability and incorporability into different decision systems, and the efficiency of being weighted to produce accurate results. See P. M. Roth, M. Hirzer, M. Köstinger, C. Beleznai, and H. Bischof, 'Mahalanobis distance learning for person re-identification' in S. Gong, M. Cristani, S. Yan, and C. C. Loy (eds.), *Person Re-Identification* (Springer, 2014), pp. 247–267.

[49] Machine learning tools often reuse elements that lie far afield from the scientific laboratories, statistical research institutes, and engineering settings in which they first took shape. See also Ariana Dongus, 'Galton's utopia – Data accumulation in biometric capitalism' (2019) 5 *Spheres: Journal for Digital Cultures* 1–16, at 11, http://spheres-journal.org/galtons-utopia-data-accumulation-in-biometric-capitalism/.

[50] Kate Crawford and Trevor Paglen, 'Excavating AI: The politics of images in machine learning training sets' (2021) 36(4) *AI & Society* 1105–1116.

[51] Shiming Xiang, Feiping Nie, and Changshui Zhang, 'Learning a Mahalanobis distance metric for data clustering and classification' (2008) 41(12) *Pattern Recognition* 3600–3612.

[52] Meredith Whittaker, Kate Crawford, Roel Dobbe, Genevieve Fried, Elizabeth Kaziunas, Varoon Mathur, Myers West, Rashida Richardson, Jason Schultz, and Oscar Schwartz, 'AI Now Report 2018' (2018), AI Now Institute.

[53] Cavazos et al., 'Accuracy comparison across face recognition algorithms'; Clare Garvie, 'Face recognition in US investigations: A forensic without the science' (5 August 2020), Webinar, UNSW Grand Challenges, online presentation, UNSW Sydney; Scheuerman et al., 'How we've taught algorithms to see identity'; Stark, 'Facial recognition is the plutonium of AI'.

how FRT is conditioned on a globalised supply chain. This includes the 'production, schematization, maintenance, inflection, and reproduction of certain [decision] rules' and how they replicate use of problematic standards in public surveillance.[54]

Indeed, there has been a 'tendency to gloss over the amount of effort that goes into developing and integrating new technologies and systems with older technologies'.[55] Computation moves fast – yet many lessons remain and are yet to be learned.

From legislative, ethical, and regulatory standpoints, it is worth noting that biometric systems and data (including use of statistical functions and facial images) are constructed on complex and interoperable supply chains involving third-party vendors needed to make these systems work. Yet there is potential incentives built within these globalised computing systems to exploit regulatory gaps and vulnerabilities that could be used against various human populations at a later date.[56] The final section examines how Mahalanobis's 100 year old experiment is relevant not only to our digital identity systems today, such as the United Nations High Commission for Refugees (UNHCR) Population Registration and Identity Management Eco-System[57] but builds on different use-cases. These include not only nation-state surveillance, such as the identification and detection of ethnic minorities in China, but the increasing datafication of animals and computerisation of biosecurity measures in agriculture that can be transferrable to human populations.[58]

3.4 DYNAMIC MATCHING STRATEGIES IN FRT EXTEND BEYOND RECOGNISING HUMAN BEINGS

To securely identify forcibly displaced persons seeking UNHCR repatriation assistance at refugee processing centres the UNHCR records biometrics such as iris, fingerprints, and facial metrics.[59] Driven in part by a Biometric Matching Engine developed by Accenture, this Population Registration and Identity Management Eco-System (PRIMES) employs a patented 'dynamic matching strategy' comprising at least two sets of biometric modalities.[60] With the advent of new, technologically

---

[54] Alexander Monea and Jeremy Packer, 'Media genealogy and the politics of archaeology' (2016) 10 *International Journal of Communication* 3141–3159, at 3144.

[55] Gates, 'Introduction', p. 11.

[56] Caroline Compton, Fleur E. Johns, Lyria Bennett Moses, Monika Zalnieriute, Guy S. Goodwin-Gill, and Jane, McAdam, 'Submission to the UNHCR's Global Virtual Summit on Digital Identity for Refugees "Envisioning a Digital Identity Ecosystem in Support of the Global Compact on Refugees"' (1 January 2019), UNSW Law Research Paper No. 19–31, https://ssrn.com/abstract=3380116 or http://dx.doi.org/10.2139/ssrn.3380116.

[57] UNHCR, 'From ProGres to PRIMES', Information Sheet 2018 (March 2018), www.unhcr.org/blogs/wp-content/uploads/sites/48/2018/03/2018-03-16-PRIMES-Flyer.pdf.

[58] Taylor, Simon Michael. "Species ex machina:'the crush'of animal data in AI." BJHS Themes (2023): 1–15.

[59] Fleur Johns, 'Data, detection, and the redistribution of the sensible in international law' (2017) 111(1) *American Journal of International Law* 57–103.

[60] A. Lodinová, 'Application of biometrics as a means of refugee registration: Focusing on UNHCR's strategy' (2016) 2(2) *Development, Environment and Foresight* 91–100.

advanced modes of biometric data gathering and analysis, some of the current 'international legal thought, doctrine, and practice are, in the main, poorly equipped to deal with them', especially in situations of forced migration.[61] One reason is the lack of manual processing options and how the introduction of machine learning can lift the collection of sensitive and personally identifiable information outside the scope of pre-existing legal methods. In grappling with new forms of quantification and statistics these systems do not just contain hundred-year old statistical decision functions but the pairing of imaging, data aggregation, and machine learning at scale. The autonomy granted to machine learning may remove abilities to interrogate the validity of the earlier datasets and matching results a system relies on to achieve a result. Such logic clusters ever increasing data collections into new 'probabilistic dependencies'.[62] Yet what this curtails are reasonable efforts to disentangle bias from standardised classifications, and how the natural divergences that occur between humans, different social groups, and their situated actions, are erased in deference to the calculative inferences instead. In the use of FRT there is always 'politics attached'. Avi Marciano illustrated this in the context of Israel where biometric standards establish hierarchies for decision making by defining particular bodies as 'ineligible' to access.[63]

Some FRTs are directly complicit in human rights abuses, including a reported detention of up to 1.5 million Uyghur Muslims in Xinjiang.[64] Owing to the increasing scale of an inescapable surveillance that the Chinese Communist Party has funded, ubiquitous CCTV systems and facial recognition are operationalised in public spaces alongside the monitoring of online communications and patterns-of-life data from mobile phones. Idealised as an all-seeing pervasive surveillance network enabled by a state manufacturing of computer vision technology, digital platforms, and data aggregation centres,[65] the simplified idea that Chinese technology and its authoritarian state surveillance system are indigenous is significantly flawed. Before China started using CCTV systems and facial pattern-matching techniques to identify ethnic minorities in Xinjiang Province, Bledsoe proposed to the Defence Department Advanced Research Projects Agency (then known as ARPA)

[61] Ibid., p. 59.

[62] Fleur Johns, 'Global governance through the pairing of list and algorithm' (2016) 34(1) *Environment and Planning D: Society and Space* 126–149.

[63] Marciano, Avi. "The politics of biometric standards: The case of Israel biometric project." Science as Culture 28, no. 1 (2019): 98–119.

[64] In September 2019, four researchers wrote to the publisher Wiley to 'respectfully ask' that it immediately retract a scientific paper. The study, published in 2018, had trained algorithms to distinguish faces of Uyghur people, a predominantly Muslim minority ethnic group in China, from those of Korean and Tibetan ethnicity. C. Wang, Q. Zhang, W. Liu, Y. Liu, and L. Miao, 'Facial feature discovery for ethnicity recognition' (2018) 9(1) *Wiley Interdisciplinary Reviews: Data Mining and Knowledge Discovery* Article ID e1278.

[65] Danielle Cave, Samantha Hoffman, Alex Joske, Fergus Ryan, and Elise Thomas, 'Mapping China's technology giants' (18 April 2019), ASPI Report No. 15, www.aspi.org.au/report/mapping-chinas-tech-giants.

that it should support Panoramic Research Laboratory in studying the feasibility of using facial characteristics to determine a person's racial background.[66] This is another instance of the politics and the power of FRT recurring and returning and re-playing into new uses, new places, and new eras, yet with similar purposes.

Western companies were involved in the creation of these systems at the start. The export of surveillance technologies from the Global North to China started in the 1970s. It is only now that Chinese technology companies are found competing with and replacing those suppliers in a globalised market.[67] The current status of FRT developed in China with known human rights and privacy violations is not adequately restricted by regulatory frameworks in Europe and the United States.[68] To better disentangle use-cases requires not only a more through mapping of globally entangled and technical supply-chains, whether through critical research or in the building of oversight capabilities such as independent risk assessments, compliance audits, or technical red-teaming in the light of such swiftly evolving material properties.

A contemporary focus on understanding FRT must therefore be concerned not only with the implementation and implications for nation and state-bound privacy law, but to make transparent infrastructural supply chains and situated origins of datasets and technical domains they were created in. This should not simply be restricted to law enforcement and public organisations being required to undertake better procurement strategies – often limited to purchasing orders or responses to requests for information – but to identify the exact sources of the FRT hardware, software, decision functions, and datasets.[69]

Indeed, there are circumstances in which we may need to look further afield. This includes so-called dual-use systems that are adopted not just from domains in nation state and military operations but those trained on animals within precision agriculture.[70] In the shift from classical identification methods to computer vision tools, the future of farming lies in the paddock-to-plate digital identification of each product. Whether for cross-border bio-security purposes or the optimisation of meat

---

[66] Raviv, 'The secret history of facial recognition'.

[67] Ausma Bernot, 'Transnational state-corporate symbiosis of public security: China's exports of surveillance technologies' (2022) 11(2) *International Journal for Crime, Justice and Social Democracy* 159–173.

[68] Yan Luo and Rui Guo, 'Facial recognition in China: Current status, comparative approach and the road ahead' (2021) 25(2) *University of Pennsylvania, Journal of Law and Social Change* 153.

[69] This includes clarifying information materials to train law enforcement personnel on using and maintaining FRT systems, including manual facial comparison, mobile device uses, and other FRT hardware. Garvie, Bedoya, and Frankle, 'The perpetual line-up'.

[70] See Simon Michael Taylor, 'Species ex machina: 'the crush' of animal data in AI.' (2023) 8 BJHS Themes, 155–169; Ali Shojaeipour, Greg Falzon, Paul Kwan, Nooshin Hadavi, Frances C. Cowley, and David Paul, 'Automated muzzle detection and biometric identification via few-shot deep transfer learning of mixed breed cattle' (2021) 11(1) *Agronomy* 2365, https://doi.org/10.3390/agronomy11112365; and Ali Ismail Awad, 'From classical methods to animal biometrics: A review on cattle identification and tracking' (2016) 123 *Computers and Electronics in Agriculture* 423–435.

FRT in 'Bloom'   57

traceability FRT is seen as a viable investment to remotely track animals. These systems commonly utilize open-source software architectures, machine learning and modular camera systems.[71] Yet in the computational transference between animal bodies, digital and data visualisation, and informational materials, we collapse into the heart of Trevor Paglen's art project titled in 'Bloom'. The visualisation and classification of *all images and all bodies* helps to establish the adoption of autonomous methods. This includes initiatives from the global accounting firm KPMG and Meat and Livestock Australia to collect data that translate into efforts to strengthen computer vision market positions. Agribusinesses are not yet treated as handling any sensitive data or training bodily surveillance systems nor are they subjected to regulatory approaches that can throw their data practices into question.[72]

As Mark Maguire suggests, a genealogical and infrastructural approach to FRT 'demands we consider how technologies are an assemblage of different elements delivered from specific contexts' yet re-made, aggregated, customised, adapted, and re-purposed for newly defined, profit-driven, and yet often speculative objectives.[73]

3.5 CONCLUSION

At the time of Bledsoe's experiments there was a meeting between the administrative management of the NYSIIS law enforcement data bases and the computer design company Systems Development Corporation (SDC) of Santa Monica, California, in September 1964.[74] The aim was to decide in what manner to proceed with the implementation of the system, and what techniques to commission for deployment. In summary, the critical inflexion point centred on: 'First buy the computer and decide what

---

[71] For animal facial recognition biometrics see Yue Lu, Xiaofu He, Ying Wen and Patrick Wang, 'A new cow identification system based on iris analysis and recognition' (2014) 6(1) *International Journal of Biometrics* 18–32.

[72] For regulatory gaps in agricultural data and privacy law, see Annie Guest, 'Are Big Ag Tech companies harvesting farmers' confidential data?' (18 February 2022), *ABC News*, Landline, www.abc.net.au/news/2022-02-19/agriculture-data-protection/100840436; also Kelly Bronson and Phoebe Sengers, 'Big Tech meets Big Ag: Diversifying epistemologies of data and power' (2022) 31(1) *Science as Culture* 1–14; and Leanne Wiseman, Jay Sanderson, Airong Zhang, and Emma Jakku, 'Farmers and their data: An examination of farmers' reluctance to share their data through the lens of the laws impacting smart farming' (2019) 90–91 *NJAS – Wageningen Journal of Life Sciences* 100301.

[73] Mark Maguire, 'The birth of biometric security' (2009) 25 *Anthropology Today* 9–14. This is also because of what has worked in the past – building on successful statistical classifications, image categorisation, and probability.

[74] SDC was called the first software company. It began as a systems engineering group for an air-defence system at the RAND in April 1955 – the same year that 'artificial intelligence' as a term was defined in a Dartmouth Conference proposal. Within a few months, RAND's System Development Division had over 500 employees developing software computing applications. For informational retrieval and database management systems see Jules I. Schwartz, 'Oral history interview with Jules I. Schwartz' (7 April 1989), Center for the History of Information Processing, Charles Babbage Institute. Retrieved from the University of Minnesota Digital Conservancy, https://hdl.handle.net/11299/107628

to put on it; (2) Or do an extensive feasibility analysis and, as a result of that study, decide on the computer (how large and powerful) and the functions to be performed.'[75] As the technical capacity of computing systems in the 1960s was nascent, SDC lacked capability to deliver the required system at scale. Yet this allowed a pause for discussion, consideration, and to recognise that computing capabilities must be defined for a particular purpose, and there should be a thorough vetting of the modular building blocks the system would contain.[76] The title of that report was 'A System in Motion', and it recognised that multiple capabilities – from query and search functions onto image recognition – could not be adequately managed and regulated when developed at once. The NYSIIS report stated the application of computers to solve recognition problems for law enforcement was a foregone conclusion. Yet the question remained whether social institutions and organisations should allow for deploying use of complete automation, especially as they function as a sum of moving, and largely unknown 'experimental parts'?[77]

Although most state departments and law enforcement undertake basic steps to adhere to industry best practices, such as compliance, testing, and legal obligations to avoid public scrutiny, these approaches often lack consistency. FRT is an experimental practice constituted by practices and elements that can be hidden from view, trialed and tested in domains unsuitable to be deemed fit-for-purpose. Whether being trained on exploitative data captured from refugees, prisoners, or operationalised on farm animals, this is called 'the deploy and comply problem' and requires public consultation and impact considerations before being put into action.[78] A prime example is the use of Clearview AI facial algorithms by New Zealand Police in 2020 without consulting the Privacy Commissioner or considering the impacts to vulnerable Indigenous groups.[79] This is indicative of multiple instances of harm,

---

[75] SDC stressed that it was imperative to get into the computer-design phase as quickly as possible. Their main fear was that if NYSIIS waited too long in getting started, they might not develop a computer system at all. A strong rebuttal was supported by the administrative management of New York State. They felt a Feasibility Report and an exhaustive systems analysis was needed to be completed first. In the end, SDC went along with this decision. See Ross Gallati, 'Identification and intelligence systems for administration of justice', in Cornog et al. (eds.), *EDP Systems in Public Management* (Rand McNally, 1968), pp. 161–162; also Silbert (1970), 'The world's first computerized criminal-justice information-sharing system', p. 116.

[76] Building Block One involved the fingerprint and an ability for the computer to search and summarise case-history capabilities; the second stage was to develop image-recognition on mug shot databases.

[77] B. G. Schumaker, *Computer Dynamics in Public Administration* (Spartan Books, 1967).

[78] Crawford and Calo consider 'this a blindspot in AI' and advocate for analyses at a systems level to consider the history of the data and algorithms being used, and to engage with the social impacts produced at every stage – dataset conception, technology design, use-case deployment and nation-state regulation. Kate Crawford and Ryan Calo, 'There is a blind spot in AI research' (2016) 538 *Nature* 311–313.

[79] New Zealand Police first contacted Clearview in January, and later set up a trial of the software; however, the high tech crime unit handling the technology appears not to have sought the necessary clearance before using it. Mackenzie Smith, 'Police trialled facial recognition tech without clearance' (13

error, oppression, and inequality that have been caused by autonomous decision and surveillance systems.[80] What is needed are efforts to trace, assess, and determine if the modular 'elements' of an FRT system are legitimate, credible, feasible, and reasonable. This challenge seeks to ringfence the 'lineage of intent' – yet can FRT systems be restricted by ethical, legal and technical guardrails to specific, deliberate, and predefined purposes?[81] This is what this book is seeking to address.

May 2020), *Radio New Zealand*, www.rnz.co.nz/news/national/416483/police-trialled-facial-recognition-tech-without-clearance. This resulted in New Zealand Police commissioning a retrospective feasibility and social impacts study owing to the pace of technological change that has outstripped law and regulation. See Nessa Lynch and Andrew Chen, 'Facial recognition technology: Considerations for use in policing' (November 2021), Report commissioned by the New Zealand Police, www.police.govt.nz/sites/default/files/publications/facial-recognition-technology-considerations-for-usepolicing.pdf.

[80] For example, IDEMIA systems have been deployed in different cultural settings with problematic results. IDEMIA supplied the biometric capture kits to the Kenyan government in 2018–2019 for its controversial national digital ID scheme, commonly known as Huduma Namba ('service number'). Data Rights filed a case before the Paris tribunal accusing IDEMIA of failing to adequately address human rights issues. See Frank Hersey, 'NGOs sue IDEMIA for failing to consider human rights risks in Kenyan digital ID' (29 July 2022), BiometricUpdate.com, www.biometricupdate.com/202207/ngos-sue-idemia-for-failing-to-consider-human-rights-risks-in-kenyan-digital-id.

[81] See Manasi Sakpal, 'How to use facial recognition technology ethically and responsibly' (15 December 2021), Gartner Insights, www.gartner.com/smarterwithgartner/how-to-use-facial-recognition-technology-responsibly-and-ethically; and also, Nicholas Davis, Lauren Perry, and Edward Santow, 'Facial recognition technology: Towards a model law' (2022), Human Technology Institute, The University of Technology, Sydney.

4

Transparency of Facial Recognition Technology and Trade Secrets

Rita Matulionyte

4.1 INTRODUCTION

Facial recognition technology (FRT) is being increasingly used by border authorities, law enforcement, and other government institutions around the world. Research shows that among the 100 most populated countries in the world, seven out of ten governments are using FRT on a large-scale basis.[1] One of the major challenges related to this technology is the lack of transparency and explainability surrounding it. Numerous reports have indicated that there is insufficient transparency and explainability around the use of artificial intelligence (AI), including FRT, in the government sector.[2] There are still no clear rules, guidelines, or frameworks as to the level and kind of transparency and explainability that should be expected from government institutions when using AI more generally, and FRT in particular.[3] The EU General Data Protection Regulation (GDPR) is among the first instruments to establish a right of explanation in relation to automated decisions,[4] but its scope is very limited.[5] The proposed EU

This chapter is a result of the project 'Government Use of Facial Recognition Technologies: Legal Challenges and Solutions' (FaceAI), funded by the Research Council of Lithuania (LMTLT), agreement number S-MIP-21-38.

[1] Paul Bischoff, 'Facial recognition technology (FRT): 100 countries analyzed' (8 June 2021), Comparitech, www.comparitech.com/blog/vpn-privacy/facial-recognition-statistics/.

[2] See, e.g., NSW Ombudsman, 'The new machinery of government: Using machine technology in administrative decision-making' (29 November 2021), State of New South Wales, www.ombo.nsw .gov.au/Find-a-publication/publications/reports/state-and-local-government/the-new-machinery-of-government-using-machine-technology-in-administrative-decision-making; European Ombudsman, 'Report on the meeting between European Ombudsman and European Commission representatives' (19 November 2021), www.ombudsman.europa.eu/en/doc/inspection-report/en/149338.

[3] See, e.g., Access Now, 'Europe's approach to artificial intelligence: How AI strategy is evolving' (December 2020), Report Snapshot, www.accessnow.org/cms/assets/uploads/2020/12/Report-Snapshot-Europes-approach-to-AI-How-AI-strategy-is-evolving-1.pdf, p. 3.

[4] Regulation 2016/679 of 27 April 2016 on the protection of natural persons with regard to the processing of personal data and on the free movement of such data, and repealing Directive 95/46/EC (General Data Protection Regulation) [2016] OJ L119/1, art 13.

[5] Sandra Wachter, Brent Mittelstadt, and Chris Russell, 'Counterfactual explanations without opening the black box: Automated decisions and the GDPR' (2018) 31 *Harvard Journal of Law & Technology* 841–847, at 842, 878, 879 ('a legally binding right to explanation does not exist in the GDPR').

Artificial Intelligence Act (Draft EU AI Act) sets minimum transparency standards to high-risk AI technologies that include FRT.[6] However, these transparency obligations are generic to all high-risk AI technologies and do not detail transparency requirements for FRT specifically.

Transparency and explainability are arguably essential to ensuring the accountability of government institutions using FRT; empowering supervisory authorities to detect, investigate, and punish breaches of laws or fundamental rights obligations; allowing individuals affected by an AI system's outcome to challenge the decision generated using AI systems;[7] and enabling AI developers to evaluate the quality of the AI system.[8] According to the proposed EU AI Act, 'transparency is particularly important to avoid adverse impacts, retain public trust and ensure accountability and effective redress'.[9]

At the same time, one should note that transparency and explainability of FRT alone would not help remedy essential problems associated with FRT use, and might further contribute to its negative impacts in some cases. For instance, if an individual learns about the government use of FRT in public spaces where public gatherings take place, this might discourage her from participating in such gatherings and thus have a 'chilling effect' on the exercise of her human rights, such as freedom of speech and freedom of association.[10] These considerations have to be kept in mind when determining the desirable levels of FRT transparency and explainability.

While there is extensive *technical* literature on transparency and explainability of AI in general,[11] and of FRT more specifically,[12] there is very limited *legal* academic discussion

---

[6] See European Commission, 'Proposal for a Regulation of the European Parliament and of the Council: Laying down harmonised rules on artificial intelligence (Artificial Intelligence Act) and amending certain Union legislative acts' (21 April 2021) (hereafter draft EU AI Act), Com 206 Final, articles 13(1), 20, 60, 62.

[7] See, e.g., OECD, 'Transparency and explainability (Principle 1.3)' (2022), OECD AI Principles, https://oecd.ai/en/dashboards/ai-principles/P7.

[8] See, e.g., Diogo V. Carvalho, Eduardo M. Pereira, and Jaime S. Cardozo, 'Machine learning interpretability: A survey on methods and metrics' (2019) 8(8) *Electronics* 832, 5–7; Leilani H. Gilpin, David Bau, Ben Z. Yuan, Ayesha Bajwa, Michael Specter, and Lalana Kagal, 'Explaining explanations: An overview of interpretability of machine learning' (3 February 2019), Working Paper, https://arxiv.org/abs/1806.00069.

[9] Draft EU AI Act, para. 38.

[10] Interview participant 2, NGO representative.

[11] See, e.g., Upol Ehsan, Q. Vera Liao, Michael Muller, Mark O. Riedl, and Justin D. Weisz, 'Expanding explainability: Towards social transparency in AI systems' (May 2021), *Proceedings of the 2021 CHI Conference on Human Factors in Computing Systems*, Article No. 82, pp. 1–19; Alejandro Barredo Arrieta, Natalia Díaz-Rodríguez, Javier Del Ser, Adrien Bennetot, Siham Tabik, Alberto Barbado, Salvador Garcia, Sergio Gil-Lopez, Daniel Molina, Richard Benjamins, Raja Chatila, and Francisco Herrera, 'Explainable artificial intelligence (XAI): Concepts, taxonomies, opportunities and challenges toward responsible AI' (2020) 58 (June) *Information Fusion* 82–115.

[12] Jonathan R. Williford, Brandon B. May, and Jeffrey Byrne, 'Explainable face recognition', *Proceedings of Computer Vision – ECCV: 16th European Conference*, Glasgow, UK (23–28 August 2020), Part XI, pp. 248–263; Wojciech Samek, Grégoire Montavon, Andrea Vedaldi, Lars Kai Hansen, and Klaus-Robert Müller (eds.), *Explainable AI: Interpreting, Explaining and Visualizing Deep Learning* (Springer International Publishing, 2019).

about the requisite extent of transparency and explainability of FRT technologies, and challenges in ensuring it, such as trade secrets. The goal of this chapter is to examine to what extent trade secrets create a barrier in ensuring transparent and explainable FRT and whether current trade secret laws provide any solutions to this problem.

This chapter first identifies the extent to which transparency and explainability is needed in relation to FRT among different stakeholders. Second, after briefly examining which types of information about AI could be potentially protected as trade secrets, it identifies situations in which trade secret protection may inhibit transparent and explainable FRT. It then analyses whether the current trade secret law, in particular the 'public interest' exception, is capable of addressing the conflict between the proprietary interests of trade secret owners and AI transparency needs of certain stakeholders. This chapter focusses on FRT in law enforcement, with a greater emphasis on real-time biometric identification technologies that are considered the highest risk.[13]

Apart from the critical literature analysis, this chapter relies on empirical data collected through thirty-two interviews with experts in AI technology. The interviews were conducted with representatives from five stakeholder groups: police officers, government representatives, non-governmental organisation (NGO) representatives, IT experts (in academia and private sector), and legal experts (in academia and private sector) from Europe, the United States, and Asia-Pacific (October 2021–March 2022, online). The data collected from these interviews is especially useful when identifying the transparency and explainability needs of different stakeholders (Section 4.2).

Keeping in mind the lack of consensus on the terms 'AI transparency' and 'AI explainability', for the purpose of this chapter we define the concepts as follows. First, we understand the 'AI transparency' principle as a requirement to provide information *about* the AI model, its algorithm, and its data. The AI transparency principle could require disclosing very general information, such as 'when AI is being used',[14] or more specific information about the AI module – for example, its algorithmic parameters, training, validation, and testing information. While this concept of transparency might require providing very different levels of information for different stakeholders, it does not include information about *how* AI decisions are being generated. The latter is covered by the principle of 'AI explainability', which we define in a narrow technical way; that is, as an explanation of *how* an AI module functions, and how it generates a particular output. Such explanations are normally provided using so called Explainable AI (XAI) techniques.[15] Generally speaking, XAI techniques might be 'global', explaining the features of the entire

---

[13] See, e.g., draft EU AI Act, arts 5, 21, 26.

[14] Such as in OECD, 'Transparency and explainability'; Australian Government, 'Australia's artificial intelligence ethics framework' (7 November 2019), Department of Industry, Science and Resources, www.industry.gov.au/data-and-publications/australias-artificial-intelligence-ethics-framework.

[15] Shane T. Mueller, Robert R. Hoffman, William Clancey, Abigail Emrey, Gary Klein, 'Explanation in human-AI systems: A literature meta-review synopsis of key ideas and publications and bibliography for explainable AI' (5 February 2019), DARPA XAI Literature Review, arXiv:1902.01876; Maja Brkan

module; or 'local', which explain how a specific output has been generated.[16] While this chapter largely focusses on FRT transparency and its possible conflict with trade secret protection, it also briefly reflects upon the need for FRT to be explainable.

In the following sections, we discuss the scope of explainability and transparency that different stakeholders need in relation to FRT in law enforcement (Section 4.2), in which situations trade secrets may conflict with these transparency and explainability needs (Section 4.3), and whether the 'public interest' defence under trade secrets law is capable of addressing this conflict (Section 4.4).

4.2 FRT TRANSPARENCY AND EXPLAINABILITY: WHO NEEDS IT AND HOW MUCH?

Before examining whether trade secrets conflict with FRT transparency and explainability principles, we need to clearly identify the level of transparency and explainability that different stakeholders require in relation to FRT. We demonstrate that different stakeholders need very different types of information, some of which is – and some is not – protected by trade secrets.

For the purpose of this analysis, we identified six categories of stakeholders who have legitimate interests in certain levels of transparency and/or explainability around FRT technologies: (1) individuals exposed to FRT; (2) police officers who directly use the technology; (3) police authorities that acquire/procure the technology and need to ensure its quality; (4) court participants, especially court experts, who need access to technical information to assess whether the technology is of sufficient quality; (5) certification and auditing bodies examining whether the FRT meets the required standards; and finally (6) public interest organisations (NGOs and public research institutions) whose purpose is to ensure, in general terms, that the technology is high quality, ethical, legal, and is used for the overall public benefit.

As could be expected, our interviews with stakeholders have shown that different stakeholders have different explainability and transparency needs in relation to FRT.

4.2.1 FRT Explainability

In terms of the explainability of FRT, few stakeholders need it as a matter of necessity. Among the identified stakeholder groups, certification and auditing bodies that examine the quality of technology might potentially find XAI techniques useful – as

---

and Gregory Bonnet, 'Legal and technical feasibility of the GDPR's quest for explanation of algorithmic decisions: Of black boxes, white boxes and fata morganas' (2020) 11(1) *European Journal of Risk Regulation* 18–50, at 18–19.

[16] Riccardo Guidotti, Anna Monreale, Salvatore Ruggieri, Franco Turini, Fosca Giannotti, and Dino Pedreschi, 'A survey of methods for explaining black box models' (2019) 51(5) *ACM Computing Surveys* 1–42.

these may help identify whether, for instance, a specific AI module is biased or contains errors.[17] For similar reasons, XAI techniques might be relied upon by public interest organisations, such as NGOs and research institutions, that have expertise in AI technologies and want to assess the quality of a specific FRT technology used by police. AI developers themselves have been using XAI techniques for a similar purpose; that is, to identify AI errors during the development process and eliminate them before deploying them in practice.[18] However, XAI techniques themselves do not currently have quality guarantees and often face issues as to quality and reliability.[19] It is thus questionable whether experts assessing the quality of AI, or FRT more specifically, would give much weigh to such explanations.

Other stakeholders – police authorities, police officers, and affected individuals – are unlikely to find explanations generated by XAI techniques useful, mainly because of the technical knowledge that is required to understand such explanations. Further, according to some interviewees, when FRT is used for identification purposes, users do not need an explanation at all as the match made by FRT could be easily double checked by a police officer.[20]

Importantly, explanations generated by XAI techniques are unlikely to interfere with trade secret protection as they do not disclose substantial amounts of confidential information. As discussed later, in order to be protected by trade secrets, information should be of independent commercial value and kept secret.[21] XAI techniques, if integrated in the FRT system, would provide explanations to the end users, which, by their nature, would not be secret. Thus, owing to its limited relevance for our debate on FRT and trade secrets, FRT explainability will not be analysed here any further.

4.2.2 FRT Transparency Needs

In contrast, transparency around FRT is required by all stakeholders, although to differing extents. Depending on the level of transparency/information needed, stakeholders could be divided into three groups: those with (1) relatively low transparency needs, (2) high transparency needs, and (3) varying/medium transparency needs.

---

[17] Interview participant 1, IT expert.

[18] Ibid.

[19] See, e.g., Zana Buçinca, Krzysztof Z. Gajos, Phoebe Lin, and Elena L. Glassman, 'Proxy tasks and subjective measures can be misleading in evaluating explainable AI systems' (2020), Proceedings of the 25th international conference on intelligent user interfaces, https://dl-acm-org.simsrad.net.ocs.mq.edu.au/doi/abs/10.1145/3377325.3377498; Julius Adebayo et al., 'Sanity checks for saliency maps' (2018) 31 *Advances in Neural Information Processing Systems* 9505, arXiv:1810.03292v3; Jindong Gu and Volker Tresp, 'Saliency methods for explaining adversarial attacks' (October 2019), Human-Centric Machine Learning (NeurIPS Workshop), https://arxiv.org/abs/1908.08413; similar from Interview participant 5, IT expert ('it's not clear to me if we'll ever come up with a particularly good explanation of how the combination of neural networks and all the technologies that go into face recognition work. Whether we'll ever be able to explain them').

[20] Interview participant 13, NGO representative.

[21] See Section 4.3.

4.2.2.1 Low Transparency Needs

Individuals exposed to FRT, and law enforcement officers directly using the technology, require relatively general non-technical information about FRT (thus 'low transparency'). Individuals have a legitimate interest in knowing where, when and for what purpose the technology is used; its accuracy levels and effectiveness; legal safeguards put around the use of this technology; and in which circumstances and how they can complain about inappropriate or illegal use of FRT.[22] After individuals have been exposed to the technology and if this has led to adverse effects (e.g., potential violation of their rights), they might require a more detailed *ex post* explanation as to why a specific decision (e.g., to stop and question the individual) was made and how FRT was used in this context. Still, they do not need any detailed technical explanations about how the technology was developed, trained, or how exactly it functions, as they do not have the technical knowledge required for the interpretation of this information.

As one of our interviewees explained (in the context of migration/border control):

> So, for example, if I am a citizen stakeholder [and] my application for a visa is denied and it's based on my looks [that suggests that I] have some criminal records, then, of course, it has impacted me and I'm not happy, and I will ask for answers. Even [if the] activities [were] rectified, still [I'll ask for] answers on how come did you make this mistake? Why did you take me wrong [as] another person and it cost me my travel to be cancelled? So, to have explainability at this level, potentially you don't need to explain all of the algorithms. It's a matter of explaining why this sort of decision was made. For example, there was this person with similar facial features and the same name; or whatever some high-level explanation of what happened in the process that explains why mistake happened, etc.[23]

Second, police officers who directly use the technology will want access to general information about how the system functions, what types of data were used to train the system, the accuracy rates in different settings, how it should be used, its limitations, and so on.[24]

In addition, these stakeholders would benefit from user-friendly explanations about, for instance, which pictures in the watch-list were found to be sufficiently similar to the probe picture and the accuracy rate with relation to that specific match.[25] This would allow police officers to assess the extent to which they could

---

[22] This type of information is being currently provided, for example, on the UK Metropolitan police website: www.met.police.uk/advice/advice-and-information/fr/facial-recognition.

[23] Interview participant 1, IT expert.

[24] Interview participant 19, law enforcement officer.

[25] Watch list is the list against which the taken image is compared. When FRT is used in law enforcement context, the watch list normally comprises images of persons who are suspected or convicted for crimes, missing persons, etc. In case of a live FRT, the probe picture is a picture taken from the passing individual.

rely on a specific FRT outcome before proceeding with an action (e.g., stopping an individual for questioning or arrest). Information needs might differ between real-time/live FRT and post FRT (i.e., when FRT is used to find a match for a picture taken some time ago), as the former is considered higher risk.[26]

4.2.2.2 High Transparency Needs

Stakeholder groups that are required to assess the quality of a FRT system – certification and auditing authorities, and court experts – have high transparency needs. In order to conduct an expert examination of FRT technology, certification and auditing bodies require access to detailed technical information about the system. This might include algorithmic parameters, training data, processes and methods, validation/verification data and processes, as well as testing procedures and outcomes.

As one of the interviewed IT experts explained:

> But if, for example, there is an audit happening. [...] then of course, at that level explainability means something completely different. It's about explaining how the system was designed, how it was being used, what sort of algorithms, what sort of data was used for the training, what sort of design and build decisions were made, and so on.[27]

Similar highly technical information could be demanded in court proceedings by court experts who are invited to assess the quality of FRT used by law enforcement authorities during legal proceedings. Detailed technical information would be necessary to provide technically sound conclusions.

4.2.2.3 Medium/Varying Transparency Needs

The third group of stakeholders might have varied information needs depending on their level of knowledge about AI technologies. Namely, law enforcement authorities, when acquiring the FRT system, would need information that allows them to judge the quality and reliability of the FRT system in question. If they have only general knowledge about FRT, they will merely want to know whether the technology meets the industry standards and whether it was certified/validated by independent bodies;[28] how accurate it is; whether it has been trialled in real life settings, the trial results, and so on. If they have expert knowledge in AI/FRT (e.g., in their IT team), they might demand more technical information, for example, about datasets on which it was trained and validated, and validation and testing information.

---

[26] For example, the draft EU AI Act treats live FRT in the law enforcement context as extremely high risk and generally bans them, with a few exceptions: see draft EU AI Act, Annex 3.

[27] Interview participant 1, IT expert.

[28] The draft EU AI Act requires all high-risk AI technologies, including FRT, to undergo certification procedures. This requirement, however, has not yet been established in other jurisdictions.

As a final stakeholder group, public interest organisations (researchers and NGOs) have a legitimate interest in accessing information about government FRT use as 'they are the ones that are most likely to initiate [...] strategic litigation and other initiatives',[29] and ensure that government is accountable for the use of this technology.[30] Similarly to law enforcement, their transparency needs will differ depending on their expertise and purpose. Those without expert knowledge in AI might be interested in general information as to which situations and purposes, and to what extent, law enforcement is using FRT; the accuracy levels and effectiveness of the technology in achieving the intended aims (e.g., whether the use of FRT led to the arrest of suspected persons or preventing a crime); and whether there have been human rights impact assessments conducted at the procurement level and their results.[31] Those with technical expertise in AI might want access to algorithmic parameters and weights, training and validation/verification data, or similar technical information, allowing them to assess the accuracy and possible bias of the technology (similar to the high level transparency discussed earlier).[32]

These three levels of transparency are relevant when determining the situations in which trade secret protection might become a barrier to ensuring the transparency demanded by stakeholders.

4.3 IN WHICH SITUATIONS MIGHT TRADE SECRETS INHIBIT TRANSPARENCY OF FRT?

There are a number of challenges in ensuring transparency around FRT.[33] One of them is trade secrets, which can arguably create barriers to ensuring transparency of AI technologies in general and FRT technologies in particular. The example often used is the *State* v. *Loomis* case decided by a US court, in which the defendant was denied access to the parameters of the risk assessment algorithm COMPAS owing to trade secrets.[34] In this section, we demonstrate that the answer is more nuanced: while trade secrets might create barriers to transparent FRT in some situations ('actual conflict' situations), they are unlikely to interfere with transparency needs in other situations ('no conflict' and 'nominal conflict' situations).

---

[29] Interview participant 21, legal expert.
[30] Interview participant 5, IT expert ('Particularly, I mean, transparency is a very useful means of regulating governments abusing their position'); similar from interview participant 2, NGO representative.
[31] Interview participant 13, NGO representative.
[32] Interview participant 2, NGO representative ('for us in civil society, knowing the parameters that were set around accuracy and the impact that might have on people of colour, might be a useful thing to know, contest the use case').
[33] Another possible challenge is government secrets (the government may not want to disclose certain information for public security reasons, for example). The challenge in ensuring FRT explainability is technical (technical ability to provide explanations of how a specific AI functions).
[34] *State* v. *Loomis* 881 N.W.2d 749, 755, 756, fn.18 (Wis. 2016), cert. denied, 137 S. Ct. 2290 (2017).

4.3.1 *The Scope of Trade Secret Protection*

In order to understand the situations in which trade secrets interfere with transparency needs around FRT, it is first necessary to clarify which information about FRT could be potentially protected by trade secrets.

Trade secrets are of special importance in protecting intellectual property (IP) rights underlying AI modules, including FRT. In contrast to other IP rights (patents, copyright), trade secrets could be used to protect any elements of AI modules as long as they provide independent commercial value and are kept secret.[35] Trade secret protection requires neither investment in the registration process nor public disclosure of the innovation.[36] While trade secret protection has its limitations, such as a possibility to reverse engineer technology protected by trade secrets,[37] and a lack of protection against third-party disclosure,[38] the software industry has so far successfully used trade secrets to protect its commercial interests.[39]

As far as trade secrets and AI are concerned, courts have already indicated that at least certain parts of AI modules can be protected as trade secrets, such as source code, algorithms, and the way a business utilises AI to implement a particular solution.[40] Keeping in mind the requirements for trade secret protection – secret nature and commercial value – a range of information about AI (including FRT) could be possibly protected by trade secrets: the architecture of the algorithm, its parameters and weights; source code in which the algorithm is coded; information about the training, validation and verification of the algorithm, including training and validation/verification data, methods and processes; real life testing information (in which settings it was tested, and the methods and outcomes of testing), and so on. All this

---

[35] See Tanya Aplin, Lionel Bently, Phillip Johnson, and Simon Malynicz, *Gurry on Breach of Confidence: The Protection of Confidential Information* (2nd ed., Oxford University Press, 2012).

[36] See, e.g., Clark D. Asay, 'Artificial stupidity' (2020) 61(5) *William and Mary Law Review* 1187–1257, 1243, Notably, significant financial costs might be incurred to ensure that information maintains secret.

[37] For more, see Tanya Aplin, 'Reverse engineering and commercial secrets' (2013) 66(1) *Current Legal Problems* 341–377.

[38] Katarina Foss-Solbrekk, 'Three routes to protecting AI systems and their algorithms under IP law: The good, the bad and the ugly' (2021) 16(3) *Journal of Intellectual Property Law & Practice* 247–258; Ana Nordberg, 'Trade secrets, big data and artificial intelligence innovation: A legal oxymoron?' in Jens Schovsbo, Timo Minssen, and Thomas Riis (eds.), *The Harmonization and Protection of Trade Secrets in the EU: An Appraisal of the EU Directive*(Edward Elgar Publishing Limited, 2020), pp. 194–220, at p. 212.

[39] See, e.g., Sylvia Lu, 'Algorithmic opacity, private accountability, and corporate social disclosure in the age of artificial intelligence' (2020) 23(99) *Vanderbilt Journal of Entertainment & Technology Law* 116–117 (contending that software industry has relied on trade secret law to protect algorithms for decades and AI algorithms are no exception).

[40] See, e.g., *LivePerson, Inc. v. 24/7 Customer, Inc.*, 83 F. Supp. 3d 501, 514 (SDNY, 2015) (finding algorithms based on artificial intelligence eligible for trade secret protection).

information is often seen by AI developers as of commercial value and kept secret,[41] and thus could be potentially protected as trade secrets.[42]

4.3.2 When is the Conflict between Trade Secrets and the AI Transparency Principle Likely to Arise?

Keeping in mind the broad range of information about the FRT that could be protected as trade secrets and the transparency needs of stakeholders (identified earlier), three types of situations could be distinguished.

4.3.2.1 No Conflict Situations

First, in some situations, there would be no conflict between stakeholder's transparency needs and trade secret protection as the information requested by the stakeholder is generally not protected by trade secrets. For instance, individuals subject to FRT would only want general information about the fact that FRT is used by a government authority, where and for what purposes it is used, and so on.[43] Similarly, police officers using the technology would only need a general understanding of how the technology functions, in which situations it could be used, its accuracy rates, and so on.[44] Owing to its generally public nature and lack of independent economic value, this information would normally not be protected as trade secrets.

4.3.2.2 Nominal Conflicts

In some other instances, 'nominal' conflict situations are likely to arise. First, certification and auditing organisations that are examining the quality of FRT technologies might require access to extensive technical information related to FRT that has commercial value and could be protected by trade secrets, such as algorithmic parameters, training, validation and verification information, and all information related to real-life trials.[45] Similar information might be requested in court proceedings by court experts who are invited to assess the reliability of the FRT system in question.[46] As discussed earlier, these types of technical information are likely to be

---

[41] Interview participant 1, IT expert.

[42] Note that even if all of this information could be 'factual' trade secrets, not all of it would qualify as 'legal' trade secrets. For a distinction between the two see Sharon K. Sandeen and Tanya Aplin, 'Trade secrecy, factual secrecy and the hype surrounding AI' in Ryan Abott (ed.), *Research Handbook on Intellectual Property and Artificial Intelligence* (Edward Elgar, 2022), pp. 442–450; see also Camilla A. Hrdy and Mark A. Lemley, 'Abandoning trade secrets' (2021) 73(1) *Stanford Law Review* 1–66.

[43] See Section 4.2.2.1. While this information could be protected as government secrets, it would not be protected as a trade secret as it does not have independent commercial value.

[44] See Section 4.2.2.1.

[45] See Section 4.2.2.2.

[46] See Section 4.2.2.2.

protected as trade secrets: AI developers consider them commercially valuable and tend to keep them secret.[47]

However, we refer to these types of situations as 'nominal' conflicts since they could be managed under existing confidentiality/trade secret rules that form part of certification/auditing processes or court procedures. Certification and auditing organisations are normally subject to confidentiality and use the confidential information provided by AI developers for assessment purposes only. Similarly, in court investigations, procedural rules determine how trade secrets disclosed during the court proceedings are protected from disclosure to third parties or to the public.[48] Since these situations are already addressed under current regulatory or governance frameworks, we will not examine them further.

4.3.2.3 Actual Conflicts

The third type of situations – related to transparency needs of law enforcement authorities and public interest organisations – are of most concern, and we refer to them as 'actual conflicts'.

Law enforcement authorities might need access to certain technical information about the FRT (e.g., training, validation and testing information) in order to evaluate its reliability before procuring it.[49] Public interest organisations, such as NGOs and research organisations, might need access to even more detailed technical information (algorithms, training and validation data, testing data) in order to provide an independent evaluation of the effectiveness of the FRT system used by law enforcement.[50] As mentioned earlier, technical information is generally considered by AI developers as commercially valuable and is likely to be kept confidential.

It is worth noting that law enforcement authorities are able to obtain certain information through contract negotiation.[51] However, it is questionable whether this solution is suitable in all cases. Owing to a lack of adequate legal advice, bargaining power, or simply the novel nature of AI technologies, law enforcement authorities might fail to negotiate for appropriate access to all essential information that will be needed during the entire life cycle of the FRT system. Government authorities using AI tools acquired from third parties have already encountered the problem

---

[47] See Section 4.3.1.
[48] For example, Court Suppression and Non-Publication Orders Act 2010 (NSW) s 9 allows a court to make a suppression or non-publication order if it is necessary to prevent prejudice to the proper administration of justice.
[49] See Section 4.2.2.3.
[50] See Section 4.2.2.3.
[51] Similar has been suggested for AI acquisition process for government institutions: see Jake Goldenfein, 'Algorithmic transparency and decision-making accountability: Thoughts for buying machine learning algorithms' in *Closer to the Machine: Technical, Social, and Legal Aspects of AI* (Office of the Victorian Information Commissioner, 2019), https://ovic.vic.gov.au/wp-content/uploads/2019/08/closer-to-the-machine-web.pdf.

of subsequently getting access to certain confidential information about the AI module.[52]

Similarly, while public interest organisations might acquire certain information about FRT used by government through freedom of information requests,[53] this solution is limited as the legislation generally protects trade secrets from public disclosure.[54] Therefore, we see both of these situations as an *actual conflict* between trade secret rights of AI developers and the AI transparency needs of two major groups of stakeholders (law enforcement authorities and public interest organisations).

4.4 DOES TRADE SECRET LAW PROVIDE ADEQUATE SOLUTIONS?

Trade secret law provides certain limitations that are meant to serve the interests of the public. Namely, in common law jurisdictions, when a breach of confidentiality is claimed, the defendant could raise a so-called public interest defence. In short, it allows defendants to avoid liability for disclosing a trade secret if they can prove the disclosure was in the public interest.[55] As explained by the House of Lords, protection of confidential information is based on the public interest in maintaining confidences, but the public interest sometimes favours disclosure rather than secrecy.[56] However, this public interest defence is of limited, if any, use in addressing the conflict between trade secrets and the legitimate transparency needs of identified stakeholders in an FRT scenario.

First, the scope of this defence is unclear.[57] Some judicial sources suggest the existence of a broad public interest defence, which is based upon freedom of the press and the public's right to know the truth.[58] Other court judgments suggest that the defence should encompass no more than an application of the general equitable defence of clean hands, namely the information that exposes a serious wrongdoing of the plaintiff should not be classified as confidential in any case (iniquity rule).[59]

---

[52] Interview participant 26, government representative.

[53] See, e.g., *Freedom of Information Act 1982* (Cth).

[54] See Elizabeth A. Rowe, 'Striking a balance: When should trade-secret law shield disclosure to the government?' 96 *Iowa Law Review* 791–835, at 804–808.

[55] For an overview of the public interest defence, see Aplin et al., *Gurry on Breach of Confidence*.

[56] *Attorney-General* v. *Guardian Newspapers Ltd* [1990] AC 109, 282 (Spycatcher case) ('although the basis of the law's protection of confidence is a public interest that confidences should be preserved by law, nevertheless that public interest may be outweighed by some other countervailing public interest which favours disclosure' (Lord Goff)) Similarly, in *Campbell* v. *Frisbee*, the UK Court of Appeal held that the confider's right 'must give way where it is in the public interest that the confidential information should be made public'. See *Campbell* v. *Frisbee* [2002] EWCA Civ 1374, [23].

[57] See Karen Koomen, 'Breach of confidence and the public interest defence: Is it in the public interest? A review of the English public interest defence and the options for Australia' (1994) 10 *Queensland University of Technology Law Journal* 56–88.

[58] See, e.g., Spycatcher case, 269 (Lord Griffiths); *Fraser* v. *Evans* [1969] 1 QB 349; *Hubbard* v. *Vosper* [1972] 2 QB 84; discussed in Trent Glover, 'The scope of the public interest defence in actions for breach of confidence' (1999) 6 *James Cook University Law Review* 109–137, at 115–116, 118.

[59] See discussion in Glover, 'The scope of the public interest defence'; *Corrs Pavey Whiting & Byrne* v. *Collector of Customs* (*Vic*) (1987) 14 FCR 434, 454 (Gummow J).

For instance, Australian courts have confirmed that disclosure in the public interest should be construed narrowly; it should limited to information affecting national security, concerning breach of law, fraud, or otherwise destructive to the public, and must be more than simply the public's interest in the truth being told.[60]

Most importantly, the defence does not provide interested stakeholders with an active right to request information about the FRT technology and its parameters. It is merely a passive defence that could be invoked by a defendant only after they have disclosed the information (or where there is an imminent threat of such a disclosure). In order to disclose the information, the defendant should already have access to the information, which is not the situation of law enforcement authorities or public interest organisations seeking information about the FRT.

The public interest defence could be possibly useful in some exceptional situations. For instance, the employee/contractor of an FRT developer might disclose certain confidential technical information about the FRT system with the public or a specific stakeholder (public authority, NGO, etc.) in order to demonstrate that the AI developer did not comply with legal requirements when developing the FRT system and/or misled the public and/or the government authority as to the accuracy of the FRT technology, for example. If breach of confidence is claimed against this person, they could argue that the disclosure served the public interest: the use of an FRT system that is of low quality or biased may lead to incorrect identification of individuals, especially ethnic or gender minorities, which may further result in the arrest of innocent people and violation of their human rights. The defendant could argue that the disclosure of technical information about such an FRT system would thus help prevent harm from occurring.

Even then, the ability of a defendant to rely on the public interest defence is questionable. For instance, the court might accept the defence if the information is disclosed to government authorities responsible for prosecuting breaches of law or fraud, as 'proper authorities' for public disclosure purposes,[61] but not to public interest organisations or the public generally.[62] While the law enforcement authority (which is also the user of FRT in this case) might qualify as a 'proper authority', a public interest organisation is unlikely to meet this criterion.

Furthermore, if a narrow interpretation of the public interest defence is applied, the defendant would have to prove that the disclosed information relates to 'misdeeds of a serious nature and importance to the country'.[63] It is questionable

---

[60] *Castrol Australia Pty Limited* v. *Emtech Associates Pty Ltd* (1980) 51 FLR 184, 513 (Rath J, quoting with approval Ungoed-Tomas J in *Beloff* v. *Pressdram* [1973] 1 All ER 241, 260); for a criticism of a narrow interpretation see Koomen, Breach of confidence and the public interest defence.

[61] See discussion in Jason Pizer, 'The public interest exception to the breach of confidence action: are the lights about to change?' (1994) 20(1) *Monash University Law Review* 67–109, at 80–81.

[62] See, e.g., *Francome* v. *Mirror Group Newspapers Ltd* [1984] 2 All ER 408.

[63] *Beloff* v. *Pressdram*, 260; see similar limitation in *Corrs Pavey Whiting & Byrne* v. *Collector of Customs*, 456 (Gummow J).

whether a low quality or biased FRT, or the AI developer hiding information about this, would qualify as a misdeed of such serious nature. More problematically, the defendant might not know whether the FRT does not meet certain industry or legal standards *until* the technical information is disclosed and an independent examination is carried out.

4.5 CONCLUSIONS

It is without doubt that transparency is needed around the development, functioning, and use of FRT in the law enforcement sector. The analysis here has shown that in some cases trade secrets do not impede the transparency around FRT needed by some stakeholders (e.g., affected individuals or direct users of FRT) and some possible conflicts could be resolved through existing arrangements and laws (e.g., with relation to the transparency needs of certification and auditing organisations, and court participants). However, trade secrets might conflict with the transparency needs of some stakeholders, especially law enforcement authorities (after acquiring the technology) and public interest organisations that might want access to confidential technical information to assess the quality of the FRT system. Unfortunately, trade secret law, with its unclear and limited public interest exception, is unable to address this conflict. Further research is needed as to how the balance between the proprietary interests of AI developers and transparency needs of other stakeholders (law enforcement authorities and public interest organisations) could be established.

5

Privacy's Loose Grip on Facial Recognition

Law and the Operational Image

Jake Goldenfein

5.1 INTRODUCTION

'Privacy' has long been central to understanding the impacts of facial recognition and related technologies. Privacy informs the intuitions, harms, and legal regimes that frame these technological systems. Privacy and data protection law already have a ready-at-hand toolkit for related practices such as closed-circuit television (CCTV) in public space, surreptitious photography, and biometric data processing. These regimes measure facial recognition applications against familiar privacy and data protection categories such as proportionality, necessity, and legality, as well as identifiability and consent. But as facial recognition becomes more widespread and diverse, and the tools, ecosystems, and supply chains for facial recognition become more visible and better understood, these privacy and data protection concepts are becoming more difficult to consistently apply.

For as long as privacy has been deployed to constrain facial recognition, analysts have been decrying its inadequacy. This research typically identifies some novel dimension of harm associated with facial recognition that evades existing regulatory strategies. This chapter proposes an alternate diagnosis for why privacy fails to deliver premised on the nature of facial recognition as a broader socio-technical system. The jurisprudence shows that privacy and data protection function as intended at the level of 'applications' such as one-to-one and one-to-many identification and identity verification systems. But emerging cases show how privacy concepts become awkward and even incoherent when addressing different dimensions of the facial recognition ecosystem – at the level of 'tools' and supply chains, such as biometric image search engines and the production of facial image datasets. Inconsistencies in how law connects to this part of the facial recognition ecosystem challenge the suitability of regulatory concepts like identifiability and consent, the nature of harm being addressed, and perhaps most fundamentally, how privacy conceptualises the nature of online images. New rules for facial recognition products and applications are being included in the in the risk-based regulatory regimes for artificial intelligence (AI) in development around the world. In the EU, these include prohibitions on *untargeted* scraping of facial images from the internet or CCTV footage to create facial recognition databases. But as described below, the industrial organisation of the facial dataset business will continue to thwart these regulatory efforts, and privacy and data protection will continue to be legal bases for litigation against companies using facial recognition today and in the future.

This chapter offers an account as to why privacy concepts lose traction in this arena. It argues that existing regulatory approaches reflect an understanding of images as primarily 'representational', whereas facial recognition demonstrates that online images are better understood as 'operational' or 'operative'. The operational image does not simply represent a referent but actively enables and participates in a sequence of automated operations. These operations take place at the level of facial recognition supply chains, where existing law struggles to find traction. Law's inability to come to terms with the operational image pushes existing legal categories to the limits of their utility.

5.2 FACIAL ANALYSIS AND IDENTIFICATION

Privacy law and emerging AI regulations have effectively addressed the 'watch list' type facial recognition applications that come up in human rights litigation. For instance, the 2020 *Bridges* v. *South Wales Police* decision found the South Wales Police (SWP) force's use of facial recognition in public to identify individuals on a watch list was a violation of Article 8 of the European Convention on Human Rights (ECHR).[1] SWP deployed their surveillance system at large public events, using CCTV towers that collected footage of individuals in public, and performed real-time facial recognition against a database of persons of interest. Despite legislation allowing for the creation of that watchlist, the exact parameters for inclusion were not clear. The practice violated the ECHR Article 8 because, while proportionate and strictly necessary for the law enforcement purpose for which it was deployed, it failed to be 'in accordance with the law' in certain respects. Specifically, the enabling legislation and applicable Codes of Conduct failed to adequately specify rules around who could be the subject of surveillance (i.e., who could be placed on a watch list in the first place), or where facial recognition systems could be deployed. The enabling law thus gave police too much discretion. These issues have also clearly informed the regulation of biometric identification by law enforcement in the EU AI Act.

But the Bridges case also highlighted some conceptual issues of interest to the argument made in this chapter. In particular, the court's conceptualisation of facial recognition as something different from both (1) police taking photographs of people in public and (2) the collection of biometric data such as fingerprints.[2] Facial recognition occupied a place somewhere between the two in terms of level of intrusion, generating some conceptual discomfort for privacy. And while this was ultimately

---

[1] *Bridges* v. *South Wales Police* [2019] EWHC 2341 (admin).
[2] Ibid., at [85], citing *S and Marper* v. *UK* [2018] Eur Court HR 1581 and *Catt* v. *UK* (European Court of Human Rights, Application no. 43514/15, 24 January 2019).

of little consequence to the court's decision, with facial recognition easily enough absorbed into a human rights proportionality analysis without having to delve deeper into facial recognition's 'in-between' character, the inability to analogise with existing police techniques for this in-betweenness was not merely a matter of novelty. This type of watch list surveillance and associated photography, including real-time (non-automated) identification, has been practised by police for decades. But facial recognition's in-between character reflected something more fundamental about the media system that automates the identification task – its operationalism.

The argument made here is that facial recognition and related techniques are a function of the operational image.[3] The central insight of operationalism is that the ontology of images has shifted from one of representation to that of an element in a sequence of operations that are typically machine executed. Mark Andrejevic and Zala Volcic, for instance, describe the 'operational enclosure' through which the operational image includes automated identification, social sorting, decision-making, and responses that enable the governance of space.[4] Their basic example is facial recognition in retail stores that, when identifying a person on a watch list, not only calls security, but also actively locks the doors. This example also exemplifies Trevor Paglen's emphasis that the audience for (operational) images is no longer humans but rather machines.[5]

The operational image reconfigures images as the communicative instruments of automated non-human visuality. Images consumed by humans are increasingly the output of machines staging what they 'see' as a derivative function. But the primary audience of an image is a complex network of machines, with human-legibility a trivial or arbitrary secondary process. As Andrejevic and Volcic note, 'In the case of facial recognition technology, there is, still, a camera with a lens, but for the purposes of recognition and response no image need be produced.'[6] The operational function of an image in the facial recognition context is, on the one hand, its capacity to communicate biometric information to other machines, which can then trigger various actions as described by Andrejevic and Volcic. On the other hand, facial images themselves have become operational through their absorption into an ecosystem and economy of image databases, search engines, and AI model training and benchmarking. In other words, online images are operationalised by the biometric supply chain. This additional operational character is revealed through the existence of companies and tools like Clearview AI, as well as the proliferating number of massive image datasets built from web-scraping and surreptitious public photography.[7]

---

3   Harun Farocki, 'Phantom images' (2004) 29 *Public* 12–22; Trevor Paglen, 'Operational images' (2014) 59 E-Flux (online); Mark Andrejevic and Zala Volcic, 'Seeing like a border: Biometrics and the operational image' (2022) 7(2) *Digital Culture & Society* 139–158; Rebecca Uliasz, 'Seeing like an algorithm: Operative images and emergent subjects' (2021) 36 *AI & Society* 1233–1241.

4   Mark Andrejevic and Zala Volcic, 'Smart cameras and the operational enclosure' (2021) 22(4) *Television & New Media* 343–359.

5   Paglen, 'Operational images'.

6   Andrejevic and Volcic, 'Smart cameras and the operational enclosure', p. 347.

7   See, e.g., Adam Harvey and Jules LaPlace 'Exposing.AI' (2021), https://exposing.ai.

Privacy and data protection law struggle to accommodate this theorisation of images and this domain of economic activity. For instance, the operational image ontology suggests images are always already enrolled in a biometric recognition process. Privacy and data protection law, however, understand images as 'representations' of a referent, amenable to subsequent human interpretation and inference. Under the GDPR, for example, images are only considered biometric data after 'specific technical processing' that renders it comprehensible to a machine.[8] In other words, privacy and data protection law insist on the separation of images and any biometric information that can be derived from them.[9] This means images alone cannot be biometric data. Various authors have pointed out that this is contrary to technical understandings of biometrics,[10] which would conceptualise every image as also a biometric sample, and the beginning of a biometric 'operation'. And as discussed Section 5.4.1.1, companies such as Clearview AI are exposing that a degree of processing of images, even if simply for aggregation in datasets, is already the default status of images online.

The following sections describe the different treatment of image and biometric data in existing law, with a focus on how the operational character of images expresses itself as conceptual confusion in how privacy addresses the tools and supply chains that make up the facial recognition ecosystem.

5.3 WHAT KIND OF DATA IS THAT?

5.3.1 *Images*

The following section spells out some of the internal ambiguities and inconsistencies that make the application of privacy and data protection to facial recognition supply chains difficult. The ambiguities exist even at the most basic definitional level. Privacy law typically deals with images that are identified, in cases where publication might diminish seclusion or reputation. Data protection law also governs anonymous images because the definition of 'personal data', the threshold for data protection's application, only requires that data be reasonably identifiable rather than identified.[11] There is a general presumption that images including a face satisfy

---

[8] *EU General Data Protection Regulation (GDPR)*: Regulation (EU) 2016/679, Art. 4(14).

[9] Ibid., Recital 51: 'The processing of photographs should not systematically be considered to be processing of special categories of personal data as they are covered by the definition of biometric data only when processed through a specific technical means allowing the unique identification or authentication of a natural person.'

[10] See, e.g., Bilgesu Sumer, 'When do the images of biometric characteristics qualify as special categories of data under the GDPR: A systemic approach to biometric data processing', IEEE International Conference of the Biometrics Special Interest Group (14–16 September 2022), referencing ISO/IEC 2382-37: 2022 Information Technology Vocabulary Part 37.

[11] *EU General Data Protection Regulation (GDPR)*: Regulation (EU) 2016/679, Art 4(1); See also *Breyer v. Bundesrepublik Deutschland* ECLI:EU:C:2016:779.

Jake Goldenfein

that definition, the processing of which then requires a 'lawful basis', the most relevant being consent or the legitimate interests of the data processor.

The presumption that images showing a person's face are always personal data is not entirely settled, however. Even European national data protection authorities give conflicting advice. For instance, the UK Information Commissioner's Office notes that an image taken in public containing recognisable faces may not be personal data if the image is not subsequently processed to learn or decide anything about any of the individuals that are imaged.[12] The German data protection authority, however, argues that all images of people contain personal data: 'photographs, whether analogue or digital, always contain personal data ... if persons can be identified on it'.[13] Advice given by other institutions is even more confusing. For instance, Oxford University's staff guidance on data protection suggests images will be personal data if individuals are the 'focus' of an image, but *not* if those individuals or groups are not the focus of the image, whatever that means.

Identification and identifiability are not always central to facial recognition and analysis, however. Not all facial recognition or analysis tasks link images to natural persons. Some may identify the same person across multiple instances of a database or across multiple cameras recording physical space. In these cases, there is an argument that facial images used in the biometric process still constitute personal information on the principle of 'singling out'. This early interpretation of 'identified' proposed by the Article 29 Working Party captures systems that distinguish an individual from a group of people without the need to connect them to a natural person.[14] Although cited several times in the jurisprudence, this definition is not necessarily authoritative.

5.3.2 *Biometric Data*

Under the GDPR, biometric data is a sub-species of personal data defined as the output of specific technical processing with a view to unique identification of a natural person.[15] It qualifies as a 'special category of personal data', requiring higher levels of protection including explicit consent for processing. The definition of 'identified' in this context is narrower than for personal data, as it requires a clear connection to a natural person. As Bilgesu Sumer notes, 'Under the current system, the threshold for identifiability for biometric data can be invoked only if there is an already identified

---

[12] Information Commissioner's Office (ICO), 'What happens when different organisations process the same data for different purposes?' (n.d.), https://ico.org.uk/for-organisations/guide-to-data-protection/guide-to-the-general-data-protection-regulation-gdpr/what-is-personal-data/what-happens-when-different-organisations-process-the-same-data-for-different-purposes/.

[13] Landesbeauftragte für Datenschutz und Akteneinsicht, 'Verarbeitung personenbezogener Daten bei Fotografien' (June 2018), www.lda.brandenburg.de/sixcms/media.php/9/RechtlicheAnforderungen Fotografie.pdf.

[14] Article 29 Working Party, 'Opinion 4/2007 on the concept of personal data (WP 136, 20 June 2007)'.

[15] *EU General Data Protection Regulation (GDPR)*: Regulation (EU) 2016/679, Art 9(1).

individual under the GDPR.'[16] Some data privacy laws, such as Australia's, include 'biometric templates' as protected 'sensitive data'. But as mentioned earlier, not all biometric templates are identified or created for the sake of identification, meaning the Australian definition raises confusing questions of whether there can be 'sensitive data' that is not also 'personal data'.

If and when biometric data constitutes personal data at all was a live question in policy discussions around the scope of data protection at the turn of the millennium. In 2003, the Article 29 Working Party suggested that biometric data is not personal data when templates are stored without images.[17] By 2012, however, that same group, without much elaboration, indicated that 'in most cases biometric data are personal data'.[18] Biometric data was not considered sensitive (or a special category of) data at that point though, because it did not reveal sensitive characteristics about the identified person. This position evolved again with the GDPR, as policymakers began describing certain intrinsically sensitive characteristics of biometric data, such as its persistence (non-changeability, non-deletability), its capacity to make bodies 'machine readable', its use in categorisation and segregation functions, and the way it could be used to track users across space without ever linking to their natural identity.[19] However, if the purpose of processing biometric data is 'categorisation' rather than unique identification of a natural person, it is still not considered processing of a special category of personal data.

Data protection (and privacy) law's relationship to biometrics – the requirement that a natural person be identified for biometric data to be considered a special category of personal data, and the related exclusion of unprocessed (or raw) images or videos from the definition of biometric data – are strongly informed by older biometric techniques. They imagine a database containing biometric information generated through enrolling an individual in a biometric system such as fingerprinting or DNA extraction. Privacy law identifies DNA and fingerprint information as especially sensitive types of identity information, necessitating rigorous protections and checks and balances.[20] But the law that developed around these techniques did not anticipate the reality that biometric 'enrolment' is no longer the only way to build a biometric system. It did not anticipate that any image contains within itself, easily coaxed out through readily available algorithmic methods, biometric data that might readily contribute to the construction of a facial image dataset or facial recognition search engine, or some other part of the biometric supply chain.

The realities of biometric supply chains and facial recognition ecosystems trouble these long held settlements undergirding existing regulatory strategies. The

[16] Sumer, 'When do the images of biometric characteristics qualify'.
[17] Article 29 Working Party, 'Working document on biometrics (WP 80, 1 August 2003)'.
[18] Article 29 Working Party, 'Opinion 3/2012 on developments in biometric technologies (WP 193, 27 April 2012)'.
[19] European Data Protection Board, 'Guidelines 3/2019 on processing of personal data through video devices (Version 2.0, 29 January 2020)'.
[20] *S and Marper* v. *UK* [2018] Eur Court HR 1581.

separation between ordinary portraits and biometric samples embedded in the data protection law does not match the reality that all images are now already also 'biometric samples' – the first step in the biometric processing pipeline. Acknowledging the operational character of images would help make sense of juridical treatments of facial recognition, under privacy and data protection, that are becoming increasingly diverse, as well as assist in drawing adequate legal attention to the processes and supply chains that make up the broader facial recognition ecosystem and economy. This is the less-visible system of circulation involving a range of corporate, government and university actors, using a variety of techniques such as web scraping and surreptitious photography, to produce products for research and profit such as benchmarking datasets, training datasets, facial recognition models, and search tools.

5.4 REPRESENTATIONALISM VERSUS OPERATIONALISM IN THE CASE LAW

5.4.1 Non-Identity Matching Cases

While images are operationalised for facial recognition through supply chains, privacy and data protection's failure to attend to the operational image manifests at all levels of the facial recognition ecosystem. Facial recognition is not always used to match a biometric template with a natural person. Facial analysis sometimes involves consumer profiling (demographics, sentiment analysis, etc.) or location tracking (i.e., identifying a person as they move through a store/space). These instances highlight some confusion and inconsistency within privacy and data protection's conceptual apparatuses.

The Office of the Australian Information Commissioner (OAIC), for instance, evaluated a profiling system used by the 7–11 chain of convenience stores. Without clear notice, 7–11 deployed a facial recognition system for demographic (age and gender) analysis of individuals that engaged with a customer feedback tablet. The system also created a faceprint (i.e., biometric template) for the sake of quality control. To ensure the same person did not give multiple survey results within a twenty-four-hour period, faceprints were stored and compared, with multiple matches within a twenty-four-hour period flagged as potentially non-genuine feedback responses.

7–11 argued that neither the images collected nor faceprints extracted were personal information because they were not collected or processed for the sake of identifying a natural person. The images were also automatically blurred when viewed by human staff. The OAIC determined, however, that the twenty-four-hour matching system 'singled out' individuals by comparing each person's faceprint against all other faceprints held in the system, which required giving them a unique identifier. Here, the images and faceprints were linked by a 'purpose', which was the pseudo-identification. Contrary to other similar legal regimes (i.e., the US State of Illinois

Biometric Information Privacy Act (BIPA),[21] and the GDPR), the OAIC even found that the *raw* images collected were biometric information, and thus sensitive information, because they were collected for the purpose of biometric identification. The recombination of image and biometric data in this case that is so explicitly rejected elsewhere would reflect some acknowledgement of the operational character of the image, but it is better understood as an outlier, representing conceptual confusion more than a considered position. It has not been replicated in subsequent OAIC determinations considering facial recognition.[22]

Other legal regimes, such as BIPA, more explicitly avoid the issue of how to conceptualise images in a biometric context. Rather than recognise images as potentially also 'biometric samples', BIPA simply excludes photographs from its definition of biometric identifiers. The *creation* of biometric information alone invokes the Act, eliding the issue of biometric data and identifiability.[23] To that end, TikTok's collection of facial landmarks used in demographic profiling for advertising and augmented reality 'filters' and 'stickers' was illegal under BIPA. Despite TikTok's arguments that all biometric data collected was anonymous, it ultimately settled the case for $92 million as questions of identifiability and anonymity (i.e., the relations of biometric information to images) are not relevant to the BIPA regime that applies as soon as biometric data has been generated.

The diversity of legal treatments and the problems associated with maintaining the separation between images and biometric data only intensifies as we move further along the facial recognition supply chain.

5.4.1.1 Clearview AI Cases

Clearview AI collects as many images of people available online as possible (approximately 1.5 billion images collected per month), storing them in a database linked to their source URLs. Clearview AI extracts biometric information from every face in every image and uses that biometric data to create a unique mathematical hash for each face. Those hashes make the image database searchable via a 'probe image' that is itself hashed and compared against the database. Any matches between the probe image and the image database are then provided to the user along with image URLs. Litigation so far has assumed the availability of the system only to law enforcement (and related entities), although Clearview AI now also provides biometric products to the private market.

---

[21] *Biometric Information Privacy Act* (740 ILCS 14/).

[22] See, e.g., Megan Richardson, Mark Andrejevic, and Jake Goldenfein, 'Clearview AI facial recognition case highlights need for clarity on law' (22 June 2022), CHOICE, www.choice .com.au/consumers-and-data/protecting-your-data/data-laws-and-regulation/articles/clearview-ai-and-privacy-law.

[23] See, e.g., *Patel* v. *Facebook* No. 18-15982 (9th Cir. 2019) – 'the development of a face template using facial-recognition technology without consent' is an invasion of a privacy interest.

Judicial treatment of Clearview AI has consistently found that the company processes personal and sensitive data, and therefore requires consent from the individuals in the images it collects. Clearview AI persistently argues that the data it processes is neither personal nor sensitive, but fails on this claim. The French data protection authority, CNIL, similarly (although somewhat circularly) stipulated in its finding against Clearview AI that images are personal data as soon as an individual can be recognised, and that Clearview AI's capacity to compare an image with another makes those images identifiable.[24] Because Clearview AI does not perform a specific processing operation for the unique identification of a natural person however, the images it collects and biometric data it extracts are not special categories of personal data. Because Clearview AI only processes personal data and not special categories of personal data, that processing *could* be lawful even without consent under GDPR Article 6, for instance if in the legitimate interests of the company. However, the court dismissed the possibility of any legitimate interest because individuals who placed their images online would not have 'reasonably expected' those images to participate in a biometric search engine that might be used for law enforcement purposes.[25] But this finding around reasonable expectations is a flimsy hook on which to hang Clearview AI's privacy violations, and explicitly rejects the operational character of images. Do individuals still expect that images published online are not used to train AI models or produce image datasets? Do individuals still believe that the function of an online image is its presentation to other humans? How long can such expectations persist?

There was a similar moment in an Australian finding against Clearview AI. The Australian regulator determined that the images collected by Clearview AI were personal data because Clearview AI's purpose is to facilitate identification.[26] And the biometric data was sensitive because the Australian definition includes biometric templates even if not used for the specific identification of a natural person. When contemplating whether Clearview AI satisfied any exceptions for processing sensitive information without consent, the OAIC indicated that the individuals whose personal and sensitive information was being collected by Clearview AI would not have been aware or had any reasonable expectation that their images would be scraped and held in a database. Further, no law enforcement exceptions applied because 'only a very small fraction of individuals included in the database would ever have any interaction with law enforcement'.[27]

---

[24] Decision 2021-134 of 1 November 2021 issuing an order to comply to the company Clearview AI (No. MDMM211166).

[25] *EU General Data Protection Regulation (GDPR):* Regulation (EU) 2016/679, Art 6(1)(f) specifies that even if data is publicly available it still requires a legal basis for processing and is not automatically available for re-use. When processing publicly available data on the basis of a legitimate interests, the European Data Protection Board suggests users need to reasonably expect that further processing.

[26] Commissioner initiated investigation into Clearview AI, Inc. (Privacy) [2021] ALCmr 54 (14 October 2021).

[27] Ibid., at [172].

Privacy's Loose Grip on Facial Recognition

These discussions of 'reasonable expectation' expose something about data privacy law's relationship to operationalism. On one hand, the breach of reasonable expectations about images law enforcement databases makes sense – there is a liberal privacy harm associated with being enrolled in a police database when a person is not deserving of suspicion. That has served as a normative boundary in privacy jurisprudence for some time. But on the other hand, this is not really enrolment in a police database: Clearview AI's database is an index of all the images on the internet that is, at the moment, primarily available only to police, but increasingly to private parties. Determining whether Clearview AI breached data privacy law with a normative standard associated with delimiting the state's policing powers,[28] does not seem adequate if we understand Clearview AI as just one of the large and growing number of image databases and biometric services that operationalise facial images by scraping the internet. What Clearview AI explicitly demonstrates is that there is no longer a police database; the internet is already an image database that is operationalised through a biometric supply chain.

Online images are sometimes viewed by humans or police, but they are primarily viewed by other machines such as web-scraping software and facial recognition algorithms for the sake of assembling the facial image datasets and searchable biometric databases that power a broader biometrics economy and ecosystem. Regulating these systems by consent (as required when defining the biometric data involved as sensitive – or a special category of personal – data) only makes sense when we imagine the internet as a media system browsed by humans,[29] where image consumption and processing is neither automatic nor at scale. Clearview AI is a jarring demonstration of the reality that humans do not browse the internet; the internet browses us.

5.4.1.2 Scraping and Dataset Cases

Clearview AI has exposed how legal settlements informed by rhetorics of 'open internet' that, for instance, stabilised the legality of web-scraping, indexing, and enabled search engines to evolve, are now straining in the context of massive data aggregation for training large machine learning models.[30] Facial recognition has its own scraping dynamics that produce not only search engines, but also facial image datasets that, while frequently produced by research teams in non-commercial contexts, have massive economic value and include a huge number of individuals. The market for datasets

---

[28] Jake Goldenfein, *Monitoring Laws* (Cambridge University Press, 2019).

[29] Chloe Xiang, 'AI is probably using your images and it's not easy to opt out' (26 September 2022), Vice: Motherboard, www.vice.com/en/article/3ad58k/ai-is-probably-using-your-images-and-its-not-easy-to-opt-out.

[30] See, e.g., Benjamin L. W. Sobel, 'A new common law of web scraping' (2021–2022) 25 *Lewis and Clark Law Review* 147–207; Vladan Joler and Matteo Pasquinelli, 'Nooscope' (2020) https://nooscope.ai/.

was estimated to be $9 billion in 2022.[31] There are a number of giant image datasets containing images of any person for whom there are a multitude of images available online – be they celebrities, political figures, or activists.[32] For instance, the 'Have I been Trained' tool can identify whether individuals are included in the notorious LAION 5B and LAION 400M datasets, used to train a substantial number of AI tools, and since refined into a large number of other industrially valuable image datasets.[33] To some extent, the new rules in the EU AI Act will prohibit this type of indiscriminate scraping by Clearview AI. But because the rules only address 'untargeted' scraping for the creation of 'facial recognition databases' it will hardly disturb the facial image dataset industry. As discussed below, apart from Clearview AI, the majority of the industry is vertically dis-integrated, meaning entities doing scraping are producing facial image datasets not biometrically identified facial recognition databases like Clearview AI.

Scraping and image datasets are often produced by companies or research institutions not themselves involved in biometric analysis or facial recognition applications, but who still perform a critical task in the facial recognition supply chain. Companies producing image datasets typically argue that images without names do not constitute personal information. Alternatively, they may claim to only index image URLs not the images themselves (i.e., making images available for other parties to download) so as to not process image data at all. If they are processing images, that processing is claimed to be legal because it is in the legitimate interests of the entity,[34] Many image datasets made available without any associated biometric information, with subsequent users performing biometric analysis to link particular individuals across multiple images. Sometimes they are simply used to test and benchmark algorithmic models, enabling a demonstration of an algorithm's efficacy.[35] These companies mostly evade privacy scrutiny and will likely avoid regulation by the AI Act. Clearview AI managed to attract legal attention for its supply chain activities because its vertical integration (i.e., because it scraped the images, ran the biometric analysis, and sold the identification service) linked those supply chains to the product / application level where privacy and data protection more comfortably apply.

Image datasets are also created without web-scraping – typically through surreptitious photography. Facial recognition in public space has different demands

---

[31] Madhumita Murgia, 'Who's using your face? The ugly truth about facial recognition' (19 April 2019), *Financial Times*, www.ft.com/content/cf19b956-60a2-11e9-b285-3acd5d43599e.

[32] Ibid.

[33] https://haveibeentrained.com/

[34] See, e.g., https://laion.ai/faq/.

[35] The diversity of actors in the facial recognition supply chain also enables problematic 'data laundering' practices. Datasets are legally constructed by research institutions using non-commercial research exceptions to copyright law, but then made available to commercial entities that use them for profit: see Andy Baio, 'AI data laundering: How academic and nonprofit researchers shield tech companies from accountability' (30 September 2022), Waxy, https://waxy.org/2022/09/ai-data-laundering-how-academic-and-nonprofit-researchers-shield-tech-companies-from-accountability/. reporting on a Meta owned generative text-video tool trained on the WebVid-10M dataset that was initially scraped from Shutterstock, as well as the XPretrain dataset released by Microsoft of millions of videos scraped from YouTube with text descriptions.

to identify verification systems that use portraits for biometric enrolment. Images scraped from the web are frequently too posed and flat-angled to produce biometric models able to identify individuals from images and video captured from more common surveillance vantage points. Facial recognition in the wild needs images of people walking around, looking at their phones, being unknowingly recorded. This is why, for instance datasets such as Brainwash, produced with a webcam in a café, capturing images of returning customers waiting to order coffee, as well as the Duke-Multi-Target, Multi-Camera Unconstrained College Student Dataset, produced with synchronised surveillance cameras taking pictures of students walking between classes from a university office window, are so valuable.[36] Data scientists are increasingly seeking access to CCTV footage for building novel datasets.[37] Although surveillance for dataset construction does not raise the same risk of real-time mass surveillance that animates privacy thinking, in the world of operationalism, those images still participate in the facial recognition ecosystem and economy, raising new critical questions that few existing legal concepts, let alone privacy, are able to answer.

A comprehensive analysis is beyond the scope of this chapter, but no legal regime clearly imposes meaningful limitations in this domain. The *HiQ* v. *LinkedIn* case seemingly upheld the legality of scraping under the US Computer Fraud and Abuse Act, even if contrary to platform terms of service.[38] Scraping does not interfere with personal property interests because there are no property rights in data. Exploitation of Creative Commons non-commercial licensed images is permissible because of the data laundering (commercial/non-commercial) techniques described in footnote 37 as well as the general copyright exemptions for research purposes.[39] Some argue that scraping images to build datasets or train algorithms does not involve market substitution or replication of any 'expressive' dimension of images, meaning it may not violate copyright anyway.[40] There are already fair use (or equivalent) exceptions for search engines in many jurisdictions.[41] The US privacy-adjacent right of publicity is unlikely to apply when a scraped image has no commercial value prior to its appropriation and exploitation and does not result in subsequent publication.[42]

---

[36] See, e.g., Harvey and LaPlace, 'Exposing.AI'.

[37] See, e.g., UC Riverside Video Computing Group. 'Datasets' (n.d.), https://vcg.ece.ucr.edu/datasets.

[38] *HiQ Labs* v. *LinkedIn Corp.*, 938 F.3d 985 (9th Cir. 2019).

[39] See, e.g., Ryan Merkley, 'Use and fair use: Statement on shared images in facial recognition AI' (13 March 2019), Creative Commons, https://creativecommons.org/2019/03/13/statement-on-shared-images-in-facial-recognition-ai/.

[40] Sobel, 'A new common law of web scraping'.

[41] See, e.g., Jonathan Band, 'Google and fair use' (2008) 3 *Journal of Business & Technology Law* 1–28.

[42] See, e.g., including for contrasting views, Wendy Xu, 'Recognizing property rights in biometric data under the right to publicity' (2020–2021) 98 *University of Detroit Mercy Law Review* 143–166; Lisa Raimondi, 'Biometric data regulation and the right to publicity: A path to regaining autonomy over our commodified identity' (2021) 16(1) *University of Massachusetts Law Review* 200–230; A. J. McClurg, 'In the face of danger: Facial recognition and the limits of privacy law' (2007) 120 *Harvard Law Review* 1870–1891.

It will be interesting to see the outcome of the pending *Vance* v. *IBM* litigation concerning IBM's refining of Flickr's YFCC100M dataset into the Diversity in Faces dataset.[43] But this case also deals only with governance of biometric information and not the images from which that biometric data is derived, meaning it will not enjoin dataset creation more generally. At the same time, industry- and research-aligned actors have started pushing in the other direction, arguing for freedoms to use and reuse datasets,[44] rights 'to process data' without consent,[45] with clear exceptions for copyright or usufructuary rights over property interests to maximise capacities to build and train machine learning models.[46]

5.5 CONCLUSION

The way privacy and data protection are configured may make sense if online images are representations of individuals, browsed by humans, at risk of certain autonomy effects; but it makes much less sense if images are already part of a socio-technical ecosystem, viewed primarily by machines, used to train and benchmark facial recognition algorithms in order to produce economic value. Privacy and data protection's representationalism struggles to grasp the mobilisation of images as supply chain components in a dynamic biometric ecology. This chapter has argued that the issues in this 'back end' of the facial recognition ecosystem are very different from those that have been typically raised in privacy discussions. Here, regulatory questions intersect with what has become a new frontier of value creation in the digital economy – facial recognition model training. The concern is no longer exclusively losing anonymity in public, but also information being captured from public spaces, not for the sake of identifying you, but for the sake of generating an archive of images of you in the wild in order to train facial recognition models and extract economic value. Once we pay attention to how facial recognition systems are built and function, privacy and data protection start to lose their grip.

---

[43] *Vance* v. *IBM* Case: 1:20-cv-00577.

[44] PIJIP, 'Joint comment to WIPO on copyright and artificial intelligence' (17 February 2020), Infojustice, https://infojustice.org/archives/42009.

[45] See, e.g., Mauritz Kop, 'The right to process data for machine learning purposes in the EU' (2021) 34 *Harvard Journal of Law & Technology – Spring Digest* 1–23.

[46] See, e.g., Inioluwa Deborah Raji, Timnit Gebru, Margaret Mitchel, Joy Buolamwini, Joonseok Lee, and Emily Denton, 'Saving face: Investigating the ethical concerns of facial recognition auditing' (2020), AAAI/ACM AI Ethics and Society Conference 2020; Vinay Uday Prabhu and Abeba Birhane, 'Large image datasets: A Pyrrhic win for computer vision?' (2020), arXiv:2006.16923.

6

Facial Recognition Technology and Potential for Bias and Discrimination

Marcus Smith and Monique Mann

6.1 INTRODUCTION

Facial recognition technology (FRT) is one of several data-based technologies contributing to a shift in the criminal justice system, and society more broadly, towards 'automated' decision-making processes. Related technologies include other forms of biometric identification and predictive policing tools. These technology-based applications can potentially improve investigative efficiency but raise questions about bias and discrimination.[1] It is important for designers of these systems to understand the potential for technology to operate as a tool that may can discriminate, furthering biases that are already entrenched in the criminal justice system.

This chapter examines how FRT contributes to racial discrimination in the criminal justice system, potentially exacerbating existing over-representation of racial minorities. From one perspective, this technology may be viewed by some as a value neutral, objective, decision-making tool, free from human prejudice and error. However, it is also recognised that FRT, and the associated algorithms, are dependent on datasets that influence its performance and accuracy.[2] If the input data is biased, so too is the algorithm, and consequently the eventual decisions and outputs. Moreover, this discriminatory potential inherent in the technology is compounded by existing discrimination and over-representation of minority groups.

The chapter is divided into four parts: the first discusses FRT, including current applications. The second discusses the potential for bias and discrimination in the criminal justice system in relation to FRT. The third moves away from a focus on technology and considers social and structural discrimination, integrating the relevant critical literature into our argument. Finally, we conclude that even if the technology could be designed in a way that was completely free from discrimination in a techno-determinist

---

[1] Avi Marciano, 'Reframing biometric surveillance: From a means of inspection to a form of control' (2019) 21 *Ethics and Information Technology* 127–136, at 134.

[2] Joy Buolamwini and Timnit Gebru, 'Gender shades: Intersectional accuracy disparities in commercial gender classification' (2018) 81 *Proceedings of Machine Learning Research Conference on Fairness, Accountability and Transparency* 1–15.

Marcus Smith and Monique Mann

sense, it may still be used to discriminate, given, for example, the long-standing over-policing and disproportionate representation of marginalised groups in the criminal justice system. This should be considered by governments when regulating FRT and by law enforcement and judicial officers making decisions that are informed by it.

6.2 FACIAL RECOGNITION APPLICATIONS AND ISSUES

The face is central to an individual's identity and, consequently, to identifying suspects in criminal investigations. The analysis of faces by law enforcement has progressed from descriptions and sketches of suspects to the contemporary biometric integrated closed-circuit television (CCTV) technology widely used around the world in both the public and private sectors today.[3] Although there are many applications of FRT, its fundamental process remains the same. FRT involves the automated extraction, digitisation, and comparison of the geometric distribution of facial features in a way that can identify individuals. It begins with a digital image of a subject's face, from which a contour map of their features is created and then converted into a digital template. An algorithm compares digital templates of facial images and ranks them according to similarity.[4]

There are two ways in which FRT is used. The first, and less controversial, is one-to-one matching. It is used to verify the identity of a person; for example, in a security feature granting access to a smartphone or to compare a person at an international border. The use of FRT expanded rapidly following the 9/11 terrorist attacks in 2001, when it was widely integrated into passports and international border control security systems, allowing the comparison of a facial template with a live image created using SmartGate technology.[5]

The second way it can be used is one-to-many searching: the focus of this chapter. One-to-many searching seeks to identify an unknown person, for example by scanning CCTV footage of a crowd or images gathered from social media sites or more widely on the internet. Police could search based on a photograph of an unknown suspect to identify them or search for a known person in a crowd in real time. The integration of FRT with CCTV to identify unknown persons in public spaces is a major change that has taken place progressively over the past twenty years, to the point where it is normalised and widely used today. Examples of this type of application include not only fixed cameras, but also cameras on vehicles, body worn cameras, and drones, to search public spaces for persons of interest using integrated FRT.[6]

More recently, FRT has been used to search images from the internet, including images uploaded to social media, from sites such as Twitter, Instagram, LinkedIn,

---

[3] Marcus Smith and Seumas Miller, *Biometric Identification Law and Ethics* (Springer, 2021).

[4] Marcus Smith, Monique Mann, and Gregor Urbas, *Biometrics, Crime and Security* (Routledge, 2018).

[5] Monique Mann and Marcus Smith, 'Automated facial recognition technology: Recent developments and regulatory options' (2017) 40 *University of New South Wales Law Journal* 121–145.

[6] *R (on the application of Bridges)* v. *Chief Constable of South Wales Police* (2020) EWCA Civ 1058.

Google, and Facebook. Facebook alone has over 250 billion images uploaded.[7] The use of Clearview AI by law enforcement agencies around the world came to light in 2020, and the company has been the subject of public debate and controversy, not least from social media and other internet companies that commenced legal action over the right to use these images. They claim its business model is in contravention of the terms of service of the websites the images were harvested from. In addition to the widespread use of the Clearview AI application by law enforcement agencies, the company also provides its services to the private sector, raising broader concerns. Clients that use the company's services for security purposes include the National Basketball Association, Bank of America, and Best Buy.[8] The use of images from the internet demonstrates how facial templates can be collected and used in ways that individuals may not be aware of and has the potential to connect many sources of data. It also provides insights into the scale of use of FRT, adding to the significance of racial discrimination and other pertinent issues in this context.[9]

There are inherent limitations in the use of FRT when deployed for the purposes of one-to-many identification that extend beyond bias and discrimination. Accuracy is impacted by factors such as the quality of images and cameras used, and the background and lighting conditions when the images were taken. Individual changes can impact on accuracy, including plastic surgery, ageing, weight gain, and facial coverings, such as the surgical masks that became commonplace during the COVID-19 pandemic.[10] In 2020, technology companies including IBM, Amazon, and Microsoft announced they would pause (or cease altogether), sales of their FRT to law enforcement and border security agencies owing to concerns around accuracy and privacy (Clearview AI was a notable exception to this position).[11] There have also been bans by some local governments in the United States – Somerville, Massachusetts, and San Francisco, California – which have outlawed any city department, including law enforcement, from using FRT.[12]

FRT has been found to be less accurate when used for the purposes of identifying people with darker skin tones, meaning that police deployment of FRT in criminal investigations can increase the likelihood that ethnic minorities will be wrongfully identified and prosecuted for crimes that they have not committed.[13] If this is not considered and addressed, it will likely increase the interaction of these individuals with police and compound their existing over-representation in the criminal justice system.

---

[7] Marcus Smith and Gregor Urbas, *Technology Law* (Cambridge University Press, 2021).

[8] Marcus Smith and Seumas Miller, 'The ethical application of biometric facial recognition technology' (2021) 37 *AI & Society* 167–175.

[9] Ibid.

[10] Smith, Mann, and Urbas, *Biometrics, Crime and Security*.

[11] Smith and Miller, 'Ethical application of biometric facial recognition technology'.

[12] Sidney Perkowitz, 'The bias in the machine: Facial recognition technology and racial disparities' (5 February 2021), MIT Schwarzman College of Computing, https://mit-serc.pubpub.org/pub/bias-in-machine/release/1?readingCollection=34db8026.

[13] Laura Moy, 'A taxonomy of police technology's racial inequity problems (2021) *University of Illinois Law Review* 139–193.

The issues we have raised in relation to racial discrimination cannot be viewed in isolation. In liberal democracies, there is ongoing tension between security, individual privacy, autonomy, and democratic accountability. The rapid growth and application of FRT in both the private and public sectors creates a power imbalance between individuals and the state (and corporations) and should be limited to specific and justified purposes (i.e., where the use of FRT is deemed to be both necessary and proportionate), with associated data and images carefully protected. As far as FRT being justified for security purposes, and privacy concerns mitigated, it must be subject to accountability mechanisms to prevent it being misused. Moreover, citizens should be informed about the potential use of their images for facial recognition and should have meaningfully consented to their use. Whether these systems are operated by public or private sector agencies or law enforcement, regulatory options should be publicly debated, and their use governed by legislation and subject to judicial review.

6.3 DATA, BIAS, AND RACIAL DISCRIMINATION

In 2020, a police investigation in Detroit involving Robert Williams received attention in the national press in the United States. Williams, an African American man, was arrested for shoplifting based on facial recognition identification. He was held for thirty hours before posting bail; but it was later established to be a false match based on his driver's licence photograph and distorted crime scene surveillance footage. The police department provided an apology and instigated a review of the use of FRT. Williams commenced litigation against the police department seeking compensation for his treatment.[14] The incident highlights the risks of inaccurate technology being used to identify suspects and relied upon in an arrest. Williams's case is one of several similar examples from across the United States that has drawn attention to the potential for racial bias to occur in relation to facial recognition, and for this to exacerbate the over-representation of minorities.

These incidents took place around the same time as the murder of George Floyd by a police officer, and the subsequent attention on the issue of racial discrimination through the Black Lives Matter movement.

The existing over-representation of minority groups in police databases will mean that they are more likely to be identified using facial recognition. Brian Jefferson notes that in the United States more than three-quarters of the black male population is listed in criminal justice databases.[15] Because facial images are included in these databases, they can also be used by analysis by FRT. Depending on the specific use cases (i.e., how the technology is deployed and the watchlists used), it is reasonable to suggest that FRT directs police towards those individuals who are already known to them.

---

[14] Drew Harwell, 'Wrongfully arrested man sues Detroit police over false facial recognition match' (13 April 2021), *Washington Post*, www.washingtonpost.com/technology/2021/04/13/facial-recognition-false-arrest-lawsuit/.

[15] Brian Jefferson, *Digitize and Punish: Racial Criminalization in the Digital Age* (University of Minnesota Press, 2020), p. 11.

FRT and Potential for Bias and Discrimination

There are also data-based reasons why minority groups may be subjected to mis-identification, or over-identification, in relation to FRT, as established by empirical studies on the issue of racial bias associated with FRT. In 2019, a National Institute of Standards and Technology (NIST) report indicated that the technology achieved significantly lower rates of accuracy in African American and Asian faces – in fact, it found that faces of these races were between 10 and 100 times more likely to be mis-identified, when compared with white male faces.[16] This is supported by other research which has found that the mis-identification rate for dark-skinned women is about 35 per cent, fifty times higher than white males.[17]

The reason for this rate of mis-identification is the data inputs that the algorithms undertaking the matching rely upon. It has been established that, on average, the datasets used to train the algorithms comprise approximately 80 per cent 'lighter skinned' subjects.[18] The issues with accuracy are therefore likely to be caused by ethnic representation in datasets used to create and train the matching algorithms. Designers of the technology need to consider the racial representation in the datasets used to train facial recognition algorithms. Failing to rectify this issue, by not proactively taking steps to include representative representation in the FRT datasets, could constitute a form of racism, whether that is intended or an oversight.[19]

This is especially concerning given that ethnic minorities are already disproportionately scrutinised by law enforcement and over-represented in the criminal justice system. Increased error rates and mis-identification by facial recognition and other new technologies may compound this serious existing problem. This should be a focus for those building facial recognition systems – designing out the potential for racial discrimination by embedding racial equality in the data used to train the algorithms. Beyond this issue, any form of identification technology should not be relied upon in isolation, but only ever used in the context of other circumstantial evidence in an investigation. However, addressing the technology will only ever be part of the solution. As Damien Patrick Williams notes, 'merely putting more Black faces in the training data will not change the fact that, at base, these systems themselves will be most often deployed within a framework of racialised and gendered carceral justice'.[20]

---

[16] Patrick Grother, Mei Ngan, and Kayee Hanaoka, *Face Recognition Vendor Test (FRVT) Part 2: Identification* (NIST, 2019).

[17] Joy Buolamwini and Timnit Gebru, 'Gender shades: Intersectional accuracy disparities in commercial gender classification' (2018) 81 *Proceedings of the 1st Conference on Fairness, Accountability and Transparency* 77–79.

[18] Ibid.

[19] Clare Garvie, Alvaro Bedoya, and Jonathan Frankle, 'The perpetual line-up: Unregulated police face recognition in America' (18 October 2016), Georgetown Law Center on Privacy and Technology, www.perpetuallineup.org/.

[20] Damien Patrick Williams, 'Fitting the description: Historical and sociotechnical elements of facial recognition and anti-black surveillance' (2020) 7 *Journal of Responsible Innovation* 74–83.

6.4 SOCIAL AND STRUCTURAL DISCRIMINATION

Police attention is not equally applied across the population; racial minorities are subject to disproportionate criminal justice system intervention. The consequences of this are most clearly seen in the disproportionate over-representation of minority groups in prisons around the world. This context is a necessary consideration when thinking about FRT and discrimination, because as we have described, technology can potentially perpetuate racial inequality. The following part of this chapter moves on from technical or technologically deterministic sources of bias and discrimination introduced above (i.e., those within the data or algorithms underpinning the technology) and adopts a broader structural and social view. It considers facial recognition as a socio-technical phenomenon and argues there is a need to dis-aggregate the technical and social dimensions to discrimination, as well as understand their interaction, and to do so it is necessary to clearly define and evaluate the use cases of technology vis-à-vis specific social and institutional contexts.

It has been recently argued that 'assisted' (rather than 'automated') facial recognition is a more suitable descriptor for the technology given the way that it is used to inform and direct police activities and operations (rather than truly 'automate' them).[21] Pete Fussey and colleagues' research examines a range of organisational, system, and operator factors, including the processes of human–computer interaction, and demonstrates how technical and environmental influences impact on the operation of facial recognition systems deployed by police. Fussey argues that 'while practitioners shape and condition the application and potential of their technological instruments, these practices, forms of action and ways of thinking are simultaneously shaped and conditioned by these technologies and the affordances they bring'.[22] They conclude that 'operator decision-making activities involving discretionary and suspicious judgements over who should be stopped once a possible identification has been articulated by the algorithm' and that 'technological capability is conditioned by police discretion, but police discretion itself is also contingent on the operational and technical environment'.[23] These are important considerations, because the roots of discrimination in policing do not stem entirely from the use of new technology in and of itself, but rather the institutions of policing and the actions of police officers in discretionary and discriminatory enforcement of the law.

Work by Simon Egbert and Monique Mann on discrimination and predictive policing technologies also draws attention to the socio-technical interactions between the inputs/outputs of predictive technologies and the street level decisions made by police.[24]

---

[21] Pete Fussey, Bethan Davies, and Martin Innes, '"Assisted" facial recognition and the reinvention of suspicion and discretion in digital policing' (2021) 61 *British Journal of Criminology* 325–344.

[22] Ibid.

[23] Ibid.

[24] Simon Egbert and Monique Mann, 'Discrimination in predictive policing: The dangerous myth of impartiality and the need for STS-analysis' in V. Badalic (ed.), *Automating Crime Prevention, Surveillance and Military Operations* (Springer, 2021), pp. 25–46.

Egbert and Mann argue that predictive policing is 'a socio-technical assemblage, encompassing not only the technical predictions themselves, but also the enactment of the predictions on the street level police – which can also have serious ramifications including discrimination'.[25] Connecting this argument to the work by Fussey, we argue that like predictive policing technologies, facial recognition technologies operate within a wider socio-technical assemblage that is shaped by the technology and wider social and structural factors such as police discretion and long-standing discrimination by police and criminal justice institutions. We contend that more attention needs to be directed to the social and structural contexts of technologies to understand their discriminatory potential when examining discrimination in policing, including in the application and use of facial recognition technologies.

Even if FRT could be designed to be perfectly 'bias free' from a technological perspective, it may still be targeted specifically against racial minorities or deployed in contexts that control and oppress them. An example of the relevance of such contextual considerations in which technology is deployed with discriminatory potential and impacts are the Smart City developments in Darwin, Australia. Pat O'Malley and Gavin Smith examine the deployment of this programme to improve public safety and public spaces, which involved the deployment of an extensive network of CCTV cameras.[26] While administrators assert that the video analytics do not include facial recognition software, there is nothing to prevent police from using facial recognition software on the CCTV footage collected. This is significant given the stark over-representation of Indigenous people in the criminal justice system in this part of Australia. For example, in 2016–2017, Indigenous people comprised 84 per cent of the prison population, and Indigenous youth comprised almost 95 per cent of those in youth detention, in addition to many other forms of disadvantage demonstrating social-economic inequality and injustice.

O'Malley and Smith argue that the Smart City technologies deployed in Darwin are 'directed at the monitoring and control of [Indigenous] people in public places' and draw attention to the 'very real prospect of the system being used to sharpen a criminalising gaze on the predominantly marginalised and excluded bodies of the Indigenous people living in and around the city'.[27] The risk is that the surveillant capabilities of the Smart City in Darwin will create negative and disproportionate impacts for Indigenous people, not only because they are already the focus on a racialized criminal justice system, but also by virtue of their daily presence in public spaces in Darwin, which is connected to social factors including unemployment and homelessness, which is in turn a consequence of Australia's colonial past and the dispossession of Indigenous people from their lands. O'Malley and Smith conclude that 'the impacts of Smart City programmes on crime control cannot be read

---

[25] Ibid., p. 25.
[26] Pat O'Malley and Gavin Smith, '"Smart" crime prevention? Digitization and racialized crime control in a smart city' (2022) 26(1) *Theoretical Criminology* 40–56, at 40.
[27] Ibid.

off in a technocratically deterministic fashion … but must be situated and analysed in specific contexts' and that the 'enduring legacies of colonialism have done much to shape the nature and implications of Smart Cities projects'.[28]

This demonstrates the importance of a focus on social, political, and historical context when thinking about how technology might be 'biased' or 'discriminatory', and the need to understand the specific use cases of policing technologies, including but not limited to FRT. Even if technologically 'bias free' forms of facial recognition were indeed available, we could assume that they will be deployed in ways that are not 'neutral' and, rather, would operate to further marginalise, discriminate against, and control certain groups, especially those that are already the most marginalised and oppressed. This is pertinent given critiques by Sara Yates that 'the narrative that [FRTs] are problematic only due to their lack of transparency and inaccuracy is faulty'.[29] Yates argues that 'if these tools are allowed to be used by law enforcement, whether they have been reformed to address the accuracy and transparency issues … they will still be used disproportionally against marginalized groups and people of colour…'.[30] A focus on addressing discrimination in FRT through only technologically deterministic approaches will not remedy broader historical social injustices and harm done by police institutions and the criminal justice system, nor will banning or outlawing facial recognition. As Yates acknowledges, 'the greatest harm from these systems does not come from these tools themselves, but instead from the unjust institutions that use them'.[31] While calling for bans on FRT may be intuitively appealing, they will not resolve institutional and systemic racism and injustices perpetrated by such institutions.

The task must be to first address these fundamental injustices, or they will recur in the guise of objective technology.[32] There is a need to disaggregate the technical and social dimensions to bias and discrimination and seek to better understand the specific use cases of technology within specific institutional and social contexts. It is necessary to understand these various sources of bias and discrimination, for example those that arise from individuals (i.e., police/operator discretion), the way the system is designed (i.e., in public places that racial minorities tend to frequent), and the wider system objectives (i.e., the reason supporting the deployment of technology in that context). Analyses of the interactive effect of social and technological factors are required in order to evaluate whether the objectives and applications of certain technologies in specific contexts are necessary and proportionate, while ensuring that individual rights are upheld (including privacy, anti-discrimination, and equality). Regulatory strategies to address this issue could be targeted according to the level of risk presented in specific contexts and specific use cases of technology.

---

[28] Ibid.

[29] Sara Yates, 'The digitalization of the carceral state: The troubling narrative around police usage of facial recognition technology' (2022) 19 *Colorado Technology Law Journal* 483–508.

[30] Ibid., p. 505.

[31] Ibid., p. 506.

[32] Damien Patrick Williams, 'Fitting the description: Historical and sociotechnical elements of facial recognition and anti-black surveillance' (2020) 7 *Journal of Responsible Innovation* 74–83.

Moving forward, there is a need to consider, implement, and evaluate measures that aim to reduce discrimination and harm in existing systems (including the criminal justice system) and design better systems. In doing so, the structural discrimination that is a feature of many systems must be addressed to ensure that existing inequalities are not perpetuated by new technologies such as facial recognition.

6.5 CONCLUSION

The use of FRT in the criminal justice system and its association with racial discrimination is an important issue for society, given the rapidly expanding application of the technology and the limited regulation in many jurisdictions. This technology may operate to further historical forms of oppression, discrimination, bias, and over-representation of minority groups in the criminal justice system. There is evidence that FRT may contribute to racial discrimination by operating with reduced accuracy, owing to the fact that the data used to inform the operation of the technology does not include sufficient representation, leading to inaccuracy and misidentification. While this issue must be dealt with, addressing it in isolation will not be sufficient. The disproportionate focus on minorities is a far bigger problem in the criminal justice system, and the extent to which FRT perpetuates this is a subset of a much bigger, complex and historically entrenched problem. Along with the data problem, this context must be considered by those operating the technology, and by law enforcement organisations and governments, and they should not over-deploy it in areas where these minority groups are concentrated.

Rather than ban the technology altogether, we need to focus on structural discrimination and inequality – calling for a widespread ban of technologies altogether, while it may be appealing to some, is not going to be productive in the long term, nor is it realistic. While there are data-based issues here that can be addressed, this step alone will not be sufficient, and there is a need to address the social issues if we are to achieve meaningful change. Technology is not the problem, nor is it the solution. In conclusion, there are two perspectives to take account of: a data perspective and a social perspective. Although they are inter-related, they need to be disaggregated, and their socio-technical interaction better understood. First, we can see that when technology is based on datasets skewed towards white populations, it does not function as accurately on minorities. Second, technology may further existing bias and racism inherent in the individuals and organisations deploying and operating it, and in terms of inequality within the criminal justice system and society more broadly. We need to ensure that there is representative racial representation in datasets (the technical issue), and ensure that it is not over-used it in areas where racial minorities are concentrated (the social issue).

7

Power and Protest

Facial Recognition and Public Space Surveillance

Monika Zalnieriute

Political freedom, generally speaking, means the right to be a participator in government, or it means nothing.[1]

7.1 INTRODUCTION

In 2018, police in India reported that the roll out of facial recognition technology (FRT) across New Delhi enabled their identification of 3,000 missing children in just four days.[2] In the United Kingdom, South Wales Police used live FRT to scan over 50,000 faces at various mass gatherings between January and August 2019 and identified nine individuals for arrest.[3] The Chinese Sharp Eyes programme, 'omnipresent, fully networked, always working and fully controllable', can take less than seven minutes to identify and facilitate apprehension of an individual among a population of nearly 5 million people.[4] In Moscow, 105,000 FRT-enabled cameras have

---

Research for this chapter has been funded by the Research Council of Lithuania (LMTLT) (Government Use of Facial Recognition Technologies: Legal Challenges and Solutions (FaceAI), agreement number S-MIP-21-38); and Australian Research Council Discovery Early Career Research Award (Artificial Intelligence Decision-Making, Privacy and Discrimination Laws, project number DE210101183). The chapter draws on and adapts some arguments developed in M. Zalnieriute, 'Facial Recognition Surveillance and Public Space: Protecting Protest Movements', *International Review of Law, Computers & Technology*, 2024 (forthcoming).

[1] Hannah Arendt, *On Revolution* (Penguin, 1977), p. 218.
[2] PTI, 'Delhi: Facial recognition system helps trace 3,000 missing children in 4 days' (22 April 2018), *Times of India*, https://timesofindia.indiatimes.com/city/delhi/delhi-facial-recognition-system-helps-trace-3000-missing-children-in-4-days/articleshow/63870129.cms.
[3] AFR South Wales, 'Deployments for Live Facial Recognition' (n.d.), www.south-wales.police .uk/police-forces/south-wales-police/areas/about-us/about-us/facial-recognition-technology/ deployments-for-live-facial-recognition/.
[4] Ryan Grenoble, 'Welcome to the surveillance state: China's AI cameras see all' (12 December 2017), *HuffPost Australia*, www.huffpost.com/entry/china-surveillance-camera-big-brother_n_5a2ff4dfe4b01 598ac484acc.

Power and Protest   97

monitored and enforced COVID-19 self-isolation orders,[5] with at least 200 violators being identified.[6]

As protest movements are gaining momentum across the world, with Extinction Rebellion, Black Lives Matter, and strong pro-democracy protests in Chile and Hong Kong taking centre stage, many governments – both in the West and in the East – have significantly increased surveillance capacity of the public sphere. City streets and squares, stations, and airports across the globe, and social media and online platforms have become equipped with sophisticated surveillance tools, enabled and made legal through a myriad of complex and ever-expanding 'emergency' laws. Irrespective of whether these events and/or political strategies are framed as 'emergencies' such as the 'war on terror' with its invisible geopolitical enemies for 9/11, or whether they were pro-democracy or anti-racism protests or connected with COVID-19, the state resort to technology and increased surveillance as a tool to control the masses and population has been similar. Examples from varied countries – ranging from China, Russia, and India to the United States and the United Kingdom – tell us that recent technological advances have enabled authoritarian and democratic governments alike to build omnipresent biometric infrastructures that systematically monitor, surveil, predict, and regulate the behaviour of individual citizens, groups, or even entire populations.

In this chapter, I focus on the chilling effect of FRT use in public spaces on the right to peaceful assembly and political protest. While technological tools have transformed protest movements widely, both amplifying and undermining them,[7] in this chapter I only focus how protest movements have been tackled with FRT and my emphasis is on *political protests* and *public spaces*. Pointing to the absence of oversight and accountability mechanisms on government use of FRT, the chapter demonstrates how FRT has significantly strengthened state power. It draws attention to the crucial role of tech companies in assisting governments in public space surveillance and curtailing protests. I argue for hard human rights obligations

---

[5] Patrick Reevell, 'How Russia is using facial recognition to police its coronavirus lockdown' (30 April 2020), *ABC News*, https://abcnews.go.com/International/russia-facial-recognition-police-coronavirus-lockdown/story?id=70299736; Sarah Rainsford, 'Russia uses facial recognition to tackle virus' (4 April 2020), *BBC News*, www.bbc.com/news/av/world-europe-52157131/coronavirus-russia-uses-facial-recognition-to-tackle-covid-19. One man, having been given a self-quarantine order, was visited by police within half an hour of leaving his home to take out the rubbish.

[6] NtechLab, 'Biometric Solution against COVID-19' (n.d.), https://ntechlab.com/en_au/solution/biometric-solution-against-covid-19/.

[7] V. Barassi, *Activism on the Web: Everyday Struggles against Digital Capitalism* (Routledge, 2015); J. Juris, 'Reflections on #occupy everywhere: Social media, public space, and emerging logics of aggregation' (2012) 39(2) *American Ethnologist* 259–279; P. Gerbaudo, *Tweets and the Streets: Social Media and Contemporary Activism* (Pluto Press, 2012); P. Gerbaudo, *The Mask and the Flag: Populism, Citizenism, and Global Protest* (Oxford University Press, 2017); Alice Mattoni, *Media Practices and Protest Politics How Precarious Workers Mobilise* (Ashgate, 2012); Lucas Melgaco and Jeffrey Monoghan, 'Introduction: Taking to the streets in the information age' in Lucas Melgaco and Jeffrey Monoghan (eds.), *Protests in the Information Age* (Routledge, 2018), pp. 1–17; D. Trottier and Christian Fuchs (eds.), *Social Media, Politics and the State* (Routledge, 2015).

Monika Zalnieriute

to bind these companies and governments, to ensure that political movements and protests can flourish in the post-COVID-19 world.

7.2 UNDERMINING PROTEST MOVEMENTS WITH FRTS

Live automated FRT, rolled out in public spaces and cities across the world, is transforming modern policing in liberal democracies and authoritarian regimes alike. The technology augments traditional surveillance methods by detecting and comparing a person's eyes, nose, mouth, skin textures, and shadows to identify individuals.[8] The live automated facial recognition can instantaneously assess the facial biometric data in the captured images against a pre-existing 'watchlist' and flag it to police officers. Some FRT tools go further, purporting to classify people by gender or race or make predictions about their sexual orientation, emotions, and intent.

This FRT has been used to tackle protest movements globally. For example, the US company Geofeedia has been marketed to law enforcement 'as a tool to monitor activists and protestors',[9] incorporating FRT use with Twitter, Facebook, and Instagram databases.[10] Rasheed Shabazz, an activist and journalist, believes that his arrest near the Black Lives Matter protests in Oakland in 2014 was as a result of the Geofeedia software.[11] This same software was also used to monitor civil unrest after the police killing of Freddie Grey and link protesters with their social media profiles.[12] Similarly, in 2020, during the protests following the killing of George Floyd in Minneapolis, Minnesota, several people were arrested and charged after being

---

[8] Andrew Guthrie Ferguson, 'Facial recognition and the Fourth Amendment' (2021) 105 *Minnesota Law Review* 1105–1106; Jagdish Chandra Joshi and K. K. Gupta, 'Face recognition technology: A review' (2016) 1 *The IUP Journal of Telecommunication* 53–54, at 53; Relly Victoria Virgil Petrescu, 'Face recognition as a biometric application' (2019) 3 *Journal of Mechatronics and Robotics* 240; Mary Grace Galterio, Simi Angelic Shavit, and Thaier Hayajneh, 'A review of facial biometrics security for smart devices' (2018) 7 (37) *Computers* 3; Ian Berle, *Face Recognition Technology: Compulsory Visibility and Its Impact on Privacy and the Confidentiality of Personal Identifiable Images* (Springer, 2020), p. 1

[9] ACLU of Northern CA, 'Police use of social media surveillance software is escalating, and activists are in the digital crosshairs' (22 September 2016), *Medium*, https://medium.com/@ACLU_NorCal/police-use-of-social-media-surveillance-software-is-escalating-and-activists-are-in-the-digital-d29d8f89c48.

[10] Matt Cagle, 'Facebook, Instagram, and Twitter provided data access for a surveillance product marketed to target activists of color' (11 October 2016), ACLU of Northern California, www.aclunc.org/blog/facebook-instagram-and-twitter-provided-data-access-surveillance-product-marketed-target; Russell Brandom, 'Facebook, Twitter, and Instagram surveillance tool was used to arrest Baltimore protestors' (11 October 2016), *The Verge*, www.theverge.com/2016/10/11/13243890/facebook-twitter-instagram-police-surveillance-geofeedia-api; Kalev Leetaru, 'Geofeedia is just the tip of the iceberg: The era of social surveillance' (12 October 2016), *Forbes*, www.forbes.com/sites/kalevleetaru/2016/10/12/geofeedia-is-just-the-tip-of-the-iceberg-the-era-of-social-surveillance/.

[11] Ali Winston, 'Oakland cops quietly acquired social media surveillance tool' (13 April 2016), *East Bay Express*, www.eastbayexpress.com/oakland/oakland-cops-quietly-acquired-social-media-surveillance-tool/Content?oid=4747526.

[12] Shira Ovide, 'A case for banning facial recognition' (9 June 2020), *New York Times*, www.nytimes.com/2020/06/09/technology/facial-recognition-software.html.

identified through the use of FRT.[13] In another case, the Detroit Police Department used FRT to identify a Black Lives Matter protester who was arrested and charged with reckless driving and resisting arrest.

Similarly, FRT has been used in many other countries. For example, 'habitual protesters' in India are included in a dataset used to monitor large crowds,[14] which is composed of 'miscreants who could raise slogans and banners'.[15] This database was used to identify dissidents at a prime ministerial rally in December 2019,[16] and also resulted in the detention of a 'handful' of individuals charged with violent crimes when it surveyed protests in New Delhi and Uttar Pradesh.[17] The Hong Kong police used FRT cameras to identify protesters and track their movements during the 2019 pro-democracy protests, which drew criticism from human rights advocates who argued that it violated the protesters' right to privacy and could lead to their persecution.[18] In 2019–2020, FRT cameras were also used in Chile to monitor and identify protesters participating in demonstrations and civil unrest, known as the *Estallido Social*.[19] The cameras were installed in public areas, including train stations and street corners, by the Chilean government to track individuals who were suspected of participating in protests or other forms of civil disobedience. In the face of mounting criticism and protests against the use of this technology, the Chilean government announced that it would suspend the use of facial recognition cameras in public spaces in early 2020.

In all these cases, FRT allowed the authorities to quickly identify individuals who were wanted for questioning or arrest. The cameras were linked to a central database containing photos and personal information of individuals who were known to have participated in previous protests or other activities that the government deemed to be illegal. Such use of FRT cameras sparked controversy and concern among civil liberties groups and privacy advocates, who argued that the technology was being used to stifle dissent and violate the rights of protesters to peacefully assemble and express their opinions. Despite these concerns, governments typically defend FRT use by framing it as a necessary measure to maintain 'public safety' and order during a time of civil unrest.

[13] Tate Ryan-Mosley and Sam Richards, 'The secret police: Cops built a shadowy surveillance machine in Minnesota after George Floyd's murder' (3 March 2020), *MIT Technology Review*, www.technologyreview.com/2022/03/03/1046676/police-surveillance-minnesota-george-floyd/.

[14] Jay Mazoomdaar, 'Delhi police film protests, run its images through face recognition software to screen crowd' (28 December 2019), *Indian Express*, https://indianexpress.com/article/india/police-film-protests-run-its-images-through-face-recognition-software-to-screen-crowd-6188246/.

[15] Vidushi Marda, 'View: From protests to chai, facial recognition is creeping up on us' (7 January 2020), *Carnegie India*, https://carnegieindia.org/2020/01/07/view-from-protests-to-chai-facial-recognition-is-creeping-up-on-us-pub-80708.

[16] Mazoomdaar, 'Delhi police film protests'.

[17] Alexandra Ulmer and Zeba Siddiqui, 'Controversy over India's use of facial recognition technology' (17 February 2020), *Sydney Morning Herald*, www.smh.com.au/world/asia/controversy-over-india-s-use-of-facial-recognition-during-protests-20200217-p541pp.html.

[18] Richard Byrne and Michael C. Davis, 'Protest tech: Hong Kong' (2020), *Wilson Quarterly*, http://wq.proof.press/quarterly/the-power-of-protest/protest-tech-hong-kong/.

[19] Michelle Corinne Liu, Jaime R. Brenes Reyes, Sananda Sahoo, and Nick Dyer-Witheford, 'Riot platforms: Protest, police, planet' (2022) 54(6) *Antipode* 1901.

In addition to such 'top-down' surveillance by public authorities in USA, India, Hong Kong, and Chile, 'horizontal' modes of surveillance have become increasingly popular.[20] This involves partially outsourcing surveillance functions to individuals and/or tech companies. A vivid example of such outsourced surveillance was the 2020 Black Lives Matter protests in Dallas, during which the police department asked individuals on Twitter to send them videos from protests that showed 'illegal activity'.[21] A larger-scale example was seen in the aftermath of the 2010 Canadian Winter Olympics riots, in which closed-circuit television (CCTV) footage was used to identify offenders, and private individuals sent the Vancouver Police Department thousands of images and helped them scour social media.[22] Similarly, tech companies such as Facebook, Twitter, and Instagram have been crucial in surveillance of protesters, as the widespread use of social media has made the monitoring of protest and dissident activities significantly easier.[23] For example, in 2014 and 2016, the US government obtained two patents that may facilitate its ability to use social-media to predict when a protest will break out.[24]

Protest movements in USA, Hong Kong, Chile, and beyond have also operated in the shadow of the global COVID-19 pandemic, and together raised questions about unprecedented levels of government power and the expanding regime of mass surveillance in public spaces. The COVID-19 pandemic has given governments a further impetus to explore FRT's health-related uses – from monitoring compliance with quarantine or social-distancing requirements to tracking (in conjunction with other biometric technologies such as thermal scanning) those who are potentially infected. COVID-19 and the latest protests in Hong Kong, Chile, and the United States have redefined the boundaries of mass surveillance and biometric tracking globally, with irreversible implications for the future exercise of government power and surveillance.

7.3 LACK OF REGULATION AND DANGERS OF FRT

Despite the increasing deployment of FRT in many city squares and streets across the globe, as many chapters in this book demonstrate, FRT use is not yet regulated.

[20] D. Trottier, 'Crowdsourcing CCTV surveillance on the internet' (2014) 15(5) *Information Communication and Society* 609; D. Trottier, 'Digital vigilantism as weaponisation of visibility' (2017) 30(1) *Philosophy and Technology* 55.

[21] Heather Kelly and Rachel Lerman, 'America is awash in cameras, a double-edged sword for protesters and police' (3 June 2020), *Washington Post*, www.washingtonpost.com/technology/2020/06/03/cameras-surveillance-police-protesters/. In protest at the request, individuals reportedly sent the police videos and images of K-pop stars.

[22] Debra Mackinnon, 'Surveillance-ready-subjects: The making of Canadian anti-masking law' in Lucas Melgaco and Jeffrey Monoghan (eds.), *Protests in the Information Age* (Routledge, 2018), pp. 151, 162.

[23] Rachel Levinson-Waldman, 'Government access to and manipulation of social media: Legal and policy challenges' (2018) 61(3) *Howard Law Journal* 531–562, at 526–531.

[24] 'U.S. Patent No. 9,892,168 BI' filed on 24 May 2016; 'U.S. Patent No. 9,794,358 BI' filed on 13 March 2014; Farrah Bara, 'From Memphis, with love: A model to protect protesters in the age of surveillance' (2019) 69 *Duke Law Journal* 197–229, at 206.

Power and Protest

Law enforcement agencies around the world are experimenting with FRT with discretion and on an ad hoc basis, without appropriate legal frameworks to govern its use nor sufficient oversight or public awareness.[25] For example, there are currently no federal regulations in the United States governing the use of FRT by law enforcement.[26] In March 2019, two US senators introduced the Commercial Facial Recognition Privacy Act, intended to ban developers and providers of commercial FRT from collecting and sharing data for identifying or tracking consumers without their consent.[27] However, this only focussed on the commercial use of FRT. Similarly, in the EU, regulation of FRT has been very limited. In February 2020, a draft EU White Paper on Artificial Intelligence appeared to call for a discussion about a temporary five-year ban on facial recognition. However, the final draft of this paper removed mention of such a moratorium.[28]

This lack of oversight of FRT use by public bodies can lead to abuses of power and violations of fundamental rights and civil liberties. As many chapters in this book demonstrate, FRT use can result in discriminatory treatment and undermining of privacy and due process, as well as other concerns. Indeed, the dangers of FRT are gradually being recognised by courts. For example, law enforcement's use of automated FRT was successfully challenged in 2020 in R *(on the application of Bridges)* v. *Chief Constable of South Wales Police ([2020] EWCA Civ 1058)* (*'Bridges'*) case, where the Court of Appeal held that the use of automated FRT by South Wales Police was unlawful because it was not 'in accordance with law' for the purposes of Article 8 of the European Convention on Human Rights.[29] In addition, South Wales Police had failed to carry out a proper Data Protection Impact Assessment and had not complied with the public sector equality duty.[30] While *Bridges* is the first successful legal challenge to police use of automated FRT worldwide, fresh lawsuits brought by non-governmental organisations in the United States and France are still pending, and they might provide different judicial responses to regulation of police FRT use.[31]

---

[25] Monika Zalnieriute, 'Burning bridges: The automated facial recognition technology and public space surveillance in the modern state' (2021) 22(2) *Columbia Science and Technology Review* 314, 284.

[26] Katja Kukielski, 'The First Amendment and facial recognition technology' (2022) 55(1) *Loyola of Los Angeles Law Review* 231.

[27] Charlotte Jee, 'A new face recognition privacy bill would give us more control over our data' (8 October 2019), *MIT Technology Review*, www.technologyreview.com/f/613129/a-new-face-recognition-privacy-bill-would-give-us-more-control-over-our-data/; Security Newswire, 'Commercial facial recognition Privacy Act of 2019 introduced' (n.d.), *Security*, www.securitymagazine.com/articles/90097-commercial-facial-recognition-privacy-act-of-2019-introduced?v=preview.

[28] Amrita Khalid, 'The EU's agenda to regulate AI does little to rein in facial recognition' (20 February 2020), Quartz, https://qz.com/1805847/facial-recognition-ban-left-out-of-the-eus-agenda-to-regulate-ai/.

[29] [2020] EWCA Civ 1058.

[30] R *(on the application of Edward Bridges)* v. *The Chief Constable of South Wales Police* [2020] Court of Appeal (Civil Division) C1/2019/2670; EWCA Civ 1058, 210 ('*Bridges (Appeal)*').

[31] *American Civil Liberties Union* v. *United States Department of Justice* (United States District Court, 31 October 2019). In October 2019 the American Civil Liberties Union (ACLU) brought an action

102   *Monika Zalnieriute*

Some jurisdictions have already regulated and limited FRT use by law enforcement. In the United States, for example, the cities of San Francisco and Berkeley have banned local agencies (including transport authorities and law enforcement) from using FRT,[32] some municipalities in Massachusetts have banned government use of facial recognition data in their communities,[33] and other US states (California, New Hampshire, and Oregon) have instituted bans on facial-recognition technology used in conjunction with police body cameras.[34] The United Kingdom also has an Automated Facial Recognition Technology (Moratorium and Review) Bill,[35] proposing to ban the use of technologies. Yet its future remains uncertain.

Therefore, not only civil right advocates, but also the courts and politicians widely recognise that FRT can be easily misused by law enforcement to target certain groups of people, such as political activists or marginalised communities, and such targeting often leads to further discrimination and injustice. Importantly, the growing prevalence of surveillance through FRT has a chilling effect on public discourse by threatening the right to protest anonymously; a notion fundamental to protest movements.

7.4 PROTEST MOVEMENTS, PUBLIC SPACE, AND THE IMPORTANCE OF ANONYMITY

Protest movements are collective actions undertaken by a group of people who come together to express their dissent, raise awareness, and advocate for change around a

---

against the US Department of Justice, the FBI, and the Drug Enforcement Agency, claiming that the public had a right to know when facial recognition software was being utilised under the Freedom of Information Act. The case was filed after the ACLU made a freedom of information request in January 2019. The DoJ, FBI, and DEA failed to produce any responsive documents. ACLU, 'ACLU challenges FBI face recognition secrecy' (31 October 2019), www.aclu.org/press-releases/aclu-challenges-fbi-face-recognition-secrecy; Conseil d'Etat, Décision n 442364 (26 April 2022), www.conseil-etat.fr/fr/arianeweb/CE/decision/2022-04-26/442364.

[32] Kate Conger, Richard Fausset, and Serge Kovaleski, 'San Francisco bans facial recognition technology' (14 May 2019), *New York Times*, www.nytimes.com/2019/05/14/us/facial-recognition-ban-san-francisco.html. The decision was made by the Board of Supervisors, who stated that the responsibility to regulate FRT will lie first with local legislators who have the capacity to move more quickly than the Federal government.

[33] Christopher Jackson, Morgan Livingston, Vetri Velan, Eric Lee, Kimberly Huynh, and Regina Eckert, 'Establishing privacy advisory commissions for the regulation of facial recognition systems at the municipal level' (2020), Science Policy Group, University of California, Berkeley, https://escholarship.org/uc/item/7qpow9rn.

[34] Max Read, 'Why we should ban facial recognition technology' (30 January 2020), *Intelligencer*, https://nymag.com/intelligencer/2020/01/why-we-should-ban-facial-recognition-technology.html; ACLU, 'California governor signs landmark bill halting facial recognition on police body cams' (8 October 2019), ACLU Northern California, www.aclunc.org/news/california-governor-signs-landmark-bill-halting-facial-recognition-police-body-cams.

[35] Lord Clement-Jones, 'Automated Facial Recognition Technology (Moratorium and Review) Bill [HL]2019–20' (2019), https://services.parliament.uk/bills/2019-20/automatedfacialrecognitiontechnologymoratoriumandreview.html/.

particular issue or cause.[36] These movements can take many different forms, ranging from peaceful demonstrations, marches, and rallies to civil disobedience, strikes, and other forms of non-violent resistance. Protest movements can emerge in response to a wide range of social, economic, political, and environmental issues. Some of the most common causes of protest movements include discrimination, injustice, corruption, inequality, environmental degradation, and war. Contemporary examples are Occupy Wall Street (2011), Arab Spring (began in 2010), Black Lives Matter (began in 2013), and the Hong Kong pro-democracy movement (began in 2019). Protest movements can also be motivated by a desire to promote social change, challenge existing power structures, and hold those in authority accountable for their actions.

Throughout history, protest movements have played a critical role in advancing social progress and promoting human rights. They have helped to raise awareness of important issues, mobilise public opinion, and influence policy and legislative changes. Examples of protest movements from history include the civil rights movement of the 1950s–1960s, the women's suffrage movement of the late nineteenth and early twentieth centuries and Vietnam anti-war protests (1960s). Today, protest movements continue to be an important tool for promoting social change and advocating for a more just and equitable world.

Protests movements require a tangible and accessible location, typically in the streets and other public places. Public space has always been central to social movements and political protests as a practical place for citizens to gather and as a symbolic place connected to wider democratic values. It provides a physical location where individuals can come together to voice their dissent, express their grievances, and demand change.[37] By occupying public spaces, protesters can create a visible and disruptive presence that draws attention to their cause, and can also serve as a symbolic representation of their struggle.

Public spaces, such as city squares, parks, and streets, are often central to the social and cultural life of a community, and their use for protests can be a powerful statement of the collective will of a group of people. Thus, public spaces are the 'ultimate area of societal interaction' and occupy a symbolic place in society given their accessibility, openness, and, according to Jens Kremer, inherent freedom.[38] When protesters occupy public spaces, they are asserting their right to participate in the democratic process and to be heard by those in power. In interrupting these public spaces, protesters 'touch upon the very core of the current structure and organization of social systems, namely the balance of power, rule of law and democratic

---

[36] John Scott and Gordon Marshall, A Dictionary of Sociology (Oxford University Press, 2009).

[37] Daniel Trottier and Christian Fuchs, 'Theorising social media, politics and the state: An introduction' in Daniel Trottier and Christian Fuchs (eds.), Social Media, Politics and the State (Routledge, 2015), pp. 3, 33; Alberto Melucci and Leonardo Avritzer, 'Complexity, cultural pluralism and democracy: Collective action in the public space' (2000) 39(4) Social Science Information 507.

[38] Jens Kremer, 'The end of freedom in public places? Privacy problems arising from surveillance of the European public space' (2017), PhD thesis, University of Helsinki, p. 5.

Monika Zalnieriute

governance'.[39] It questions the ability of government authorities to maintain the integrity of these shared spaces,[40] thus challenging existing power structures.

Historically, protesters have taken the right to protest anonymously largely for granted; a right that is now becoming increasingly more fragile. The right to anonymity has been fundamental to social movements and protesting, as these events require the population to feel confident and safe in their ability to gather in public spaces and manifest their disagreement with the status quo. This is impossible if they fear surveillance tools can be weaponised against them to suppress and punish their dissent. The sense of safety necessary to facilitate robust democratic participation stems from an understanding that an individual, in the act of demonstrating, is expressing something larger than themselves by joining in a collective. They thus sacrifice their individual voice for the benefit of social disruption, and in return are granted the key right that protesters have enjoyed for centuries; the right of anonymity. The anonymity earned by protesters in public spaces has been increasingly challenged and eroded by surveillance infrastructure.

While the relative anonymity of the individual during protest gatherings has typically 'neutralised' the effect of surveillance, they have been increasingly subject to 'counter-neutralization technologies' that require those individuals to take more active steps to circumvent identification.[41] Of course, protest movements have long devised resistance strategies against surveillance. For example, protesters can break a system a surveillance system by flooding it, rendering surveillance inoperable or impractical.[42] Typical examples include crude forms of neutralisation such as disabling phone lines, wearing masks, and destroying cameras. For example, Hong Kong protesters in 2019 used lasers and broke smart lampposts that they believed contained FRT software.[43] With FRT, protestors are given two choices: first, they can wear a mask and risk arrest and the collection of biometric information in the form of criminal records, or second, they can do without a mask and risk collection of biometric data through FRTs.[44]

Surveillance technologies dealing with political protests have become the norm in many countries, and scholars have theorised about the chilling effect of surveillance on dissent.[45] Monitoring, tracking, and detaining individual protesters for

---

[39] Ibid., p. 73.

[40] Christoph Burgmer, 'Protestbewegung: Warum einen öffentlichen Platz besetzen?' [Why occupy a public space?] (3 October 2014), *Deutschlandfunk*, www.deutschlandfunk.de/protestbewegung-warum-einen-oeffentlichen-platz-besetzen.1184.de.html?dram:article_id=299327.

[41] G. T. Marx, 'Security and surveillance contests: Resistance and counter- resistance' in T Balzacq (ed.), *Contesting Security. Strategies and Logics* (Routledge, 2015), pp. 15, 23.

[42] G. T. Marx, *Windows into the Soul: Surveillance and Society in an Age of High Technology* (University of Chicago Press, 2016), p. 160.

[43] Byrne and Davis, 'Protest tech'.

[44] Mackinnon, 'Surveillance-ready-subjects', p. 161.

[45] Melgaco and Monoghan, 'Introduction', p. 7; Luis Fernandez, *Policing Dissent: Social Control and the Anti- Globalization Movement* (Rutgers University Press, 2008); P. Gillham, 'Securitizing America: Strategic incapacitation and the policing of protest since the 11 September 2001 terrorist attacks' (2011)

Power and Protest 105

their actions in public places significantly shifts the power balance between the state and individuals. Surveillance of political protests undermines the individual as a 'free autonomous citizen', and negatively impacts democracy and the rule of law.[46] Protestors become disempowered in relation to their body and biological information,[47] which is not only threatening, in one sense, to discrete individuals,[48] but in another to discretise protesters, breaking down their collective image. Pervasive surveillance tools can be understood as disciplinary, as they are able to threaten and realise retribution against individual protesters who would otherwise have been lost in a sea of voices, but it is in another sense indicative of a 'controlled' society in which surveillance is ubiquitous.[49]

7.5 PROTECTING PROTESTERS FROM ABUSE: POTENTIAL WAYS TO REGULATE

Given the danger that FRT surveillance in public spaces poses to political protests, the rights to peaceful assembly and association, and wider democratic participation, legislatures should regulate or entirely ban the use of FRT in policing and law enforcement. Regulation of FRT use is a necessary step to ensure the chilling effect of FRT on political expression and freedom of assembly is eliminated.

The chilling effect on freedom of speech and assembly is even stronger in some jurisdictions, such as Australia. This is because, unlike many other jurisdictions discussed in this book, Australia has no human rights protection enshrined in its Constitution and no national human rights legislation.[50] Only three out of eight Australian states and territories have state-level human rights Acts. For this reason, in its recent report, the Australian Human Rights Commission has urged Australia's federal, state, and territory governments to enact legislation regulating FRT.[51]

What are the ways to protect protesters and protest movements from abuse by public authorities? Recent literature related to AI and accountability has recommended

5(7) *Sociology Compass* 636; P. Gillham, B. Edwards, and J. Noakes, 'Strategic incapacitation and the policing of Occupy Wall Street protests in New York City, 2011' (2013) 23(1) *Policing and Society* 81; Jeffrey Monoghan and K. Walby, 'Making up "terror identities": Security intelligence, Canada's integrated Threat Assessment Centre, and social movement suppression' (2012) 22(2) *Policing and Society* 133; Jeffrey Monoghan and K. Walby, '"They attacked the city": Security intelligence, the sociology of protest policing, and the anarchist threat at the 2010 Toronto G20 Summit' (2012) 60(5) *Current Sociology* 653.

[46] Irena Nesterova, 'Mass data gathering and surveillance: The fight against facial recognition technology in the globalized world', *SHS Web of Conferences* 74, 03006, www.shs-conferences.org/articles/shsconf/pdf/2020/02/shsconf_glob2020_03006.pdf, pp. 2–3, 6.

[47] J. Pugliese, *Biometrics: Bodies, Technologies, Biopolitics* (Routledge, 2012).

[48] T Monahan, 'Dreams of control at a distance: Gender, surveillance, and social control' (2009) 9(2) *Cultural Studies – Critical Methodologies* 286; Mackinnon, 'Surveillance-ready-subjects', p. 162.

[49] Melgaco and Monoghan, 'Introduction', p. 9; Gilles Deleuze, 'Postscript on the societies of control' (1992) 59 October 3; Zygmunt Bauman and David Lyon, *Liquid Surveillance: A Conversation* (Polity Press, 2013).

[50] Australian Human Rights Commission, 'How are human rights protected in Australian law?' (2015) https://humanrights.gov.au/our-work/rights-and-freedoms/how-are-human-rights-protected-australian-law.

[51] Australian Human Rights Commission, 'Human rights and technology: Final report' (March 2021).

106   *Monika Zalnieriute*

several avenues, including regulation,[52] the development of technical methods of explanation,[53] the promoting of auditing mechanisms,[54] and the creation of standards of algorithmic accountability in public and private bodies.[55] Law, of course, should also play a role.

7.5.1 *Privacy Law*

Privacy law provides one avenue to regulate police use of FRT in public spaces.

Scholars have long argued that public activities deserve privacy protections, and that the simple act of being 'in public' does not negate an individual's expectation of privacy.[56] However, as Jake Goldenfein in Chapter 5 of this book suggests, privacy law has severe limitations when regulating the use of FRT. For example, the US Fourth Amendment, under current Supreme Court jurisprudence, has been viewed as an unlikely protection against FRT for two reasons: first, jurisprudence has typically ignored pre-investigatory surveillance,[57] and secondly, it has failed to encompass identification of information already exposed to the public.[58] In relation to the Fourth Amendment, Douglas Fretty questions whether Constitutional protection will require the Supreme Court to confirm the 'right of the people to be secure' or simply display how insufficient the Fourth Amendment is in safeguarding individuals beyond the scope of their private spaces.[59] Drawing on recent US Supreme Court cases concerning GPS tracking and other technologies and

[52] Marion Oswald, 'Algorithm-assisted decision-making in the public sector: Framing the issues using administrative law rules governing discretionary power' (2018) 376(2128) *Philosophical Transactions of the Royal Society A*, https://royalsocietypublishing.org/doi/abs/10.1098/rsta.2017.0359; Andrew Tutt, 'An FDA for algorithms' (2017) 69 *Administrative Law Review* 83.

[53] Brent D. Mittelstadt, Chris Russell, and Sandra Wachter, 'Explaining explanations in AI', *Proceedings of FAT* '19: Conference on Fairness, Accountability, and Transparency (FAT* '19)*, Atlanta, GA, ACM, New York (29–31 January 2019).

[54] Brent Mittelstadt, 'Auditing for transparency in content personalization systems' (2016) 10 *International Journal of Communication* 4991; Pauline T. Kim, 'Auditing algorithms for discrimination' (2017) 166 *University of Pennsylvania Law Review Online* 189.

[55] Corinne Cath et al., 'Artificial intelligence and the "good society": The US, EU, and UK approach' (2018) 24 *Science and Engineering Ethics* 505.

[56] Tjerk Timan, Bryce Clayton Newell, and Bert-Jaap Koops (eds.), *Privacy in Public Space: Conceptual and Regulatory Challenges* (Edward Elgar, 2017); Bryce Clayton Newell, Tjerk Timan, and Bert-Jaap Koops, *Surveillance, Privacy and Public Space* (Routledge, 2019); N. A. Moreham, 'Privacy in public places' (2006) 65(3) *The Cambridge Law Journal* 606; Joel Reidenberg, 'Privacy in public' (2014) 69(1) *University of Miami Law Review* 141; Helen Fay Nissenbaum, 'Towards an approach to privacy in public: Challenges of information technology' (1997) 7(3) *Ethics & Behaviour* 207; Beatte Roessler, 'Privacy and/in the public sphere' (2016) 1 *Yearbook for Eastern and Western Philosophy* 243.

[57] Elizabeth Joh, 'The new surveillance discretion: Automated suspicion, big data, and policing' (2016) 10 *Harvard Law & Police Review* 15, 33.

[58] Orin Kerr, 'The case for the third-party doctrine' (2009) 107 *Michigan Law Review* 561, 566; Ferguson, 'Facial recognition and the Fourth Amendment', pp. 16–17.

[59] Douglas A. Fretty, 'Face-recognition surveillance: A moment of truth for Fourth Amendment rights in public places' (2011) 16(3) *Virginia Journal of Law & Technology* 430, 463.

Power and Protest

the Fourth Amendment,[60] Andrew Ferguson suggests that the Supreme Court is cognisant of the need to adapt Fourth Amendment jurisprudence to emerging technologies.[61] He identifies six key principles in adapting the Fourth Amendment to deal with modern concerns. First, technological searches cannot be viewed as equivalent to pre-technological police investigatory modes.[62] Secondly, there must be a general presumption against the large-scale aggregation of data.[63] Thirdly, there must be a general presumption against the long term storage and ongoing use of aggregated data.[64] Fourthly, the ability to track and trace an individual must be a relevant factor in considering the application of the Fourth Amendment.[65] Fifthly, the concept of anti-arbitrariness must be transposed to a digital setting to act against automated technologies that do not require probable cause.[66] Sixthly, monitoring technologies must not be so over-reaching as to grossly permeate civil society.[67] However, the Fourth Amendment offers limited support in the protection of protest movements from FRT surveillance in public spaces.

7.5.2 *Discrimination Law*

Could discrimination law provide a better avenue to regulate police use of FRT in public spaces? The emerging consensus in an increasing body of academic research is that FRTs are not 'neutral',[68] but instead reinforce historical inequalities.[69] For example, studies have shown that FRT performs poorly in relation to women, children, and individuals with darker skin tones.[70]

---

[60] *United States* v. *Jones* [2012] US Supreme Court 565 U.S. 400; *Carpenter* v. *United States* [2018] United States Supreme Court 138 S. Ct.; *Riley* v. *California* [2014] United States Supreme Court 573 US 373.

[61] Ferguson, 'Facial recognition and the Fourth Amendment', p. 21.

[62] Ibid., pp. 21–23: 'Anti-equivalence principle'; *Carpenter* v. *United States* 2219.

[63] Ferguson, 'Facial recognition and the Fourth Amendment', pp. 23–24: 'Anti-aggregation principle'.

[64] Ibid., pp. 24: 'Anti-permanence principle'.

[65] Ibid., pp. 24–26: 'Anti-tracking principle'.

[66] Ibid., pp. 26–27: 'Anti-arbitrariness principle'.

[67] Ibid., pp. 27–28: 'Anti-permeating surveillance principle'.

[68] Clare Garvie, Alvaro Bedoya, and Jonathan Frankle, '*The perpetual line-up*: Unregulated police face recognition in America' (18 October 2016), Georgetown Law Center on Privacy and Technology, www .perpetuallineup.org/; Brendan F. Klare, Mark J. Burge, Joshua C. Klontz, Richard W. Vorder Bruegge, and Anil K. Jain, 'Face recognition performance: Role of demographic information' (2012) 7 *IEEE Transactions on Information Forensics and Security* 1789; Joy Buolamwini and Timnit Gebru, 'Gender shades: Intersectional accuracy disparities in commercial gender classification' (2018) 81 *Proceedings of Machine Learning Research* 1, http://proceedings.mlr.press/v81/buolamwini18a/buolamwini18a.pdf.

[69] Matthew Schwartz, 'Color-blind biometrics? Facial recognition and arrest rates of African-Americans in Maryland and the United States' (2019), Thesis in partial fulfilment of a Masters in Public Policy, Georgetown University, p. 15.

[70] Salem Hamed Abdurrahim, Salina Abdul Samad, and Aqilah Baseri Huddin, 'Review on the effects of age, gender, and race demographics on automatic face recognition' (2018) 34 *The Visual Computer* 1617–1630; Jacob Snow, 'Amazon's face recognition falsely matched 28 members of Congress with mugshots' (26 July 2018), ACLU, www.aclu.org/blog/privacy-technology/surveillance-technologies/ amazons-face-recognition-falsely-matched-28.

This bias and discrimination can be introduced into the FRT software in three technical ways: first, through the machine learning process, based on the training data set and system design; secondly, through technical bias incidental to the simplification necessary to translate reality into code; and thirdly, through emergent bias that arises from users' interaction with specific populations.[71] Because the training data for FRTs in the law enforcement context comes from photos relating to past criminal activity,[72] minority groups and people of colour are over-represented in FRT training systems.[73] In some jurisdictions, such as the United States, people of colour are at a much higher risk of being pulled over,[74] searched,[75] arrested,[76] incarcerated,[77] and wrongfully convicted than white women.[78] Therefore, police use of FRT to repress political protests can produce a large number of false positives – as it is already functioning in a highly discriminatory environment; and this can impact on the freedom of assembly and association of those already marginalised and discriminated against. However, discrimination law alone offers limited support in the protection of protest movements from FRT surveillance in public spaces.

7.5.3 Holding Private Companies Accountable for FRT Surveillance of Public Spaces

Private actors are also playing a role in the increasing surveillance of public spaces by stifling protest movements and political participation worldwide, and we need to

[71] Rebecca Crootof, '"Cyborg justice" and the risk of technological–legal lock-in' (2019) 119(1) *Columbia Law Review* 1, 8; Batya Friedman and Helen Fay Nissenbaum, 'Bias in computer systems' (1996) 14 *ACM Transactions on Information Systems* 330, 333–336.

[72] Henriette Ruhrmann, 'Facing the future: Protecting human rights in policy strategies for facial recognition technology in law enforcement' (May 2019), CITRIS Policy Lab, https://citrispolicylab.org/wp-content/uploads/2019/09/Facing-the-Future_Ruhrmann_CITRIS-Policy-Lab.pdf, p. 46; Garvie, Bedoya, and Frankle, 'The perpetual line-up'.

[73] Ruhrmann, 'Facing the future', p. 63; Garvie, Bedoya, and Frankle, 'The perpetual line-up'.

[74] Nusrat Choudhury, 'New data reveals Milwaukee police stops are about race and ethnicity' (23 February 2018), ACLU, www.aclu.org/blog/criminal-law-reform/reforming-police/new-data-reveals-milwaukee-police-stops-are-about-race-and; Frank R. Baumgartner, Derek A. Epp and Kelsey Shoub, *Suspect Citizens What 20 Million Traffic Stops Tell Us about Policing and Race* (Cambridge University Press, 2018).

[75] 'Choudhury, 'New data reveals'; Camelia Simoiu, Sam Corbett-Davies, and Sharad Goel, 'The problem of infra-marginality in outcome tests for discrimination' (2017) 11(3) *The Annals of Applied Statistics* 1193; Lynn Lanton and Matthew Durose, 'Police behavior during traffic and street stops, 2011' (September 2013), US Department of Justice, www.bjs.gov/content/pub/pdf/pbtss11.pdf.

[76] NAACP, 'Criminal Justice Fact Sheet' (n.d.), www.naacp.org/criminal-justice-fact-sheet/; Megan Stevenson and Sandra Mayson, 'The scale of misdemeanor justice' (2018) 98 *Boston University Law Review* 371.

[77] Ashley Nellis, 'The color of justice: Racial and ethnic disparity in state prisons' (13 October 2021), The Sentencing Project, www.sentencingproject.org/publications/color-of-justice-racial-and-ethnic-disparity-in-state-prisons/.

[78] Samuel Gross, Maurice Possley, and Klara Stephens, *Race and Wrongful Convictions in the United States* (National Registry of Exonerations, 2017), www.law.umich.edu/special/exoneration/Documents/Race_and_Wrongful_Convictions.pdf.

Power and Protest

insist on holding them accountable. Private companies, such as telecommunications service providers and tech giants, have been co-operating with law enforcement agencies and developing the technical infrastructure needed for public space surveillance. This includes police purchasing and using privately developed FRT technology or image databases, both of which often happen in secret. For example, IBM, one of the world's oldest (and largest) technology companies,[79] has recently collaborated with repressive governments by providing FRT software. Best known for its famous personal computers, in recent years the company's focus has shifted to AI and FRT.[80] A detailed report by *The Intercept* published in March 2019 revealed that in 2012 IBM provided police forces in the Philippines with video surveillance technology, which was subsequently used to perpetuate President Duterte's war on drugs through extra-judicial killings.[81] The brutal and excessive crime suppression tactics of the Davao police were well known to local and international human rights organisations.[82]

At the time, IBM defended the deal with Philippines, saying it 'was intended for legitimate public safety activities',[83] but claimed that it had ceased provision of its technology to the Philippines in 2012. However, it took at least several years for IBM to stop providing general purpose FRT software to law enforcement (e.g., IBM mentioned its Face Capture technology in a public disclosure in 2013 and 2014, related to its Davao City project).[84] The company's practice of providing authoritarian regimes with technological infrastructure is not new and dates back to the 1930s, when IBM supplied the Nazi Party with unique punch-card technology that was used to run the regime's censuses and surveys to identify and target Jewish people.[85]

Because of such close (and often secretive) collaboration between private tech companies and governments, we need to think of new ways to hold the companies providing the FRT infrastructure accountable – not just in aspirational language, but in law. Currently, in many countries, the application of human rights laws is limited to government bodies only (anti-discrimination and data protection laws being the primary exceptions of horizontal application).[86] The same is true

---

[79] Encyclopedia Britannica, 'IBM: Founding, history, & products', www.britannica.com/topic/International-Business-Machines-Corporation.

[80] Eric Reed, 'History of IBM: Timeline and facts' (24 February 2020), *TheStreet*, www.thestreet.com/personal-finance/history-of-ibm.

[81] George Joseph, 'Inside the video surveillance program IBM built for Philippine strongman Rodrigo Duterte' (20 March 2019), *The Intercept*, https://theintercept.com/2019/03/20/rodrigo-duterte-ibm-surveillance/.

[82] Ibid.

[83] Ibid.

[84] Ibid.

[85] Edwin Black, *IBM and the Holocaust: The Strategic Alliance between Nazi Germany and America's Most Powerful Corporation-Expanded Edition* (Crown Publishers, 2001).

[86] Monika Zalnieriute, 'From human rights aspirations to enforceable obligations by non-state actors in the digital age: The case of internet governance and ICANN' (2019) 21 *Yale Journal of Law & Technology* 278.

of international human rights law. This leaves private companies in the human rights gap. However, as I have argued elsewhere in detail, existing efforts focussing on voluntary 'social and corporate responsibility' and ethical obligations of private tech companies are insufficient and incapable of tackling the challenges that these technologies pose to freedom of expression and association.[87] Moreover, a lot of those efforts have merely been 'transparency washing' – performatively promoting transparency and respect for human rights while acting in ways that undermine both.[88]

The problem of the human rights gap is greater in some jurisdictions, such as Australia, which lacks a federal level human rights framework and where governments often remain unaccountable for public space surveillance. Therefore, we need to demand change and accountability from governments, police, and tech companies. We should not continue to rely on the 'goodwill' of tech companies, when they promise to 'respect' our right to protest and our freedom of association and assembly. We need to demand hard legal obligations for private actors because of the significant role they play in increasing public space surveillance and infrastructure. We need data protection and human rights laws that bind companies, to ensure that political movements and protests can flourish and that communities whose rights to peaceful assembly and association have been curtailed via FRT technologies can access an effective remedy.

7.5.4 *Outright Bans on Police Use of FRT*

Of course, even with all the limits that could be placed by law, police use of FRT in public spaces is problematic in itself – owing to the centrality of public space and anonymity for protest movements. It is thus not surprising that many scholars, activists, regulators, and politicians have turned to arguing for bans on FRT use. For example, US scholar Ferguson advocates for a blanket ban on facial surveillance, a probable cause requirement for facial identification, a ban or probable cause-plus standard for facial tracing, and limitations to facial verification at international borders in addition to increased accountability for error, bias, transparency, and fairness.[89]

Proposals to ban FRT have also been coming from sources outside the academic realm; with informal resistance groups such as the developers of the website Fight for the Future running a project called Ban Facial Recognition, which operates an interactive map of where and how the government is using FRT around the United States.[90] Further, the United Kingdom's Equality and Human Rights

---

[87] Ibid.

[88] Monika Zalnieriute, '"Transparency-washing" in the digital age: A corporate agenda of procedural fetishism' (2021) 8(1) *Critical Analysis of Law* 39.

[89] Ferguson, 'Facial recognition and the Fourth Amendment', pp. 63–73.

[90] 'Ban Facial Recognition', www.banfacialrecognition.com/.

Commission,[91] and the Australian Human Right Commission,[92] have recently called on governments to introduce a moratorium on the use of FRT in policing and law enforcement before legislation regulating the use of FRT and other biometric technology is formally introduced.

7.6 CONCLUSION

If the government and law enforcement can resort to FRT without any restrictions or safeguards in place, the right to protest anonymously will be curtailed and political discourse in our democracies will be stifled. For example, the High Court of Australia – Australia's apex court – has emphasised the centrality of the right to protest to Australian democracy: besides casting their vote in elections, Australians have no other avenues through which to voice their political views.[93] Adapting Hannah Arendt's famous quote used at the beginning of this chapter, political freedom must enable a right to participate in government. And in many instances, the only way to do that, in addition to voting, is through political protest.

Before FRTs develop further and become even more invasive, it is imperative that this public surveillance infrastructure is limited. We need laws restraining the use of FRT in our public spaces, and we need hard legal obligations for those who develop and supply law enforcement with them. The reforms could start with an explicit ban (or at least suspension) on police use of FRT in public spaces, pending independent scrutiny of the discriminatory impacts the technology may have against women and other protected groups.[94] These proposed changes are not drastic. In fact, they are a modest first step in the long journey ahead to push back against escalating surveillance of the public sphere worldwide.

---

[91] For example, the UK Equality and Human Rights Commission had, in March 2020, called on suspension; see Equality and Human Rights Commission, 'Facial recognition technology and predictive policing algorithms out-pacing the law' (12 March 2020), www.equalityhumanrights.com/en/our-work/news/facial-recognition-technology-and-predictive-policing-algorithms-out-pacing-law.

[92] Australian Human Rights Commission, '*Human Rights and Technology Final Report*' (1 March 2021), https://tech.humanrights.gov.au/downloads?_ga=2.200457510.901905353.1624842000-1160604841.1624842000.

[93] *Brown* v. *Tasmania* [2017] HCA 43.

[94] For example, the UK Equality and Human Rights Commission had, in March 2020, called on suspension; see Equality and Human Rights Commission, 'Facial recognition technology'.

8

Faces of War

Russia's Invasion of Ukraine and Military Use of Facial Recognition Technology

Agne Limante

8.1 INTRODUCTION

Shortly after Russia launched large-scale military action on Ukraine on 24 February 2022, Clearview AI (a US-based facial recognition company) announced that it had given its technology to the Ukrainian government to be used for military purposes in Russia's attack on Ukraine.[1] In mid-March 2022, it was reported that Ukraine's Ministry of Defence started using facial recognition technology (FRT).[2] In such a way, simply and effectively, without long-lasting political debate and academic or civil society discussions, FRT was brought to a new profitable market and joined a list of tools that can be employed for military purposes.

While the Russian war against Ukraine is not the first time that FRT has been used in a military setting, this conflict has brought the military use of this technology to a different level: FRT was offered openly at the outset of the war to one of the sides, being promptly accepted by the Ukrainian authorities and tested on the ground for a variety of objectives. Before 2022, there was only minimal evidence of FRT employment for military purposes. One might recall that in 2019, Bellingcat, a Netherlands-based investigative journalism group specialising in fact-checking and open-source intelligence, used FRT to help identify a Russian man who had filmed the torture and killing of a prisoner in Syria,[3] or that in 2021, Clearview AI signed a contract with the Pentagon to explore putting its technology into augmented reality glasses.[4] It has also been reported that Israel performs surveillance of Palestinians

---

[1] BBC, 'Ukraine offered tool to search billions of faces' (14 March 2022), *BBC News*, www.bbc.com/news/technology-60738204.

[2] Paresh Dave and Jeffrey Dastin, 'Exclusive: Ukraine has started using Clearview AI's facial recognition during war' (14 March 2022), *Reuters*, www.reuters.com/technology/exclusive-ukraine-has-started-using-clearview-ais-facial-recognition-during-war-2022-03-13/.

[3] BBC, 'How facial recognition is identifying the dead in Ukraine' (13 April 2022), *BBC News*, www.bbc.com/news/technology-61055319.

[4] kwono321, 'Clearview AI working on A.R. goggles for Air Force security' (3 February 2022), *Days Tech*, https://daystech.org/clearview-ai-working-on-a-r-goggles-for-air-force-security/.

Faces of War 113

using a facial recognition program.[5] However, these cases only provide evidence of incidental use or potential future application of FRT for military purposes.

This chapter discusses how FRT is employed by both sides in Russia's war against Ukraine. In particular, it examines how Ukraine engages FRT in the country's defence, testing the different possibilities this technology offers. It also acknowledges the use of FRT on the other side of the conflict, elaborating on how it is used in Russia to suppress society's potential opposition to the war. The chapter focusses on the potential and risks of using FRT in a war situation. It discusses the advantages that FRT brings to both sides of the conflict and underlines the associated concerns.

8.2 FRT IN THE BATTLEFIELD: UKRAINE

Ukraine began exploring the possibilities of FRT use in the military during the first month of the war. There was no time for elaborate learning or training, and the FRT was put directly into the battlefield, applying creative thinking and a trial-and-error approach. As a result, the Ukraine war can be seen as a field trial for FRT, where, faced with the pressing need to defend its territory and people, the country referred to collective efforts to generate ideas on innovative ways to employ modern technologies and is putting them into practice and checking what works well.

It should be admitted that the FRT developed by Clearview AI (perhaps the most famous and controversial facial recognition company) worked for the interests of Ukraine, owing to its enormous database of facial images. The company has harvested billions of photos from social media companies such as Facebook, Twitter, and Russian social media sites (Vkontakte).[6] Such a method of database creation attracted wide criticism in peacetime,[7] but proved beneficial in war, enabling access to facial images of Russian citizens, including soldiers.

---

[5] Elizabeth Dwoskin, 'Israel escalates surveillance of Palestinians with facial recognition program in West Bank' (8 November 2021), *Washington Post*, www.washingtonpost.com/world/middle_east/israel-palestinians-surveillance-facial-recognition/2021/11/05/3787bf42-26b2-11ec-8739-5cb6aba30a30_story.html.

[6] BBC, 'How facial recognition is identifying the dead'.

[7] In Europe, Clearview AI's services have been condemned by, for instance, the Swedish DPA, the French DPA, the Italian DPA, and the UK Information Commissioner's Office. See European Data Protection Board, 'Swedish DPA: Police unlawfully used facial recognition app' (12 February 2021), https://edpb.europa.eu/news/national-news/2021/swedish-dpa-police-unlawfully-used-facial-recognition-app_es; Commission Nationale de l'Informatique et des Libertés, 'Facial recognition: The CNIL orders CLEARVIEW AI to stop reusing photographs available on the internet' (16 December 2021), www.cnil.fr/en/facial-recognition-cnil-orders-clearview-ai-stop-reusing-photographs-available-internet; European Data Protection Board, 'Facial recognition: Italian SA fines Clearview AI EUR 20 million' (17 March 2022), https://edpb.europa.eu/news/national-news/2022/facial-recognition-italian-sa-fines-clearview-ai-eur-20-million_en; Information Commissioner's Office, 'ICO fines facial recognition database company Clearview AI Inc more than £7.5 m and orders UK data to be deleted' (23 May 2022), https://ico.org.uk/about-the-ico/media-centre/news-and-blogs/2022/05/ico-fines-facial-recognition-database-company-clearview-ai-inc/.

One might think that collecting facial images of military personnel, especially those of a higher rank, from social networks might be a challenge – as they are less likely to reveal their identity. But this is not entirely true. While persons who post frequently on social media can be identified more easily, facial recognition systems can also identify and verify those who do not even have social accounts. It is enough that a family member, friend, co-worker, or person also serving in the army post a picture where the person is seen. The technology can even single out a face in a crowd picture and compare it with the face in question. Face recognition can also be used where only some people from a group (e.g., a military unit) have been identified, with the rest of the group being identified through content from any of the identified members. Even if a person appears on the internet in a randomly taken picture, it might also be helpful information allowing their gradual recognition.[8]

Here, several ways in which the Ukrainian authorities employed FRT in its efforts to fight Russia are discussed. The author would like to note that the list might be not exhaustive as, at the time of writing (September 2022), the war continues, and part of the information remains undisclosed.

8.2.1 *Identification of Dead*

Being probably the first country in the world to use FRT for such a purpose, Ukraine has made the headlines by announcing that it is employing FRT to recognise fallen Russian soldiers.[9] Many discussions have arisen regarding this controversial idea, its objectives, ethical issues, and effects in case of a mismatch.

Identification of the dead is typically a task for forensic experts. Methods such as examining DNA, dental data, and physical appearance can be used to identify the deceased and have proven reliable. While in peacetime this information is usually available, in wartime experts might be faced with limited data availability, both in the case of nationals of the country in question and soldiers or civilians of the enemy state. Obtaining pre-death samples of enemy fighters' DNA or dental data is challenging, if not impossible, and in a majority of cases requires too much effort to be of value to a country at war.

In such a situation, the FRT becomes a particularly handy tool, as all is needed is to take a picture of a dead soldier and run it through the database. In the first fifty days since Russia's invasion of Ukraine, Ukrainian officials are stated to have run more than 8,600 facial recognition searches on dead or captured Russian soldiers, identifying

---

[8] Pictures of soldiers might be useful in many ways. Another possible use of images is geoprofiling, employed at public and private level. A background of a picture often allows the identification of the location where the picture was taken, in a war situation enabling identification of the position of the enemy. Kyiv media cites the situation where using a dating website a hacker group received a picture of a Russian soldier standing next to a military base, thus allowing the detection – and then elimination – of the enemy. *KyivPost* post on Facebook, 5 September 2022.

[9] FRT-based identification of fallen soldiers can also be performed on soldiers on any side of the conflict; however, it is more relevant with regard to enemy personnel.

some of them.[10] Why was FRT used this way, especially towards the deceased? An unprecedented strategy was developed by Ukraine. After the bodies were identified, the Ukrainian officials (as well as civil activists) contacted the families of the deceased Russian soldiers to inform them about the death of their relative. As recognised by Ukraine's Digital Transformation Minister, this served two purposes. On the one hand, it could be perceived as a method to inform the families, providing them with information on their beloved ones and allowing them to retrieve the bodies. On the other hand, it was seen as a tool for Ukrainians to overcome Russian propaganda and denial of the human costs of the war.[11] In other words, such FRT employment worked as a political counter-offensive and was one of Ukraine's strategies in endeavours to inform Russians, who had limited access to non-state-controlled information or were simply ignorant, about the war hostilities and death of Russian soldiers.[12]

This second objective of informing Russian families about the death of their relatives fighting in Ukraine nevertheless appeared to be challenging to accomplish. Again, Ukrainians had to develop their own model to fulfil this goal, as FRT had not been used in this way before and thus there were no experiences to learn from. Theoretically, it would have been possible only to send information to the relatives that their family member had died in a field. However, in the light of constant Russian claims as to 'fakes' being spread by the Ukrainians,[13] this would not have been enough – some evidence needed to be added. From the other perspective, accompanying information about the death of a soldier with pictures of his abandoned corpse or lifeless face, which allegedly was done from the Ukrainian side in several instances, might be interpreted as psychological violence towards the family members or even psychological warfare. Instead of encouraging Russian mothers and fathers to start opposing the war, such a strategy had a risk of bringing the opposite results of anger and claim of disregard for human dignity and humiliation by the enemy.

8.2.2 *Identification and Verification of the Identity of Persons of Interest*

Another possible use of FRT in a war zone is identifying persons of interest who come within eyeshot of military personnel or public authorities and verifying their identity. Such identification and verification might be employed in different contexts and serve various needs.

---

[10] Drew Harwell, 'Ukraine is scanning faces of dead Russians, then contacting the mothers' (15 April 2022), *Washington Post*, www.washingtonpost.com/technology/2022/04/15/ukraine-facial-recognition-warfare/.

[11] Sara Sidner, 'Ukraine sends images of dead Russian soldiers to their families in Russia' (n.d.), *CNN Video* (including interviews with Ukraine officials), www.cnn.com/videos/world/2022/05/13/ukraine-face-recognition-russian-soldiers-lead-sidner-pkg-vpx.cnn.

[12] This strategy was employed at the beginning of the conflict, but it lost its initial scale within a few months.

[13] The term 'fake' (Rus. фейк) has entered the Russian language and is used on a regular basis in the politics, media, and everyday life. It has become a keyword that is used to raise doubts as to any information published by Ukraine or Western countries that conflicts with the information disseminated by Russian-controlled media.

As public sources state, the Ukrainian government used FRT at checkpoints to help identify enemy suspects (Russian infiltrators or saboteurs, covert Russian operatives posing as Ukrainian civilians).[14] At the time of writing, however, it is impossible to obtain data on the extent and how effectively FRT was employed in checkpoints. But it can be claimed that FRT has considerable potential in this regard, especially if specific persons are sought – although systemic use of FRT at checkpoints might be complicated during wartime owing to technical and time constraints.

FRT could also be (and likely was) employed when identifying and interviewing captured soldiers. This limits the ability of captured soldiers to deny their links with the army or present false or misleading information. It also allows additional psychological pressure to be put on an enemy soldier, who is well aware he has been identified.

It might also be tempting to publish a video interview with a captured enemy soldier, aligning it with his image (alone or with family members) retrieved from social media. Similar to notification of families about killed Russian soldiers, this could be a strategy to encourage Russian society to oppose the war. In this regard, it should be taken into account that Article 13(2) of the Geneva Convention (III) prescribes that prisoners of war must be protected from insults and public curiosity, whether these take place at the same time or not. The International Committee of the Red Cross commentary (of 2020) on Article 13 of the Geneva Convention (III) underlines that the prohibition of exposing prisoners of war to 'public curiosity' also covers the disclosure of photographic and video images, recordings of interrogations in public communication channels, including the internet, as this practice could be humiliating and jeopardise the safety of the prisoners' families and of the prisoners themselves once they are released (para. 1624).[15] The Committee suggests that any materials that enable individual prisoners to be identified must normally be regarded as subjecting them to public curiosity and, therefore, may not be transmitted, published, or broadcasted (if there is a compelling public interest in revealing the identity of a prisoner – for instance, owing to their seniority or because they are wanted by justice – then the materials may exceptionally be released, but only insofar as they respect the prisoner's dignity) (para. 1627).

8.2.3 Combating Misinformation, Denial, and Propaganda

As noted earlier, one of the objectives of Ukrainian authorities when using the information retrieved by FRT is combating the misinformation and denial of Russian citizens regarding the human costs of war and propaganda related to the war itself.

---

[14] BBC, 'How facial recognition is identifying the dead'.

[15] International Committee of the Red Cross, 'Convention (III) relative to the Treatment of Prisoners of War. Geneva, 12 August 1949. Commentary of 2020, Art. 13 : Humane treatment of prisoners' (2020), https://ihl-databases.icrc.org/applic/ihl/ihl.nsf/Comment.xsp?action=openDocument&documentId=3DEA78B5A19414AFC125858500434BD#:~:text=1626%E2%80%83%E2%80%83More%20compellingly,international%20tribunals%20subsequently.

In Russia, information published by Ukraine or Western countries on dead and captured Russian soldiers, as well as war atrocities committed by Russian soldiers, is dealt with using a simple strategy: denying the information, raising doubts about its truthfulness and blaming the other side. Russian commentators often claim that the faces are not of Russian soldiers, that the situation is staged, or that actors are involved.[16]

In fact, during wartime, both sides could be falsifying information while simultaneously denying accurate information, damaging their policy. FRT, however, allows published material to be more precise and evidence-based, as faces can be linked to the name and family name, place of residence, and photos taken from social media profiles. It also simplifies cross-checking information published by the other side, and thus is a tool in an information war.

An example of using FRT to verify public information concerned the sinking of the Russian warship *Moskva* in the Black Sea south of Ukraine. When the Russian state held a ceremony for the surviving sailors and officers who had been on the ship, many people wondered if these were actual sailors from the *Moskva*. Bellingcat ran the pictures through Russian facial recognition platform FindClone using images in Russian social media, and found that most of the men were indeed Russian sailors from Sevastopol.[17]

8.2.4 *Identification of War Criminals*

Historically, photographic and other visual evidence has been used to prosecute war crimes, promote accountability, and raise public awareness of abuses.[18] FRT has a high potential to improve such usage of visual tools and to contribute to the process of bringing those responsible to justice, as well as identifying guilty soldiers who it might otherwise be complicated to single out.

Ukraine does not deny that it uses facial recognition to identify Russian soldiers suspected of war crimes or caught on camera looting Ukrainian homes and storefronts. It acknowledges that from the beginning of the conflict it has deployed this technology to identify war criminals, and will continue to do so.[19] For instance, Ukraine's Digital Transformation Minister (Mykhailo Fedorov) shared on Twitter

---

[16] For example, 1TV, 'Украина и Великобритания сняли антироссийский фейк, поместив туда символику нацистов. Новости. Первый канал' (3 June 2022), www.1tv.ru/news/2022-06-03/430410-ukraina_i_velikobritaniya_snyali_antirossiyskiy_feyk_pomestiv_tuda_simvoliku_natsistov.

[17] Lizzy O'Leary, 'How facial recognition tech made its way to the battlefield in Ukraine' (26 April 2022), *Slate*, https://slate.com/technology/2022/04/facial-recognition-ukraine-clearview-ai.html.

[18] Aoife Duffy, 'Bearing witness to atrocity crimes: Photography and international law' (2018) 40 *Human Rights Quarterly* 776.

[19] Ministry of Digital Transformation, Ukraine, 'Як Розпізнавання Обличчя Допоможе Знайти Всіх Воєнних Злочинців' (9 April 2022), Interview (directed by Міністерство цифрової трансформації України), www.youtube.com/watch?v=fUKQM7BXryc.

and Instagram the name, hometown, and personal photo of a man who, according to him, was recorded shipping looted clothes from a Belarus post office to his home in Russia. The Ukrainian official added, 'Our technology will find all of them', presumably referring to FRT.[20] He also noted that 'many killers have already been identified who terrorised civilians in Bucha and Irpen. In a short time, we will establish all the information about these people.'[21] The Chief Regional Prosecutor (Ruslan Kravchenko), in an interview with a news portal, also acknowledged the use of FRT to identify the Russian soldiers suspected of criminal offences, giving an example of how a Russian soldier who murdered a civilian was identified by FRT and later confirmed by the witness.[22] There were more reported recognitions later.[23]

If FRT can successfully identify war criminals in Russia's war against Ukraine, there is a slight hope that this could (at least to some extent) deter soldiers from committing war crimes in the future. One has to admit, though, that any false matches may lead to wrongful accusations of war crimes (see Section 8.4.1). Therefore, FRT should only be seen as an investigative lead, but not as definitive evidence. The risk of a false match can be minimised by performing additional analysis on the person concerned. Such further searches can prove to be particularly fruitful where context-related information can be found (e.g., videos and photos confirming the person was fighting in Ukraine, his statements and pictures, communication with relatives, photos and articles on his previous military activity and visibility).[24]

8.3 FRT IN RUSSIA: A GOVERNMENT'S TOOL IN ITS EFFORT TO STIFLE ANTI-WAR PROTESTS

During the war against Ukraine, the FRT in Russia mainly, though not exclusively,[25] served a different purpose – to stop any anti-war protests.[26] While marches and mass

---

[20] Mykhailo Fedorov [@FedorovMykhailo], Post, Twitter (7 April 2022), https://twitter.com/FedorovMykhailo/status/1512101359411154953: 'After events in Bucha, I am launching the #russian-looters column. Our technology will find all of them. Shchebenkov Vadym stole more than 100 kg of clothes from UA families and sent them from Mozyr, Belarus, to his hometown of Chita. It is 7 thousand km away.'

[21] 'FEDOROV', Telegram, (9 April 2022), https://t.me/zedigital/1546.

[22] Sidner, 'Ukraine sends images of dead Russian soldiers'.

[23] For example, Oleksandr Topchij and Vitlij Saenko, 'Завдяки відео CNN встановлено особу росіянина, який розстріляв двох цивільних на Київщини' (2 September 2022), *Unian*, www.unian.ua/society/zavdyaki-video-cnn-vstanovleno-osobu-rosiyanina-yakiy-rozstrilyav-dvoh-civilnih-na-kijivshchini-novini-kiyeva-11964534.html.

[24] See 'Tactical OSINT Analyst' [@OSINT_Tactical], Post, Twitter (1 March 2022), https://twitter.com/OSINT_Tactical/status/1498694344781484037.

[25] Russia also uses FRT to survey the areas close to the border zone to identify the enemy and saboteurs, for example. *Moscow Times*, 'Russia to expand high-tech surveillance to Ukraine border areas – Kommersant' (20 June 2022), www.themoscowtimes.com/2022/06/20/russia-to-expand-high-tech-surveillance-to-ukraine-border-areas-kommersant-a78043.

[26] There is no doubt that the potential of FRT has a negative impact on freedom of assembly. Facial recognition systems integrated in street surveillance cameras significantly reduce the chances of

rallies against Russia's attack on Ukraine were taking place all over Europe, protests in Russia had been sporadic and small-scale. In Moscow, with a population of more than 12 million, the number of protesters never exceeded a few thousand. Large numbers of protesters were also never seen on the streets in other cities.

There are different reasons for this. On the one hand, the small number of Russians who expressly oppose Russian aggression might be interpreted to confirm overall society's support for the current government, prevailing approval of the policies being pursued, and agreement with the arguments put forward by the authorities as to the validity and necessity of the 'special operation' (the term used in Russia to refer to the attack on Ukraine). This support arguably stems from strong influence of national mass media, general mentality, and from the iconisation of Russia as a superpower and even 'true-values protector',[27] which has to be respected and abided by. On the other hand, owing to the massive arrests of protesters, those opposing the war see it as dangerous to protest.

From the very beginning of the invasion of Ukraine, Russian authorities effectively stopped any anti-war protest efforts. In addition to prohibiting protests against the Russian military attack on Ukraine and traditional street arrests, Russia employed FRT to track down and apprehend anti-war protesters. Analysis of online posts and social media reveals that Russian citizens are in no doubt that Big Brother is literally watching them, and that the FRTs used by the authorities in public spaces will prevent them from remaining unidentified and simply being part of the crowd.

According to Human Rights Watch, Russian authorities have been integrating public surveillance systems with FRT across the country and using these technologically advanced systems to identify and prosecute peaceful protesters since 2017.[28] The authorities do not deny this information and do not comment on the details of the extent of use, thus reinforcing the deterrent effect.[29] Already back in 2017, it was announced on the official website of the Mayor of Moscow that more than 3,500 cameras had been connected to the Joint Data Storage and Processing Centre, including more than 1,600 cameras in the entrances of residential

---

people remaining anonymous, which is often crucial during protests. Particularly in countries where freedom of assembly is restricted and where administrative or criminal liability for anti-government rallies can be imposed, the likelihood of being identified, even after a rally, encourages people to refuse to express their opinions or ideas and to take part in the democratic process (the chilling effect).

[27] See, e.g., LIFE, 'Путин: Россия никогда не откажется от любви к Родине и традиционных ценностей' (9 May 2022), https://life.ru/p/1492826.

[28] Human Rights Watch, 'Submission by Human Rights Watch on Russia to the Human Rights Committee' (15 February 2022), www.hrw.org/news/2022/02/15/submission-human-rights-watch-russia-human-rights-committee.

[29] While in Europe and many other Western countries companies offering face recognition platforms faced a lot of criticism and even fines, personal data protection seems to be much less stringent in Russia. Face recognition platforms in Russia boast wide use by private individuals. See VestiRu, 'FindFace: российская программа распознавания лиц завоевывает мир (22 February 2016), www.vesti.ru/article/1656323.

buildings, with many closed-circuit television cameras in the city also reportedly being connected to a facial recognition system.[30] Additional cameras were placed during later years, and after the start of the war, surveillance was increased in the places where protests typically take place.[31] The collection of biometric data also continues to be strengthened. For instance, in May 2022, Russian authorities demanded that the four largest state-owned banks hand over their clients' biometrics to the government.[32] To ensure that the biometric data is collected from the practically entire adult population, the laws were amended in July 2022 to oblige banks and state agencies to enter their clients' biometric data, including facial images and voice samples, into a central biometrics database. This measure, which does not require clients' consent to share data with the government, came into force in March 2023.[33]

Human Rights Watch stated in its submission to the Human Rights Committee on Russia on 10 February 2022 that the use of FRT, including for police purposes, is not regulated by Russian law. It highlighted that such use in the context of peaceful protests contradicts the principle of legal certainty by interfering with the rights to liberty and security by using methods that are not adequately supervised or provided for by law. It also violates the rights to privacy and peaceful assembly and is used in a discriminatory manner on the basis of political opinion. Human Rights Watch suggested that the Committee urge the Russian government to end the use of facial recognition during peaceful protests and ensure that all government use of facial recognition is strictly regulated by law.[34] It is not likely that Russia intends to implement this proposal in the near future, as the FRT has proved to be a powerful tool to control protests against the country's policies.

---

[30] ОВД-Инфо, 'Как Власти Используют Камеры и Распознавание Лиц Против Протестующих' (17 January 2022), https://reports.ovdinfo.org/kak-vlasti-ispolzuyut-kamery-i-raspoznavanie-lic-protiv-protestuyushchih. The use of FRTs to stop protests in the country caught the attention of the international community in 2019, when women's rights activist Ms Popova filed a lawsuit after being detained for an unauthorised picket in 2018. Ms Popova claimed that the video used in her case file contained evidence of the use of FRT. In September 2019, Ms Popova and the politician Mr Milov filed another lawsuit alleging that the authorities use the technology to collect data on public protesters. However, Russian national courts rejected both claims, as well as all other similar claims. Human Rights Watch, 'Moscow's use of facial recognition technology challenged'(8 July 2020), www.hrw.org/news/2020/07/08/moscows-use-facial-recognition-technology-challenged.

[31] After March 2022, additional surveillance cameras, presumably with facial recognition, were installed on Nevsky Avenue in St Petersburg, where some anti-war protests had been held.

[32] *Moscow Times*, 'Russian banks to share clients' biometric data with the state – Kommersant' (31 May 2022), www.themoscowtimes.com/2022/05/31/russian-banks-to-share-clients-biometric-data-with-the-state-kommersant-a77844.

[33] Federal Law of July 14, 2022 No. 325-FZ On amendments to Articles 14 and 14-1 of the Federal Law 'On Information, Information Technologies and Information Protection' and Article 5 of the Federal Law 'On Amendments to Certain Legislative Acts of the Russian Federation', Official Publication of Legal Acts, Russia. http://publication.pravo.gov.ru/Document/View/0001202207140096?index=3&rangeSize=1.

[34] Human Rights Watch, 'Submission by Human Rights Watch on Russia'.

8.4 CONCERNS ASSOCIATED WITH THE USE OF FRT IN WARTIME

While there is no doubt that the FRT brings many advantages to both sides of the conflict, it also raises a number of concerns. The main ones are the possibility of false identification, misuse of FRT, and problems associated with its continued use after the war.

8.4.1 *False Identification*

One of the significant risks linked to the use of FRT is false identification. FRT might produce inaccurate results; moreover, the input data determines the accuracy of FRT systems. This might be forgotten in wartime stress, especially considering the limited training for persons using it.

As to the recognition of dead soldiers, there is little research about FRT effectiveness in the case of deceased or distorted bodies. One recent study recognised that decomposition of a person's face could reduce the software's accuracy, though, according to researchers, overall the research results were promising.[35] Similar findings were presented in academic research on automatic face recognition for humanitarian emergencies, which concluded that automatic recognition methods based on deep learning strategies could be effectively adopted as support tools for forensic identification.[36] However, it has to be taken into account that the quality of the photos obtained in a war scenario can be substantially different from those taken under optimal conditions. Poor image quality, poor lighting, changes in faces after death, and injuries could lead to false positives or negatives.

When Ukraine started running FRT on dead Russian soldiers, it received a lot of criticism. This largely revolved around the idea that sending pictures of dead bodies to their relatives could constitute psychological violence and that any false-positive recognition of a dead soldier and subsequent notification of his family about his death would cause distress to the family. One could argue, however, that this second point might be slightly exaggerated. To cause stress, the misidentified family must first actually have a son at war in Ukraine, and second, they must have the option to try to contact him or his brothers in arms and verify the information received. Furthermore, one might expect that, at least currently, when FRT is taking its first steps as a military technology, its ability to identify fallen enemy soldiers remains

---

[35] David Cornett, David Bolme, Dawnie W. Steadman, Kelly A. Sauerwein, and Tiffany B. Saul, 'Effects of postmortem decomposition on face recognition' (1 September 2019), Oak Ridge National Lab, Oak Ridge, TN, United States, www.osti.gov/biblio/1559672#:%7E:text=During%20the%20early%20 stages%20of,have%20little%20effect%20on%20detection.

[36] Ruggero Donida Labati, Danilo De Angelis, Barbara Bertoglio, Cristina Cattaneo, Fabio Scotti, and Vincenzo Piuri, 'Automatic face recognition for forensic identification of persons deceased in humanitarian emergencies' (2021), *2021 IEEE International Conference on Computational Intelligence and Virtual Environments for Measurement Systems and Applications (CIVEMSA)*, https://ieeexplore .ieee.org/document/9493678/.

considerably limited. The Ukrainian side tested the possibilities of identifying deceased soldiers and the impact of such identification on the Russian people; however, currently Ukraine focusses its war efforts on eliminating as many enemy soldiers as possible, and recognition of the dead ones is not on the priority list.

More problematic would be a mismatch by facial recognition performed in the warzone on live persons and when identifying the enemy. This could lead to the eventual prosecution (or even killing) of wrongly identified persons. Thus, FRT in no case should become a single tool to define the fate of a person, as the technical mistake could lead to fatal outcomes. Of particular importance to avoid false positives when using the FRT in a war context is to double-check a face recognition match using alternative intelligence and contextual information. While at the stage of after-war investigation of war crimes, FRT will most likely be used as a complementary source of information, double-checking its results, it is less realistic to assume such control in the fog of war.

8.4.2 Misuse of FRT

In an active war zone, it is difficult to guarantee only limited use of FRT or to enforce any restrictions on the use of the technology. It is a challenge to ensure that FRT is used only for the purposes it is designated or by the authorised persons.

As FRT is a new technology in a war zone with little legal regulation in place, it is tempting to experiment with it and its possibilities. This allows the almost uncontrolled proliferation of FRT uses. If the deployment of FRT on the battlefield proves effective for identifying enemy soldiers, this may lead to its incorporation into systems that use automated decision-making to direct lethal force. This possibility only increases with the development of the accuracy of the FRT. The more precise the tool actually is, the more likely it will be incorporated into autonomous weapons systems that can be turned not only on invading armies, but also on, for instance, political opponents or members of specific ethnic groups.[37]

Another issue is the possibility of the unauthorised use of FRT. One strategy to mitigate this risk is to create a clearly established system that verifies the identity and authority of any official who is utilising it. The administrator of a body using the FRT should be able to see who is conducting searches and what those searches are. Moreover, the system should be designed with the possibility to revoke entry from a distance, disabling the possibility of use in case of abuse.[38] However, legal instruments should be developed and personnel trained to implement such a control.

---

[37] Darian Meacham and Martin Gak, 'Face recognition AI in Ukraine: Killer robots coming closer?' (30 March 2022), *openDemocracy*, www.opendemocracy.net/en/technology-and-democracy/facial-recognition-ukraine-clearview-military-ai/.

[38] See 'At war with facial recognition: Clearview AI in Ukraine' (17 May 2022), Interview with Hoan Ton-That, CEO of Clearview AI, at kwono321, Days Tech, https://daystech.org/at-war-with-facial-recognition-clearview-ai-in-ukraine/.

8.4.3 *Continued Use after the War*

Modern technologies share one common feature – once people learn to use them, the technologies spread, and their usage intensifies. This phenomenon has been observed in Ukraine: in September 2022, it was announced that additional cameras with facial recognition were already planned for installation in public places in the Kyiv region; with the declared goal being to counter sabotage and intelligence groups and search for saboteurs.[39]

It is likely that authorities who get comfortable with using FRT during wartime will be willing to continue its use after the war ends. It is thus difficult to anticipate that FRT introduced during a war will not endure throughout peacetime. In such a situation, the issues related to privacy, discrimination, and other concerns explored in this volume, which are less concerning in wartime, become important.

The subsequent use of information gathered during the conflict, including images of battlefield victims, raises another set of concerns. In the case of the Russia–Ukraine military conflict, the Clearview AI database is considerably enriched with pictures of deceased persons or persons who were interviewed or simply checked at a checkpoint during wartime. While the legality of harvesting pictures from social networks causes doubts, even more ethical and legal issues arise as to images taken of dead persons or persons who were not informed about the collection of their data (which would be naive to expect in a war zone). When FRTs are employed in the EU for border control and migration, the sensitive data required for facial identification is collected by public agencies, the data subject is informed, and EU law strictly regulates the process. Naturally, the use of FRT in a war zone differs materially in this regard.

8.5 CONCLUDING REMARKS: FRT – A NEW TOOL OF MILITARY TECHNOLOGY?

Any war is a tragedy for human society, but it also acts as a step in the further development of technologies. This is evident in the current Russian war against Ukraine. The conflict in Ukraine represents a coming of age for a number of advanced technologies, from drones to commercial satellites, loitering munitions, and FRT. As Lauren Kahn notes, Ukrainian steppes have been transformed into a proving ground for next-generation technologies and military innovations in this war.[40]

---

[39] Віолетта Карлащук, 'На Київщині встановлять понад 250 камер з розпізнаванням обличчя' (9 September 2022), *Суспільне | Новини*, https://suspilne.media/279898-na-kiivsini-vstanovlat-ponad-250-kamer-z-rozpiznavannam-oblicca/?.

[40] Lauren Kahn, 'How Ukraine is remaking war. Technological advancements are helping Kyiv succeed' (29 August 2022), *Foreign Affairs*, www.foreignaffairs.com/ukraine/how-ukraine-remaking-war?utm_medium=promo_email&utm_source=lo_flows&utm_campaign=registered_user_welcome&utm_term=email_1&utm_content=20220907.

From the perspective of FRT companies, the contribution of FRT to the Ukrainian war effort, in terms of proving ground and use, yields valuable data and – at the same time – visibility and even an advertisement for FRT companies. It is also difficult to argue against the fact that offering FRT technology to Ukraine during the war was a wise choice because it created a chance for the technology to prove its worth. Likely, companies whose products are being deployed in this conflict (both in Ukraine and in Russia) in a short time will become defence contractors offering their FRT as military technology.

In such a way, the broad and effective deployment of modern tools in Ukraine in its efforts to stop Russia's military invasion is bringing emerging technologies into the mainstream of the military. In an era where technology reigns, it comes as no surprise that artificial intelligence is being employed for military purposes. FRT is advancing and spreading, and it might safely be projected that FRT will be a well-established military – and propaganda – tool in a decade or two. While one can argue that bringing FRT to war is dangerous and should be avoided because of the associated risks, it would be naive to believe that this will not happen. What can be done, though, is to develop international standards on the accepted use of FRT for military purposes – work that awaits the international community in the near future.

PART II

Facial Recognition Technology across the Globe: Jurisdictional Perspectives

9

Government Use of Facial Recognition Technologies under European Law

Simone Kuhlmann

State actors in Europe, in particular security authorities, are increasingly deploying biometric methods such as facial recognition for different purposes, especially in law enforcement, despite a lack of independent validation of the promised benefits to public safety and security. Although some rules such as the General Data Protection Regulation (GDPR) and the Law Enforcement Directive (LED) are in force, a concrete legal framework addressing the use of facial recognition technologies (FRTs) in the EU so far does not exist. Given the fact that the technology is processing extremely sensitive personal data, is not always working reliably, and is associated with risks of unfair discrimination, a general ban on any use of artificial intelligence (AI) for automated recognition of human features at least in publicly accessible spaces has been demanded.[1] Against this background, this chapter adopts a fundamental rights perspective and examines whether and to what extent government use of FRT can be accepted under European law.

9.1 GOVERNMENT USE OF FACIAL RECOGNITION TECHNOLOGIES WITHIN THE EU

The government use of FRT in the EU is limited so far. With Austria, Finland, France, Germany, Greece, Hungary, Italy, Latvia, Lithuania, Slovenia, and the Netherlands, eleven countries are already using FRT, with an upward trend, but the deployments are primarily experimental and localised so far.[2] It is mainly used by security authorities for the purposes of prevention, investigation, detection, and

---

[1] European Data Protection Board (EDPB), 'EDPB & EDPS call for ban on use of AI for automated recognition of human features in publicly accessible spaces, and some other uses of AI that can lead to unfair discrimination', Press Release (21 June 2021), https://edpb.europa.eu/news/news/2021/edpb-edps-call-ban-use-ai-automated-recognition-human-features-publicly-accessible_en; European Parliament resolution of 6 October 2021 on artificial intelligence in criminal law and its use by the police and judicial authorities in criminal matters.

[2] 'Biometric & behavioural mass surveillance in EU member states' (2021), Report for the Greens/EFA in the European Parliament, p. 36 et seq.

prosecution of criminal offences as well as the prevention of threats to public security. In addition to the most controversial use of FRT for (mass) surveillance, especially in publicly accessible spaces, FRT is primarily used among law-enforcement agencies in the EU for the purposes of forensic authentication so far.[3] The typical scenario is to match the photograph of a suspect (e.g., extracted from previous records or closed-circuit television footage) against an existing database of known individuals (e.g., a national biometric database, a driver's licence database) for *ex-post* identification in a criminal investigation. Finally, on grounds of efficiency, FRT is also increasingly used by law enforcement agencies as a tool for analysing large amounts of video footage, for instance to search for a specific person or to track a person over multiple videos, since a manual analysis can be very time and resource consuming.[4]

9.2 SUITABILITY DESPITE ACCURACY CONCERNS

A ban on use of FRT for law enforcement purposes is still discussed under the recurring argument that the performance of such systems is not yet appropriate. The sufficient accuracy rates cannot be achieved in real life settings, the errors are unequally distributed in the referenced population, and minorities are discriminated against.[5]

If methods or systems are not reliable and mistakes occur when implementing the method or the system in practice, its use by state authorities may be unlawful. Under European law, the exercise of recognised rights and freedoms can be limited only if such limiting measures are appropriate and necessary to achieve the objectives (see Art. 52 para. 1 EU Charter of Fundamental Rights (CFR)). If this is lacking, the measures are disproportionate and thus unlawful. However, the European Court of Justice (CJEU) allows a wide margin of assessment to the legislator to assess the suitability of the measure. Only if, having regard to its objective, the measure is manifestly inappropriate, can the legality of a measure be affected. As long as the objective is promoted in any way, the measure is presumed to be appropriate, even if the employed method is not wholly reliable. Hence, the CJEU assessed the storage of biometric fingerprints in passports and travel documents for the purpose of preventing illegal entry to the EU as generally suitable, despite a not inconsiderable error rate.[6] The court came to the same conclusion with relation to the automated analysis of passenger name records (PNR) for the purposes of preventing, detecting, investigating, and prosecuting terrorist offences and serious crime.[7] With regard to

---

[3] Ibid., p. 38.

[4] Stephan Schindler, 'Biometrische Videoüberwachung – Zur Zulässigkeit biometrischer Gesichtserkennung in Verbindung mit Videoüberwachung zur Bekämpfung von Straftaten' (2020), p. 211; Gerrit Hornung and Stephan Schindler, 'Das biometrische Auge der Polizei' (2017) 5 ZD 203.

[5] European Parliament resolution of 6 October 2021 on artificial intelligence in criminal law and its use by the police and judicial authorities in criminal matters.

[6] CJEU, Case 291/12, *Michael Schwarz* v. *Stadt Bochum* [2013], ECLI:EU:C:2013:670, p. 43.

[7] CJEU, Case 817/19, *Ligue des droits humains* v. *Conseil des ministres* [2022], ECLI:EU:C:2022:491, pp. 123–124.

Government Use of FRT under European Law

the automated matching of PNR data with patterns, which is comparable in its functioning to facial recognition systems, the CJEU stated that the possibility of 'false negatives' and the fairly substantial number of 'false positives' resulting from the use of the system may limit the appropriateness of the system. However, automated processing has indeed already made it possible to identify air passengers presenting a risk in the context of the fight against terrorist offences and serious crime; this is why the system is not inappropriate.[8] Moreover, according to the CJEU, the appropriateness of the system essentially depends on the proper functioning of the subsequent verification of the results obtained under those processing operations by non-automated means.[9]

The FRT technologies have made real progress towards accuracy in the last years, owing to the use of convolutional neural networks. Despite this, the accuracy and error rates of FRT systems depend strongly on the task and the conditions under which the technology is used, as well as the quality of training and comparison data.[10] The one-to-one variant has become extremely accurate.[11] It is used to confirm a person's identity on the basis of clear reference images, such as recognising the rightful owner of a passport or smartphone (verification/authentication). On standard assessments such as the Facial Recognition Vendor Test (FRVT) of the National Institute of Standards and Technology (NIST), accuracy scores can be as high as 99.97 per cent.[12] This is, with some reductions in accuracy, true even if the face is partially covered by a mask.[13] The reason for this is that the one-to-one variant is comparatively simple. In one-to-one situations, one typically deals with standardised images often produced under ideal conditions (e.g., consistency in lighting and positioning), which correspondingly leads to a lower number of inaccuracies.

The situation is quite different if FRT is used in the one-to-many variant,[14] which receives most attention in the debate. This variant serves to determine an unknown person's identity by comparing a facial image with a large volume of known faces (identification). For example, it can be used to identify specific offenders or suspects or track down missing persons or victims of kidnapping.[15] Compared with the verification systems, the pictures of individuals used for identification purposes were usually captured remotely and in real life settings ('in the wild'), where the subjects

---

[8] Ibid., p. 123.

[9] Ibid., p. 124.

[10] Davide Castelvecch, 'Beating biometric bias' (2022) 587 *Nature* 348.

[11] Ibid., p. 349; William Crumpler, 'How accurate are facial recognition systems – And why does it matter?' (14 April 2020), Center for Strategic and International Studies, www.csis.org/blogs/technology-policy-blog/how-accurate-are-facial-recognition-systems-%E2%80%93-and-why-does-it-matter.

[12] Crumpler, 'How accurate are facial recognition systems?'.

[13] Mei Ngan, Patrick Grother, and Kayee Hanaoka, 'Ongoing Face Recognition Vendor Test (FRVT), Part 6B: Face recognition accuracy with face masks using post-COVID-19 algorithms' (November 2020), NISTIR 8331, https://doi.org/10.6028/NIST.IR.8331.

[14] Castelvecchi, 'Beating biometric bias', p. 349.

[15] For more examples see EDPB, Guidelines 05/2022 on the use of facial recognition technology in the area of law enforcement, Version 1.0, p. 9.

do not know they are being scanned. They may not be looking directly at the camera and/or may be obscured by objects or shadows. Accordingly, the accuracy rates tend to be far lower when compared with the controlled setting. For example, NIST's FRVT found that, when using footage of passengers entering through boarding gates (a relatively controlled setting), the best FRT system had an accuracy rate of 94.4 per cent.[16] In contrast, leading algorithms identifying individuals walking through a sporting venue – a much more challenging environment – had accuracies ranging between 36 per cent and 87 per cent, depending on camera placement.[17] These different uses with a broad range of accuracy could cause fundamental rights concerns.

9.3 FUNDAMENTAL RIGHTS CONCERNS

The government use of FRT interferes with the European fundamental right guarantees. First of all, the initial video recording, the subsequent retention of the footage, and the comparing of the footage with database records for the purpose of identification (matching) constitutes an interference with the right to data protection, as set out in Article 8 CFR and Article 16 Treaty on the Functioning of the European Union (TFEU).[18] Both regulations ensure identical protection of personal data against processing, including in particular the image of a person recorded or, rather, the unique facial features extracted in a template. In addition, the right to private life implemented in Article 7 CFR and Article 8 European Convention on Human Rights (ECHR) might also be violated, depending on how and for what purpose the technology is used. Article 7 CFR protects privacy to ensure the development, without outside interference, of the personality of each individual in his relations with other human beings.[19] The protection guaranteed by Article 7 CFR and Article 8 ECHR extends primarily to private zones (a person's home or private premises). However, there can also be interaction in a public context, which may fall within the scope of private life, when the person can have the reasonable expectation to be in private (e.g., private conversation in a screened area).[20] Such expectation cannot exist in a public space where everyone is visible to any member of the public.[21]

Accordingly, the use of FRT by authorities is not necessarily inconsistent with Article 7 CFR and the right to private life, as long as the video recording is made in

---

[16] Patrick Grother, George Quinn, and Mei Ngan, 'Face in Video Evaluation (FIVE): Face recognition of non-cooperative subjects' (March 2017), NISTIR 8173, https://doi.org/10.6028/NIST.IR.8173.

[17] Ibid.

[18] European Parliamentary Research Service (EPRS), 'Regulating facial recognition in the EU' (September 2021), p. 10.

[19] ECtHR, *Niemietz* v. *Germany*, judgment of 16 December 1992, Series A no. 251-B, pp. 33–34, § 29; *Botta* v. *Italy*, judgment of 24 February 1998, Reports of Judgments and Decisions 1998-I, p. 422, § 32.

[20] ECtHR, *P.G. and J.H.* v. *the United Kingdom*, no. 44787/98, § 56; *Peck* v. *the United Kingdom*, no. 44647/98, § 57.

[21] See ECtHR, *Uzun* v. *Germany*, judgment, no. 35623/05, § 44.

a public space where one cannot expect to be in private and is used solely for the purpose of identification. This applies at least as long as the recording is not stored systematically and permanently.[22] If FRT is used to gain inferences about the person and their personality, for example, their behaviour, whereabouts, movement patterns, contacts, or personal characteristics such as sexual or political orientation, Article 7 CFR might be violated, as the respect of private life includes the protection of private information and free development of personality.[23]

Furthermore, depending on the task for which the technology is used, FRT may affect other fundamental rights. For instance, if authorities deploy facial recognition systems in the context of public protests, during the protest or *ex-post*,[24] to identify participants or locate individuals suspected of offending, interference with the freedom of assembly according to Article 12 CFR and Article 11 ECHR comes into consideration.[25] In addition, there might a violation of a person's freedom of opinion and expression as guaranteed by Article 11 CFR. Assemblies and protests are legally protected as spaces for the collective expression of opinions. The use of FRT and the consequent possibility of identification and traceability may discourage individuals from exercising their right to freedom of peaceful assembly as well as their right to freedom of expression.[26]

9.4 LAWFULNESS UNDER THE EUROPEAN RIGHTS FRAMEWORK

These interferences with European fundamental rights do not make the government use of FRT generally inadmissible. Fundamental rights enshrined in the CFR and, in particular, the rights of data protection and private life, are not absolute rights; they must be considered in relation to their function in society and can be limited under certain circumstances.

9.4.1 *Specific Legal Bases*

First of all, Article 52(1) CFR requires a specific legal basis for any limitations to fundamental rights.[27] Thus, the specific legal basis is required that authorises the

---

[22] Ibid.

[23] See ECtHR, *Niemietz* v. *Germany*, judgment of 16 December 1992, Series A no. 251-B, pp. 33–34, § 29; *Botta* v. *Italy*, judgment of 24 February 1998, Reports of Judgments and Decisions 1998-I, p. 422, § 32.

[24] For example, the police in Hamburg used FRT after the G20 summit in 2017 to identify offenders from private recordings and police videos as well as image and video material from S-Bahn stations and from the media.

[25] Schindler, 'Biometrische Videoüberwachung', p. 384.

[26] See 'Impact of new technologies on the promotion and protection of human rights in the context of assemblies, including peaceful protests' (2020), Report of the United Nations High Commissioner for Human Rights.

[27] EDPB, Guidelines 05/2022 on the use of facial recognition technology in the area of law enforcement, Version 1.0, p. 13.

deployment of FRT systems. The EU currently has no competence to comprehensively and conclusively regulate the powers of member states' public authorities to intervene in the processing of personal data.[28] It is therefore up to the member states to create regulations precisely describing the applications and the conditions for the use of FRT.[29] A recourse to the GDPR is not possible, as police data processing for the purpose of preventing and prosecuting criminal offences, which are as described earlier currently the main application field in the EU, is not covered by its scope (see Art. 2(2) lit. d GDPR).

When adopting a legal basis for the use of FRT in law enforcement, the member states must observe the general requirements of the LED.[30] It regulates the processing of personal data by competent authorities for the purposes of the prevention, investigation, detection, or prosecution of criminal offences including the prevention of threats to public security. The LED imposes some restrictions on the processing of special categories of personal data such as biometric data. For instance, the Directive permits the processing and saving of biometric data for the purpose of uniquely identifying a natural person only where 'strictly necessary' and, *inter alia*, subject to appropriate safeguards for the rights and freedoms of the data subject (see Art. 10 LED). Automated decisions based on biometric data are completely prohibited unless suitable measures to safeguard the data subject's rights and freedoms and legitimate interests are in place (see Art. 11(2) LED).

9.4.2 *Specific, Explicit, and Legitimate Purpose*

Secondly, according to Article 52(1) and the first sentence of Article 8(2) CFR, as well as the requirements of the LED, the legal basis must specify in detail the purposes for which facial biometric data may by processed and by whom.[31] It must lay down clear and precise rules governing the scope and application of the measure in question.[32] In particular, the conditions and circumstances in which authorities are empowered to resort to any measures of secret surveillance and collection of data must be sufficiently clearly defined.[33] The reason for this is twofold: On the

---

[28] Art. 16(2) TFEU only empowers the EU to adopt rules relating to the protection of individuals with regard to the processing of personal data by the member states when carrying out activities that fall within the scope of EU law and on the free movement of such data.

[29] Schindler, 'Biometrische Videoüberwachung', p. 404; see also Vera Lúcia Raposo, 'The use of facial recognition technology by law enforcement in Europe: A non-Orwellian draft proposal' (2022) *European Journal on Criminal Policy and Research*, https://doi.org/10.1007/s10610-022-09512-y.

[30] See in detail EDPB, Guidelines 05/2022 on the use of facial recognition technology in the area of law enforcement, Version 1.0, p. 17 ff.

[31] EDPB, Guidelines 05/2022, p. 13; EPRS, 'Regulating facial recognition in the EU', p. 14; Raposo, 'The use of facial recognition technology'.

[32] CJEU, Case 293/12 and 594/12, *Digital Rights Ireland Ltd* v. *Minister for Communications, Marine and Natural Resources* [2014], ECLI:EU:C:2014:238, 54; Case 203/15 and 698/15, *Tele2 Sverige AB* v. *Post- och telestyrelsen* [2016], ECLI:EU:C:2016:970, 109.

[33] ECtHR, *Shimovolos* v. *Russia*, no. 30194/09, § 68.

one hand, it should be possible for a person affected to foresee the scope and the application of the measures in question. On the other hand, the legal basis should define and restrict the authorities' scope of action. General clauses that allow the processing of personal data for public interest purposes are, therefore, insufficient for the use of FRT. For instance, in a UK case, the Court of Appeal overturned a first instance decision and concluded that the legal framework – a Surveillance Camera Code – did not qualify as legal basis, because it was imprecise and afforded individual police officers too much discretion.[34] The court considered that it was not clear who could be placed on the watchlist, nor was it clear that there were any criteria for determining where FRT can be deployed.[35]

The specified purpose for which the data processing is authorised in the legal basis must, according to the second sentence of Article 52(1) CFR, genuinely meet the objectives of the general interest recognised by the EU or meet the need to protect the rights and freedoms of others.[36] The fight against crime in order to ensure public security, which is the main purpose of FRT in the EU so far, in principle constitutes such an objective of general interest according to the case-law of the CJEU,[37] as well as European law. In several passages in the European Treaties, the European legislator expresses the role of the EU as an 'area of freedom, security and justice' (see Art. 67(1) TFEU), in which the 'prevention and combating of crime' (see Art. 3(2) TEU, Art. 67(3) TFEU) constitutes an objective of general interest. The ECHR also recognises the legitimacy of such purposes. According to Article 8(2) ECHR, an interference by a public authority can *inter alia* be accepted in the 'interests of national security, public safety or the prevention of disorder or crime', which includes the detection of crimes that have already been committed.[38]

The purpose and extent to which the government use of FRT can be permitted under the European legal framework depends on the degree of interference with fundamental rights. Depending on the application and task, the deployment of FRT by authorities can affect these fundamental rights in different degrees. If authorities solely use the technology *ex post* to identify a person who committed a crime, and, for this purpose, match the image of the suspect against an existing database, the infringement of the fundamental rights is rather limited.[39] In this case, the conduct of the affected person causes the data processing, and the data used for matching are sometimes already available in the authorities' databases. The situation is quite different when FRT is used by safety authorities in publicly accessible spaces for the purpose of prevention, detection, and prosecution of crime, as well as for the detection of persons

---

[34] Judgement in Case No. C1/2019/2670, Court of Appeal, 11 August 2020, 90–96.
[35] Ibid.
[36] See EDPB, Guidelines 05/2022, p. 14.
[37] CJEU, Case 293/12 and 594/12, *Digital Rights Ireland Ltd* v. *Minister for Communications, Marine and Natural Resources* [2014], ECLI:EU:C:2014:238, 42; see also Case C-145/09, *Land Baden-Württemberg* v. *Panagiotos Tsakouridis* [2010], EU:C:2010:708, 45–47.
[38] See ECtHR, *S. and Marper* v. *The United Kingdom*, nos. 30562/04 and 30566/04, 100.
[39] See Schindler, 'Biometrische Videoüberwachung', p. 613.

of interest.[40] In this case, images are captured of the face of anyone who passes within the range of the camera, without a justification that their conduct might have a link, even an indirect or remote one, with crime and without any differentiation, limitation, or exception. Consequently, it can be described as a general, indiscriminate (mass) surveillance, where the interference with the fundamental rights and freedoms is wide ranging and must be considered to be particularly serious.[41] From a fundamental rights perspective, it must be considered that the deployment of FRT is generally more sensitive than conventional video surveillance. Unlike the latter, FRT is capable (for some applications in near real-time) to associate the footage with a specific person and the information already available about them, which enables the collection of further sensitive data and conclusions about the person's behaviour. In addition, an official announcement of the use of FRT in a certain area reduces the intensity of the infringement of fundamental rights but does not abrogate it.[42]

The extent of interference with fundamental rights caused by the deployment of FRT does not solely depend on the number of affected people, but also lies in the design of the system. If the recorded facial images from a public space are deleted automatically and immediately after the comparison with the database fails to find a match, the interference is not so severe.[43] However, if the authorities store the facial images including the information when and where the image was taken, systematically (e.g., in a biometric reference database) and for a longer period of time (e.g., to verify the identity of the affected person, hold it for later matching, or to draw inferences regarding behaviour or personality), then a considerable intrusive weight must be assumed. Further, the crucial factor is not only the length of data storage, but also the amount and type of data additionally collected when the facial image is taken. Finally, the secrecy of FRT use is also significant for the degree of interference, as it does not allow the person concerned to evade the technology or seek legal protection. This applies both for the deployment of FRT in certain areas and the storage of facial images (for instance from social media) in a reference database for later matching attempts.

9.4.3 Lessons Learned from the Case Law Concerning Data Retention

From the numerous CJEU decisions on data retention, such as those dealing with the storage of data for the purpose of the prevention and prosecution of serious crime arising in connection with the use of telecommunication services, we know

---

[40] Ibid., p. 608 et seq.
[41] See in this regard CJEU, Case 293/12 and 594/12, *Digital Rights Ireland Ltd* v. *Minister for Communications, Marine and Natural Resources* [2014], ECLI:EU:C:2014:238, 57–65.
[42] Mario Martini, 'Gesichtserkennung im Spannungsfeld zwischen Sicherheit und Freiheit' (2022), 1–2 NVwZ-Extra 6.
[43] See BVerfG, Urt. v. 18.12.2018, *Kfz-Kennzeichenkontrolle 2*, ECLI:DE:BVerfG:2018:rs20181218.1 bvr014215, 47–51.

that the general preventive and indiscriminate retention of traffic and location data is not compatible with the fundamental rights under Articles 7, 8, and 11 CFR. This is the case even when such data retention is conducted for the purposes of combating serious crime, preventing serious threats to public security and equally safeguarding national security.[44] The CJEU considers the collection of data for these purposes to be permissible only if it is based on certain personnel, geographical, and temporal criteria, which limit the data processing to what is strictly necessary.[45] These limits may, in particular, be determined according to the categories of persons concerned. For instance, these activities may only target people whose data are likely to reveal a link with serious crime offences. Alternatively, they may be set by using a geographical criterion, where the competent national authorities consider that there exists, in one or more geographical areas, a situation characterised by a high risk of preparation for a commission of serious criminal offences.[46] According to the CJEU, those areas may include places with a high incidence of serious crime and places that are particularly vulnerable to the commission of serious criminal offences, such as places or infrastructure that regularly receive a very high volume of visitors, or strategic locations such as airports, stations, or tollbooth areas.[47]

Moreover, in one of its recent decisions on data retention, the CJEU has clarified that the processing of data relating to the civil identity of a user solely for the purpose of identifying the user concerned can be justified by the objective of preventing, investigating, detecting, and prosecuting criminal offences in general.[48] This is assuming that the data does not provide information other than that necessary for identification purposes, such as contact details of the user or information on the communication sent. Hence, if the data provides further information that allows precise conclusions concerning the private lives of the persons concerned, only the objectives of combating serious crime or preventing serious threats to public security are capable of justifying public authorities having access to a set of such traffic or location data.[49]

Finally, according to the CJEU, there have to be minimum safeguards to ensure that the persons whose data have been retained have sufficient guarantees to effectively protect their personal data against the risk of abuse and against any unlawful

---

[44] CJEU, Case 293/12 and 594/12, *Digital Rights Ireland Ltd* v. *Minister for Communications, Marine and Natural Resources* [2014], ECLI:EU:C:2014:238, 51; Case 140/20, *G.D.* v. *Commissioner of An Garda Síochána* [2022], ECLI:EU:C:2022:258, 101.

[45] See CJEU, Case 511/18, 512/18 and 520/18, *La Quadrature du Net* v. *Premier ministre* [2020], ECLI:EU:C:2020:791, 147; C-203/15 and C-698/15, *Tele2 Sverige AB* v. *Post- och telestyrelsen* [2016], EU:C:2016:970, 108.

[46] See CJEU, Case 511/18, 512/18 and 520/18, *La Quadrature du Net* v. *Premier ministre* [2020], ECLI:EU:C:2020:791, 148–150; Case-203/15 and C-698/15, *Tele2 Sverige AB* v. *Post- och telestyrelsen* [2016], EU:C:2016:970, 111.

[47] See CJEU, Case 511/18, 512/18 and 520/18, *La Quadrature du Net* v. *Premier ministre* [2020], ECLI:EU:C:2020:791, 150.

[48] Ibid., paras. 158–159; Case 746/18, *H.K.* v. *Prokuratuur* [2021], ECLI:EU:C:2021:152, 34.

[49] CJEU, Case 746/18, *H.K.* v. *Prokuratuur* [2021], ECLI:EU:C:2021:152, 35.

access and use of that data.[50] The need for such safeguards is greater when personal data is subject to automatic processing and when there is a significant risk of unlawful access to the data.[51] Therefore, in addition to technical and organisational measures to ensure the protection and security of the data and their full integrity and confidentiality, there is a need for substantive and procedural rules that regulate the access to the data and to their subsequent use by authorities.[52] The legal rules that authorise the data processing, must restrict the purposes for which authorities are allowed to use the data to what is strictly necessary. The accepted safeguard against the risks of automatic processing is, apparently also from the CJEU, the individual review of the results by non-automated means, often called 'human in the loop'.[53] It should only be noted in passing since this kind of safeguarding is a dubious idea for many reasons, especially while there is so much literature and studies on deficits in human decision-making.

9.5 CONSEQUENCES FOR THE GOVERNMENT USE OF FRT

When trying to adopt these guidelines given by the European fundamental rights framework and the associated case-law concerning data retention in the use of FRT, it must be considered that facial recognition systems process data of similar or even higher sensitivity than traffic or location data. The processing of facial biometric data does not only enable the identification and verification of individuals. The systematic collection and evaluation of such data might – as described earlier – lead to conclusions about persons' behaviour and whereabouts; apart from the fact that increasing attempts are being made to draw inferences about individual personal attributes from facial appearance, such as sexual or political orientation or violent tendencies.[54] However, the face is a highly personal feature that cannot simply be amended, given that FRT even works if the face is partially covered.[55] Accordingly, the existing rules addressing the processing of biometric data – the GDPR and LED – impose particularly high requirements on the processing of such data and only permit it for the prevention of threats to high-priority legal interests, including the prosecution of serious criminal offences.

The analysis shows that, despite the interference with fundamental rights such as privacy or data protection as well as possible high error rates, the European

---

[50] CJEU, Case 293/12 and 594/12, *Digital Rights Ireland Ltd* v. *Minister for Communications, Marine and Natural Resources* [2014], ECLI:EU:C:2014:238, para. 54; Case 746/18, *H.K.* v. *Prokuratuur* [2021], ECLI:EU:C:2021:152, 48.

[51] Case 293/12 and 594/12, *Digital Rights Ireland Ltd* v. *Minister for Communications, Marine and Natural Resources* [2014], ECLI:EU:C:2014:238, para. 55; Case 511/18, 512/18 and 520/18, *La Quadrature du Net* v. *Premier minister* [2020], ECLI:EU:C:2020:791, 132.

[52] See Case 293/12 and 594/12, *Digital Rights Ireland Ltd* v. *Minister for Communications, Marine and Natural Resources* [2014], ECLI:EU:C:2014:238, 61–66.

[53] Case 817/19, *Ligue des droits humains* v. *Conseil des ministres* [2022], ECLI:EU:C:2022:491, para. 203.

[54] See Michael Kosinki, 'Facial recognition technology can expose political orientation from naturalistic facial images' (2021) 11 *Scientific Reports* 100, https://doi.org/10.1038/s41598-020-79310-1.

[55] See Ngan, Grother, and Hanaoka, 'Face recognition accuracy with face masks'.

Government Use of FRT under European Law

fundamental rights framework does not preclude government deployment of FRT in principle. However, a specific legal basis is required, defining clearly and precisely the purposes for which and by whom FRT can be used, who has access to the generated data, and how to proceed with the data once collected (e.g., retention and deletion periods). The law must not only consider the various applications and sectors where FRT can be used, but also address the different phases of the use, including the creation of a reference dataset and its deployment.[56] Furthermore, safeguards against abuse and any external (unauthorised) use are needed as well.

A government use of FRT for general preventive and indiscriminate mass surveillance purposes, in which individuals are recorded without a reasonable suspicion, would not be compatible with the European fundamental rights framework. In particular, establishing a state-owned biometric reference database with face images of persons without any specific reason (e.g., in order to be able to easily identify individuals in the future), would be contrary to fundamental rights. It would be nothing else but general and indiscriminate data retention. Hence, only individuals who have given the authorities a reason to do so, because they are dangerous or are suspected of having committed a crime, for example, may be recorded in the reference database. A deployment of FRT in publicly accessible spaces can only be allowed if it serves to avert threats to high-priority legal interests or to prosecute serious criminal offences. Such deployment should be geographically limited to high-risk areas or to areas with high probability of locating wanted persons.[57] This is likely to apply even if the facial image is deleted automatically and immediately after the comparison with the database is completed and no matches are found. The use of FRT systems is therefore conceivable, for instance, when tracking terrorists or serious criminals in highly frequented areas or strategic locations, such as airports, stations, or tollbooth areas. It could also be used for the surveillance of events or places where the risk of serious criminal offences is high. Moreover, the deployment of FRT may also be compatible with fundamental rights if it is used for *ex-post* identification of criminals, terrorists, or other persons of interest, or as a tool for the effective image and video evaluation (e.g., to recognise or track individuals in a video recording). Most importantly, the decisive factor for using FRT, which complies with fundamental rights, is that the incoming data should not be stored longer than necessary for the intended purposes and cannot be used for other purposes.

9.6 CONCLUSION

The analysis here leads to the conclusion that the government use of FRT can be permissible under the European fundamental rights framework if subjected to

---

[56] See Council of Europe, 'Consultative Committee of the Convention for the protection of individuals with regard to automatic processing of personal data, Convention 108' (28 January 2021), Guidelines on facial recognition, p. 8.

[57] A limitation to categories of persons is not technically possible when deployed in public spaces.

specific and strict conditions. In order to allow FRT use, a legislator should provide a specific legal basis regulating the deployment of FRT that is compatible with fundamental rights. In light of this, the EU AI-Act,[58] which provides general limitations to FRT use,[59] will not be sufficient as a legal basis, especially for the present main application of FRT by authorities: the prevention and prosecution of crime. There should be a legal basis directly legislated by the member states,[60] as the protection of national security as well as law enforcement fall under the legislative competence of the states and not the EU. In addition, an empirical study of the real effectiveness of FRT would be sensible and desirable considering the fundamental rights violations before widespread use. So far, the advocates of this technology have failed to provide enough evidence to prove that this technology can genuinely ensure public safety and security.

---

[58] Proposal for a Regulation of the European Parliament and of the Council laying down harmonized rules on Artificial Intelligence and amending certain Union Legislative Acts, COM (2021) 206 final.

[59] The AI-Act only contains limitations for the use of real-time remote biometric identification systems deployed in publicity accessible space for the purpose of law enforcement (see Art. 5(1) lit. d of the Commission's AI-Act Proposal). However, the Commission's original AI-Act Proposal is silent regarding other modalities of FRT for law enforcement purposes, such as when this technology does not take place in real-time or it is not performed in public spaces. Only the proposals made by the European Parliament address these deployment modalities of FRT, see European Parliament, P9_TA(2023)0236.

[60] Recognised by Art. 5(4) of the AI-Act Proposal.

10

European Biometric Surveillance, Concrete Rules, and Uniform Enforcement

Beyond Regulatory Abstraction and Local Enforcement

Paul De Hert and Georgios Bouchagiar

10.1 INTRODUCTION

In the era of biometric mass surveillance, novel technological implementations have led to an unprecedented monitoring of sensitive data. Among other purposes, this data has been used to discriminate based on certain characteristics (from sex to ethnic or social origin), contrary to multiple protective declarations, or draw insights into people's emotions. Such applications call for concrete regulatory intervention that is expressly targeted at practices that may interfere with fundamental human rights, including the right to privacy and personal data protection.

Despite promising initiatives, such as the European Citizens' Initiative's 'Civil society initiative for a ban on biometric mass surveillance practices', which was registered by the European Commission in 2021,[1] regulators have failed to readily intervene (before the materialisation of the harm) with a view to banning, halting, or sanctioning certain intrusive practices. Although this failure might to some extent be justified by lengthy law-making procedures, there is an acute social need to protect people's facial and other biometric data from constant watching by public or private actors, including for-profit firms, whose exercise of surveillance activities appears unregulated or under-regulated.

After discussing new challenging trends in the technological arena, this chapter emphasises the need for concrete rules surrounding specific technological uses and their possible harms. Technological uses (and misuses) can have a global reach,

---

[1] The procedure of collecting signatures for the 'Civil society initiative for a ban on biometric mass surveillance practices' (initiated at the beginning of 2021) is ongoing. See: Commission Implementing Decision (EU) 2021/360 of 19 February 2021 on the extension of the periods for the collection of statements of support for certain European citizens' initiatives pursuant to Regulation (EU) 2020/1042 of the European Parliament and of the Council (notified under document C(2021) 1121) (2021) OJ L69/9; Commission Implementing Decision (EU) 2021/944 of 3 June 2021 on the extension of the periods for the collection of statements of support for certain European citizens' initiatives pursuant to Regulation (EU) 2020/1042 of the European Parliament and of the Council (notified under document C(2021) 3879).

meaning they pose a global risk, with a potential for global harm that may affect numerous citizens simultaneously. Hence, there is a need for precise law-making *and* uniform enforcement – via joint-intervention and collaboration between regulatory entities around the globe – with a view to halting, banning, and sanctioning targeted practices interfering with fundamental human rights.

Section 10.2 discusses trends such as remote biometric surveillance, biometric monitoring targeted at classifying people on legally protected grounds, biometric processing drawing inferences on emotions or intentions, and traditional practices, such as closed-circuit television (CCTV) surveillance, whose regulation appears to require updating. It then makes the argument that these four trends must become a warning for regulators, because they have resulted in the emergence of new needs of the citizens.

Section 10.3 summarises findings of our comparative study of US initiatives that regulate facial recognition or biometric data processing. Relying on these initiatives, we highlight three regulatory building blocks for the EU. First, concreteness and precision of the law: US legal texts appear clear and expressly targeted at technological uses, vulnerable groups, or coercive state powers. Second, bright-line bans: the US prohibition-agenda includes moratoria and other techniques that may, in some instances, reach the level of unconditionality. Third, practical organisation of remedies: it is not only the civil/administrative route that citizens can follow; rather, many areas, from competition and market to criminal law, are combined to enhance effectiveness of protection.

Since the surveillance-effect appears ubiquitous and the technological reach seems transnational, the solution may lie not only in concrete law-making, but also in uniform or global enforcement. Section 10.4 discusses the 2021 Clearview-case to demonstrate that in this targeted case, joint scrutiny by different national entities and joint regulatory intervention (via rigorous investigations), had a positive effect and led to a considerable degree of enhanced protection for those affected by the firm's mass surveillance practices. Section 10.5 summarises, comments, and makes more concrete recommendations.

10.2 BIOMETRIC SURVEILLANCE: FOUR CRITICAL TRENDS

New technological implementations have allowed for an unprecedented regime of observation, rendering the people and their biometric data particularly vulnerable to unregulated or under-regulated state and business practices.

First, remote biometric surveillance may be aimed at matching citizens to reference datasets without their knowledge.[2] In the absence of concrete laws targeted

---

[2] European Parliamentary Research Service, 'Person identification, human rights and ethical principles: Rethinking biometrics in the era of artificial intelligence' (16 December 2021), European Union, p. I, refers to 'remote biometric identification' as 'AI systems used for the purpose of identifying natural persons at a distance through the comparison of a person's biometric data with the biometric data contained in a reference database, and without prior knowledge of the user of the AI

European Biometric Surveillance

at such practices, states can hardly guarantee their citizens that firms – whose for-profit activities may be exercised around the globe and operate without enhanced checks and balances (known from public law) – will not collect this data unnoticed. Neither can it be guaranteed that firms will not share collected biometric data with law enforcement, who may subsequently exploit such data and inferences in the name of national security or the need to effectively fight against crime. In the Clearview case (discussed in Section 10.4), citizens became explicitly exposed to a giant firm's mass processing and excessive sharing of sensitive data with law enforcement agencies around the world.

Second, biometric monitoring can be targeted at classifying people based on specific attributes, ranging from gender and age to political views.[3] With no specific regulation, citizens are unaware of how they may be protected against these unfairly discriminative practices – as discrimination on such bases is expressly prohibited under the Charter of Fundamental Rights of the European Union and the European Convention on Human Rights (ECHR).[4] Such protections are particularly important in an era when sensitive data is processed in an uncontrollable data-tsunami-fashion that becomes sharable with various state entities, and given that the European Court of Human Rights has held the view (and emphasised) for more than a decade that mere retention/collection of personal data may raise serious privacy-concerns.[5]

Third, biometric watching can today be directed to processing with the further objective of drawing inferences on emotions or even intents.[6] Orwellian fears become relevant if citizens could suffer any detriment or mistreatment on the basis

---

system whether the person will be present and can be identified', www.europarl.europa.eu/stoa/en/document/EPRS_STU(2021)697191.

3 European Parliamentary Research Service, 'Person identification', p. I, defines 'biometric categorisation' as 'AI systems used for the purpose of assigning natural persons to specific categories, such as sex, age, hair colour, eye colour, tattoos, ethnic origin or sexual or political orientation, on the basis of their biometric data'.

4 Charter of Fundamental Rights of the European Union (2012) OJ C326/391, Art. 21. '1. Any discrimination based on any ground such as sex, race, colour, ethnic or social origin, genetic features, language, religion or belief, political or any other opinion, membership of a national minority, property, birth, disability, age or sexual orientation shall be prohibited. 2. Within the scope of application of the Treaties and without prejudice to any of their specific provisions, any discrimination on grounds of nationality shall be prohibited [...].' European Convention on Human Rights (as amended by Protocols Nos 11, 14 and 15 supplemented by Protocols Nos 1, 4, 6, 7, 12, 13 and 16), Art. 14. 'The enjoyment of the rights and freedoms set forth in this Convention shall be secured without discrimination on any ground such as sex, race, colour, language, religion, political or other opinion, national or social origin, association with a national minority, property, birth or other status [...].'

5 *S and Marper v. the United Kingdom*, Application Nos 30562/04 and 30566/04 (ECtHR, 4 December 2008) 121. 'The Court [...] reiterates that the mere retention and storing of personal data by public authorities, however obtained, are to be regarded as having direct impact on the private life interest of an individual concerned, irrespective of whether subsequent use is made of the data [...].'

6 European Parliamentary Research Service, 'Person identification, human rights and ethical principles' , p. I, sees 'emotion recognition' as 'AI systems used for the purpose of identifying or inferring emotions or intentions of natural persons on the basis of their biometric data'.

of ideas, feelings, or thoughts that, as regulators would agree, must stay untouched by any law or practice.

Fourth, old-school surveillance, for instance via CCTV systems, is no more old-school. With new applications and improvements of old technologies, citizens have come to realise that legal regimes, introduced to regulate old technological implementations, have failed to evolve and are apparently lagging behind rapidly developing tech-trends.[7] Gone are the days of a simple CCTV camera announced by an information notice that a location is under surveillance. These notices are hardly effective against powerful cameras capable of capturing detailed images from miles away.

These developments, leading to ubiquitous monitoring of all earth-citizens, must become a three-prong warning for regulators. *First*, although surveillance practices are very well targeted at citizens and their sensitive data, laws are not. Especially at the EU level, laws have remained untargeted, general, abstract, and neutral. Technologies such as cameras or drones are unmentioned in the 2016 General Data Protection Regulation (GDPR) or the 2016 Law Enforcement Directive (LED).[8] Much criticism has also surrounded recent efforts in the proposed AI Act to address more expressly certain emerging or materialised harms,[9] (potentially) caused by biometric and other un(der)regulated technologies.[10] *Second*, regulatory responses and checks, such as proportionality assessments performed by courts, must focus on and properly balance what is actually at stake, without fearing that they might look

---

[7] On old (CCTV) modes of surveillance that keep being subjected to new soft law, in light of technological developments and further implementations, see: ICO, 'Video surveillance (including guidance for organisations using CCTV)' (n.d.): 'Traditional closed circuit television (CCTV) also continues to evolve into more complex artificial intelligence (AI) based surveillance systems. These can process more sensitive categories of personal data [...] The ways in which the technology is used also continue to develop. This includes connected databases utilising Automatic Number Plate Recognition (ANPR) or the use of Facial Recognition Technology (FRT) in public spaces [...]', https://ico.org.uk/for-organisations/guide-to-data-protection/key-dp-themes/guidance-on-video-surveillance/.

[8] Paul De Hert and Georgios Bouchagiar, 'Visual and biometric surveillance in the EU. Saying "no" to mass surveillance practices?' (2022) 27(2) *Information Polity* 193.

[9] See, among many others, European Parliamentary Research Service, 'Person identification, human rights and ethical principles', 53ff, finding regulatory failures and gaps and suggesting, among others, more specific and targeted regulation and bans on certain uses.

[10] Although some of these efforts and AI-proposals appear promising, it remains to be seen whether they will be effectively realised. See Maximilian Gahntz, Mark Surman, and Mozilla Insights, 'How to make sure the EU's AI Act delivers on its promise' (25 April 2022), Mozilla Foundation, https://foundation.mozilla.org/en/blog/how-to-make-sure-the-eu-ai-act-delivers-on-its-promise/#:~:text=The%20draft%20AI%20Act%20includes,before%20they%20can%20be%20deployed. In our view, these efforts need to be taken seriously. Regulators simply *must* provide the citizen a response to materialised, detected, or emerging risks and harms. At least those states that see themselves as pioneers in a tech-field should make themselves analogously responsibilised towards those affected by their technological expertise and uses. Compare Els Kindt, 'Biometric data processing: Is the legislator keeping up or just keeping up appearances?' in Gloria González, Rosamunde Van Brakel and Paul De Hert (eds.), *Research Handbook on Privacy and Data Protection Law* (Edward Elgar, 2022), pp. 375, 396: '[T]he responsibility of the States to regulate the automated use of unique and other human characteristics cannot be underestimated: Any State claiming a pioneer role in the development of new technologies bears special responsibility for "striking the right balance" [...].'

political or too activist.[11] This risk is only heightened when a regulatory framework is lacking or too vague. *Third*, fundamental human rights demand priority and enforcement – an argument closely linked to the second point. While the risk-based, cost/benefit rationale already underlying many fields, from environment to data protection,[12] could entertain utilitarianism-advocates, it cannot and should not replace the logic of the 'fundamental'. There are certain sensitive areas where financial interests and security must not be over-prioritised; where fundamental human rights cannot be outweighed by being attributed numerical values in a mathematical fashion.[13]

These technological trends and regulatory challenges must catch the eye of the regulator; for the watching of anyone anywhere, their sorting into whatever classes on whatever bases and for whatever purposes, the foreseeing of people's thoughts and feelings, and the rebirth of old-school technologies escaping old-school laws have given birth to new citizens' needs.

10.3 REGULATORY STRATEGY: FOCUS ON CONCRETE TECHNOLOGICAL USES AND THEIR POSSIBLE HARM

The need for bright-line rules directed to concrete technological uses and possible harms has long been identified and stressed in privacy-related contexts;[14] and, in recent publications, we have resorted to the US legal regime and its piecemeal approach to make concrete recommendations that might be useful for EU audiences.[15] More concretely, we have digested about fifteen US-initiatives at federal,

---

[11] See, on the refusal of the judges in *Bridges* to test the proportionality of facial recognition systems, Nóra Ni Loideain, Chapter 11 in this volume. See also De Hert and Bouchagiar, 'Visual and biometric surveillance in the EU'.

[12] See, among others, Gabe Maldoff, 'White Paper – The risk-based approach in the GDPR: Interpretation and implications' (March 2016), IAPP, https://iapp.org/resources/article/the-risk-based-approach-in-the-gdpr-interpretation-and-implications/; Gianclaudio Malgieri, 'Malgieri & Ienca on European Law Blog: "The EU regulates AI but forgets to protect our mind"' (7 July 2021), Gianclaudio Malgieri, European Law Blog, www.gianclaudiomalgieri.eu/2021/07/07/malgieri-ienca-on-european-law-blog-the-eu-regulates-ai-but-forgets-to-protect-our-mind/; European Commission, 'Environmental risks' (n.d.), https://ec.europa.eu/environment/risks/index_en.htm.

[13] Compare with Orla Lynskey on the possible role of law in this area: either shaping proportionate surveillance or banning facial recognition since it affects the core of individual and collective rights and interests. Orla Lynskey, 'Keynote address in facial recognition in the modern state' (15 September 2022), *UNSW Allens Hub*, https://allenshub.unsw.edu.au/events/facial-recognition-modern-state.

[14] See, among others, McKay Cunningham, 'Next generation privacy: The internet of things, data exhaust, and reforming regulation by risk of harm' (2014) 2(2) *Groningen Journal of International Law* 115, 142, 144. 'Privacy laws should focus on data use, not collection. Privacy laws should identify and address the specific harm or risk associated with the use of sensitive data in particular contexts […]'; Paul De Hert, 'The future of privacy – Addressing singularities to identify bright-line rules that speak to us' (2016) 2(4) *European Data Protection Law Review* 461.

[15] Paul De Hert and Georgios Bouchagiar, 'Facial recognition, visual and biometric data in the US. Recent, promising developments to regulate intrusive technologies' (2021) 7(29) *Brussels Privacy Hub* https://brusselsprivacyhub.eu/publications/wp729; De Hert and Bouchagiar, 'Visual and biometric surveillance in the EU'.

state, and local level. These initiatives refer either to biometrics or to face recognition.[16] On biometrics there is the federal 2020 National Biometric Information Privacy Act, which aims to tackle biometric data exploitation by private entities. What caught our attention was the setting out of concrete bans on specific manners of obtaining, exploiting, and sharing biometric data:

> A private entity may not collect, capture, purchase, receive through trade, or otherwise obtain a person's or a customer's biometric identifier or biometric information [...] may not sell, lease, trade, use for advertising purposes, or otherwise profit from a person's or a customer's biometric identifier or biometric information [...] may not disclose, redisclose, sell, lease, trade, use for advertising purposes, otherwise disseminate, or profit from such biometric identifier or biometric information [...].[17]

In the same vein, the 2008 Illinois Biometric Information Privacy Act sets out a number of targeted prohibitions on the processing (again, mainly obtaining, profiting, and disseminating) of biometrics by private entities (prohibitions that will play a crucial bright-line-rule role in the Clearview case discussed in Section 10.4).[18] We also appreciated the imposition of a standard of care (regarding storing, communicating, and securing) that ensures biometrics are treated in a similar way to, or are more shielded than, other confidential and sensitive information in that industry:

> No private entity may collect, capture, purchase, receive through trade, or otherwise obtain a person's or a customer's biometric identifier or biometric information [...] No private entity [...] may sell, lease, trade, or otherwise profit from a person's or a customer's biometric identifier or biometric information [...] No private entity [...] may disclose, redisclose, or otherwise disseminate a person's or a customer's biometric identifier or biometric information [...] A private entity [...] shall [...] store, transmit, and protect from disclosure all biometric identifiers and biometric information using the reasonable standard of care within the private entity's industry [...] store, transmit, and protect from disclosure all biometric identifiers and biometric information in a manner that is the same as or more protective than the manner in which the private entity stores, transmits, and protects other confidential and sensitive information [...].[19]

Similar is the 2009 Texas Business and Commerce Code Sec 503.001 'Capture or Use of Biometric Identifier' (obviously influenced by the Illinois Act), which forbids the capturing, disclosing, or exploiting of biometrics in commercial contexts, save

---

[16] For full reference of these initiatives, see: De Hert and Bouchagiar, 'Facial recognition, visual and biometric data in the US'; De Hert and Bouchagiar, 'Visual and biometric surveillance in the EU'.

[17] Federal 2020 National Biometric Information Privacy Act, section 3(b)–(d).

[18] For a list of lawsuits, based on Illinois Biometric Information Privacy Act and revealing that some actors are becoming nervous and uneasy in light of risks connected with FRTs and machine learning-implementations, see Debra Bernard, Susan Fahringer, and Nicola Menaldo, 'New biometrics lawsuits signal potential legal risks in AI' (2 April 2020), Perkins Coie, www.perkinscoie.com/en/news-insights/new-biometrics-lawsuits-signal-potential-legal-risks-in-AI.html.

[19] 2008 Illinois Biometric Information Privacy Act, section 15(b)–(e).

for exceptional circumstances. It further requires that when securing biometrics, 'reasonable care' must be shown and that any measures taken must have the same level of protection (or be more shielding) than the measures taken to store their own confidential data.

The 2019 California's Assembly Bill No. 1215 is expressly aimed at forbidding biometric surveillance by law enforcement through cameras. There is not much to say about such a clear-cut provision targeted at avoiding abuse of law enforcement powers: 'A law enforcement agency or law enforcement officer shall not install, activate, or use any biometric surveillance system in connection with an officer camera or data collected by an officer camera [....].'[20]

The 2020 California Privacy Rights Act is an EU-like tool targeted at businesses and the protection of consumers. Not only does it use GDPR-like terminology, but it also grants consumers various GDPR-like rights (including the right to correct inaccurate data or opt out of automated decision making), imposes on businesses GDPR-like obligations (such as the duty to conduct audits or risk assessments), and includes GDPR-like principles (such as data minimisation, purpose limitation, and storage limitation).

The 2020 Indiana House Bill 1238 imposes on law enforcement actors a duty to conduct a 'surveillance technology impact and use policy', make that policy available to the public, and update it prior to altering the technology's function or purpose. Interestingly, these duties are set out using brief and simple phrasing:

> Requires a state or local law enforcement agency [...] that uses surveillance technology to prepare a surveillance technology impact and use policy [...] and post the policy on the agency's Internet web site [...] Specifies the information that must be included in the policy [...] Requires an agency to post an amended policy before implementing any enhancements to surveillance technology or using the technology in a purpose or manner not previously disclosed through the existing policy [...].[21]

The 2020 New York's Assembly Bill A6787D aims to protect children by suspending the use of biometric technologies (including face recognition) in public and private schools. It does so through a moratorium on purchases and uses of technologies for a concrete period of time or until these technologies are proven safe: 'Public and nonpublic elementary and secondary schools [...] shall be prohibited from purchasing or utilizing biometric identifying technology for any purpose, including school security, until July first, two thousand twenty-two or until the commissioner authorizes such purchase or utilization [...] whichever occurs later [...].'[22]

The 2021 proposed Virginia's Senate Bill 1392 focusses on private for-profit entities that process significant amounts of personal data, including biometrics. This

---

[20] 2019 California's Assembly Bill No. 1215, section 2(b).
[21] House Bill 1238.
[22] New York's Assembly Bill, subdivision 2.

Bill offers clear rules protecting biometric data as sensitive personal information, whose processing is in principle prohibited. What we found novel, compared with the GDPR-regime, is the prohibition on discrimination against consumers: 'A controller shall not discriminate against a consumer for exercising any of the consumer rights [...] including denying goods or services, charging different prices or rates for goods or services, or providing a different level of quality of goods and services to the consumer [...].'[23]

Moving on to the US initiatives on face recognition, the proposed federal 2019 Commercial Facial Recognition Privacy Act bans the use of face recognition technology (FRT) by private actors (save where there is consent and, where possible, notification) for the purposes of facial recognition data collection, discrimination, purposes other than those of initial processing, and the sharing of facial recognition data. Though conditional, the ban on discrimination is, again, a novelty, when compared with the EU regime: '[I]t shall be unlawful for a controller to knowingly [...] use the facial recognition technology to discriminate against an end user in violation of applicable Federal or State law [...].'[24]

The federal 2020 Facial Recognition and Biometric Technology Moratorium Act forbids the federal government from using face recognition or other biometric technology until expressly allowed by the law: '[I]t shall be unlawful for any Federal agency or Federal official [...] to acquire, possess, access, or use in the United States (1) any biometric surveillance system; or (2) information derived from a biometric surveillance system operated by another entity [...] The prohibition [...] does not apply to activities explicitly authorized by an Act of Congress [...].'[25]

Washington's Engrossed Substitute Senate Bill 6280 (2020) is targeted at state/local authorities using facial recognition services and imposes several concrete duties (such as conduct of accountability reports that are reviewable by the public), as well as restrictions (such as preventing the application of the technology to persons on concrete discriminatory grounds). What appeared interesting to us (in addition to the regulator's concern about discrimination) was the clear ban on reliance upon the facial recognition service as the only basis for establishing 'probable cause' in criminal contexts or image-tampering in face recognition contexts. Nothing similar or even close to this exists in the LED:

> A state or local law enforcement agency may not use the results of a facial recognition service as the sole basis to establish probable cause in a criminal investigation [...] may not substantively manipulate an image for use in a facial recognition service in a manner not consistent with the facial recognition service provider's intended use and training [...].[26]

---

[23] Senate Bill 1392, section 59.1-574, subsection A.
[24] Federal 2019 Commercial Facial Recognition Privacy Act, section 3(a)(2–4).
[25] Federal 2020 Facial Recognition and Biometric Technology Moratorium Act, section 3(a)–(b).
[26] Engrossed Substitute Senate Bill 6280, section 11(5), (7).

European Biometric Surveillance

The 2020 New Jersey's Assembly Bill 989 is targeted at subjecting facial recognition technologies to accuracy- and bias-checking; again, the focus is placed on avoiding discrimination on concrete grounds: 'The testing and auditing is required to determine whether there is a statistically significant variation in the accuracy of the facial recognition systems on the basis of race, skin tone, ethnicity, gender, or age of the individuals portrayed in the images, whether or not those categories are applied individually or in combination [...].'[27]

Portland's ordinances (2020) ban the application of face recognition to public spaces and by private entities, as well as the use of FRTs by the city's public actors ('bureaus'). Portland clearly says 'no' to both state and private entities.

Baltimore's ordinance (2021) prohibits, first, the city of Baltimore from obtaining a face recognition system and contracting other entities with a view to using such systems (some biometric security systems are exempted) and, second, private actors from obtaining, retaining, accessing, or using a face recognition system or information gathered from such a system (certain biometric security systems and Maryland's Image Repository System are exempted). Remarkably, in case of violation of the provisions on the ban related to private actors, the ordinance provides not only for civil, but also for criminal remedies: '§ 18-3. Penalties [...] Any person who violates any provision of this subtitle is guilty of a misdemeanor and, on conviction, is subject to a fine of not more than $1,000 or imprisonment for not more than 12 months or both fine and imprisonment [...] Each day that a violation continues is a separate offense [...].'[28]

After analysing these US texts, we detected three key ideas that encapsulate the overall approach followed by the US regulators:[29]

Concreteness and precision: We appreciated the unambiguous clarity of the US initiatives, which appear to have clear objectives and target concrete and intrusive technological uses. Compared with the EU regime, US provisions are more demanding with respect to various requirements. *First*, although some bans are conditional upon consent, the latter goes beyond the EU model – demanding not only that consent be 'informed', 'specific', and so forth (terms also present in the GDPR), but also focussing on the independent, genuine will of the person concerned, who must be free from outside control. These demands make the US prohibition stronger and more honest than the EU's ban, which is accompanied by a long list of exceptions.[30] *Second*, some duties and prohibitions concretely set

---

[27] Assembly Bill 989.

[28] Ordinance 'Surveillance Technology in Baltimore', 'Article 19. Police Ordinances', 'Subtitle 18. Surveillance'.

[29] For full analysis of our conclusions, see: De Hert and Bouchagiar, 'Facial recognition, visual and biometric data in the US'; De Hert and Bouchagiar, 'Visual and biometric surveillance in the EU'.

[30] A good example of this can be found in Federal 2020 National Biometric Information Privacy Act, section 2(4): 'The term written release means specific, discrete, freely given, unambiguous, and informed written consent given by an individual who is not under any duress or undue influence of an entity or third party at the time such consent is given; or [...] in the context of employment, a release executed by an employee as a condition of employment [...].'

out in the US texts are completely absent in the EU. These include the prohibition on discrimination, the prohibition on profiting, the application of standards of care, and the treatment of biometric data as particularly sensitive and confidential information.

Bright-line bans: We saw explicit prohibitions on certain technologies or surveillance practices, often reaching the level of unconditionality. In this regard, Portland and its ordinances very well illustrate how both private and public actors can be prohibited from using FRTs. Remarkably, the US prohibitions aim to protect vulnerable groups (such as children) and anticipate, or probably avoid, possible abuses of coercive powers (for instance, by prohibiting law enforcement from using surveillance cameras). Even where ban-techniques, such as moratoria, can end upon the (future) introduction of laws that would allow for relevant uses, the United States demands that such laws be particularly detailed in various terms, ranging from lists of authorised entities to operation-standards, auditing duties and compliance-mechanisms. Probably, the best example is given by section 3(a)–(b) of the Federal 2020 Facial Recognition and Biometric Technology Moratorium Act quoted earlier.[31]

Practical organisation of remedies: We found the United States's supremacy in combining several legal fields (e.g., market, competition or criminal law/procedure) with a view to enhancing effectiveness of their remedy-scheme. Good examples can be found in the 2019 Commercial Facial Recognition Privacy Act (section 4(a)),[32] and in the Ordinance 'Surveillance Technology in Baltimore'.[33]

One could argue that the EU's general approach allows for an always-present regime covering any technological implementation; and, in our recent EU–United States comparative analysis, we addressed pros and cons of both general and concrete law-making, finding persuasive arguments for both approaches.[34] However, in our opinion, what makes bright-line regulation more desirable (and more protective) is

---

[31] '[I]t shall be unlawful for any Federal agency or Federal official [...] to acquire, possess, access, or use in the United States (1) any biometric surveillance system; or (2) information derived from a biometric surveillance system operated by another entity [...] (t)he prohibition set forth in subsection (a) does not apply to activities explicitly authorized by an Act of Congress that describes, with particularity (1) the entities permitted to use the biometric surveillance system, the specific type of biometric authorized, the purposes for such use, and any prohibited uses; (2) standards for use and management of information derived from the biometric surveillance system, including data retention, sharing, access, and audit trails; (3) auditing requirements to ensure the accuracy of biometric surveillance system technologies, standards for minimum accuracy rates, and accuracy rates by gender, skin color, and age; (4) rigorous protections for due process, privacy, free speech and association, and racial, gender, and religious equity; and (5) mechanisms to ensure compliance with the provisions of the Act [...].'

[32] 'A violation of section 3 shall be treated as a violation of a rule defining an unfair or deceptive act or practice [...].'

[33] 'Any person who violates any provision of this subtitle is guilty of a misdemeanor and, on conviction, is subject to a fine of not more than $1,000 or imprisonment for not more than 12 months or both fine and imprisonment [...].'

[34] De Hert and Bouchagiar, 'Facial recognition, visual and biometric data in the US'.

the very principle of legality.[35] If laws are general and abstract by-design, then they risk becoming human rights-incompatible by default. If law enforcement and other state actors are not told by the lawmaker in simple, clear, and detailed language what they can and cannot do, not only are citizens under-protected, but also regulators are confused. Experience has indeed shown that lack of bright-line-rule-setting has confused and puzzled regulators, who may not be able to fully foresee or tell the legal grounds upon which proposed bans can be introduced.[36]

Today, with the tremendous challenges posed by the global reach of any anywhere-based tech-firm,[37] as well as the mass adoption of latest technologies and pilot programmes in both private and public arenas,[38] we encounter concrete risks from concrete uses (from school-areas involving vulnerable children to work environments obliging employees to be surveilled) that appear to demand concrete rule-setting.[39] And, in our view, effectiveness of such precise rule-making can be enhanced by uniform enforcement aimed at scrutinising, banning, or sanctioning specific surveillance practices. At least one case, namely Clearview (discussed in Section 10.4), can support the claim that the ideal solution can include both precise rule-making *and* uniform enforcement.

10.4 REGULATORY STRATEGY: UNIFORM ENFORCEMENT

In May 2021, several national data protection authorities and organisations submitted complaints against Clearview, an American face recognition-tech firm. The firm

---

[35] Paul De Hert and Gianclaudio Malgieri, 'One European legal framework for surveillance: The ECtHR's expanded legality testing copied by the CJEU' in Valsamis Mitsilegas and Niovi Vavoula (eds.), *Surveillance and Privacy in the Digital Age. European, Transatlantic and Global Perspectives* (Hart, 2021), p. 255.

[36] See, for instance, European Parliament, 'Parliamentary questions' (13 August 2021), European Parliament: 'In a joint opinion, the European Data Protection Supervisor (EDPS) and the European Data Protection Board (EDPB) have called for a general ban on the use of AI for the automated recognition of human features – such as of faces, gait, fingerprints, DNA, voice, keystrokes and other biometric or behavioural signals – in publicly accessible spaces. The EDPS and EDPB recommend tightening the draft EU Artificial Intelligence Act, as they consider that the current proposal does not cover a wide enough scope. 1. To what extent does the Commission take the views of the EDPS, EDPB and the 175 civil society organisations mentioned in the article above into account? 2. Does the automated recognition of human features constitute interference with the fundamental rights of EU citizens? 3. Is the Commission aiming to ban the automated recognition of human features? If so, on what grounds? [...]', www.europarl.europa.eu/doceo/document/E-9-2021-003888_EN.html.

[37] There is a discussion on serious challenges in the US in an interview of Helena Wootton and Stewart Dresner with Justin Antonipillai, Privacy Laws & Business, 'Privacy Paths' podcast, Episode 17: 'US privacy laws most likely to be adopted and when' (10 November 2021), www.privacylaws.com/podcasts/.

[38] On smart-contracting-programmes in the EU agenda targeted at the public sphere, from voting to establishing digital identities, see, among others, EU Blockchain, 'Observatory and forum' (n.d.), www.eublockchainforum.eu/initiative-map.

[39] On face recognition in schools, see Asress Adimi Gikay, 'On facial recognition technology in schools, power imbalance and consent: European data protection authorities should re-examine their

had in its hands the (allegedly) largest known database (more than 3 billion facial images). With its AI technology, it searches for human (face) photographs in the web, stores them on its proprietary database, and sells access to other firms or law enforcement authorities.[40]

Elsewhere, we have critically approached the Clearview-case, questioning the legal grounds for data collection and further processing, as well as doubting the lawfulness of sharing practices – particularly in relation to EU law enforcement authorities.[41] These concerns were recently shared by two national authorities.

Upon joint scrutiny conducted by the United Kingdom's Information Commissioner's Office (ICO) and the Office of the Australian Information Commissioner (OAIC), initiated in July 2020, these authorities gathered evidence from the web and searched separately for uses of relevant data by their law enforcement entities.[42] After stressing the global nature of the digital space and the resulting need for a global regulatory approach, they highlighted new challenges posed by Clearview's practices.[43] According to the ICO's preliminary opinion, the firm had probably failed to comply with data protection laws in various respects (including unfair processing, lack of mechanisms to avoid forever-storage, no legal basis, and opaque processing).[44] After expressing its intent to impose on the firm a provisional

---

approach' (20 December 2021), EU Law Analysis, http://eulawanalysis.blogspot.com/2021/12/on-facial-recognition-technology-in.html. On recent initiatives in the United States, introducing concrete duties to employers who use monitoring technologies, see Hunton Andrews Kurth, 'New York State requires private employers to notify employees of electronic monitoring' (12 November 2021), Hunton Privacy Blog, www.huntonprivacyblog.com/2021/11/12/new-york-state-requires-private-employers-to-notify-employees-of-electronic-monitoring/#more-20908. This refers to New York's law A.430/S.2628, introduced in 2021 (effective from May 2022), demanding private employers to give employees prior written notice (before hiring) of their monitoring technologies.

[40] Privacy International, 'Challenge against Clearview AI in Europe' (2 June 2021), EDRi, https://edri.org/our-work/challenge-against-clearview-ai-in-europe/.

[41] De Hert and Bouchagiar, 'Visual and biometric surveillance in the EU'.

[42] OAIC, 'OAIC and ICO conclude joint investigation into Clearview AI' (3 November 2021), www.oaic.gov.au/updates/news-and-media/oaic-and-ico-conclude-joint-investigation-into-clearview-ai.

[43] Ibid. 'Our digital world is international and so our regulatory work must be international too, particularly where we are looking to anticipate, interpret and influence developments in tech for the global good [...] The issues raised by Clearview AI's business practices presented novel concerns in a number of jurisdictions. By partnering together, the OAIC and ICO have been able to contribute to an international position, and shape our global regulatory environment [...].'

[44] ICO, 'ICO issues provisional view to fine Clearview AI Inc over £17 million' (29 November 2021), https://ico.org.uk/about-the-ico/news-and-events/news-and-blogs/2021/11/ico-issues-provisional-view-to-fine-clearview-ai-inc-over-17-million/. 'The ICO's preliminary view is that Clearview AI Inc appears to have failed to comply with UK data protection laws in several ways including by [...] failing to process the information of people in the UK in a way they are likely to expect or that is fair [...] failing to have a process in place to stop the data being retained indefinitely [...] failing to have a lawful reason for collecting the information [...] failing to meet the higher data protection standards required for biometric data (classed as 'special category data' under the GDPR and UK GDPR) [...] failing to inform people in the UK about what is happening to their data; and asking for additional personal information, including photos, which may have acted as a disincentive to individuals who wish to object to their data being processed [...].'

fine and after issuing its provisional notice to halt processing and erase relevant data,[45] the ICO imposed a fine of £7.5 million and ordered deletion.[46] While it was clarified that the firm's services are no longer offered in the United Kingdom, the ICO stated that there is no guarantee that Clearview will stop processing data of UK citizens, in light of its opaque practices.[47]

What the Clearview-case can reveal is that uniform enforcement, collaboration (in the sense of looking for ways to make different approaches work), and co-ordination can successfully tackle the transnational, global reach, risk, and potential harm of surveillance practices. The success is not the imposition of the huge fine; rather, it is the desire of the regulators (ICO and OAIC), which was actually expressed and materialised via rigorous investigations and targeted application of the law, to a concrete technological use: Clearview's risky, opaque, and harmful practice, exercised at global level, potentially affecting each individual citizen.

Such global exercise can very well be halted and sanctioned by collaborating regulators at national level(s). One could claim that Clearview's fine and order to delete data may fail to 'frighten' gigantic firms; albeit, if collaboration between national authorities were embraced by various states, then analogous fines and orders imposed/issued by various domestic entities could have a considerable impact on the financial status of Clearview and similar big firms. Indeed, state authorities, finding absence of a legal basis, have taken steps in that direction and against Clearview: Italy, for example, imposed a fine of EUR 20 million,[48] and France ordered the firm to halt processing.[49] For a further discussion of the Clearview case, we refer to the discussion by Orla Lynskey, insisting on the limits of a European human rights approach.[50] Judges and data protection authorities are inclined to avoid general statements about facial recognition and limit their intervention to cases involving facial recognition brought before them. The UK and French data protection authorities demand 'settled evidence' about the negative impact of this technology. Rather than banning a technology, they opt for prohibiting a certain processing activity. The Greek and Italian data protection authorities did indeed ban the Clearview

---

[45] Ibid.

[46] ICO, 'Clearview AI Inc.' (26 May 2022), https://ico.org.uk/action-weve-taken/enforcement/clearview-ai-inc-mpn/.

[47] ICO, 'ICO issues provisional view'. 'Clearview AI Inc's services are no longer being offered in the UK. However, the evidence we've gathered and analysed suggests Clearview AI Inc were and may be continuing to process significant volumes of UK people's information without their knowledge. We therefore want to assure the UK public that we are considering these alleged breaches and taking them very seriously [...].'

[48] Hermes Center and Reclaim Your Face, 'Italian DPA fines Clearview AI for illegally monitoring and processing biometric data of Italian citizens' (23 March 2022), EDRi, https://edri.org/our-work/italian-dpa-fines-clearview-ai-for-illegally-monitoring-and-processing-biometric-data-of-italian-citizens/.

[49] CNIL, 'Facial recognition: The CNIL orders CLEARVIEW AI to stop reusing photographs available on the internet' (16 December 2021), www.cnil.fr/en/facial-recognition-cnil-orders-clearview-ai-stop-reusing-photographs-available-internet.

[50] Lynskey, 'Keynote address in facial recognition in the modern state'.

processing activity, but only for future collection and processing of data through the company's facial recognition system. The Italians moreover only ordered the company to erase the data relating to individuals in Italy. The United Kingdom's ICO only 'banned' the web scraping by Clearview, but did not put a ban on Clearview's facial recognition activities.

While in the EU Clearview's abuses were sanctioned with fining and halting-orders, in Illinois, the firm was given a clear, quasi-permanent, and almost *erga omnes*-ban. More concretely, the American Civil Liberties Union (ACLU), a US-based organisation fighting for human rights and freedoms, brought its case against the giant firm, claiming violation of the Illinois Biometric Information Privacy Act. On 11 May 2022, there was a settlement accepted by the court, under which Clearview is permanently prohibited from offering its services to numerous private entities in the entire United States, as well as all entities (including the police) of the state of Illinois (the latter ban for the following five years).[51] The result is a settlement with compromises.[52] Clearview AI settled the lawsuit without admission of liability. There is a nationwide 'Private Entity Ban',[53] supplemented with an 'Illinois State Ban' (no facial recognition services for state or local government entities including Illinois law enforcement),[54] but for the law enforcement services outside Illinois there is also a law enforcement friendly 'Savings Clause',[55] a shaky system to prevent further web scraping without consent for Illinois residents, and with no obligation to delete past collected data.[56] It is not simple to compare the outcomes of this settlement with the preceding outcomes

[51] For the text of the settlement, see www.aclu.org/cases/aclu-v-clearview-ai. See also ACLU, 'In big win, settlement ensures Clearview AI complies with groundbreaking Illinois biometric privacy law' (9 May 2022), www.aclu.org/press-releases/big-win-settlement-ensures-clearview-ai-complies-with-groundbreaking-illinois. See also Security.nl, 'Clearview AI beperkt gebruik van massale gezichtsherkenningsdatabase' (10 May 2022), www.security.nl/posting/752955/Clearview+AI+beperkt+gebruik+van+massale+gezichtsherkenningsdatabase.

[52] Compare Arti, 'Clearview *Ai vs ACLU* lawsuit is nothing but a facade of fake hopes and claims' (18 May 2022), Analytics Insight, www.analyticsinsight.net/clearview-ai-vs-aclu-lawsuit-is-nothing-but-a-facade-of-fake-hopes-and-claims/.

[53] Clearview AI has agreed to a nationwide injunction barring access to the Clearview App by (1) any private entity or private individuals unless such access is compliant with BIPA; or (2) any governmental employee not acting in his or her official capacity.

[54] Clearview has agreed to a five-year injunction against access to the Clearview App (1) by Illinois state and local agencies and their contractors; (2) by any private entity located in Illinois even if permissible under BIPA; and (3) by employees of Illinois state and local agencies and their contractors, whether in their individual or official capacities.

[55] There will be no restrictions on Clearview's ability to work with or contract with (1) third parties outside Illinois; (2) federal agencies whether in Illinois or outside Illinois; and (3) state or local government agencies outside Illinois.

[56] This is the 'Opt-Out Program' for Illinois residents in the settlement, by which an Illinois resident will be allowed to submit a photo to Clearview and compel Clearview, on a best-efforts basis, to block search results and prevent any future collection of facial recognition data or images of such person. A last element of the settlement is 'Illinois Photo Screening', in which Clearview has agreed, on a best-efforts basis, not to access or use any of its existing 'Illinois-based' facial recognition data.

in the EU. Within the state of Illinois, the Illinois Biometric Information Privacy Act has delivered some of its promises and even more: Clearview is permanently banned, nationwide, from making its faceprint database available to most businesses and other private entities. The company also has to cease selling access to its database to any entity in Illinois, including state and local police, for five years. The Illinois Act was already used successfully to settle facial recognition practices by Facebook,[57] and IBM,[58] and has clearly brought the message to the United States that even for publicly available data, a citizen may claim that processing personal data without consent violates the law.[59]

Two remarks before concluding. First, in the EU, national authorities successfully defended citizens' rights and freedoms by jointly investigating the firm's practices and, after seeing the harm done, enforced the law and proceeded to various sanctions including halting and fining. Second, in the United States, there was a forever – and almost toward-any-party – ban prohibiting Clearview from selling its technology. Clearly enough, if the United States's clear law-making was combined with the EU's uniform enforcement, citizens would be better and more effectively protected against surveillance practices.

10.5 CONCLUSION: PRECISE RULE-MAKING AND UNIFORM ENFORCEMENT AS A TWOFOLD SOLUTION AGAINST UNDESIRED SURVEILLANCE PRACTICES

This analysis has shown that new technological trends, from monitoring of emotions to attempts to predict feelings, can pose novel, serious challenges that existing laws have failed to adequately tackle. This has in turn created new needs for global citizens: in particular, enhanced protection against increasing tech-interference. Looking to other jurisdictions for insights into how their targeted and precise regulations may better address new threats can offer useful lessons. Indeed, the US approach could offer insights into how specific uses and concrete harms could be more effectively avoided. Our argument for supremacy of the US initiatives is neither to dignify nor to deify the United States. Rather, it is to support the view that targeted and precise law-making is a matter of legality; in its absence, laws risk violating human rights by simply being abstractly designed. This is a claim we have already raised in previous publications;[60] in this chapter, we have engaged in a meta-analysis to further argue

---

[57] On the *In re Facebook Biometric Information Privacy Litigation* settlement of 2020, see J. Cleary, 'Facial recognition: Clearview-ACLU settlement charts a new path for BIPA and the First Amendment' (2022) *September The National Law Review* 1.
[58] On *Vance v. IBM* and *Janecyk v. International Business Machines*, see D. Bernard, Susan Fahringer, and Nicola Menaldo, 'New biometrics lawsuits signal potential legal risks in AI' (2020) 3/5, *The Journal of Robotics, Artificial Intelligence & Law* 353–356.
[59] Ibid.
[60] De Hert and Bouchagiar, 'Facial recognition, visual and biometric data in the US'; De Hert and Bouchagiar, 'Visual and biometric surveillance in the EU'.

that effectiveness of bright-line-ruling can be enhanced by uniform enforcement. The Clearview-section exemplifies how collaboration in enforcing the rules can work.

In our opinion, precise laws banning, halting, and sanctioning certain practices are not to be seen as vengeance; as revenge, fighting back against firms and their mass and over-surveilling technologies. Rather, they are to be seen as sincere manifestations of legality. And, when uniformly enforced, they are to be seen as honest manifestations of fairness. If numerous firms are bringing technologies into the market, into the court, into the law enforcement area, into the school, into the employment arena, and into any other domain one might imagine, technologies could be abused by strong entities such as the state, and used against weak parties such as the individual citizen; it would therefore make sense to demand that multiple actors (from investigating entities to administrative supervisory authorities) jointly enforce precise rules from various areas, such as competition or criminal law.

With these recommendations, we do *not* suggest that all tech-pioneers be treated as possible criminals, who should be chased by the entire enforcement-mechanism for designing technologies that might then be abused by the state. Such a far-reaching scenario, an *erga omnes*-regime attacking any tech-developer, would probably *not* be desirable. What is desirable in our opinion is a targeted, clear, and rigorous scheme applicable to those disrespecting legality and fairness at the detriment of anyone – from our children to our neighbours, ethnic or other minorities. If, for instance, a law bans our kids being watched in classrooms or when they play in the schoolyard, because such a monitoring would have a hostile impact on their personality development, their freedom of expression, their privacy, or their very dignity, then maybe the tech-developer that violated that law by selling surveillance cameras to schools should have its criminal record permanently marked to remind society of the harm suffered by those kids. Even though, in this example, no blood was spilled and no kid died of the camera-watching, citizens may want to remember the detriment this for-profit designer caused to our kids, their personality, their freedom of expression, their privacy, and their dignity – things any citizen would die and spill blood for.

11

Lawfulness and Police Use of Facial Recognition in the United Kingdom

Article 8 ECHR and Bridges v. South Wales Police

Nora Ni Loideain

11.1 INTRODUCTION

Police use of facial recognition is on the rise across Europe and beyond.[1] Public authorities state that these powerful algorithmic systems could play a major role in assisting them to prevent terrorism, reduce crime, and to more quickly locate and safeguard vulnerable persons (online and offline).[2] There is also an international consensus among policymakers, industry, academia, and civil society, that these systems pose serious risks to the rule of law and several human rights integral to the existence of a democratic society.[3] These include the rights to private life, freedom of expression, freedom of assembly and association, and equality as guaranteed under the European Convention on Human Rights (ECHR).[4]

---

[1] Nessa Lynch et al., *Facial Recognition Technology in New Zealand* (The Law Foundation, 2020); European Digital Rights, *The Rise and Rise of Biometric Mass Surveillance in the EU* (EDRi, 2021); US Government Accountability Office, 'Facial recognition technology, GAO-21-526' (2021); House of Lords, 'Technology rules? The advent of new technologies in the justice system' (2022), HL Paper 180; Nicola Kelly, 'Facial recognition smartwatches to be used to monitor foreign offenders in UK' (5 August 2022), *The Guardian*; Laura Kayali, 'French privacy chief warns against using facial recognition for 2024 Olympics' (24 January 2023), *Politico*.

[2] World Economic Forum, 'A policy framework for responsible limits on facial recognition' (3 November 2022), pp. 15–18.

[3] Big Brother Watch, '*Face off: The lawless growth of facial recognition in the UK*' (May 2018), pp. 9–19; Pete Fussey and Daragh Murray, 'Independent report on the London metropolitan police's services trial of live facial recognition technology' (July), pp. 5–6; Information Commission's Office, 'The use of live facial recognition technology by law enforcement in public places' (2019), ICO Opinion; Kate Crawford, 'Regulate facial recognition technology' (2019) 572 *Nature* 565; European Digital Rights, *The Rise and Rise of Biometric Mass Surveillance*, pp. 12–13; Biometrics, Forensics and Ethics Group, 'Briefing note on the ethical issues arising from public–private collaboration in the use of live facial recognition technology' (2021), UK Government; Sarah Bird, 'Responsible AI investments and safeguards for facial recognition' (21 June 2022), Microsoft Azure AI; Matthew Ryder KC, *Independent Legal Review of the Governance of Biometric Data in England and Wales* (Ada Lovelace Institute, 2022); Information Commissioner's Office, 'ICO fines facial recognition company Clearview AI Inc more than £7.5 m' (May 2022); Clothilde Goujard, 'Europe edges closer to a ban on facial recognition' (20 September 2022), *Politico*.

[4] On the risks of unlawful discrimination from AI-based systems used for predictive policing, see EU Agency for Fundamental Rights (FRA), '*Bias in algorithms: AI and discrimination*' (2022), FRA

In response to these 'profound challenges', policymakers and researchers have called for law reform that would provide greater clarity on the limits, lawfulness, and proportionality of facial recognition and other emerging AI-based biometric systems (such as gait and emotion recognition).[5] Consequently, some local and state governments in the United States have placed legal restrictions or banned law enforcement use of facial recognition technologies.[6] During the pre-legislative stages of the proposed EU AI Act, the European Parliament has also issued calls for a ban on the use of private facial recognition databases in law enforcement.[7] The world's first case examining the legality of a facial recognition system deployed by police, *Bridges v. South Wales Police*, thus remains an important precedent for policymakers, courts, and scholars worldwide.[8]

This chapter focusses on the role and influence of the right to private life, as enshrined in Article 8 ECHR and the relevant case law of the European Court of Human Rights (ECtHR), in the 'lawfulness' assessment of the police use of live facial recognition (LFR) in *Bridges*. A framework that the Court of Appeal for England and Wales ultimately held was 'not in accordance with the law' for the purposes of Article 8(2) and therefore in breach of Article 8 ECHR.[9] The analysis also considers the emerging policy discourse prompted by *Bridges* in the United Kingdom (UK) surrounding the need for new legislation.[10] This marks a significant shift away from the current AI governance approach of combining new ethical standards with existing law.[11]

Report, pp. 36–48; FRA, 'Facial recognition technology: Fundamental rights considerations in law enforcement' (2019), FRA Paper, pp. 27–28.

[5] Bethan Davies, Martin Innes, and Andrew Dawson (2018), 'An evaluation of South Wales Police's use of automated facial recognition' (September 2018), Report, Crime & Security Research Institute, Cardiff University, p. 43; Crawford, 'Regulate facial recognition technology'; Information Commission's Office, 'The use of live facial recognition technology', pp. 21–22; House of Lords, 'Technology rules?', pp. 76–77. See generally European Data Protection Board and European Data Protection Supervisor, 'EDPB-EDPS Joint Opinion 5/2021' (18 June 2021).

[6] Kashmir Hill, 'How one state managed to actually write rules on facial recognition' (27 February 2021), *New York Times*.

[7] European Parliament, 'Report on artificial intelligence in criminal law and its use by the police and judicial authorities in criminal matters' (2021), Report-A9-0232/2021.

[8] *R (Bridges) v. South Wales Police* [2019] EWHC 2341, High Court; [2020] EWCA Civ 1058, Court of Appeal.

[9] [2020] EWCA Civ 1058 [210]. Other legal issues addressed in *Bridges*, concerning proportionality, data protection, and equality law, are beyond the scope of this chapter. On these areas, see Lorna Woods, 'Automated facial recognition in the UK' (2020) 6 *European Data Protection Law Review* 455; Monika Zalnieriute, 'Burning bridges: The automated facial recognition technology and public space surveillance in the modern state' (2021) 22 *Columbia Science & Technology Law Review* 284; Joe Purshouse and Liz Campbell, 'Automated facial recognition and policing' (2022) 42 *Legal Studies* 209.

[10] Biometrics and Surveillance Camera Commissioner, 'Annual report 2022' (2023), UK Government, p. 6; House of Lords, 'Technology rules?', pp. 27–32; Ryder, *Independent Legal Review*, pp. 62–67.

[11] See generally Julia Black and Andrew Murray, 'Regulating AI and machine learning' (2019) 10(3) *European Journal of Law and Technology*.

11.2 FACIAL RECOGNITION SYSTEMS IN LAW ENFORCEMENT: LEGAL AND TECHNICAL ISSUES

Within a legal context, the use by public authorities of any preventive measures that will indiscriminately capture and analyse the biometric data of a vast number of innocent individuals raises significant questions. These include whether rule of law requirements developed for ensuring adequate limits, safeguards, and oversight for police surveillance systems in the pre-Internet era, such as closed-circuit television (CCTV), remain adequate and relevant to facial recognition systems and other modern internet-enabled and automated monitoring systems; furthermore, whether such novel and powerful AI-based technologies are strictly necessary in a democratic society and respect the presumption of innocence.[12] Privacy and data protection concerns have also been raised regarding the transparency and oversight challenges posed by the increasing role of the private sector within the areas of law enforcement and public security. These developments range from law enforcement use of data-driven tools and systems developed by industry, including commercial facial recognition software,[13] to tasking industry itself with law enforcement functions.[14]

11.2.1 *Facial Recognition Systems in Law Enforcement: Issues of Accountability and Bias*

The use of AI-based biometric systems for law enforcement purposes raises several legal and technical issues. First, there are transparency and accountability challenges that may hinder adequate independent auditing and oversight of their overall efficiency and societal impacts. These stem from the opaque design and operation of commercial facial recognition systems, including intellectual property issues, what training datasets are used, the risk of those datasets being unfairly biased, and how exactly these automated decisions and recommendations are being made (and fairly assessed) by public authorities.[15] The second concerns scientific evidence that facial

---

[12] Deryck Beyleveld and Roger Brownsword, 'Punitive and preventing justice in an era of profiling, smart prediction, and practical preclusion' (2019) 15 *International Journal of Law in Context* 198. See generally Andrew Ashworth and Lucia Zedner, *Preventive Justice* (Oxford University Press, 2014).

[13] For instance, multiple US public authorities have used Clearview commercial facial recognition software for law enforcement purposes since 2020: see US Government Accountability Office, 'Facial recognition technology', pp. 26–28.

[14] See Nora Ni Loideain, 'Cape Town as a smart and safe city: Implications for privacy and data protection' (2017) 4 *International Data Privacy Law* 314; Nadezhda Purtova, 'Between the GDPR and the police directive' (2018) 8 *International Data Privacy Law* 52; Orla Lynskey, 'Criminal justice profiling and EU data protection law' (2019) 15 *International Journal of Law in Context* 162; Sarah Brayne, *Predict and Surveil* (Oxford University Press, 2020); Helen Warrell and Nic Fildes, 'Amazon strikes deal with UK spy agencies to host top secret material' (25 October 2021), *Financial Times*; Litska Strikwerda, 'Predictive policing' (2020) 94 *The Police Journal* 259; Stanisław Tosza, 'Internet service providers as law enforcers and adjudicators' (2021) 43 *Computer Law & Security Review*.

[15] Linda Geddes, 'Digital forensics experts prone to bias, study shows' (31 May 2021), *The Guardian*; FRA, 'Bias in Algorithms', p. 19.

recognition software currently designed and developed by industry, and subsequently used for law enforcement, is biased with a greater risk of false identifications ('false positives') for women and people from black, Asian, and other minority ethnic backgrounds.[16] There is then a risk that such groups may be disproportionately affected by this technology. This is particularly problematic given the need for public trust in police powers being used lawfully and responsibly and existing evidence of racial bias across the UK justice system (and indeed in other jurisdictions), with resulting harms including false arrests and over-policing of already vulnerable communities.[17]

11.2.2 Facial Recognition Systems in Law Enforcement: 'Real-Time' and Historical

Police trials of industry-developed facial recognition systems have been taking place in the UK since 2014.[18] Automated facial recognition (AFR) implies that a machine-based system is used for the recognition either for the entire process or assistance is provided by a human being. Live automated one-to-many matching involves near real-time video images of individuals with a curated watchlist of facial images. In a law enforcement context, this is typically used to *assist* the recognition of persons of interest on a watchlist, which means that police are required to verify or over-ride a possible match identified by the system (a system alert) and decide what actions to take (if any).[19] However, as regulators and scholars highlight, much uncertainty in UK law (and in laws across Europe) surrounds the complex legal framework governing police use of real-time access and historical (retrospective/post-event) of LFR and other biometric identification systems.[20]

In the case of historical (post-event) facial recognition systems, individual's facial data are compared and identified in searches by public authorities after the event

---

[16] Joy Buolamwini and Timnit Gebru, 'Gender shades: Intersectional accuracy disparities in commercial gender classification'(2018), *Proceedings of Machine Learning Research 81 Conference on Fairness, Accountability, and Transparency*, pp. 1–15; US National Institute of Standards and Technology (NIST), 'NIST study evaluates effects of race, age, sex on face recognition software' (19 December 2019).

[17] Dominic Casciani, 'Sarah Everard's murder and the questions the Met police now face' (2 October 2021), *BBC News*; UK Government, 'The Lammy Review: An independent review into the treatment of, and outcomes for, Black, Asian and minority ethnic individuals in the criminal justice system' (2017); Kashmir Hill, 'Wrongfully accused by an algorithm' (24 June 2021), *New York Times*; Jane Bradley, '"Troubling" race disparity is found in UK prosecution decisions' (8 February 2023), *New York Times*.

[18] *BBC News*, 'Leicestershire police trial facial recognition software' (15 July 2014); Fussey and Murray, 'Independent report'.

[19] Biometrics, Forensics and Ethics Group, 'Briefing note', p. 4.

[20] Woods, 'Automated facial recognition', p. 561; Zalnieriute, 'Burning bridges', p. 287; Nora Ni Loideain, 'A trustworthy framework that respects fundamental rights? The draft EU AI Act and police use of biometrics' (4 August 2021), Information Law & Policy Centre; European Data Protection Board and European Data Protection Supervisor, 'EDPB-EDPS Joint Opinion 5/2021'; Biometrics and Surveillance Camera Commissioner, 'Annual Report 2022', pp. 59–60.

Lawfulness of Facial Recognition in the UK

with images previously collected through various sources. These include custody photographs and video footage from CCTV, body-worn police cameras, or other private devices. Both the ECtHR and the Court of Justice of the EU (CJEU) view *real-time* access to these automated biometric systems, as opposed to searching through previously collected facial images, as inherently more invasive.[21] Yet these judgments do not explain why tracking a person's movements or attendance at certain events (such as public protests) over months or years should be viewed as less invasive of their privacy than one instance of real-time identification, particularly given the capacity of these automated systems to identify thousands of individuals using facial images in only a few hours.[22]

Such legal uncertainty would be less likely if these issues had already been addressed in a clear legislative framework regulating law enforcement use of facial recognition systems. As the UK House of Lords rightly points out, while they play 'an essential role in addressing breaches of the law, we cannot expect the Courts to set the framework for the deployment of new technologies'.[23] In other words, it is not the function of courts to provide a detailed and comprehensive legal framework for police powers, though they may provide careful scrutiny of the current law and its application in specific circumstances. This brings us to Article 8 ECHR and its relevance to the landmark case of *Bridges* where police use of LFR was (ultimately) held not to have met the legality requirements of Article 8(2).

11.3 JUSTIFYING AN INTERFERENCE WITH ARTICLE 8 ECHR

11.3.1 *Police Collection of Biometric Data: An Interference with Article 8(1)*

Th ECtHR has described the negative obligation to protect against arbitrary interference by a public authority with a person's private life 'as the essential object' of Article 8 ECHR.[24] It is also well-established case law that the mere storage of data 'relating to the private life of an individual' for the prevention of crime constitutes an interference with the right to respect for private life.[25] The ECtHR Grand Chamber has further held that it is irrelevant if this information collected by interception or other secret measures has not been subsequently accessed, used, or disclosed.[26]

---

[21] *Ben Faiza v. France* [2018] ECHR 153; Joined Cases C-511/18, C-512/18, C-520/18, *La Quadrature du Net and Others*, judgment of 6 October 2020 (ECLI:EU:C:2020:791) [187].

[22] Ni Loideain, 'A trustworthy framework'.

[23] House of Lords, 'Technology rules?', p. 50. See generally Robert Baldwin, Martin Cave, and Martin Lodge, *Understanding Regulation* (Oxford University Press, 2011).

[24] *M.D. and Others v. Spain* [2022] ECHR 527 [52].

[25] *Leander v. Sweden* (1987) 9 EHRR 433 [48]; *Catt v. United Kingdom* [2019] ECHR 76 [93].

[26] *Amann v. Switzerland* (2000) ECHR 87 [69].

Public information has also been held to fall within the scope of private life when it is systematically collected and stored by public authorities.[27]

In determining whether the retention of this personal data involves any 'private-life' aspects, the ECtHR will have due regard to the specific context in which the information has been recorded and retained, the nature of the records, the way in which these records are used and processed, and the results that may be obtained.[28] These standards all derive from the long-established principle in ECHR case law that 'private life' is 'a broad term *not* susceptible to exhaustive definition'.[29] As a result, this concept has been interpreted broadly by the Strasbourg Court in cases involving Article 8 ECHR and any data collection, retention, or use by public authorities in a law enforcement context. Even if no physical intrusion into a private place occurs, surveillance can still interfere with physical and psychological integrity and the right to respect for private life. For instance, in *Zakharov v. Russia*, the ECtHR Grand Chamber held Russia laws providing security agencies and police *remote* direct access to the databases of mobile phone providers to track users contained several 'defects' owing to a lack of adequate safeguards to ensure against abuse, thereby constituting a breach of Article 8 ECHR.[30]

The ECtHR has also shown itself to be particularly sensitive to the 'automated processing' of personal data and the unique level of intrusiveness on the right to private life posed by the retention and analysis of biometric data for law enforcement purposes, particularly DNA.[31] Biometric data (DNA, fingerprints, facial images) are a highly sensitive source of personal data because they are unique to identifying an individual and may also be used to reveal other sensitive information about an individual, their relatives, or related communities, including their health or ethnicity. Consequently, the ECtHR has held that even the capacity of DNA profiles to provide a means of 'identifying genetic relationships between individuals' for policing purposes thus amounts to a privacy interference of a 'highly sensitive nature' and requires 'very strict controls'.[32]

At the time of writing, there has been no judgment to date in which the ECtHR has been required to specifically review the compatibility of police use of a LFR system with Article 8 ECHR. This is surely, however, an important question on the horizon for the Strasbourg Court, particularly as the technology has already featured in the legal analysis of related case law. In *Gaughran v. United Kingdom*, the ECtHR highlighted as a factor the possibility that the police 'may also apply facial recognition and facial mapping techniques' to the taking and retention of a custody

---

[27] *M.M. v. United Kingdom* [2012] ECHR 1906 [187]

[28] *Gaughran v. United Kingdom* [2020] ECHR 144 [63]–[70]; *M.D. and Others v. Spain* [54].

[29] *S and Marper v. United Kingdom* (2009) 48 EHRR 50 [66] (emphasis added).

[30] *Zakharov v. Russia* (2016) 63 EHRR 17.

[31] *S and Marper v. United Kingdom* [66]–[86]; *Gaughran v. United Kingdom* [63]–[70].

[32] *Gaughran v. United Kingdom* [81]. On law enforcement use of this technique in the UK, see Biometrics and Forensics Ethics Group, *Should We Be Making Use of Genetic Genealogy to Assist in Solving Crime?* (UK Government, 2020).

Lawfulness of Facial Recognition in the UK

photograph taken on the applicant's arrest in its determination that this clearly amounted an interference with Article 8(1).[33] Current jurisprudence therefore leaves little doubt that the collection, retention, or analysis of an individual's facial image for the prevention of crime (irrespective of where or how it was acquired) amounts to an interference with the right to private life, as guaranteed under Article 8 ECHR.

11.3.2 *The Legality Requirements under Article 8(2): The Traditional Approach*

Under the traditional approach of the ECtHR in its assessment of whether an interference with Article 8(1) is justified, there is a two-stage test. First, as noted earlier, the ECtHR assesses whether the complaint falls within the scope of Article 8(1) and whether the alleged interference by the contracting state (such as the UK) has engaged Article 8(1). If so, the ECtHR will then examine whether the interference with one of the protected interests in Article 8(1) (in this instance, 'private life') meets the conditions of Article 8(2). The three conditions examined during this second stage concern whether the interference is 'in accordance with the law' (legality), pursues one of the broadly framed legitimate aims under Article 8(2) (including the prevention of crime), and whether it is 'necessary in a democratic society' (proportionality). If a measure is determined not to have satisfied the requirements of the legality condition, the ECtHR will not proceed to examine the proportionality condition.[34]

The traditional approach of the ECtHR, when determining if an interference meets the legality condition under Article 8(2), requires that the contested measure satisfy two principles. The measure must have 'some basis in domestic law' and, secondly, must also comply with the rule of law.[35] In its early jurisprudence, the ECtHR established that the principle of having some basis in domestic law comprises legislation and judgments.[36] The second principle focusses on the 'quality' of the domestic law, which involves meeting the tests of 'accessibility' and 'foreseeability'.[37] As police operation and use of surveillance measures by their very nature are not open to full scrutiny by those affected or the wider public, the ECtHR has stated that it would be 'contrary to the rule of law for the legal discretion granted to the executive or to a judge to be expressed in terms of an unfettered power'.[38]

Thus, as part of the Article 8(2) foreseeability test, the ECtHR developed six 'minimum' safeguards the basis in domestic law should address to avoid abuses of power in the use of secret surveillance. These comprise: the nature of the offences where the measure may be applied; a definition of the categories of people that may be

---

[33] *Gaughran v. United Kingdom* [68]–[70].

[34] On the traditional approach of the ECtHR regarding the legality condition, see generally Geranne Lautenbach, *The Concept of the Rule of Law and the European Court of Human Rights* (Oxford University Press, 2013).

[35] *Malone v. United Kingdom* (1985) 7 EHRR 14 [67].

[36] *Huvig v. France* [1990] ECHR 9 [28].

[37] *Zakharov v. Russia* [228].

[38] *Weber and Saravia v. Germany* [2006] ECHR 1173 [94] (admissibility decision).

subjected to this measure; a limit on the duration of the measure; the procedures to be followed for the examination, use, storage of the obtained data; precautions to be taken if data is shared with other parties; and the circumstances in which obtained data should be erased or destroyed.[39] With regard to police use of emerging technologies, the ECtHR has consistently held that such measures 'must be based on a law that is *particularly precise* ... especially as the technology available for use is continually becoming more sophisticated'.[40] The ECtHR has further stressed, in cases where biometrics have been retained for policing purposes, that the need for data protection safeguards is 'all the greater' where 'automatic processing' is concerned.[41]

This traditional approach, and the resulting legality standards developed and applied therein in landmark Article 8 ECHR judgments, have shaped and brought about notable legal reforms in domestic laws governing data retention and secret surveillance by public authorities across Europe.[42] Scholars have long recognised this impact by highlighting the major role played by this Article 8 ECHR jurisprudence in entrenching and ratcheting up data privacy standards in EU countries and within the legal system of the EU.[43] Based on these Article 8 ECHR standards, these minimum legality requirements seem no less than essential to ensuring adequate accountability and oversight of police surveillance powers. Indeed, as the ECtHR points out, this is an area 'where abuse is potentially so easy in individual cases and could have such harmful consequences for democratic society as a whole'.[44] However, more recent case law dealing with Article 8 ECHR and the legality of police powers has diverged from this lauded approach.

11.3.3 *The Legality Requirements under Article 8(2): The à la carte Approach*

Two key developments in its jurisprudence have contributed to the departure of the ECtHR from its previously lauded role for setting minimum standards in the review of laws governing government surveillance and police investigatory powers across Europe.

---

[39] *Huvig v. France* [1990] ECHR 9 [34]; *Big Brother Watch v. United Kingdom* [2021] ECHR 439 [335]. Although established in the 1990s, some scholars refer to the six foreseeability safeguards as the 'Weber criteria' following *Weber and Saravia*.

[40] *Huvig v. France* (1990) 12 EHRR 547 [32]; *Zakharov v. Russia* [229] (emphasis added).

[41] *S and Marper v. United Kingdom* [103]; *M.K. v. France* [2013] ECHR 341 [35]; *Aycaguer v. France* [2017] ECHR 587 [38].

[42] See, for instance, Lorena Winter, 'Telephone tapping in the Spanish criminal procedure' (2007) 13 *Jura* 7; John Spencer, 'Telephone-tap evidence and administrative detention in the UK' in Marianne Wade and Almir Maljevic (eds.), *A War on Terror?* (Springer, 2010); T. J. McIntyre and Ian O'Donnell, 'Criminals, data protection, and the right to a second chance' (2017) 58 *The Irish Jurist* 27.

[43] David Feldman, 'Secrecy, dignity or autonomy? Views of privacy as a civil liberty' (1994) 47(4) *Public Law* 54–58; Aileen McHarg, 'Reconciling human rights and the public interest' (1999) 62 *Modern Law Review* 671; Lee Bygrave, *Data Privacy Law: An International Perspective* (Oxford University Press, 2014), p. 86; see generally Nora Ni Loideain, *EU Data Privacy Law and Serious Crime* (Oxford University Press, 2024).

[44] *Klass v. Germany* [1978] ECHR 4 [56]; *Zakharov v. Russia* [233].

11.3.3.1 The Hierarchy of Intrusiveness

First, the ECtHR has established that the scope of the safeguards required to meet legality requirements under Article 8(2) will depend on the nature and extent of the interference with the right to private life.[45] This means that the ECtHR will not apply the same strict-scrutiny approach regarding what requirements must be met by interferences it considers to be less intrusive and thus affect an individual's rights under Article 8(1) less seriously.[46] Accordingly, the ECtHR may assess a measure to be justified interference with Article 8 ECHR even if the domestic legal basis does not incorporate the six minimum foreseeability safeguards.[47] Application of this 'hierarchy of intrusiveness' principle is clearly evident in the general legality assessments of the High Court and Court of Appeal in *Bridges* discussed in Section 11.4.

11.3.3.2 The Joint Analysis of Legality and Proportionality

Secondly, and perhaps more importantly, scholars have raised concerns regarding a shift away from the traditional approach of the ECtHR in its Article 8 ECHR case law dealing with data retention and state surveillance. This often takes the form of an assessment that combines the legality and proportionality conditions under Article 8(2) and conflates separate principles and requirements under the distinct conditions of legality and proportionality.[48] From a rule of law perspective, this shift away from the traditional approach to the Article 8(2) stage of assessment is highly problematic as it makes less systematic and clear what is already a case-by-case analysis by the ECtHR. The resulting assessment of the domestic law is often ad hoc, patchy, and invariably less detailed regarding what specific standards contracting states should be satisfying if a contested measure is to be considered compatible with Article 8 ECHR.

Thus, as Murphy rightly notes, this joint analysis has resulted in the ECtHR applying less scrutiny of the accessibility and foreseeability legality tests, thereby serving to weaken the substantive protection of the right to respect for private life provided under Article 8 ECHR.[49] Indeed, the ECtHR may also determine (without

---

[45] *P.G. and J.H. v. United Kingdom* [2001] ECHR 550 [46].

[46] Janneke Gerards, *General Principles of the European Convention on Human Rights* (Cambridge University Press, 2019), p. 222.

[47] See, for instance, *Breyer v. Germany* [2020] ECHR 95. The CJEU has also followed the Art. 8 ECHR jurisprudence of the ECtHR and applies what this author describes as the 'hierarchy of intrusiveness' in its landmark data retention judgments: Ni Loideain, *EU Data Privacy Law*.

[48] Marie-Helen Murphy, 'A shift in the approach of the European Court of Human Rights in surveillance cases' (2014) *European Human Rights Law* 507; Kirsty Hughes, 'Mass surveillance and the European Court of Human Rights' (2018) *European Human Rights Law* 589; Nora Ni Loideain, 'Not so grand: The *Big Brother Watch* ECtHR Grand Chamber Judgment' (28 May 2021), Information Law & Policy Centre.

[49] Murphy, 'A shift in the approach', p. 513. See further Ni Loideain, *EU Data Privacy Law*.

164   *Nora Ni Loideain*

any detailed reasoning) that no rule of law assessment at all be undertaken and that the Article 8(2) stage assessment proceed directly to an examination of the proportionality condition. *Catt v. United Kingdom* illustrates the application of this à la carte approach to the requirements of Article 8(2), where the legality condition assessment is entirely omitted despite being the core issue before the ECtHR.

11.3.3.3 *Catt v. United Kingdom*: The Danger of Ambiguous Common Law Police Powers

The main facts in *Catt* involve the overt collection and subsequent retention of more than sixty records (including a photograph) on an 'Extremism database' concerning the applicant's attendance at protests between 2005 and 2009. The applicant was never charged or accused of any violent conduct as part of these protests.[50] An instrumental factor in *Catt* and *Bridges* is the broad scope of the 'common law' in England and Wales, which allowed for the police collection and storage of information in both cases.[51] Based on the undefined scope of these police powers, and the lack of clarity regarding what fell within the concept of 'domestic extremism', the ECtHR in *Catt* states that there was 'significant ambiguity over the *criteria* being used by the police to govern the collection of the data in question'.[52] A year later, in *Bridges*, the Court of Appeal would also criticise the same lack of clarity surrounding the criteria and limits underpinning the use of LFR by South Wales Police (SWP).

    The Article 8(2) assessment in *Catt* then takes a curious turn. Following a bald statement that the question of whether the collection, retention, and use of the applicant's personal data is in accordance with the law is 'closely related to the broader issue of whether the interference was necessary in a democratic society', the ECtHR observes that it is not necessary for the legality condition to be examined.[53] The ECtHR proceeds to then hold that the retention of the applicant's personal data on this police database, and the fact that this retention occurred based on no 'particular inquiry', constituted a disproportionate interference with Article 8 ECHR.[54] The ECtHR was particularly critical that the applicant's personal data in *Catt* could potentially have been retained indefinitely owing to 'the absence of any rules setting a definitive maximum time limit on the retention of such data'.[55] The ECtHR further observes that the applicant was 'entirely reliant' on the application of 'highly flexible safeguards' in non-legally binding guidance to ensure the proportionate

---

[50] *Catt v. United Kingdom* [8]. The applicant was twice arrested for being part of demonstrations that blocked a public highway.

[51] Ibid., [34]. No specific case law is provided in *Catt v. United Kingdom* regarding the basis for these police powers.

[52] Ibid., [97] (emphasis added).

[53] Ibid., [106].

[54] Ibid., [33], [124]–[128].

[55] Ibid., [106] [124]–[128].

Lawfulness of Facial Recognition in the UK   165

retention of his data.[56] In other words, as Woods rightly points out, this is 'hardly a ringing endorsement of broad common law powers'.[57]

However, despite its recognition of the 'danger' posed by the ambiguous approach to the scope of data collection under common law police powers,[58] the ECtHR sidesteps dealing with the lack of any clear legal basis or any assessment of the six minimum foreseeability safeguards. By departing from the traditional approach in its assessment of Article 8 ECHR, the ECtHR stops short of any detailed scrutiny of these requirements under the legality condition of Article 8(2). This allows the ECtHR to avoid addressing whether the 'common law' basis for police collection of personal data in the UK provides the 'minimum degree of legal protection' to which citizens are entitled under the rule of law in a democratic society.[59] Indeed, the curious decision of the ECtHR not to deal with these clear legality issues, and the resulting lax approach, is subject to strong criticism from members of the Strasbourg Court itself in *Catt*.[60] The latter stressed that the unresolved 'quality of law' questions posed by the contested common law police powers is actually 'where the crux of the case lies'.[61] This à la carte approach to the rule of law requirements in *Catt* is also clearly evident in the assessment of the LFR system by the national courts in *Bridges*, examined in Section 11.4.

11.4 BRIDGES V. SOUTH WALES POLICE: THE 'LAWFULNESS' OF AFR LOCATE

11.4.1 *Background and Claimant's Arguments*

This landmark case involves two rulings, the most significant being the Court of Appeal judgment delivered in 2020.[62] The claimant/appellant was Edward Bridges, a civil liberties campaigner who lived in Cardiff. His claim was supported by Liberty, an independent civil liberties organisation. The defendant was the Chief Constable of SWP. SWP is the national lead on the use of AFR in policing in the UK and has been conducting trials of the technology since 2017.[63] The software used by SWP for LFR in public places was developed by NEC (now North Gate Public Services (UK) Ltd).[64] In *Bridges*, AFR Locate was deployed by SWP via a live feed from

---

[56] Ibid., [119]. Since 2013, this guidance has been issued by the College of Policing.
[57] Woods, 'Automated facial recognition', p. 460.
[58] *Catt v. United Kingdom*, [123].
[59] As held in the leading case law on Art. 8 ECHR, lawfulness, and police powers: *Malone v. United Kingdom* (1985) 7 EHRR 14; *Huvig v. France* (1990) 12 EHRR 528; *Valenzuela v. Spain* (1999) 28 EHRR 483.
[60] *Catt v. United Kingdom*. See Separate Opinion of Judge Koskelo joined by Judge Felici [12]–[15].
[61] Ibid.
[62] [2019] EWHC 2341; [2020] EWCA Civ 1058.
[63] [2020] EWCA Civ 1058, paras 10–26. The Metropolitan Police also conducted ten trials of LFR technology between 2016 and 2019: Fussey and Murray, 'Independent report'.
[64] [2020] EWCA Civ 1058, para. 10. NEC has been awarded contracts for providing facial recognition systems to other police services since 2014, including the Metropolitan Police and Leicestershire Police.

CCTV cameras to match any facial images and biometrics with watchlists compiled from existing custody photographs. SWP would be alerted to a possible match by the software (subject to meeting a threshold level set by SWP) and the police would verify the match, determining whether any further action was required, such as making an arrest, if the match was confirmed.[65]

Mr Bridges challenged the lawfulness of SWP's use of the AFR Locate system in general, and made a specific complaint regarding two occasions when his image (he argued) was captured by the system. The first occasion was in a busy shopping area in December 2017, the second at a protest attended by the claimant in March 2018.[66] Regarding the legality requirements of Article 8 ECHR and use of this LFR system by SWP, the claimant submitted two main arguments. First, there is 'no legal basis' for the use of AFR Locate and thus SWP did not, as a matter of law, have power to deploy it (or any other use of AFR technology). Secondly, even if it was determined that some domestic basis in law existed, it was not 'sufficient' to be capable of constituting a justified interference under Article 8(2).[67] This contrasts with legal provisions under the Police and Criminal Evidence Act 1984 and its related Code of Practice, which specifically state the circumstances that apply to police collection and use of DNA and fingerprints.[68]

The claimant submitted that to satisfy the legality condition of Article 8(2) there must be a legal framework that specifies the following five safeguards. First, the law should specify the circumstances and limits by which AFR Locate may be deployed, such as only when there is 'reasonable suspicion' or a 'real possibility' that persons who are sought may be in the location where AFR Locate is deployed. Secondly, the law should place limits on where AFR Locate may be deployed. Thirdly, the law should specify the 'classes of people' that may be placed on a watchlist, further arguing that this be limited to 'serious criminals at large'. Fourthly, the law should state the sources from where images included in watchlists may be obtained. Finally, the law should provide 'clear rules relating to biometric data obtained through use of AFR Locate'. This should include how long it may be retained and the purposes for which such information may (or may not) be used.[69]

The claimant thus challenged the absence of any accessible or foreseeable legal framework (in legislation or any related Code of Practice) that explicitly and clearly regulates the obtaining and use of AFR technology by SWP (or any police force) in England and Wales. In her role as an intervener before the High Court in *Bridges*, the then Information Commissioner (the statutory regulator of UK data protection law) made similar arguments. While she did not seek to limit the categories of persons who might be included on watchlists, her submission was that the 'categories

---

[65] Davies, Innes, and Dawson, 'An evaluation of South Wales Police's use', p. 13.

[66] [2020] EWCA Civ 1058, paras 27–30.

[67] [2019] EWHC 2341 [63].

[68] Ibid., [64].

[69] Ibid.

Lawfulness of Facial Recognition in the UK

of who could be included on a watchlist needed to be specified by law'. She also submitted that the purposes for which AFR Locate could be used should be specified in law. Finally, she argued that any use of AFR Locate, and any decision as to who should be included on a watchlist, needed to be the subject of 'independent authorisation'.[70]

11.4.2 *Police Collection, Use, Retention of a Facial Image: An Interference with Article 8(1)*

Both the High Court and the Court of Appeal engage in detail, and at length, with the Article 8 ECHR case law of the ECtHR in their assessments that SWP use of AFR Locate amounted to an infringement with the Article 8(1) rights of the applicant. As the High Court states: 'Like fingerprints and DNA, AFR technology enables the extraction of unique information and identifiers about an individual allowing his or her identification with precision in a wide range of circumstances. Taken alone or together with other recorded metadata, AFR-derived biometric data is an important source of personal information.'[71] This determination is unsurprising for two reasons.

First, as noted earlier, the ECtHR has consistently held that the collection and use of biometric data using automated processing for police purposes constitutes an interference with Article 8(1). Secondly (and perhaps more importantly), none of the parties contested that use of the AFR Locate system by SWP constitutes an interference with Article 8(1).[72] Nevertheless, as the first judgment worldwide to hold that a police force's use of LFR constituted an interference with Article 8 ECHR, this assessment in *Bridges* represents an important legal precedent in European human rights law and international human rights law.

11.4.3 WAS SWP DEPLOYMENT OF AFR LOCATE 'IN ACCORDANCE WITH THE LAW' UNDER ARTICLE 8(2)?

11.4.3.1 *High Court Finds Common Law Powers 'Amply Sufficient': No Breach of Article 8 ECHR*

With respect to there being a lack of a specific statutory legal basis for SWP's use of LFR, SWP and the Secretary of State submitted to the High Court that the police's common law powers constituted 'sufficient authority for use of this equipment'.[73] The High Court accepted this argument. In its reasoning, the High Court cited

[70] Ibid.
[71] Ibid., [62].
[72] Ibid., [57].
[73] Ibid., [68].

at length previous caselaw where the extent of the police's common law powers has generally been expressed in very broad terms. In particular, the High Court relied heavily on the controversial majority verdict in the UK Supreme Court case of *Catt*.[74] The High Court gave considerable weight to a specific passage by Lord Sumption JSC who states in *Catt* that at 'common law the police have the power to obtain and store information for policing purposes … [provided such] powers do not authorise intrusive methods of obtaining information, such as entry onto private property or acts … which would constitute an assault'.[75]

The High Court then observed that the 'only issue' for it then to consider is whether using CCTV cameras fitted with AFR technology to obtain the biometric data of members of the public in public amounts to an 'intrusive method' of obtaining information as described by Lord Sumption JSC in *Catt*. Observing that the AFR Locate system method of obtaining an image 'is no more intrusive than the use of CCTV in the streets', the High Court held that such data collection did not fall outside the scope of police powers available to them at common law.[76] Regarding the use of watchlists within the AFR Locate system, the High Court swiftly concluded that as the relevant images were acquired by way of police photography of arrested persons in custody, the police already have explicit statutory powers to acquire, retain, and use such imagery under the Police and Criminal Evidence Act 1984.[77] The High Court also took no issue with the ambiguity of the broadly-framed scope for watchlists that may cover any 'persons of interest' to the police. The grounds for such reasoning being that the compilation of any watchlists 'is well within the common law powers of the police … namely "all steps necessary for keeping the peace, for preventing crime or for protecting property"'.[78]

The High Court briefly refers to the general requirements of accessibility and foreseeability, but there is no mention (or any engagement with) the six minimum safeguards implicitly raised in the claimant's submission on legality. Instead, the court distinguishes the need for AFR Locate to have 'detailed rules' or any independent oversight to govern the scope and application of police retention and use of biometrics (as set out in the ECtHR jurisprudence) on two grounds. First, that facial recognition is 'qualitatively different' from the police retention of DNA that provides access to a very wide range of information about a person and, secondly, it is not a form of covert (or secret) surveillance akin to communications interception.[79] In addition to the common law, the High Court stresses that the legal framework comprises three layers, namely existing primary legislation, codes of practice,

---

[74] This judgment was subsequently reviewed by the ECtHR (see Section 11.3.3.3).
[75] [2019] EWHC 2341 [71].
[76] Ibid., [75].
[77] Ibid., [76].
[78] Ibid., [77].
[79] Ibid., [82]–[83].

and SWP's own local policies, which it considered to be 'sufficiently foreseeable and accessible'.[80]

In dismissing the claimant's judicial review on all grounds, the High Court held the legal regime was adequate 'to ensure the appropriate and non-arbitrary use of AFR Locate', and that SWP's use to date of AFR Locate satisfied the requirements of the UK Human Rights Act 1998 and data protection legislation.[81]

11.4.3.2 'Fundamental Deficiencies' in the Law: Court of Appeal Holds Breach of Article 8 ECHR

In stark contrast to the High Court judgment, the Court of Appeal held the use of the AFR Locate system by SWP to have breached the right to respect for private life, as protected under Article 8 ECHR of the UK Human Rights Act 1998, because of 'two critical defects' in the legal framework that leave too much discretion to individual officers.[82] The Court of Appeal highlights that the guidance (not legally binding) in the Surveillance Camera Code of Practice 2013 did not contain any requirements as to the content of local police policies as to who can be put on a watchlist. Nor does it contain any guidance as to what local policies should contain 'as to where AFR can be deployed'.[83]

The Court of Appeal further criticised the fact that SWP's local policies did 'not govern who could be put on a watchlist in the first place … [and] leave the question of the location simply to the discretion of individual police officers'.[84] Thus, the Court of Appeal took issue with 'fundamental deficiencies' of the legal framework relating to two areas of concern, namely two safeguards from the established ECtHR Article 8 ECHR case law on the six minimum foreseeability safeguards: 'The first is what was called the "who question" at the hearing before us. The second is the "where question" … In relation to both of those questions too much discretion is currently left to individual police officers.'[85]

11.4.4 Beyond Bridges: Moves towards Regulating Police Use of Facial Recognition?

The Court of Appeal judgment represents a clear departure from the legality assessment of the High Court, particularly its determination that SWP's use of LFR does not satisfy the requirement of Article 8 ECHR (via the UK Human Rights Act 1998)

---

[80] Ibid., [84]. The primary legislation is the Data Protection Act 2018, which does not specifically refer to facial recognition technology.
[81] [2020] EWCA Civ 1058 [61].
[82] Ibid., [120].
[83] Ibid.
[84] Ibid., [129]–[130].
[85] Ibid., [91].

of being 'in accordance with the law'. This assessment was long-awaited by civil society and scholars who had consistently raised concerns that police deployment in England and Wales of LFR trials risked being assessed as unlawful if challenged before the courts. Two key issues were the lack of a specific legal basis authorising police use of AFR and a lack of clarity regarding the foreseeability of the applicable circumstances and safeguards by which police services across England and Wales are lawfully permitted to use these automated systems.[86] Indeed, the former Biometrics Commissioner observed in his 2017 Annual Report that the development and deployment of automated biometric systems in use by police at that time was already 'running ahead of legislation'.[87]

The Court of Appeal judgment in *Bridges* thus provides some clarity regarding the 'deficiencies' to be addressed by the current legal framework applied specifically by SWP and its deployment of a specific LFR system. Critically, however, the Court of Appeal also states that *Bridges* is 'not concerned with possible use of AFR in the future on a national basis', only the local deployment of AFR within the area of SWP.[88] Thus, the legality of police use of facial recognition systems (real-time and post-event) across the UK remains a subject of intense debate. Over 80,000 people have signed a petition (organised by UK-based non-governmental organisation Liberty) calling on the UK Government to ban all use of facial recognition in public spaces.[89] In 2022, a House of Lords report and a review on the governance of biometrics in England and Wales (commissioned by the Ada Lovelace Institute) both called for legislation that would provide greater clarity on the use, limits, and safeguards governing facial recognition and other AI-based biometric systems.[90]

In the wake of the *Bridges* case, the Biometrics and Surveillance Camera Commissioner (BSCC) for England and Wales and civil society has also highlighted concerns regarding wide-ranging guidance from the College of Policing,[91] which gives police services considerable discretion regarding the criteria of persons who may be placed on a watchlist for LFR use. The Commissioner has noted that the broad and general scope of such guidance means LFR is not limited to the identification of suspects but may even include potential victims on such watchlists, providing police with a level of discretion that has 'profound' implications for constitutional freedoms.[92] A Data Protection Impact Assessment (DPIA) published by

---

[86] See, for instance, Fussey and Murray, 'Independent report', pp. 8–9. The former Biometrics Commissioner also raised issues regarding the lack of any specific legal basis for the use of LFR systems: Office of the Biometrics Commissioner, 'Annual Report 2017' (2018), UK Government, p. 86.

[87] Ibid.

[88] [2020] EWHC 2341, para. 159.

[89] Liberty, 'Resist facial recognition' (n.d.), Online petition, https://action.libertyhumanrights.org.uk/page/50456/petition/1.

[90] House of Lords, 'Technology rules?', p. 31; Ryder, *Independent Legal Review*, pp. 62–67.

[91] College of Policing, 'Authorised Profession Practice (APP) on live facial recognition' (last updated 21 March 2022), www.college.police.uk/app/live-facial-recognition/live-facial-recognition.

[92] Alexander Martin, 'Police warned against "sinister" use of facial recognition to find potential witnesses and not just suspects' (4 April 2022), Sky News.

SWP concerning their use of LFR confirms the broad criteria for those persons that may be placed on a watchlist, including witnesses and persons 'who are or *may be* victims of a criminal offence'.[93]

It is also important to stress that the standards set out by the College of Policing APP are not legally binding. They also do not constitute a statutory code of practice. In direct reference to its legal context, the APP states that its function is to provide 'direction to [police] forces that will *enable them* to ensure that their deployment of overt LFR [complies] with applicable legal requirements'.[94] An important caveat, however, for police services across England and Wales immediately follows. The APP implicitly acknowledges that such guidance is insufficient in of itself to ensure the lawfulness of LFR and proceeds to specifically advise police that they should obtain 'expert legal advice' to support their use of these systems.[95]

In terms of developing the foreseeability safeguards as part of the legality requirements of Article 8(2) ECHR, it is submitted that legislation should require law enforcement authorities using facial recognition systems to make publicly available the 'threshold value' being applied by public authorities when using these systems. Where the system has been acquired from the private sector, this information should also explain if (and why) public authorities have chosen to depart from the default threshold value set by the company that has provided any facial recognition system(s) to public authorities. Independent scientific research examining the facial recognition systems being used by SWP, and the Metropolitan Police Service,[96] has specifically stated that false positive identifications 'increase at lower face-match thresholds and start to show a statistically significant imbalance between demographics with more Black subjects having a false positive than Asian or White subjects'.[97] Thus, using a system with a lower threshold value increases the number of matching results but also increases the risk of unfair bias against certain societal groups by law enforcement, and should consequently be accompanied by the necessary justification and safeguards. Such information should also be shared in Data Protection Impact Assessments in order to alert regulators (and other independent oversight bodies) of the increased risk of bias posed towards

---

[93] SWP DPIA, 4–5 (emphasis added). The DPIA further states that: 'It is possible that the personal data of individuals aged under 18 years, those under 13 years, a person with a disability or vulnerable adults will be processed where there is a policing need and it is deemed to be necessary and proportionate to locate and/or safeguard these individuals.' See further www.south-wales.police .uk/police-forces/south-wales-police/areas/about-us/about-us/facial-recognition-technology/live-facial-recognition-documents/.

[94] College of Policing, 'Authorised profession practice', p. 5.

[95] Ibid.

[96] The largest police force in England and Wales.

[97] National Physical Laboratory, 'Facial recognition technology in law enforcement equitability study' (March 2023), NPL Report MS 43, para. 1.4.5. https://science.police.uk/site/assets/files/3396/ frt-equitability-study_mar2023.pdf. See further Davies, Innes, and Dawson, 'An evaluation of South Wales Police's use' and their findings and recommendations regarding false positives and threshold value settings by SWP in their trials of FRT in 2019.

certain groups and the safeguards being adopted by public authorities to address and mitigate these risks.

11.5 CONCLUSIONS

While some valuable guidance has been provided by the Court of Appeal in *Bridges*, which draws (albeit in a limited way) on the lauded legality case law of the ECtHR dealing with Article 8 ECHR and police investigatory powers, the current patchwork of law governing police use of facial recognition in the UK falls short of lawful and trustworthy public policy.

As the UK House of Lords rightly points out, it is not for the courts to set the framework for the deployment of new technologies. This chapter argues that the reasoning for this is threefold. First, court judgments are not systematic, comprehensive, or evidence based. Secondly, they represent ad hoc reviews of problematic public policymaking that only occur when (and if) a legal challenge is brought before them. Thirdly, the courts will assess only a narrow scope of issues relevant to that specific case. The implications posed by the lack of an accessible and foreseeable framework for police use of AFR in the UK are significant. This gap represents a source of confusion and legal uncertainty for policymakers, police, industry, courts, and citizens, thereby giving rise to gaps and patchy protection of affected rights and safeguards, including but not limited to the right to private life. These all serve to undermine adequate and effective compliance, oversight, evaluation, and thus public trust in the use of these novel and increasingly sophisticated police powers.

There is, however, a post-*Bridges* discourse on lawfulness that has moved towards enacting a law specifically tailored to regulating use of facial recognition. Such reform could address the current obscurity and uncertainty in the current patchwork of legal rules in England and Wales governing the limits and safeguards underpinning police use of facial recognition, particularly the compilation and application of watchlists. This legislation could then meet the accessibility and foreseeability tests under the legality condition of Article 8 ECHR, the 'minimum degree of legal protection' to which citizens are entitled under the rule of law in a democratic society.[98] Such reform would also enable 'greater certainty and accountability' around police use of AI-based biometric surveillance systems and other emerging technologies.[99]

---

[98] As held by the ECtHR in its leading case law dealing with Art. 8 ECHR, lawfulness, and police powers: *Malone v. United Kingdom* (1985) 7 EHRR 14; *Huvig v. France* (1990) 12 EHRR 528; *Valenzuela v. Spain* (1999) 28 EHRR 483.

[99] Biometrics and Surveillance Camera Commissioner, 'Annual Report'.

12

Does Big Brother Exist?

Facial Recognition Technology in the United Kingdom

Giulia Gentile

12.1 INTRODUCTION

Facial recognition technology (FRT) functions by analysing key facial features to generate a mathematical representation of them, and then comparing these against the mathematical representation of known faces in a database to determine possible matches. This is based on digital images (still or from live camera feeds). In a policing context, FRT is used to help verify the identities of persons 'of interest' to police. State-operated surveillance involving FRT is hardly a novel phenomenon in the United Kingdom (UK). The UK has been the crib of the use of FRT. A technology that initially was used by public entities, it is now widespread also in the private sector.[1] According to a recent study, there are more than 6 million closed-circuit television (CCTV) cameras in the UK, more per citizen than in any country apart from China.[2] These cameras can take images of faces they film and compare them against a pre-defined database of images to determine if there is a match. That means they can be used to quickly identify individuals even in crowded areas such as shopping centres, airports, railway stations, and city streets. Even when a face is partially covered – by a cap or glasses, for example – they can still usually match it up with a stored image.[3]

The extensive presence of FRT in the UK raises concerns from the angle of democracy and individual freedoms: is the UK becoming an 'Orwellian' society where all individuals are monitored, identified, and potentially controlled? As observed in the literature, mass surveillance has immediate implications on privacy rights, but the knowledge gathered through monitoring can be used to compress

---

[1] See comments throughout this chapter.

[2] Silkie Carlo, 'Britain has more surveillance cameras per person than any country except China. That's a massive risk to our free society' (17 May 2019), *Time*, https://time.com/5590343/uk-facial-recognition-cameras-china/.

[3] Scutum, 'Facial recognition CCTV cameras' (n.d.), www.scutumlondon.co.uk/security-surveillance-systems/cctv-surveillance-cameras/cctv-products/facial-recognition-cctv-cameras/.

other individual freedoms.[4] It follows that regulation on FRT should strive to minimise the interferences with privacy, and thus other individuals' rights, if democratic values of human dignity and pluralism are to be truly achieved.

Several non-governmental organisations (NGOs) protecting privacy rights established in the UK became the centre of important strategic litigation to protect privacy rights.[5] For instance, in the *Bridges* case,[6] supported by the NGO Liberty, the Court of Appeal has not only invalidated the use of facial recognition technology by South Wales Police (SWP), but also raised the attention to some unsolved issues regarding the use of FRT for law enforcement. As a matter of fact, notwithstanding the presence of multiple legal sources governing FRT, several legal and ethical issues are still unsolved. Clear legislation on FRT is missing.[7] In which circumstances should FRT not be used? What information duties should be discharged by those utilising FRT? What remedies should exist for individuals to address abuses of this technology? These are only some of the questions that should be addressed by legislators in order to prevent the emergence of an Orwellian society. What the future holds for FRT in the UK remains to be seen. Uncertainty is even higher in light of Brexit and the potential reforms to be introduced in the UK on the data protection framework.[8]

This chapter outlines the framework on FRT in the UK and offers reflections on the future of this technology in that jurisdiction. It is structured as follows. First, it discusses the uses of FRT in the UK and the public perceptions surrounding this technology. Second, it explores the UK relevant legal framework, and highlights its gaps. Third, the chapter discusses the *Bridges* saga and its implications. Fourth, the chapter highlights selected regulatory matters on FRT that are currently unsettled and on which legislative guidance appears necessary to prevent the establishment of an Orwellian society in the UK. Conclusions follow.

12.2 FRT IN THE UK: BETWEEN PUBLIC AND PRIVATE

To assess the impact of FRT in the UK, we need first to explore its use in this jurisdiction. The first observation is *the extensive use of this technology by both private*

---

[4] European Parliament, 'The US Surveillance programmes and their impact on EU citizens' fundamental rights' (2013), www.europarl.europa.eu/RegData/etudes/note/join/2013/474405/IPOL-LIBE_NT(2013)474405_EN.pdf; José R. Augustina and Gemma Galdon Clavell, 'The impact of CCTV on fundamental rights and crime prevention strategies: The case of the Catalan Control Commission of Video Surveillance Devices' (2011) 27(2) *Computer Law and Security Review* 168–174.

[5] See further references in this chapter.

[6] [2020] EWCA Civ 1058.

[7] Kay L. Ritchie, Charlotte Cartledge, Bethany Growns, An Yan, Yuqing Wang, Kun Guo, Robin S. S. Kramer, Gary Edmond, Kristy A. Martire, Mehera San Roque, and David White, 'Public attitudes towards the use of automatic facial recognition technology in criminal justice systems around the world' 2021 16(10) *PLoS ONE*.

[8] UK Government, 'Data: A new direction' (23 June 2022), Department for Digital, Culture, Media & Sport, www.gov.uk/government/consultations/data-a-new-direction/outcome/data-a-new-direction-government-response-to-consultation.

Does Big Brother Exist? 175

and public entities. Starting from the public sector, the first CCTV system in the UK was set up in 1953 in London for the Queen's coronation.[9] By the 1960s, permanent CCTV began to cover certain London streets. Since then, the reach of CCTV surveillance has expanded in sporadic bursts, with many cameras installed in response to the 1990s IRA attacks and then again after 9/11 and the London Underground bombing.[10] Currently, CCTV cameras embed FRT that allows the identification of individuals against the information included in databases managed by law enforcement bodies. Policy documents produced by Metropolitan Police and the College of Policing indicate that FRT can be used to improve the fight against crime and make people's lives safer.[11] Moreover, the British government specifies that CCTV serves four purposes: the detection of crime and emergency incidents, the recording of events for investigations and evidence, direct surveillance of suspects, and the deterrence of crime.[12] In the past, critics argued there is little evidence to support the proposition that its use has reduced levels of crime. An internal report dated 2009 produced by London's Metropolitan Police revealed that only one camera out of every 1,000 had been involved in solving a crime.[13]

However, recent documents produced by the Metropolitan Police indicate that the main advantage of using FRT is that of making manhunts more effective. It was observed that many manhunts for offenders wanted for very serious offences such as murder involve hundreds of officer and staff hours. When aggregated together, manhunts cost many thousands of policing hours across London. By comparison, the four recent trial deployments of live facial recognition (LFR) resulted in eight arrests.[14] It was also reported that LFR deployments provide opportunities for police officers to engage with a person potentially wanted by the police and the courts. Another relevant comparative metric for LFR is the policing outcomes resulting from 'stop and search'. According to a report published in February 2020 by the Metropolitan Police,[15] 13.3 per cent of stops resulted in an arrest in 2019. By contrast, 30 per cent of engagements following an adjudicated alert from the LFR system

---

[9] Philipp Chertoff, 'Facial recognition has its eye on the U.K.' (7 February2020), Lawfare, www.lawfareblog.com/facial-recognition-has-its-eye-uk.

[10] Ibid.

[11] Metropolitan Police Service, 'Facial recognition' (2022), www.met.police.uk/advice/advice-and-information/fr/facial-recognition. College of Policing, 'Live facial recognition technology guidance published' (22 March 2022), www.college.police.uk/article/live-facial-recognition-technology-guidance-published.

[12] Parliamentary Office of Science and Technology, 'Postnote: CCTV', Number 175 (April 2022), www.parliament.uk/globalassets/documents/post/pn175.pdf.

[13] Christopher Hope, '1,000 CCTV cameras to solve just one crime, Met Police admits' (25 August 2009), *The Telegraph*, www.telegraph.co.uk/news/uknews/crime/6082530/1000-CCTV-cameras-to-solve-just-one-crime-Met-Police-admits.html.

[14] National Physical Laboratory and Metropolitan Police Service, 'Metropolitan Police Service live facial recognition trials' (February 2020), www.met.police.uk/SysSiteAssets/media/downloads/central/services/accessing-information/facial-recognition/met-evaluation-report.pdf.

[15] Ibid.

resulted in the arrest of a wanted person.[16] While the enhancement of public security and safety via FRT is a valuable goal, we should not lose sight of the significant implications of this technology on individual freedoms.

Such implications are amplified by the substantial employment of FRT by private entities in the UK. For instance, Clearview AI has collected more than 20 billion images of people's faces and data from publicly available information on the internet and social media platforms all over the world, including in the UK, to create an online database. The Information Commissioner's Office (ICO) has recently sanctioned this company for violation of data protection rules.[17] Further examples are supermarkets such as Tesco, Budgens, and Sainsbury, and start-ups such as Yoti and Facewatch. Such private entities utilise FRT in different fashions. For instance, Yoti, an FRT software, is used in UK cinemas to verify the age of customers,[18] while a growing number of businesses use Facewatch to share CCTV images with the police and identify suspected shoplifters entering their store.[19] Such widespread use of FRT by private entities is likely to cause invasive interferences with individual entitlements. Let us consider, for instance, the employment of FRT in supermarkets and in the workplace. The data gathered through FRT used in supermarkets might increase the potential for profiling consumers and thus limiting their choices based on selected biometric features.[20] Similarly, the use of FRT by employers could potentially facilitate profiling and monitoring employees' behaviours and even emotional states. As a result, employees may be controlled and ultimately prevented from exercising their fundamental rights, such as the freedom of expression. Constraining and regulating the use of this technology by private entities becomes essential to prevent indiscriminate restrictions of fundamental rights.

Another peculiarity of the use of FRT in the UK is that, especially in the field of law enforcement, the deployment of this technology has occurred *via partnerships between private entities providing digital services or infrastructures and public entities*. For instance, the Japanese technology company NEC provides cameras to the Metropolitan Police and SWP.[21] There is no transparency on how NEC was identified as supplier to SWP. The only publicly available information is contained in a series of statements published by NEC's and SWP's websites.[22] This example

---

[16] Ibid.

[17] ICO, 'ICO fines facial recognition database company Clearview AI Inc more than £7.5 m and orders UK data to be deleted' (23 May 2022), https://ico.org.uk/about-the-ico/media-centre/news-and-blogs/2022/05/ico-fines-facial-recognition-database-company-clearview-ai-inc/.

[18] Sofi Summers, 'UK Cinema Association partners with digital identity provider Yoti to ease "proof of age" challenges at cinemas' (27 May 2022), www.yoti.com/blog/uk-cinema-association-partners-yoti-proof-of-age/.

[19] Chris Vallance. 'Facial recognition "watch-list" trial in UK stores', *BBC* (16 December 2005), www.bbc.co.uk/programmes/p03c7srr.

[20] Shoshana Zuboff, 'Big other: Surveillance capitalism and the prospects of an information civilization' (2015) 30 *Journal of Information Technology* 75–89.

[21] NEC, 'South Wales Police – Smarter recognition, safer community' (n.d.), www.necsws.com/case-studies/public-safety/facial-recognition/facial-recognition-south-wales-police.

[22] Ibid.

raises the question of how the selection of specific technologies provided by private entities may shape public services. As a subsequent matter, the issue arises as to what values, principles and rules should guide public–private partnerships in the field of law enforcement, especially when dealing with the processing of sensitive personal data.

The diffusion and evolution of FRT in the UK has led to the development of a system in which civil society has been crucial in casting light on the issues attached to FRT technology and its impact on individuals' rights. The *establishment of numerous privacy-related NGOs* appears to be a direct consequence of the spread in use of this technology on the UK territory. To name but a few, Privacy International, Liberty, Open Rights Group, and Big Brother Watch were all born out of the concerns surrounding mass surveillance in the UK.[23] These entities have contributed to many strategic litigation cases that have shaped the legal landscape of FRT regulation in the UK. The *Bridges* case, discussed in Section 12.4, is an instance of strategic litigation relating to FRT driven by the NGO Liberty. It is difficult to draw a clear connection between the work of civil society in the field of FRT and the impact of advocacy and strategic litigation on public awareness regarding the FRT challenges and risks. However, recent studies have highlighted that the UK public has a contradictory stance with reference to this technology.

In a study conducted by Steinacker and his colleagues involving more than 6,000 respondents, it was observed that while an overall of 43 per cent of respondents supported the use of surveillance, 26 per cent opposed it.[24] In the same study, 39 per cent of the interviewees expressed the view that FRT increases privacy violations and 53 per cent were of the opinion that FRT enhances surveillance.[25] These findings were confirmed by a study conducted by the Ada Lovelace Institute in 2019. The Institute commissioned YouGov to conduct an online survey with over 4,000 responses from adults aged sixteen and above. The survey asked respondents to express their views on a range of uses of FRTs in a number of settings including law enforcement, education, and in the private sector.[26] The report found that support for the use of FRT depends on the purpose. Notably, the study found that 49 per cent of the respondents supported its use in policing practices with the presence of appropriate safeguards, but 67 per cent opposed it in schools, 61 per cent on public transport, and a majority of 55 per cent wanted restrictions placed on its use by police.[27]

---

[23] See https://privacyinternational.org; www.libertyhumanrights.org.uk; www.openrightsgroup.org; https://bigbrotherwatch.org.uk.

[24] Léa Steinacker, Miriam Mechel, Genia Kostka, Damian Borth, 'Facial recognition: A cross-national survey on public acceptance, privacy and discrimination' (2020), https://arxiv.org/pdf/2008.07275.pdf.

[25] Ibid.

[26] Ada Lovelace Institute, 'Beyond face value: Public attitudes to facial recognition technology' (September 2019), www.adalovelaceinstitute.org/wp-content/uploads/2019/09/Public-attitudes-to-facial-recognition-technology_v.FINAL.pdf.

[27] Steinacker et al., 'Facial recognition'.

In light of these findings, it appears that the public perception of FRT in the UK depends on the use of that technology. While this research illustrates that individuals appreciate the potential of FRT in the field of security and law enforcement, the general impression emerging from these surveys is that there is still a lack of awareness regarding the full consequences and impact of FRT on individual rights beyond privacy. This conclusion is further strengthened when one considers the significant gaps existing in the UK regulatory approach to FRT. It is argued that were the implications of FRT on individual rights' protection entirely appreciated, a stronger social resistance against FRT would emerge in light of the current limited framework. The attention on safety and security as one of the advantages of FRT would most likely be reassessed against the worrisome implications that mass surveillance, and ultimately a police state, would have on individual freedoms. The following paragraphs outline the UK legal framework on FRT and its limits.

12.3 THE LEGAL FRAMEWORK

Until 2019, the Law Enforcement Facial Images and New Biometrics Oversight and Advisory Board oversaw the police use of automated facial recognition (AFR), LFR custody images, and new biometrics. The last meeting of the Board took place in September 2019 and alternative governance arrangements are now in place.[28] Currently, two bodies supervise the use of FRT: the ICO and the Biometric and Surveillance Camera Commissioner. The legal framework governing FRT in the UK is multi-layered. It is composed of human rights law, but also by data protection and law enforcement rules. As a result, the rights to privacy and data protection, being the most immediately entitlements affected by FRT, are to be balanced with public security and law enforcement objectives.

The starting point for analysing the UK FRT framework is the Human Rights Act, which gives effect to Article 8 ECHR, protecting the right to privacy, in the UK territory. In addition, the Data Protection Act (DPA) of 2018,[29] which transposed the EU's General Data Protection Regulation (GDPR) in the UK, plays a crucial role in governing FRT. This Act provides the duties for controllers and processors and rights for data subjects. It grants enhanced protection for sensitive personal data,[30] and imposes specific requirements for personal data used in the context of law enforcement.[31] While under EU law data protection is a fundamental right, in the post-Brexit era data protection has lost this status since the EU Charter of Fundamental

---

[28] UK Government, 'Law enforcement facial images and new biometrics oversight and advisory board' (n.d.), www.gov.uk/government/groups/law-enforcement-facial-images-and-new-biometrics-oversight-and-advisory-board.

[29] Data Protection Act 2018, www.legislation.gov.uk/ukpga/2018/12/contents/enacted.

[30] See section 42.

[31] See part 3 of the DPA 2018.

Rights is no longer binding in the UK.[32] Additionally, the UK GDPR framework may be subject to evolution in light of recent plans of the UK Government to depart from the EU legislation and case law.[33]

The Protection and Freedoms (PoFA) Act 2012 is also of relevance, since it regulates the use of evidential material, including biometric material that may be gathered through FRT. Furthermore, mention should be made of the Surveillance Camera Code of Practice, originally published in 2013 and amended in November 2021. This code is an implementation of Section 29(6) of PoFA and is to be taken into account by a relevant authority in the exercise of its functions when involving the operation or use of any surveillance camera systems, or the use or processing of images or other information obtained by virtue of such systems. The code sets out twelve guiding principles, such as that there should be effective review of audit mechanisms to ensure respect for legal requirements, policies, and standards. While this code applies to public authorities, private entities are not constrained by it. The ICO has issued guidance harmonising the Surveillance Camera Code of Practice with the GDPR requirements.[34] In this sense, the guidance has a broader scope than the code. In addition, we should mention that public authorities using FRT technology have produced policy and guidance documents. To name but one example, the Metropolitan Police have issued several LFR policy documents, including Data Protection Impact assessments and the 'Standard operating procedure'.[35] Similarly, SWP has produced multiple documents stating their approach to the deployment of FRT.[36] Finally, several guidance documents, such as those issued by the British Security Industry Association regarding the ethical and legal use of AFR,[37] or the Data Ethical Framework prepared by the UK Government, provide directives on the employment of FRT.[38] The effects and status of these guidance documents is unclear. While they may be used to guide the action of

---

[32] Marco Galimberti, 'Farewell to the EU Charter: Brexit and fundamental rights protection' (2021) (1) Nordic Journal of European Law 36–52.

[33] UK Government, 'Data: A new direction', Department for Digital, Culture, Media & Sport (10 September 2021), www.gov.uk/government/consultations/data-a-new-direction.

[34] ICO, 'Checklist for limited CCTV systems' (n.d.), https://ico.org.uk/for-organisations/uk-gdpr-guidance-and-resources/cctv-and-video-surveillance/guidance-on-video-surveillance-including-cctv/checklist-for-limited-cctv-systems/.

[35] Metropolitan Police, 'Data protection impact assessment' (n.d.), www.met.police.uk/SysSiteAssets/media/downloads/force-content/met/advice/lfr/impact-assessments/lfr-dpia.pdf; Metropolitan Police, 'Standard Operating Procedure (SOP) for the overt deployment of Live Facial Recognition (LFR) technology' (29 November 2022), www.met.police.uk/SysSiteAssets/media/downloads/force-content/met/advice/lfr/policy-documents/lfr-sop.pdf.

[36] See South Wales Police, 'Facial recognition technology', www.south-wales.police.uk/police-forces/south-wales-police/areas/about-us/about-us/facial-recognition-technology/.

[37] See BSIA, 'Automated facial recognition: A guide to ethical use' (1 January 2021), BSIA Artificial Intelligence Series, www.bsia.co.uk/zappfiles/bsia-front/public-guides/form_347_automated_facial%20recognition_a_guide_to_ethical_and_legal_use-compressed.pdf.

[38] UK Government, 'Data ethics framework' (16 September 2020), Central Digital and Data Office, www.gov.uk/government/publications/data-ethics-framework/data-ethics-framework-2020.

public authorities, whether or not they are binding is allegedly different from the law.[39]

Overall, the private use of FRT appears less regulated than the public enforcement. However, the presence of a more developed legislative framework for the public sphere does not equate to effective FRT regulation in that sector. In 2019, the London Policing Ethics Panel advanced several recommendations concerning LFR, such as that there should be enhanced ethical governance of policing technology field research trials, and that regulation of new identification technologies should be simpler.[40] The ICO also issued an opinion on the use of LFR technology by law enforcement authorities in public places, which concluded that the use of that technology should meet the threshold of strict necessity.[41] For example, it was suggested that FRT could be used to locate a known terrorist but not indiscriminately in order to identify suspects of minor crimes.[42] The 2022 report of the Minderoo Centre for Technology and Democracy found that the use of FRT by the UK police did not meet fundamental rights standards.[43] Yet, as mentioned, private parties may also be extremely intrusive when utilising FRT. One may wonder whether this different treatment for private bodies, which are subject to less cumbersome duties when utilising FRT, is at all justified.

In the UK, the ICO, former Biometrics Commissioner, and former Surveillance Camera Commissioner have all argued that the law relating to biometric technologies is no longer fit for purpose.[44] The same point was advanced by the Court of Appeal of England and Wales in August 2020 in its judgment on the *Bridges* case, concluding that there were 'fundamental deficiencies' in the legal framework surrounding the police use of facial recognition.[45] The next paragraphs offer an overview of this case, which is pivotal in identifying existing regulatory gaps concerning FRT in the UK.

---

[39] Giulia Gentile, '"Verba volant, quoque (soft law) scripta?" An analysis of the legal effects of national soft law implementing EU soft law in France and the UK' in M. Eliantonio, E. Korkea-Aho, and O. Stefan (eds.), *EU Soft Law in the Member States: Theoretical Findings and Empirical Evidence* (Hart Publishing, 2021), pp. 79–98.

[40] Ritchie et al., 'Public attitudes'.

[41] ICO, 'The use of live facial recognition technology by law enforcement in public places' (31 October 2019), https://ico.org.uk/media/about-the-ico/documents/2616184/live-frt-law-enforcement-opinion-20191031.pdf.

[42] Ritchie et al., 'Public attitudes'.

[43] See Evani Radiya-Dixit, 'A sociotechnical audit: Assessing police use of facial recognition' (October 2022), Minderoo Centre for Technology and Democracy, www.mctd.ac.uk/wp-content/uploads/2022/10/MCTD-FacialRecognition-Report-WEB-1.pdf; Vikram Dodd, 'UK police use of live facial recognition unlawful and unethical, report finds' (27 October 2022), *The Guardian*, www.theguardian.com/technology/2022/oct/27/live-facial-recognition-police-study-uk?CMP=share_btn_tw.

[44] See Ada Lovelace Institute, 'The Citizens' Biometrics Council' (March 2021), www.adalovelaceinstitute.org/wp-content/uploads/2021/03/Citizens_Biometrics_Council_final_report.pdf.

[45] [2020] EWCA Civ 1058 (*Bridges*) para. 91.

12.4 THE *BRIDGES* CASE

The case concerned the deployment of AFR Locate, a technology that involves the capturing of digital images of members of the public, which were then processed and compared with digital images of persons on a watchlist compiled by SWP. The claimant in the case, Edward Bridges, supported in his action by the NGO Liberty, raised complaints against the use of this technology against him on two occasions and against the use of AFR Locate in general. The watchlists used in the deployments contested by Mr Bridges included, among others, persons wanted on warrants, individuals who were unlawfully at large having escaped from lawful custody or persons simply of possible interest to SWP for intelligence purposes.

At first instance, the Divisional Court declared that Article 8 ECHR was not violated. This was because of 'the common law powers of the police to obtain and store information for policing purposes, and [the fact] that the compilation of the watchlists is both authorised under the Police and Criminal Evidence Act 1984 and within the powers of the police at common law'.[46] The court also found that DPA 2018 and the Code of Practice on the Management of Police information provided a legal basis for the use of AFR Locate. Overall, the 'accordance with the law' requirement laid down in Article 8(2) ECHR was satisfied. Furthermore, the Divisional Court rejected the pleas based on data protection law. Of interest is the way in which the court delineated the scope of the margin of appreciation enjoyed by the ICO. Notably, it concluded that it was for the ICO to assess whether the documents adopted by the SWP complied with Section 42(2) of the DPA 2018, requiring the adoption of a policy document by public entities processing personal data for law enforcement purposes. The court also rejected the claim that SWP had failed to comply with the Equality Act 2010.

Mr Bridges challenged the Divisional Court's judgment and was granted leave to appeal. In its judgement, the Court of Appeal began by considering whether the interference of privacy rights caused by the SWP was in accordance with the law, as demanded by Article 8(2) ECHR. While it found that the action of the SWP was carried out pursuant to a legal basis, it embraced a relativist approach: it advanced the view that 'the more intrusive the act complained of, the more precise and specific must be the law said to justify it'.[47] After acknowledging that the technology involved in the case was different from that considered in previous judgments,[48] the court held that 'the legal framework that the Divisional Court regarded as being sufficient to constitute the "law" for the purposes of Article 8(2) is on further analysis insufficient'.[49] In particular, the Court of Appeal argued that two issues remained

---

[46] Ibid., para. 38.
[47] Ibid., para. 82, citing *R (Wood) v Metropolitan Police Commissioner* [2009] EWCA Civ 414.
[48] *S v UK* Apps nos. 30562/04 and 30566/04 (ECHR, 4 December 2008) and R *(Catt) v Association of Chief Police Officers* [2015] UKSC 9.
[49] EWCA Civ 1058 *(Bridges)* para. 90.

open under the framework in place, the 'who' and the 'where' questions. As a matter of fact, the applicable law did not clarify who could be placed on the watchlist, nor was it clear that there were any criteria for determining where AFR Locate could be deployed. On this issue, the court advanced the view that the legislator should provide clearer guidance on the erasure of data of individuals who are captured by FRT but do not match the identity of any person included in the watchlist. Subsequently, the judgment moved on to the analysis of the Surveillance Camera Code of Practice. The court noted that 'the guidance does not contain any requirements as to the content of local police policies as to who can be put on a watchlist. Nor does it contain any guidance as to what local policies should contain as to where AFR can be deployed.'[50] The court also assessed the documents issued by the SWP, and concluded that they too left unsolved the 'who' and 'where' questions. As a result, the first ground submitted by Mr Bridges concerning the violation of the legal basis requirement under Article 8 ECHR was well founded.

The court then tackled the second ground raised by Mr Bridges; that is, whether the SWP complied with principle of proportionality in the deployment of AFR Locate. The judgment found that the Divisional Court did not err in the assessment of proportionality. While the appellant had suggested that the balancing under proportionality should consider not only the FRT's impact on a single individual, but also on the public as a whole, the Court of Appeal held that the assessment of proportionality should occur as a matter of legal principle,[51] and therefore not in abstract terms. The second ground was thus dismissed.

However, the court allowed the appeal on the third ground submitted by Mr Bridges, notably that the data protection impact assessment (DPIA) carried out by the SWP did not comply with the DPA 2018 requirements. On this issue, the Court of Appeal ruled that, since SWP had failed to comply with Article 8 ECHR, and especially the 'in accordance with the law' requirement, the DPIA was not compliant with the DPA 2018.

Subsequently, the Court of Appeal evaluated whether the SWP had failed to respect Section 35 of the DAP 2018, detailing the first data protection principle. The combined reading of Sections 35, 42 and Schedule 8 DPA 2018 requires public entities processing personal data for law enforcement purposes to have appropriate policy documents in place. The Court of Appeal held that, since the ICO had found that the SWP documents contained sufficient information in compliance with Section 42(2) DPA, the Divisional Court did not err in law. The fact that the ICO had later revised the guidance on FRT and law enforcement could not change the validity of the ICO's opinion on the policy documents. Putting it differently, the updated guidance of the ICO could not have retroactive effects and invalidate the policy documents adopted by SWP.

[50] Ibid., para. 120.
[51] Ibid., para. 139.

Finally, the court considered whether SWP had breached the Equality Act 2010. To address this plea, the court evaluated the robustness of the verifications carried by SWP with reference to the potential biases entailed by the FRT. The court observed that 'SWP have never sought to satisfy themselves, either directly or by way of independent verification, that the software program in this case does not have an unacceptable bias on grounds of race or sex. There is evidence [...] that programs for AFR can sometimes have such a bias.'[52] As a result, the court concluded that the safeguards employed by the SWP were insufficient, and therefore this ground of appeal was allowed.

The *Bridges* saga prompts several observations. First, it demonstrates that the central provision in the reasoning of the parties as well as the court in drawing the boundaries for the use of FRT was the fundamental right to privacy protected under the ECHR. By contrast, the data protection framework was employed to 'compensate' and strengthen the fundamental right to privacy. Through the prism of Strasbourg case law, Article 8 ECHR appears to offer ample guidance to courts on how to achieve the protection of privacy even in the face of technological advancements such as FRT.[53] Second, the *Bridges* case showcases the intersectionality of FRT. This technology does not only impact privacy and data protection rights, but also other fundamental entitlements, such as the right not to be discriminated against. Yet additional fundamental rights could be found to intersect with the use of FRT, such as the freedom of expression or the right to liberty. Third, the case suggests that different understanding of the principle of proportionality and its interplay with fundamental rights can allow for stricter or laxer scrutiny over the employment of FRT. In *Bridges*, the Court of Appeal did not consider the 'necessity' requirement or the 'stricto sensu' proportionality; rather, it carried a soft scrutiny over the choices of the SWP. Hence, owing to the malleability of proportionality, one may wonder whether this is an effective principle to carry a precise scrutiny over the deployment of this technology and its implications. The answer to this matter depends on personal views on the very principle of proportionality. Fourth, one may wonder how much 'law' is needed to regulate FRT. While the Court of Appeal considers that it is not the place of the judges to dictate what the law should look like, at the same time it cast light on selected drawbacks and limitations emerging from the current framework. The Court of Appeal invited the legislator to clarify the 'who' and 'where' questions and to detail rules on the deletion of personal data for individuals captured by FRT. One could think of additional questions and issues that require legislative action. Indeed, the *Bridges* saga highlighted only selected open questions concerning the use of FRT in the UK. The future of FRT regulation in the UK will depend on how the uncertainty surrounding these issues is tackled.

---

[52] Ibid., para. 199.
[53] Ibid.

12.5 THE FUTURE OF FRT IN THE UK

While the *Bridges* case has powerfully illustrated some of the crucial gaps in the current framework on FRT, there are further unsletted matters. To name but a few: For what purposes and in what contexts is it acceptable to use FRT to capture an individual's image? What checks and balances should be in place to ensure fairness and transparency in the use of FRT? What accountability mechanisms should be established for different usages? The list could continue. Several NGOs have produced reports partially addressing these matters. Interestingly, there seems to be convergence towards the (at least partial) halting of FRT under the current rules. For instance, the Ada Lovelace Institute commissioned the Ryder Review,[54] published in June 2022, which recommended that the use of live FRT should be suspended until the adoption of a legally binding code of practice governing its use. The presence of binding rules identifying accountable entities and means of redress for individuals are considered as crucial to enhance the protection of individuals against FRT technology.[55] The report specified that the code should not only address the public use of the technology, but also its deployment by private parties. Furthermore, the Mideroo report on the use of FRT,[56] published in October 2022, went as far as calling for a ban of FRT in the context of police activities. The report justified this recommendation in light of the blatant violations of fundamental rights by way of deployment of FRT by the police.

Interestingly, these proposals are to a certain extent in line with the position of EU institutions. For instance, the European Data Protection Board called for a general ban on any use of AI for an automated recognition of human features in publicly available spaces, as well as for AI systems categorising individuals from biometrics into clusters.[57] Moreover, in the European Parliament there is growing consensus on banning the use of this technology.[58] Whether the UK legislator and authorities involved in the regulation of FRT will reach a similar conclusion requiring the suspension, if not the banning, of FRT remains to be seen. In July 2022, Liberty published a tweet indicating that the Metropolitan Police used FRT at Oxford Circus. As a result, thousands of people walking in that area were monitored and captured

---

[54] See Ada Lovelace Institute, 'The Ryder Review' (June 2022), www.adalovelaceinstitute.org/wp-content/uploads/2022/06/The-Ryder-Review-Independent-legal-review-of-the-governance-of-biometric-data-in-England-and-Wales-Ada-Lovelace-Institute-June-2022.pdf.

[55] See Julia Black and Andrew D. Murray, 'Regulating AI and machine learning: Setting the regulatory agenda' (2019) 10(3) *European Journal of Law and Technology*, https://eprints.lse.ac.uk/102953/4/722_3282_1_PB.pdf.

[56] See Radiya-Dixit, 'A sociotechnical audit'.

[57] See EDPB, 'Joint opinion 5/2021 on the proposal for a Regulation of the European Parliament and of the Council laying down harmonised rules on artificial intelligence' (18 June 2021), EDPB and EDPS, https://edpb.europa.eu/system/files/2021-06/edpb-edps_joint_opinion_ai_regulation_en.pdf.

[58] See Clothilde Goujard, 'Europe edges closer to a ban on facial recognition' (20 September 2022), *Politico*, www.politico.eu/article/europe-edges-closer-to-a-ban-on-facial-recognition/.

by cameras. Such overt and extensive use of FRT in the UK might signify that this jurisdiction is still far away from undergoing a serious reconsideration of FRT's limited benefits and high risks. However, several crucial changes to the current rules seem necessary. These reforms should involve increasing public awareness of the implications of FRT as well as enhancing transparency on the deployment of that technology. Another point that future legislation should tackle is how to ensure that public–private partnerships involving the digitisation of public services respect public goods and values. The opaque co-operation between NEC and SWP suggests that the public is unable to scrutinise how public entities build their co-operation with private digital providers, and therefore how much power private parties have in shaping the public sphere. Until the day such legislation is in place, it is legitimate to ask: 'Does Big Brother exist in the UK?'

12.6 CONCLUSION

The UK has been a crib for the development and deployment of FRT. Since the 1950s, this technology has been largely used in the public sphere, and especially for law enforcement purposes. However, FRT has rapidly expanded, and it is now omnipresent, having landed also in the private sector. As a result, the UK legal order offers a remarkable case study to reflect on the future of FRT regulation. The existing FRT framework in the UK is multi-layered but also fragmented and incomplete. The loopholes of the rules currently in place became evident in the *Bridges* saga. While the first instance court considered the use of FRT by SWP lawful, the Court of Appeal identified violations of Article 8 ECHR, data protection rules, and the Equality Act 2010. Accordingly, the UK judicature has revealed the power of fundamental rights in regulating FRT and cast light on the limits of existing rules. In particular, the Court of Appeal observed that the legislator should clarify who can be placed on watchlists and where the FRT can be employed. Yet additional questions remain open, beyond those identified by the *Bridges* case: For what purposes and in what contexts is it acceptable to use FRT to capture an individual's image? What checks and balances should be in place to ensure fairness and transparency in the use of FRT? What accountability mechanisms should be established for different usages? The list could continue. Several NGOs have called for halting or even banning FRT in the UK. There is general consensus that the current UK framework is insufficient. Until the point when the UK legislator takes charge of enhancing regulation relating to FRT, it is legitimate to ask: 'Does Big Brother exist?'

13

Facial Recognition Technologies in the Public Sector

Observations from Germany

Andreas Engel

13.1 INTRODUCTION

Facial recognition technologies (FRTs) have raised concerns in Germany,[1] and have not been put to use on a widespread basis. This may not be expected to change in the near future, as the current coalition treaty between the German government parties rejects comprehensive video surveillance and the use of biometric measurement for surveillance purposes.[2]

This reluctance to put FRT to use may explain why, so far, the use of FRT has seldom come before German courts: Only fifty-three court decisions out of a total of 1.6 million decisions of German courts in the legal database *juris* include a textual reference to 'Gesichtserkennung', the German term for facial recognition.[3] A search for 'Biometrie', equivalent to 'biometrics', yields 991 decisions.[4] However, many of these latter decisions only have a tenuous link to FRT. These numbers suggest that FRT has rarely been the subject-matter of legal proceedings in Germany.

Nevertheless, there are individual instances in which FRT is already being employed – or has been employed – in the public sphere in Germany. Three prime

---

[1] See, e.g., Der Bundesbeauftragte für den Datenschutz und die Informationsfreiheit, 'Bundesdatenschutzbeauftragter mahnt Zurückhaltung bei Gesichtserkennung an' (2019), www.bfdi .bund.de/SharedDocs/Pressemitteilungen/DE/2019/02_Zur%C3%BCckhaltungbeiGesichtserkennung .html; Dirk Heckmann, 'Gesichtserkennung muss streng reguliert werden' (2020), jurisPR-ITR 16/2020 Anm. 1; see also Marie-Theres Tinnefeld, '… fertig ist das Gesicht – eine Betrachtung im Spiegel digitaler Gesichtserkennungssysteme' (2018) *MMR* 777; Amélie P. Heldt, 'Gesichtserkennung: Schlüssel oder Spitzel? Einsatz intelligenter Gesichtserfassungssysteme im öffentlichen Raum' (2019) *MMR* 285. Note that the manuscript was, by and large, finalized in December 2022, with only minor edits being made in the subsequent publishing process.

[2] Koalitionsvertrag 2021–2025 zwischen SPD, Bündnis 90/Die Grünen und FDP, pp. 15, 86, www.bundesregierung.de/breg-de/service/gesetzesvorhaben/koalitionsvertrag-2021-1990800.

[3] The search via www.juris.de was conducted on 15 September 2022. For the relevance and limitations of such searches, see, e.g., Andreas Engel, 'The ECHR in the German Legal System – A qualitative and quantitative introduction' in Matteo Fornasier and Marella Stanzione (eds.), *The European Convention on Human Rights and Its Impact on National Private Law: Italo-German Perspectives* (Intersentia, 2023), parts 3.1 and 3.2.

[4] The search via www.juris.de was conducted on 15 September 2022.

FRTs in the Public Sector

examples of real-life use cases of FRT in the public sector in Germany will be discussed in further detail.

The first example concerns the pilot study involving the continuous use of FRT without specific cause, conducted at the Berlin Südkreuz train station (which has received a high degree of public attention). The second example is the use of FRT in the aftermath of the G20 riots in Hamburg. Here, FRT was employed to analyse video recordings from mass gatherings to identify suspects. As a third example, FRT cameras are being used in the city of Görlitz to combat serious border crime. In Görlitz, FRT is employed for a limited time and for specific cause. Hence, these examples illustrate different scenarios of the application of FRT. They will be discussed in turn to illustrate specific requirements and challenges, particularly with a view to the varying degree of detail of relevant legal provisions.

13.2 CONSTITUTIONAL FRAMEWORK FOR FRT IN THE PUBLIC SECTOR IN GERMANY

All cases of FRT use take place within the constitutional framework of the Grundgesetz (Basic Law – GG). FRT mainly raises concerns with regard to the right to informational self-determination (Art. 2 (1) in conjunction with Art. 1 (1) GG), which has first been recognised in a decision by the Bundesverfassungsgericht (Federal Constitutional Court – BVerfG) on the 1983 Federal Census Act.[5] Additionally, and depending on the specific context, FRT may affect other fundamental rights, such as the right to assemble (Art. 8 (1) GG).[6] And, even more fundamentally, the BVerfG has acknowledged that the constitution entails a ban on total surveillance,[7] and underlines its importance as part of Germany's constitutional identity: 'It is an integral part of the constitutional identity of the Federal Republic of Germany that the state may not record and register the exercise of freedoms by citizens in its entirety.'[8] So far, the BVerfG has not decided a case that directly involved the use of FRT. Absent a pertinent judgment, a recent decision by the BVerfG on automatic licence plate recognition (ALPR) may provide orientation, and guidelines for FRT can be derived *a fortiori* from this decision.[9] As Martini points out, both ALPR and FRT aim

---

[5] BVerfGE 65, 1; for a recent discussion see, e.g., Philipp Lassahn, 'Datenschutz und Personenschutz' (2022) 61 *Der Staat* 407.

[6] See in particular Heldt, 'Gesichtserkennung', 285, 288. On issues of discrimination, see Stephan Schindler, *Biometrische Videoüberwachung* (Nomos, 2021), pp. 641–666.

[7] See also Timo Rademacher, '*Predictive Policing* im deutschen Polizeirecht' (2017) 142 *AöR* 366, 399 et seq. for an extensive discussion of the reasons for such a ban in the context of predictive policing.

[8] BVerfGE 125, 260, 324, para. 218, translation provided by the BVerfG, www.bverfg.de/e/rs20100302_1bvr025608en.html; see Mario Martini, 'Gesichtserkennung im Spannungsfeld zwischen Sicherheit und Freiheit' (2022) 41(1–2) *NVwZ-Extra* 7 fn. 97 with further references to the jurisprudence of the BVerfG.

[9] BVerfGE 150, 244; cf. Martini, 'Gesichtserkennung im Spannungsfeld zwischen Freiheit und Sicherheit', 7; Stephan Schindler, 'Noch einmal: Pilotprojekt zur intelligenten Videoüberwachung am Bahnhof Berlin Südkreuz' (2017) ZD-Aktuell 5799; for an in-depth-comparison, see Schindler, Biometrische Videoüberwachung, pp. 199–201.

188   *Andreas Engel*

at automated surveillance of the public sphere and would lend themselves as tools for permanent surveillance.[10] Personal data collected via ALPR or FRT can be used to draw inferences about the persons monitored.[11] While ALPR uses information that may indirectly relate to persons, FRT surveillance directly pertains to biometric data. Thus, even higher legal standards would apply to FRT than for ALPR.[12]

Specifically, in its decision on ALPR, the BVerfG has first ascertained the broad scope of the right to informational self-determination (which would be relevant both for ALPR and FRT): 'The right to informational self-determination covers threats and violations of personality that arise for the individual from information-related measures, especially under the conditions of modern data processing.'[13]

The right to informational self-determination applies even in the public sphere, where individuals have an interest in ensuring that their personal information is not collected and stored without their consent (which, again, equally concerns ALPR and FRT): 'Even when individuals go out in public, the right to informational self-determination protects their interest in ensuring that the associated personal information is not collected in the course of automated information collection for storage with the possibility of further exploitation.'[14]

Different stages of data processing have to be distinguished and need respective justification, in particular the collection, the storage and the use of data: 'Regulations that allow for the handling of personal data by government authorities generally justify various interventions that build on each other. In particular, a distinction must be made in this respect between the collection, storage and use of data.'[15]

For all stages of data processing, the basic principles of proportionality, clarity of legal rules, and certainty apply:[16]

> As encroachments on the right to informational self-determination, authorizations for automated license plate checks must be measured against the principle of proportionality. Accordingly, they must pursue a legitimate purpose, be suitable for achieving the purpose, necessary and proportionate in the strict sense of the term. At the same time, they must comply with the principles of clarity of legal rules and certainty, particularly in the area of data processing.[17]

[10] Martini, 'Gesichtserkennung im Spannungsfeld zwischen Freiheit und Sicherheit', p. 7.
[11] Ibid.
[12] But see VG Hamburg, BeckRS 2019, 40195 para. 104–105, hinting at a possible distinction for cases where FRT is applied in the context of crime.
[13] BVerfGE 150, 244, para. 37.
[14] Ibid., para. 39.
[15] Ibid., para. 42.
[16] Regarding the basic principles of proportionality, see, e.g., Bernd Grzeszick, 'Art. 20 GG' in Rupert Scholz, Matthias Herdegen, and Hans H. Klein (eds.), *Dürig/Herzog/Scholz, Grundgesetzkommentar* (98th ed., CH Beck, 2022), paras 109 et seq. with further references. Regarding clarity of legal rules, see, e.g., Udo di Fabio, 'Art. 2 GG' in Dürig/Herzog/Scholz, Grundgesetzkommentar, para. 184, 186. Regarding certainty, see, e.g., Bernd Grzeszick, 'Art. 20 GG' in Dürig/Herzog/Scholz, Grundgesetzkommentar, paras 58 et seq. with further references, also on the relation between legal clarity and certainty.
[17] BVerfGE 150, 244, para. 82.

Proportionality in this context is understood in a narrower sense, as a prohibition of excessiveness. The pursued purpose must be proportionate to the impact on the individuals' right to informational self-determination (the comparatively deeper impact of FRT on individual rights would affect this analysis accordingly, and a more important purpose would be required): 'The principle of proportionality in the narrower sense as a prohibition of excessiveness is only satisfied ... if the purpose pursued is not disproportionate to the weight of the intervention entailed.'[18] To be justified, automated licence plate checks must be prompted by a sufficiently concrete, objectively determined reason. Furthermore, the conditions for a check must meet a certain threshold and allow for compliance review.[19] Checks cannot be carried out arbitrarily or without a valid reason.

Furthermore, the BVerfG stressed that surveillance measures must serve 'to protect legal interests of at least considerable weight or a comparably weighty public interest'.[20] It is crucial to note that FRT raises additional concerns about privacy and the potential for misuse. Thus, the standard for the use of FRT would be higher than for automated licence plate checks.

Moreover, the general framework for surveillance measures must also be proportionate in a broader sense of the term; that is, in an overall assessment:

> In this respect, the legislature must preserve the balance between the type and intensity of the impairments of fundamental rights on the one hand and the causes justifying the interference on the other hand, for instance by establishing requirements regarding the threshold for the exercise of powers, the necessary factual basis, or the weight of the protected legal interests.[21]

From these considerations, the BVerfG derives more specific procedural requirements to protect individual rights: 'In addition, the proportionality requirements include requirements relating to transparency, individual legal protection and supervisory control as well as regulations on data use and deletion for all individual acts.'[22]

13.3 APPLICATION IN SPECIFIC FRT USE CASES

This general framework sets the standard for the application of FRT in specific cases and its legal basis. In this section, the chapter discusses in turn the aforementioned instances in which FRT has already been applied: a pilot study that entailed the continuous use of FRT without specific cause at Berlin Südkreuz (Section 13.3.1), the use of FRT for analysis of video recordings from mass gatherings at the G20

---

[18] Ibid., para. 90.
[19] Ibid., paras 91, 112.
[20] Ibid., para. 95.
[21] Ibid., para. 100.
[22] Ibid., para. 101.

Andreas Engel

summit in Hamburg (Section 13.3.2), and the use of FRT for a limited time and with specific cause in the city of Görlitz (Section 13.3.3).

13.3.1 Permanent Use of FRT without Specific Cause

The federal police (Bundespolizei) from 2017 to 2018 conducted a study at Berlin Südkreuz train station to test the feasibility of the permanent use of FRT in the public sector.[23] The study comprised two phases and was conducted with volunteer test subjects. A reference database was built with pictures of these subjects. During the study, the participants passed by the cameras at Berlin Südkreuz train station and were thus monitored.

As its main conclusion from the study, the federal police stated that the technology employed makes it possible to detect and identify people in crowds automatically.[24] The federal police considered the test scores of the systems as 'excellent' (*'ausgezeichnet'*):[25] During phases 1 and 2 of the study, the average hit rate of the three individual systems employed was 68.5 per cent and 82.8 per cent, respectively. The average false hit rate was 0.12–0.25 per cent in phase 1 and 0.07 per cent in phase 2. The overall system – interconnecting the three individual systems – had an average hit rate of 84.9 per cent in phase 1 and 91.2 per cent in phase 2, with a false hit rate of 0.67 per cent and 0.34 per cent, respectively. These results indicate that the individual and overall systems had relatively high hit rates, with relatively low rates of false hits.

Against this background, the federal police concluded that 'the state of the art FRT systems ... can make a valuable contribution to ensuring security in train stations',[26] indicating a positive attitude towards a potential future use of FRT.

Notably, FRT measures at a train station, such as Berlin Südkreuz, would arguably not conflict with the ban on total surveillance.[27] Even if, at the specific venue, FRT is employed permanently and without specific cause, its application would not cover the exercise of freedoms by citizens in its entirety: As FRT is only used at a specific venue, it only serves to monitor citizens at this venue, but not their conduct elsewhere.[28]

---

[23] See, generally, Bundespolizeipräsidium Potsdam, 'Biometrische Gesichtserkennung' des Bundespolizeipräsidiums im Rahmen der Erprobung von Systemen zur intelligenten Videoanalyse durch das Bundesministerium des Innern, für Bau und Heimat, das Bundespolizeipräsidium, das Bundeskriminalamt und die Deutsche Bahn AG am Bahnhof Berlin Südkreuz – Abschlussbericht – p. 36 et seq, www.bundespolizei.de/Web/DE/04Aktuelles/01Meldungen/2018/10/181011_abschlussbericht_gesichtserkennung_down.pdf;jsessionid=37519C29A2E21493673F09F9BD416715.1_cid289?__blob=publicationFile&v=1; Schindler, 'Pilotprojekt zur intelligenten Videoüberwachung'; Kai Wendt, 'Einsatz von intelligenter Videoüberwachung: BMI plant Testlauf an Bahnhöfen' (2017) ZD-*Aktuell* 2017, 5724; Schindler, Biometrische Videoüberwachung, pp. 195 et seq. (and pp. 190 et seq. for further examples).

[24] Bundespolizeipräsidium Potsdam, 'Biometrische Gesichtserkennung', p. 7.

[25] Ibid., pp. 7–8, 23 et seq.; for a more critical view, see the assessment by the Chaos Computer Club, Germany's largest association of hackers, www.ccc.de/en/updates/2018/debakel-am-suedkreuz.

[26] Bundespolizeipräsidium Potsdam, 'Biometrische Gesichtserkennung', p. 38.

[27] Cf. BVerfGE 125, 260 (324, para. 218).

[28] Cf. Martini, 'Gesichtserkennung im Spannungsfeld zwischen Freiheit und Sicherheit', pp. 7–8.

FRTs in the Public Sector

For the pilot study, the monitored individuals had consented beforehand to the use of FRT. However, without such consent, future permanent employment of FRT without specific cause would need a legal basis consistent with individuals' constitutional rights and legal protections.

At first glance, an existing provision might cover such cases. According to Sec. 27, sentence 1 no. 2 Bundespolizeigesetz (Law on Federal Police – BPolG), which has a broad scope of application, 'the federal police may use automatic image capture and image recording devices to ... detect dangers to [certain specified objects, including train stations or airports], or to persons or property located there'.[29]

However, Sec. 27, sentence 1 no. 2 BPolG does not address FRT specifically and does not meet the procedural requirements that the BVerfG outlined for ALPR, such as transparency, individual legal protection, and supervisory control or regulations on data use and deletion for all individual acts. While BPolG does contain procedural rules (see in particular Sec. 29 et seq. BPolG on data processing and data use), arguably more specific provisions would be required for FRT,[30] as the permanent use of FRT at specific venues would amount to a new level of intensity.[31]

Similar problems arise for provisions in police laws of the Länder (German states) that allow video recordings in general but are not written for FRT specifically.[32]

13.3.2 Use of FRT for Analysis of Video Recordings from Mass Gatherings

A second example, which has even been before a court, concerns the use of FRT for specific cause, the analysis of videos of riots. Hamburg police collected video and image files of the riots at the July 2017 G20 summit in Hamburg.[33] These videos and photos were partly taken by the police themselves, partly from video surveillance recordings from certain S-Bahn stations, partly from relevant recordings accessible on the internet, and partly from privately created image files.[34] The files collected were merged into one large collection of images. Using facial recognition software (which had been specially procured), the police created a reference database that contained digital (biometric) extracts of the faces ('templates') that had been identified by the software in the images of the basic file.[35] The number of templates in

---

[29] On this provision and FRT, see ibid., pp. 8–9 (with a discussion of further provisions at pp. 9–11).

[30] Ibid., p. 8.

[31] Ibid., p. 6; Schindler, 'Biometrische Videoüberwachung', pp. 608–613.

[32] See the list of provisions at Michael W. Müller and Thomas Schwabenbauer, 'G. Informationsverarbeitung im Polizei- und Strafverfahrensrecht' in Matthias Bäcker, Erhard Denninger, and Kurt Graulich (eds.), Handbuch des Polizeirechts (7th ed., CH Beck, 2021), paras 662 (video surveillance in general) and 672 (video surveillance of objects in danger). See, in more detail, Martini, 'Gesichtserkennung im Spannungsfeld zwischen Freiheit und Sicherheit', p. 9.

[33] On the riots, see, e.g., www.dw.com/en/raids-in-four-european-countries-over-hamburg-g20-riots/a-43969633.

[34] VG Hamburg, BeckRS 2019, 40195, para. 3; see also Schindler, Biometrische Videoüberwachung, pp. 214–216.

[35] VG Hamburg, BeckRS 2019, 40195, para. 4.

the database supposedly exceeded 100,000.[36] The database was not connected to or linked with other official databases.

For individual search sweeps, the police made the images of individual crime suspects file-compatible with this software and fed them into the reference database. Hits identified and flagged by the software were further confirmed by clerks. The individual search runs took place on the order of the public prosecutor's office.[37]

The Hamburg Commissioner for Data Protection and Freedom of Information ordered the police to delete this database. Whether this order was lawful hinged upon, inter alia, whether the creation and use of this database conformed with data protection laws.

The Verwaltungsgericht Hamburg (Hamburg Administrative Court – VG Hamburg) held that the order was unlawful. The court saw Sec. 48 (1) Bundesdatenschutzgesetz (Federal Data Protection Act – BDSG) as a sufficient legal basis for the measures in question, even though the provision is written in very broad terms: 'The processing of special categories of personal data [which includes biometrical data, Sec. 46 no. 14 BDSG] is only permitted if it is absolutely necessary for the performance of the task.' According to the VG Hamburg, 'Sec. 48 (1) BDSG is unquestionably a provision on data protection.'[38] According to the court, no more specific legal provision existed for the processing of personal data carried out by the police. Therefore, the court held the provision to be applicable.[39]

Consequently, the VG had to assess whether the use of FRT in this context was 'absolutely necessary' in the sense of Sec. 48 (1) BDSG. The court concluded it was, as a similar review of the data collected by humans would require far too much time and hence would not be a feasible alternative:

> [T]he plaintiff argues ... that processing the image material contained in the basic file by human evaluators would far exceed the time frame for effective criminal prosecution and would take years. The defendant does not dispute the validity of this consideration ... Thus, it is self-evident to consider the establishment and use of the reference database as indispensable.[40]

[36] Jan Mysegades, 'Keine staatliche Gesichtserkennung ohne Spezial-Rechtsgrundlage' (2020) NVwZ 852.
[37] VG Hamburg, BeckRS 2019, 40195, para. 5.
[38] Ibid., para. 75.
[39] Ibid., para. 75. Holger Greve, '§ 48 BDSG' in Martin Eßer, Philipp Kramer and Kai von Lewinski (eds.), *Auernhammer, DSGVO/BDSG* (8th ed., Carl Heymanns, 2023), para. 5 explains in more detail that the use of general clauses is acceptable even in the law of data protection. Greve argues that in cases where fundamental rights are gravely affected by new technologies, Sec. 48 BDSG can apply only for an interim period until the legislator has had the time to draft a more specific provision: Ibid., para 8. For a broader and deeper analysis of the role of general clauses in data protection law, see Nikolaus Marsch and Timo Rademacher 'Generalklauseln im Datenschutzrecht' (2021) 54 *Die Verwaltung* 1, with similar conclusions.
[40] VG Hamburg, BeckRS 2019, 40195, para. 81.

In a second step, the VG considered the constitutionality of the relevant provision.[41] The court held it was decisive that the Hamburg Commissioner for Data Protection and Freedom of Information had not sufficiently engaged with Sec. 48 (1) BDSG and had not tried to come to an interpretation of the norm that would conform with the constitution.[42] The court pointed to a set of aspects that would have merited further analysis by the commissioner.

Among these, the following aspects are of particular interest in the present enquiry: The VG observed that closer scrutiny of the measure's impact on constitutional rights would have been required and that the measure in question might be distinguishable from surveillance without a specific reason. In that context, the court remarked that in the individual search runs, the software would not use further, but suppress, biometric data of the large number of unsuspected persons.[43] Moreover, the court contrasted the measures taken by the police with ALPR, which would amount to a structure that citizens might view as a system of general surveillance. The court pointed out that the analysis of a given set of videos from a specific event might not trigger the exact same concerns.[44]

This decision raised heavy criticism, in particular by Mysegades.[45] Mysegades argues that even in view of the primacy of the law,[46] if Sec. 48 BDSG was an insufficient legal basis for the measure in question, the Hamburg Commissioner for Data Protection and Freedom of Information was able to deem the measure taken by the police illegal (for lack of a sufficient legal basis).[47]

And, indeed, Mysegades puts forwards reasons to doubt that Sec. 48 BDSG was a sufficient legal basis for the measures taken. He points out that the BVerfG in its decision on ALPR established criteria that would apply irrespective of whether an entire surveillance system is being established. Rather, specific aspects would have to be put into consideration, such as the (high and indeterminate) number of uninvolved persons being surveyed, the covert nature of the measure, and a feeling of citizens that they

---

[41] Here, the specific procedural facts of the case were also discussed. As the Hamburg Commissioner for Data Protection and Freedom of Information had issued an administrative act, the principle of the primacy of law came into play. The VG – obiter – expressed grave doubts whether the administrative act – as a decision by the executive branch for an individual case – could at all apply, as it might override statutory law, VG Hamburg, BeckRS 2019, 40195, paras 93 et seq.

[42] In this context, see Greve, '§ 48 BDSG', para. 21 on how Sec. 48 BDSG conforms with the constitution.

[43] VG Hamburg, BeckRS 2019, 40195, para. 101.

[44] Ibid., para. 102–103.

[45] Mysegades, 'Keine staatliche Gesichtserkennung', p. 852. On Sec. 48 (1) BDSG and FRT, see also Martini, 'Gesichtserkennung im Spannungsfeld zwischen Freiheit und Sicherheit', pp. 9–10; Marion Albers and Anna Schimke, '§ 48 BDSG' in Heinrich Amadeus Wolff and Stefan Brink (eds.), *BeckOK Datenschutzrecht* (42nd ed., CH Beck, 2022), paras 11–12; Frank Braun, '§ 48 BDSG' in Peter Gola and Dirk Heckmann (eds.), *DS-GVO/BDSG* (3rd ed., CH Beck, 2022), para. 10; Florian Albrecht, '§ 32 NPOG' in Markus Möstl and Bernhard Weiner (eds.), *BeckOK Polizei- und Ordnungsrecht Niedersachsen* (25th ed., CH Beck, 2022), para. 14b; Moritz Votteler, '48 BDSG' in Andreas Decker, Johann Bader and Peter Kothe (eds.), *BeckOK Migrations- und Integrationsrecht* (13th ed., CH Beck, 2022), para. 5.

[46] Cf. Greve, § 48 BDSG, para. 21.

[47] Mysegades, 'Keine staatliche Gesichtserkennung', pp. 852–853.

were being monitored, which might flow from the broad ambit of the measure taken.[48] In particular, Mysegades contests an argument of the VG regarding the societal impact of the measures. While the VG argued that only those bystanders were being subjected to surveillance and further scrutiny who had willingly gone to the places where riots took place, Mysegades points out that Article 8 (1) GG protects the freedom to assemble, and that this freedom is infringed upon if future participants of assemblies feel the chilling effect of potentially being affected by FRT if they partake in assemblies.[49]

Moreover, Mysegades emphasises that when drafting Sec. 48 BDSG, the legislator had no intention for it to apply to FRT. When the provision was passed, the pilot study at Berlin Südkreuz (see Section 13.3.1) was already under way. Thus, it stands to reason that the legislator could and would have created a more specific provision for the highly contentious and sensitive issue of FRT use.[50]

Additionally, in its analysis of whether the measure was 'absolutely necessary', the VG refers to the necessity of automatic recognition measures for search sweeps within the data collected. Mysegades points out two issues with this approach.[51] The VG in its judgment does not provide a legal basis for all the individual steps of data processing and data collection. This also affects the court's analysis of whether the measure was absolutely necessary. The court held that automatic data processing was absolutely necessary, as processing the data collected by humans would not have been possible within a reasonable time frame. With this approach, the necessity of data processing is being linked to the data collected in the first step. However, the judgment does not answer whether and on what legal basis the data collection itself was justified.[52] One might expect such discussion to be linked to an over-arching goal of the measure, such as prosecution (or, in other scenarios, prevention) of crime.[53]

Lastly, the court could also have considered and given more weight to further risks for citizens' rights, such as potential abuse of the data collected, and, at the same time, the long period of time during which data was possibly stored.[54]

13.3.3 Use of FRT for a Limited Time and with Specific Cause in the City of Görlitz

The third and final example concerns the use of FRT for a specific purpose: FRT is being used in Görlitz, the easternmost city in Germany, located near the Polish and Czech borders. Since 2019, FRT cameras have been used there to combat serious

---

[48] Ibid., p. 854.
[49] Ibid.
[50] Ibid.
[51] Ibid., p. 855.
[52] See also Braun, '§ 48 BDSG', para. 10: the decision 'shows how not to' assess whether a measure was 'absolutely necessary'.
[53] On the background of the provision and for more details on the test whether a measure is absolutely necessary, see Greve, '§ 48 BDSG', para. 15.
[54] Mysegades, 'Keine staatliche Gesichtserkennung', p. 855.

border crime.[55] Görlitz is part of a corridor that is under video surveillance for a distance of 30 km. This use of FRT technology is aimed at addressing severe crimes and enhancing security in the area.

This application of FRT has its legal foundation in Section 59 Gesetz über die Aufgaben, Befugnisse, Datenverarbeitung und Organisation des Polizeivollzugsdienstes im Freistaat Sachsen (Law on the Tasks, Powers, Data Processing and Organisation of the Police Enforcement Service in the Free State of Saxony – SächsPVDG)[56]:

> Use of technical means to prevent severe cross-border crime
> (1) The police may, in order to prevent cross-border crime [as enumerated] collect personal data by the open use of technical means to make image recordings of traffic on public roads and to record information on the place, time and direction of use in order to compare it automatically with other personal data. This applies to road sections in the border area with the Republic of Poland and the Czech Republic up to a depth of 30 kilometres, insofar as facts justify the assumption that the road section in question is of outstanding importance for cross-border crime because it is regularly used as a venue for the commission of criminal acts within the meaning of sentence 1 or for the transfer of property or assets resulting from these criminal acts. The outstanding importance for cross-border crime must be evident from facts documented by the police. Technical and organisational measures must be taken to ensure that such means are not used either individually or in combination on a widespread or continuous basis.
>
> (2) Personal data in the sense of paragraph 1 may only be further processed to the extent that it is automatically compared with personal data of specific persons who are under police surveillance for the prevention of criminal offences within the meaning of paragraph 1 sentence 1.
> The data collected has to be deleted by automated means after ninety-six hours at the latest, unless the automated comparison revealed a match, and the data are required for the prevention or prosecution of criminal offences within the meaning of paragraph 1 sentence 1.
>
> (3) Measures pursuant to paragraph 1, including the determination of those persons whose data are absolutely necessary for [their] identification are to be processed for automated comparison, may only be ordered by the President of the State Criminal Police Office (Landeskriminalamt) or of a Police Directorate or by an official commissioned by them for this purpose. At the latest after the expiry of six months, the ordering police station shall check whether the conditions for the order still exist. The result of the examination has to be documented. The basis for the decision, including the findings in accordance with paragraph 1 sentence 3, which led to the respective operation, have to be documented for each measure.

---

[55] Martini, 'Gesichtserkennung im Spannungsfeld zwischen Freiheit und Sicherheit', p. 11.
[56] For a discussion of this provision, see in particular ibid., pp. 11–13, which also addresses concerns with regard to Art. 10 JHA Directive.

Andreas Engel

(4) The necessity, practical application, and effects of the provisions of paragraphs 1 to 3 have to be examined by the state government. The state government has to report to the Landtag on the result of the evaluation three years after this Act comes into force.[57]

This provision has been drafted specifically for FRT measures.[58] Section 59 SächsPVDG allows the collection and recording of data (image recordings) to compare them automatically with other personal data. This provision, therefore, addresses many of the issues raised by the BVerfG and in the discussion of the measures by the police after the G20 riots. In contrast with Section 48 (1) BDSG, this provision is written in more detail and thus appears less problematic as a basis for FRT measures.

In the first place, the provision clearly states its purpose – it is directed at the prevention of grave cross-border crime. Pertinent crimes are explicitly enumerated in paragraph 1 sentence 1 and include human trafficking, gang theft, robbery, and severe cases of drug trafficking.

To conform with the ban on total surveillance,[59] technical and organisational measures must be put in place to ensure that such means are not used either individually or in combination on a widespread or continuous basis (paragraph 1 sentence 4).

As regards proportionality in a narrower sense,[60] it appears particularly relevant that the provision clearly states and restricts its geographic scope to road sections in the border area, that is with the Republic of Poland and the Czech Republic up to a depth of 30 kilometres.[61] Furthermore, concrete facts documented by the police must justify the assumption that the road section in question is of outstanding importance for cross-border crime, and according to paragraph 1 sentence 4, organisational measures must guarantee FRT is not applied on a widespread basis. However, Martini points out two regards in which this provision may not be sufficiently determinate in view of the requirement of legal certainty: it may not be sufficiently clear (1) when a road section is of outstanding importance for cross-border crime and (2) how far 'road sections' extend.[62]

The use of FRT is also limited in further respects. There is a time limit on the storage of data, and personal data may only be further processed to the extent that it is automatically compared with the personal data of specific persons who are already under surveillance for enumerated crimes. The data collected shall be deleted by automated means after ninety-six hours *at the latest*. If FRT procedures can be completed in a shorter time, the wording 'at the latest' may be viewed as a further guarantee of proportionality, requiring an earlier deletion where possible.

---

[57] Translation by the author.
[58] Sächsischer Landtag, Drucksache (LT-Drs) 6/14791, p. 186; Martini, 'Gesichtserkennung im Spannungsfeld zwischen Freiheit und Sicherheit', p. 11.
[59] See BVerfGE 125, 260, 324, para. 218.
[60] Cf. BVerfGE 150, 244, para. 90.
[61] Cf. Martini, 'Gesichtserkennung im Spannungsfeld zwischen Freiheit und Sicherheit', p. 12.
[62] Ibid.

Section 59 (3) includes further procedural safeguards. Measures have to be based on a specific order and may only be ordered by the President of the State Criminal Police Office or of a police directorate or by an official commissioned, and have to be re-assessed as to whether the conditions for the order still exist (sentence 2). As a further procedural safeguard, the factual basis for this decision and pertinent findings by the police *shall be documented for each measure*. Again, potential criticism might be directed at the maximum period of six months for a re-assessment of the measure, but the wording 'at the latest' allows for a shorter period. Martini argues that further safeguards might be needed concerning supervision and transparency, and in particular, given the gravity of FRT, a decision by a court (instead of a member of the executive) might be in order.[63]

13.4 CONCLUSION

So far, FRT has only been employed in individual cases in Germany. The BVerfG has acknowledged that a ban on total surveillance is part of Germany's constitutional identity. For individual measures, constitutional key considerations concern their proportionality, the clarity of legal rules, and certainty. Furthermore, specific procedural safeguards are required.

This arguably amounts to a high threshold for FRT measures, as the examples discussed show. The permanent use of FRT without specific cause cannot be based on the existing provision Section 27, sentence 1 no. 2 BPolG, as it is not sufficiently specific. The use of FRT for analysis of video recordings from mass gatherings (as after the G20 riots) based on Section 48 (1) BDSG was viewed in a positive light by an administrative court. However, commentators raise the issues of legal clarity and certainty, and point out that the administrative court has not sufficiently explained the proportionality of the measures in this instance. Finally, even a very specific provision on the use of FRT for a limited time and with specific cause has been criticised for a potential lack of proportionality and for not being specifically determinate in certain regards.

---

[63] Ibid., p. 12.

14

A Central-Eastern Europe Perspective on FRT Regulation

A Case Study of Lithuania

Eglė Kavoliūnaitė-Ragauskienė

14.1 INTRODUCTION

In Lithuania, rather than being determined by the intrinsic needs of society, legal regulation of face recognition technology (FRT) came merely as a part of the EU's general data protection framework. Prior to this, the rules governing facial image usage of private persons were regulated mainly by the Civil Code of the Republic of Lithuania,[1] which provides that if a photo (or a part thereof), portrait, or other image of a natural person is to be reproduced, sold, displayed, and printed, the person may be photographed only with their consent – but this is not required if these actions are related to the person's social activities, their official position, the requirement of law enforcement authorities or if the photograph is taken in a public place. However, a person's photo (or part of it) taken in these cases may not be displayed, reproduced, or sold if this would degrade the person's honour, dignity, or professional reputation.[2] In terms of the work of law enforcement institutions, as will be seen from the analysis presented in this chapter, the laws regulating the work of separate law enforcement institutions or laws regulating specific activities of law enforcement (as a general rule) provide that the law enforcement institutions may collect and process personal data, usually without specifying the regime applicable to the collection and processing of biometric data.

As in all of the EU member states, law enforcement institutions in Lithuania have to adhere to EU standards of FRT usage, especially those laid down in the Directive (EU) 2016/680 of the European Parliament and of the Council of 27 April 2016 on the protection of natural persons with regard to the processing of personal data by competent authorities for the purposes of the prevention, investigation, detection, or prosecution of criminal offences or the execution of criminal penalties, and on the free movement of such data (the Law Enforcement

---

[1] Civil Code of the Republic of Lithuania (Identification code 1001010ISTAIII-1864).
[2] Art. 2.22 of the Civil Code of the Republic of Lithuania.

Directive).[3] However, each country also has local national standards that transpose other requirements to the FRT framework and its practical use.

From the perspective of the effectiveness of legal regulation, it should be noted that a country might have a very definite and clear legal rule or a set of rules regulating a particular field of social relations; however, this regulation may rendered as declarative and not implemented in practice. In Lithuania there are some examples of such, and one of the most prominent involves the legal regulation of lobbying activities. At the time of consideration of the Law on Lobbying Activities in the Parliament of Lithuania, one of the Members of Parliament noted that the relations that were going to be regulated were little known in Lithuanian society, so the law was not expected to be accepted in practice. He also said during the parliamentary session that it looked as if the law was aiming to 'prepare cosmonaut suits and then see if there would be cosmonauts willing to try them on'.[4] Indeed, this law (adopted in 2000) was one of the worst examples of legislation in Lithuania, as lobbying activities were practised despite what was stated in it until 2018 – when the law was amended significantly, this time following broad discussions with stakeholders and society. This and similar examples imply that in order for legislation to be applied in practice, it needs to fit both the legal culture and legal system of a country as well as fall in line with the views of wider society.

Keeping this in mind and recognising that society has an important role in controlling the implementation of legal acts, especially where they relate to human rights, the proper implementation of FRT regulations also relies on society and related interest groups deeming them necessary, otherwise they may remain declarative and void. If public awareness and pressure to have a law implemented properly are high, the implementing institutions are forced to take action. Usually, strong players in the performance of social control are non-governmental organisations (NGOs), especially where regulations or their improper implementation pose a threat to human rights. Therefore, it is of major importance that society and NGOs accept and understand the need and the usage of FRT in law enforcement institutions.

This section analyses the regulation of FRT usage by Lithuanian law enforcement institutions, as well as the public discussion relating to FRT usage in the media, NGO involvement, and other types of social control. Finally, the chapter considers what changes may be brought to national regulation of FRT by the EU Artificial Intelligence Act.

---

[3] Directive (EU) 2016/680 of the European Parliament and of the Council of 27 April 2016 on the protection of natural persons with regard to the processing of personal data by competent authorities for the purposes of the prevention, investigation, detection or prosecution of criminal offences or the execution of criminal penalties, and on the free movement of such data, and repealing Council Framework Decision 2008/977/JHA. [2016] OJ L 119, pp. 89–131.

[4] Alvidas Lukošaitis, 'Lobizmas užsienio šalyse ir Lietuvoje: teisinio reguliavimo ir institucionalizacijos problemos' 2(62) *Politologija* 3–42, at 34.

14.2 LEGAL FRAMEWORK FOR THE USE OF FRT IN LAW ENFORCEMENT IN LITHUANIA

In general, the basis for the use of biometric data (including facial recognition data) in Lithuania is the Law Enforcement Directive,[5] which was transposed into the Law of the Republic of Lithuania on the Legal Protection of Personal Data Processed for the Prevention, Investigation, Disclosure or Prosecution of Criminal Offences, Execution of Sanctions or National Security or Defence and other legal acts.[6] Biometric data are classified as a special category of personal data that reveal racial or ethnic origin, political opinions, religious or philosophical beliefs, or trade union membership; they include genetic data and data concerning health or a person's sex life or sexual orientation. Processing of these personal data categories is only allowed when strictly necessary, subject to appropriate safeguards for the rights and freedoms of the data subject, and only where it is authorised by the EU or Lithuanian law – for example, when it is needed to protect the vital interests of the data subject or another person; or when such processing relates to data that are manifestly made public by people themselves.[7]

In Lithuania the collection and use of facial images on the one side, and processing of personal data such as biometric data, on the other, are regulated in law enforcement institutions by different laws and other legal acts. For example, the Law on Police of the Republic of Lithuania provides that with a person's consent and/or in cases established by law, police officers are entitled to take photos and make audio or video recordings. Without a person's consent, a police officer can take pictures of unidentified persons, persons in a helpless condition, unidentified corpses, risk group persons, and temporarily detained persons; they can be measured and their external features described, audio or video recordings can be made, fingerprints can be taken, samples can be taken for genetic testing to perform typification or for comparative research and identification, and all these data can be processed.[8] The law also states that the police can process personal data necessary for the implementation of police tasks, including the personal code, without the consent of the data subject, and that when processing data, the police have the right to collect them using technical means.[9]

The Penal Code provides that the Probation Service may receive data, documents, and other information necessary for the execution of public service sentences (or to get acquainted with this information) from the state, municipalities,

---

[5] Directive (EU) 2016/680, pp. 89–131.

[6] Law of the Republic of Lithuania on the Legal Protection of Personal Data Processed for the Prevention, Investigation, Disclosure or Prosecution of Criminal Offenses, Execution of Sanctions or National Security or Defence (Identification code 111010ISTAoXI-1336).

[7] Law of the Republic of Lithuania on the Legal Protection of Personal Data, Art. 8.

[8] Law on Police of the Republic of Lithuania (Identification code 100101oISTAIII-2048), Art. 22(1).

[9] Law on Police of the Republic of Lithuania, Art. 9(1) and (2).

and other institutions, bodies, or organisations with state information resources. The Probation Service is also entitled to process the personal data of convicted persons.[10]

In criminal procedure there is a general requirement that the use of technical means and their results are also subject to the requirements of public information, personal data protection, the right to inviolability of private life, and the protection of personal honour and dignity established in other laws.[11] This means that all steps in criminal procedure involving the use of biometric data should be in line with the previously mentioned provisions of the Law of the Republic of Lithuania on the Legal Protection of Personal Data Processed for the Prevention, Investigation, Disclosure or Prosecution of Criminal Offenses, Execution of Sanctions or National Security or Defence. It is therefore quite natural that, for example, the Law on Prosecution of the Republic of Lithuania,[12] or the Law on Financial Crime Investigation Service,[13] do not mention handling of any type of personal data at all.

However, a number of laws regulating the activities of law enforcement institutions do not provide clear wording on the possibility of collecting and using facial images. For example, the Law on Intelligence of the Republic of Lithuania provides only that state intelligence institutions have a right to process personal data, without clarifying what kinds of data these might be, and the provision for the performance of particular activities after having received a court permit only mentions 'access to a person's home, other premises or vehicles, their inspection and recording',[14] without a clear reference to collection or use of facial images. Similarly, the Law on Criminal Intelligence does not provide clear grounds for collecting and using facial images; it does not speak about handling personal data at all. This law only mentions that criminal intelligence activities (meaning the activities of criminal intelligence officers in collecting, recording, evaluating, and using available information about criminal intelligence objects) must be carried out in accordance with the procedure established by the law, and that methods of collecting criminal intelligence information are agency activity, survey, inspection, control inspection; controlled transportation; imitation of a criminal act; ambush; tracking; covert operation; and tasks of law enforcement authorities. However, this law also mentions that human rights and freedoms cannot be violated during criminal intelligence activities. Individual limitations of these rights and freedoms are temporary and can only be applied in accordance with the procedure established by law, in order to protect the rights and freedoms of another person, property, or

---

[10] Penal Code of the Republic of Lithuania (Identification code 1021010ISTA00IX-994), Art. 43(1).

[11] Code of Criminal Procedure of the Republic of Lithuania (Identification code 1021010ISTA00IX-785), Art. 260(4).

[12] Law on the Prosecution of the Republic of Lithuania (Identification code 0941010ISTA000I-599).

[13] Law on Financial Crime Investigation Service of the Republic of Lithuania (Identification code 1021010ISTA00IX-816).

[14] Law on Intelligence of the Republic of Lithuania (Identification code 1001010ISTAIII-1861), Art. 9(2) and Art. 13(1).

public and state security.[15] The Code of Administrative Offences also generally states that investigative activities may include photography, video recording, audio and video recording, footprints and casts, plans and diagrams, and other recording techniques.

Regarding the activities of the Special Investigation Service, the handling of personal data is indirectly mentioned in the law that regulates the institution's analytical intelligence activities. It is stated that analytical anti-corruption intelligence means analytical activity carried out by the Special Investigation Service, which includes the collection, processing, comparison of information on corruption and related phenomena with other public or classified information available to the Service, obtaining qualitatively new data that is the result of these information processing processes, and use by and provision to state or municipal institutions and officials authorised to make significant decisions in terms of reducing the prevalence of corruption. The possibility of using available biometric data is provided, as in order to achieve its operational goal and implement the tasks assigned to it, the Special Investigation Service has the right to receive relevant documents from all public institutions.[16] Additional rules are applied in respect of the collection and usage of facial images and the usage of biometric data in the process of issuing identity documents and migration.[17]

Thus, it can be stated that the legal rules on the collection and usage of facial images and generating/usage of biometric data in Lithuania are rather fragmented and vague. As may be seen, in most cases it is stated that law enforcement institutions may collect and process personal data needed for the fulfilment of their duties without specifying any additional restrictions or criteria. Based on the personal nature of biometric data and the rigorous collection and processing of facial images, in accordance with the laws provided here, it is possible that every person may be affected: not only those who are subject to the issuance of personal identity documents or involved in migration issues, or those in any way involved in criminal proceedings or other proceedings that relate to national security and state interests, but also any other persons who act or appear in public places.

The second important issue is that the legal acts implementing the provisions of laws stray even further from the requirements applied to data collection and

---

[15] Law on Criminal Intelligence of the Republic of Lithuania (Identification code 1121010ISTA0XI-2234), Art. 2(7) and 8) and Art. 5(1).

[16] Law on Special Investigation Service of the Republic of Lithuania (Identification code 1001010ISTAIII-1649), Art. 8(1) and (9).

[17] Law on Identity Card and Passport of the Republic of Lithuania (Identification code 2014-21281); Law on the Legal Status of Foreigners of the Republic of Lithuania (Identification code 1041010ISTA0IX-2206), Law on Service Passport of the Republic of Lithuania (Identification code 1001010ISTAIII-1527), Order of the Minister of the Interior of the Republic of Lithuania on the Approval of Rules on Issuing Driving Licences for Motor Vehicles (Identification code 1082310ISAK001V-328), Order of the Minister of the Interior of the Republic of Lithuania on the Approval of Requirements for Personal Document Photos (Identification code 1022310ISAK00000569), etc.

Central-Eastern Europe Perspective on FRT Regulation 203

processing. For example, based on the provision of the Law on Police (the police have the right to collect and process personal data necessary for the implementation of their tasks without the consent of the data subject), all municipalities in Lithuania have adopted separate rules on the use of video surveillance cameras and the data they record.[18] Video surveillance may be established with the aim 'to identify persons who may have committed administrative offences and criminal acts'. Consequently, this means that cameras can be established in any public place and may collect video data on all persons appearing there.

Still, a nonetheless important issue is the processing of the video surveillance data and other facial images. According to the aforementioned and related legal acts, facial images can be stored in a number of databases (which are usually interlinked): the Police Information System and other police department registers and information systems, the Criminal Intelligence Information System; databases of detention facilities (prisons, probation offices, etc.); court and other authorities' databases; databases of institutions issuing identity documents; databases of the Migration Department and the State Border Guard Service; databases of the state enterprise Regitra, which issues driving licences; databases of institutions issuing personal documents; and municipal databases.[19]

In this context it is important that according to the law, as well as to the Law Enforcement Directive and the General Data Protection Regulation (GDPR),[20] 'biometric data' means personal data resulting from specific technical processing relating to the physical, physiological, or behavioural characteristics of a person, which allow or confirm the unique identification of that person. The definition of biometric data in GDPR (as well as in the Law Enforcement Directive) has generally been restricted to mean a technically defined digital representation of bodily traits that has been processed for machine or algorithmic analysis. This is suggested by the wording that data have to be subject to 'specific technical processing'. Speaking more broadly, data processing systems do not need all of the data, but instead rely on extracting meaningful sub-parts from voice or image data, which can then be easily compared to existing 'templates' in a database. This implies that photographs and

---

[18] For example, see Order of Biržai District Municipal Council. On the approval of the description of the procedure for handling video surveillance cameras installed in the territory of the municipality of Biržai district and their fixed video data (Identification code 2022-05136); Order of Tauragė District Municipal Council. On the approval of the description of the procedure for the use of video surveillance cameras installed in public spaces of the Tauragė district municipality and their fixed data (Identification code 2022-07557), Order of Kaišiadorys District Municipal Council. Regarding the approval of the description of the procedure for the use of video surveillance cameras and their fixed data installed in the territory of the municipality of Kaišiadorys district (Identification code 2022-13200).

[19] For more information, see TELEFI Project, 'Towards the European level exchange of facial images' (7 February 2020), Legal analysis for TELEFI project, www.telefi-project.eu/sites/default/files/TELEFI_LegalAnalysis.pdf

[20] Regulation (EU) 2016/679 of the European Parliament and of the Council of 27 April 2016 on the protection of natural persons with regard to the processing of personal data and on the free movement of such data, and repealing Directive 95/46/EC (General Data Protection Regulation) (2016) OJ L 119.

video images of faces are expressly excluded from the definition of biometric data both in GDPR and the Law Enforcement Directive.[21] Therefore, there is a difference between the regulatory rules applied in respect of data images (which may be regarded as personal data) and images processed with FRT technology (which then is regarded as biometric data).

To summarise, in Lithuania there is quite a significant gap between the regulatory rules that set requirements for FRT from a data protection perspective and rules regulating activities of separate law enforcement institutions and law enforcement activities. Although the standards of data protection in general seem to be sufficient, the specific laws on law enforcement institutions solely provide the possibility to collect and process personal data, including facial images, without making it known whether FRT will be used to process such images or not. Therefore, there is a possibility that the general data protection rules are only declarative and not enforced in practice. Thus, in order to understand whether the legal regulation of FRT usage in Lithuanian law enforcement is sufficient, a deeper analysis of the practical implementation of regulatory rules on the usage of FRT in Lithuania is needed.

14.3 FRT USAGE IN PRACTICE

According to the respondents to the Government Use of Facial Recognition Technologies: Legal Challenges and Solutions project,[22] the volume of FRT usage in law enforcement institutions is not clear. In the course of this project the team sought to interview representatives from the institutions that are responsible for (or directly participate in) the processing of personal data, including facial images and biometric data. However, only very few representatives were willing to participate, whereas others stated they had insufficient knowledge of or competence in these issues. Moreover, according to a couple of respondents from the private sector, who were trying to investigate the use of FRT in the context of human rights, the representatives of law enforcement institutions disclosed to them that they felt comfortable as they benefited from having considerable latitude for when and how to use FRT as a result of the vague legal background.

As an example of insufficient regulatory basis for handling biometric data, including facial data processed using FRT, the case of the Register of Habitoscopic Data of the Republic of Lithuania may be analysed. This is a component of the Internal Affairs Information System – a general system for storing detailed personal identification data in a single database, which stores data on convicted persons, persons who have served a sentence of arrest or fixed-term imprisonment in the Republic of

---

[21] Amba Kak, 'Regulating biometrics: Global approaches and urgent questions' (1 September 2020), AI Now Institute, https://ainowinstitute.org/publication/regulating-biometrics-global-approaches-and-open-questions, p. 20.

[22] Government use of facial recognition technologies: Legal challenges and solutions (Face-AI). Project funded by the Research Council of Lithuania, contract No. S-MIP-21–38.

Central-Eastern Europe Perspective on FRT Regulation

Lithuania, temporarily detained persons suspected of having committed a criminal act, wanted persons, identification marks of unidentified dead bodies or unknown helpless persons, and other categories. This data is used by pre-trial investigation institutions, border protection, customs, the prosecutor's office and other law enforcement institutions in order to ensure the prevention of criminal acts and the fight against crime. It processes personal data for the following purposes: (1) to investigate criminal acts and ensure their prevention, organise, and carry out the search for persons, as well as to identify both unidentified corpses and unknown helpless persons according to personal identification marks; and (2) to determine the identity of a person in order to ensure the control of the movement of foreigners who have been detained by the competent control authorities for illegally crossing the state border by sea, land, or air from a third country and who have not been returned to that country.[23] The Register of Habitoscopic Data contains data on the external characteristics of a person, obtained by photographing, measuring, and describing the person's appearance. According to this definition and the list of processed data presented in the same Order, the Register of Habitoscopic Data processes personal data that does not fall under the definition of biometric personal data, meaning no additional rules on the processing of biometric data should apply. The Order does not mention or otherwise provide grounds for processing of FRT-related biometric data. However, there was a public announcement in the media about the reorganisation and improvement of the Register of Habitoscopic Data through the 'Modernisation of Register of Habitoscopic Data using advanced technologies of face recognition and identification tag search' project.[24] The project description states:

> [I]n the course of project activities, the Personal Face Biometric Recognition subsystem of the Register of Habitoscopic Data was modernized; using advanced facial biometric recognition technologies, the accuracy, performance, and reliability of personal facial biometric recognition was improved. Facial biometric recognition functions of the Register of Habitoscopic Data were modernised using high- facial biometric recognition software (NeoFace Watch, manufactured by NEC Corporation), which enables software users to perform facial biometric recognition (1:1; 1:N) in indirect mode, using digital facial photographs, and face-to-face biometric recognition (N:N) in live mode using real-time IP video cameras. Purchased facial biometric recognition software also includes a specially designed

---

[23] Order of Minister of the Interior of the Republic of Lithuania: On the reorganisation of the departmental register of identification marks of persons who have served a sentence of arrest or fixed-term imprisonment into a Register of Habitoscopic data (Identification code 1132310ISAK001V-440), para. 4.

[24] 'As part of the project funded by the Internal Security Fund, the Habitoscopic Data Register was modernised to introduce advanced biometric recognition technologies for a person's face.' IRD, 'Įgyvendinant Vidaus saugumo fondo lėšomis finansuojamą projektą modernizuotas Habitoskopinių duomenų registras – įdiegtos pažangios asmens veido biometrinio atpažinimo technologijos' (5 April 2020), https://ird.lt/lt/naujienos/igyvendinant-vidaus-saugumo-fondo-lesomis-finansuojama-projekta-modernizuotas-habitoskopiniu-duomenu-registras-idiegtos-pazangios-asmens-veido-biometrinio-atpazinimo-technologijos.

software component for smart devices. The 'Face Recognition' application of a smart device provides an opportunity for mobile face recognition of a person, that is, taking a picture of a person with a phone and performing a search (recognition) of the face image of such a person based on the captured face image data in the database of the Register of Habitoscopic Data.[25]

The Police Department website provides information about a related project. It is stated that:

> [This aims to] create a uniform system for collecting personal identification marks and biometric data and submitting them to the Register of Habitoscopic Data of the Ministry of the Interior of the Republic of Lithuania. After the implementation of the project, sixteen specialised workstations for collecting personal identification marks and biometric data and submitting them to the Register of Habitoscopic Data were established in the main police commissariats and detention centres of the country's counties. It became possible to capture images of unidentified persons, take biometric data, as well as other data of an event related to a person, process them in police custody and detention facilities, register them, and transfer them to be recorded in the Register of Habitoscopic Data. After arresting a person suspected of having committed a crime, it is possible to promptly compare the person's biometric data with the data contained in the HDR – in this way, this data will be used to reveal criminal acts faster, determine the identity of the person, conduct investigations more efficiently, conduct forensic investigations faster, and, with better quality, ensure crime prevention, public order, and public safety.[26]

However, as mentioned earlier, there is no legal ground for processing biometric personal data in the Register of Habitoscopic Data, nor are there security measures to be applied in order to ensure the protection of biometric personal data based on the criteria established in the Law Enforcement Directive and the Law of the Republic of Lithuania on the Legal Protection of Personal Data Processed for the Prevention, Investigation, Disclosure or Prosecution of Criminal Offenses, Execution of Sanctions or National Security or Defence. Furthermore, there are no terms for storage of biometric data (data processed by facial recognition technologies that allows identification of a specific person) in the Register of Habitoscopic Data.

Moreover, the Order of the Minister of the Interior establishing the Register of Habitoscopic Data allows the linking of the Register of Habitoscopic Data with other state registers (Residents' Register, Addresses' Register, Register of Application

---

[25] IRD, 'Įgyvendinant Vidaus saugumo fondo lėšomis finansuojamą projektą modernizuotas Habitoskopinių duomenų registras – įdiegtos pažangios asmens veido biometrinio atpažinimo technologijos' (4 May 2020), https://ird.lt/lt/naujienos/igyvendinant-vidaus-saugumo-fondo-lesomis-finansuojama-projekta-modernizuotas-habitoskopiniu-duomenu-registras-idiegtos-pazangios-asmens-veido-biometrinio-atpazinimo-technologijos.

[26] Lietuvos policija, 'Sukurta vienoda asmens atpažinimo žymių ir biometrinių duomenų rinkimo Sistema' (13 August 2020), Lietuvos policija, https://policija.lrv.lt/lt/naujienos/sukurta-vienoda-asmens-atpazinimo-zymiu-ir-biometriniu-duomenu-rinkimo-sistema.

of Preventive Measures, Official Register of Wanted Persons, Unidentified Corpses and Unknown Helpless Persons, Register of Suspected, Accused and Convicted Persons, Official Register of Criminal Acts, Register of Dactyloscopic Data, Register of DNA Data, Register of Foreigners, and Register of Events registered by the Police). However, in the description of the 'Modernisation of Register of Habitoscopic Data using advanced technologies of face recognition and identification tag search' project, it is stated that 'three new integration interfaces have been created: with the Integrated Criminal Procedure Information System (IBPS), the Register of Administrative Offences (ANR), and the Lithuanian National Second Generation Schengen Information System (N.SIS)'. In other words, the Register of Habitoscopic Data has interconnections with other registers that are not found in the relevant regulatory document.

The Ministry of the Interior of the Republic of Lithuania was officially asked to provide an explanation of the differences between the current regulatory framework for the operation of the Register of Habitoscopic Data and the declared updates to the register, which are said to have been already implemented.[27] However, no response was received.

Such a situation implies not only that the regulation of collection of facial images (which falls outside the scope of 'biometric data' definition) and the processing of such images to generate biometric data is not regulated properly, but also that the current practices (given no information is provided about any unpublished legal regulations – which is unlikely given the requirements of transparency in the field of human rights and data protection) are likely to be in breach of the existing legal basis for such activities. First, as already mentioned, the data and information, as regulated by the Order of the Minister of the Interior on the Register of Habitoscopic Data, would be limited only to facial images and their description, with digital processing using FRT not being mentioned. The use of FRT brings the activities of the

---

[27] On 14 June 2022, an official letter was sent from the Law Institute of the Lithuanian Centre for Social Sciences to the Ministry of the Interior kindly requesting to indicate the legal basis on which biometric personal data are processed in the Register of Habitoscopic Data and to indicate what security measures are applied in order to ensure the protection of biometric personal data based on the criteria established in the law; to specify the Register of Habitoscopic Data (including database archive) storage terms of biometric data (data processed by facial recognition technologies that allow identification of a specific person) and the legal basis for their regulation; to indicate whether there are integrations of the Register of Habitoscopic Data with other databases/registries (e.g., the register of events registered by the police or the traffic accident information system), to submit the legal act/s regulating Order/s No. 1V-440 linking of registers/databases not mentioned in the Order itself; to specify which data not mentioned in the Order are transferred between the Registers. Finally, it was asked to provide legal regulation (references to specific legal acts and their structural parts, and if these legal acts are not published publicly – to attach their copies), establishing restrictions on the processing of personal images obtained from other registers with FRTs and to describe how this is implemented in practice (e.g., if a person is suspected of having committed an administrative offence, will the image of the suspect from the available video/photo material be processed by facial recognition technology in all cases, and in which cases is this not done), and to indicate the specific legal regulation.

Register to a different level of legal requirement – that is, the obligation to conform with the rules applicable to biometric data processing. Second, the interconnections between the Register of Habitoscopic Data and other registers are not clear. It appears that in practice there are links to more registers than provided in the relevant Order of the Minister of the Interior, however, it is not clear what data could be exchanged. It should also be noted that a special Order of the Commissioner General of the Police restricts the transfer of facial image data (received via public surveillance cameras) to state registers to situations when there is a need to verify or specify information on a particular criminal or administrative offence.[28] However, it is still plausible that all facial images of both recognised and unrecognised persons, who may be captured by video or photo cameras established for public surveillance by accident and without taking any part in an offence, could be automatically processed for facial biometric data.

14.4 PUBLIC ACCEPTANCE OF THE USAGE OF FRT BY GOVERNMENT AUTHORITIES IN LITHUANIA

To begin with, the issues surrounding FRT usage by Lithuanian government authorities are not commonly mentioned in media, NGOs, or social networks. Similarly, as with all advances in artificial intelligence (AI), FRT is welcomed positively as a facilitator of general life in Lithuania. For example, the Strategy of Artificial Intelligence in Lithuania encourages integrating AI, including FRT, into all economic sectors. Specifically, regarding the public sector, it is stated that AI will be helpful in the field of crime control, optimising the daily work of public institutions and improving the provision of public services.[29] In particular, the optimisation of work is a rather attractive promise for most institutions – for example, the Kaunas Information Technology School carried out the 'Attendance Marking Powered by Face Recognition' project, which revealed that teachers would save time significantly if attendance of students was checked by using FRT rather than manually.[30] Moreover, FRT was even suggested as a practical solution for simplifying the checking of persons who had been vaccinated against COVID-19, with proposals to use FRT instead of the official 'opportunities passport' system, which was declared to be

---

[28] Lietuvos Policijos Generalinis Komisaras, 'Order of the Commissioner General of the Police Department under the Ministry of the Interior of the Republic of Lithuania on the approval of rules for processing data captured by video surveillance in police institutions' (19 February 2020), Paras 3 and 4. Lietuvos Policijos Generalinis Komisaras, https://policija.lrv.lt/uploads/policija/documents/files/Vaizdo%20stebejimo%20duomenu%20tvarkymo%20taisykles.pdf.

[29] Ministry of Economics and Innovation of the Republic of Lithuania, 'Strategy of artificial intelligence in Lithuania' (n.d.), https://eimin.lrv.lt/uploads/eimin/documents/files/DI_strategija_LT(1).pdf.

[30] Paulius Briedis, 'Attendance marking powered by Face Recognition' (2022) (KA2 Strategic partnerships project, Introducing artificial intelligence to vocational schools in Europe No. 2020-1-LT01-KA202-078015), https://docs.google.com/presentation/d/1L6Gj5yI8mgR-V3g83OicVE bydoIYJ5_KmKsVsvX3wKM/edit?fbclid=IwARoM7z5PuhnE2qNz1K42p61tPquS4O8dHK-ievqNY 7FRHbjoFNleFW8b6po#slide=id.g12cc187cc22_2_842.

Central-Eastern Europe Perspective on FRT Regulation

'outdated'.[31] In Lithuania the case law on application of FRT is a rarity. However, a recent court decision directly relating to FRT usage demonstrates how the argument about convenience may easily transform into an argument about public interest. The State Data Protection Inspection challenged an order made by a university regarding the procedure for students' remote examinations and measures related to the processing of personal data in order to ensure fair behaviour during examinations. This document established that the following personal data will also be processed during the state-level emergency brought about by COVID-19: surveillance photos, facial biometric data, audio recording of the exam. In this case the court declared that the rules of the university were legitimate as they were necessitated by public interest.[32]

Quite a strong argument with the public in favour of FRT use is the possibility of increasing public safety. Municipal institutions boast that they have introduced surveillance cameras that increase the safety of citizens. For example, the Mayor of Marijampolė municipality publicly announced that the network of sixty-four video surveillance cameras installed in 2020 has raised security in the city to a new level:

> Let's start with the fact that stationary cameras were placed at all entrances to the city, monitoring the flow of cars and scanning their licence plates. It is extremely useful for investigating various crimes, such as thefts, robberies from homes or shops. At the same time, it also has a preventive effect, since thieves try to bypass the monitored cities – they don't want their vehicles or themselves to be captured.[33]

Or, for example, a local internet news portal of Mažeikiai district proudly presents:

> Almost half a dozen stationary and another fifteen mobile video surveillance cameras in Mažeikiai help to ensure the safety and order of residents in the city. With them, surveillance is performed in the busiest streets and intersections of the city, in public spaces, and near waste management container sites, and transmitted in real time to the monitoring console.[34]

It seems that residents are confident and satisfied with such usage of FRT in public places. People have even complained that the video cameras do not adequately ensure safety, as upon an accident the recording is too blurry or badly angled so that not all persons captured can be identified:

---

[31] Dovydas Vitkauskas, 'Galimybių pasą turėtų keisti veido atpažinimo Sistema' (7 October 2021), Delfi, www.delfi.lt/verslas/nuomones/dovydas-vitkauskas-galimybiu-pasa-turetu-keisti-veido-atpazinimo-sistema.d?id=88361491.

[32] LRT.lt, 'Teismas: Vilniaus universitetas galėjo naudoti veido atpažinimo funkciją per atsiskaitymus' (13 May 2022), www.lrt.lt/naujienos/mokslas-ir-it/11/1693760/teismas-vilniaus-universitetas-galejo-naudoti-veido-atpazinimo-funkcija-per-atsiskaitymus.

[33] Telia, 'Marijampolėje gyventojų saugumą užtikrina stiklinės akys: tokio poveikio nesitikėjo' (13 April 2022), Delfi.lt, www.delfi.lt/uzsakomasis-turinys/premium/marijampoleje-gyventoju-sauguma-uztikrina-stiklines-akys-tokio-poveikio-nesitikejo.d?id=89958475.

[34] Mažeikių rajono savivaldybė, 'Vaizdo stebėjimo kameros mieste – daugiau saugumo ir tvarkos' (14 January 2021), Budas.lt, www.budas.lt/regionu-naujienos/naujienos-mazeikiuose/41960-vaizdo-stebejimo-kameros-mieste-daugiau-saugumo-ir-tvarkos.

It is declared that Vilnius is safe, we see advertisements, billboards, how many cameras are attached. Oh, it turns out that when there is an incident in the middle of the day, not at night, not in a corner, not somewhere behind the trees, when we start to investigate, it turns out that those cameras are of very poor quality, hung up high. Here, perhaps, is the question I would like to raise – why do we need cameras, if, as declared, safe Vilnius is not safe at all in Cathedral Square?[35]

Moreover, FRT in public places is used not only for safety reasons, but also for fun: in Vilnius there was a two-year experiment in which researchers' devices measured the face temperature, breathing rate, heartbeat, and emotions of any passers-by. The explanation was that this experiment was intended to substitute for a public poll on how people feel at a given moment in a given place, as it was a much more precise way to do so.[36]

On the other side, certain aspects of FRT usage have also been criticised in the media. For example, it has been widely and critically discussed that Lithuanian institutions are using video surveillance cameras made in China, which raises doubts as regards the safety of the data recorded and potentially threatens state security.[37] Moreover, the potential for the misappropriation of FRT footage was revealed to the public in a well-known case concerning a policeman who had published online a video that had been recorded in a police car in which a drunk women took off her clothes.[38]

Nonetheless, these examples of the usage of FRT being publicly criticised are rather rare, and public attention is paid only to cases that raise state security issues or where there is a manifest infringement of professional duties. The overall attitude of Lithuanian society towards FRT usage seems to be positive – at least this is what can

[35] Živilė Kairytė, '16-metį vilnietės sūnų užpuolė Katedros aikštėje: skubiai prašo pagalbos' (30 August 2022), TV3.lt, www.tv3.lt/naujiena/gyvenimas/16-meti-vilnietes-sunu-uzpuole-katedros-aiksteje-skubiai-praso-pagalbos-n1185568.

[36] Made in Vilnius, 'Mokslininkai Vilniaus gatvėse matuoja praeivių emocijas, temperatūrą bei kvėpavimo dažnį' (24 December 2019), Delfi.lt, www.delfi.lt/miestai/vilnius/mokslininkai-vilniaus-gatvese-matuoja-praeiviu-emocijas-temperatura-bei-kvepavimo-dazni.d?id=83040699.

[37] Paulius Vaitekėnas, 'Kaune gyventojus stebi žmonių sekimu pagarsėjusios kinų kameros: fiksuos žmonių veidus ir KET pažeidimus' (29 January 2020), LRT.lt, www.lrt.lt/naujienos/eismas/7/1137677/kaune-gyventojus-stebi-zmoniu-sekimu-pagarsejusios-kinu-kameros-fiksuos-zmoniu-veidus-ir-ket-paz eidimus?fbclid=IwAR1VKjHQEWAWLVo3d5IJJpvYCvo9ZLlgovZtkGpfAJPiaLvFIgMxA23HFMo; Ignas Jačauskas, 'NKSC: kiniškos vaizdo stebėjimo kameros turi saugumo spragų' (29 May 2020), Diena. lt, www.diena.lt/naujienos/lietuva/salies-pulsas/nksc-kiniskos-vaizdo-stebejimo-kameros-turi-saugumo-spragu-969413; LRT tyrimai, 'Lietuvos vadovus saugo kameros, kurių bijo amerikiečiai' (29 January 2020), LRT.lt, www.lrt.lt/naujienos/lrt-tyrimai/5/1137518/lrt-tyrimas-lietuvos-vadovus-saugokameros-kuriu-bijo-amerikieciai?fbclid=IwAR2Y9BLDthGBeGX4RrNa9vozrDww6E3myMXUoiJFwJELIPTb e8znM-mVaKY; Valdemaras Šukšta, '"Kiniška akis" Kaune: nors palaiminimo miesto gatvėse naudoti kameras dar negauta, policija tyliai jas jau išmėgina' (19 November 2021), LRT.lt, www.lrt.lt/naujienos/lietuvoje/2/1541495/kiniska-akis-kaune-nors-palaiminimo-miesto-gatvese-naudoti-kameras-dar-negauta-policija-tyliaijas-jau-ismegina.

[38] Andrius Vaitkevičius, 'Į viešumą pateko Vilniaus policininkų darytas vaizdo įrašas – skandalas neišvengiamas' (29 January 2020), Lrytas.lt, www.lrytas.lt/lietuvosdiena/kriminalai/2020/01/20/news/i-viesuma-pateko-vilniaus-policininku-darytas-vaizdo-irasas-skandalas-neisvengiamas-13326794.

Central-Eastern Europe Perspective on FRT Regulation

be seen from media sources. It seems that priority is given to the vast development of FRT and other AI technologies because the public can benefit from increased convenience and safety, while human rights issues related to threats to privacy, discrimination, or false accusation are left aside. Indeed, no civil society organisations in Lithuania prioritise threats posed by usage of FRT and AI. Therefore, it may be assumed that public discourse is driven by the position of state institutions and any developers' interests in this field – thus a critical standpoint is lacking.

14.5 WHAT IMPACT ON FRT USAGE BY LAW ENFORCEMENT INSTITUTIONS IS EXPECTED UPON THE APPLICATION OF THE EU ARTIFICIAL INTELLIGENCE ACT?

As has been noted, the fragmented regulatory basis and rather weak public control of FRT usage in Lithuania could lead to the uncontrolled usage of FRT in law enforcement. Hopefully, the application of the EU Artificial Intelligence Act may bring about some changes to this situation. In April 2021, the European Commission presented the draft Artificial Intelligence Act, which is intended to introduce high standards for an EU trustworthy AI paradigm. It sets out core horizontal rules for the development, trade, and use of AI-driven products, services, and systems across all industries within the territory of the EU. This proposal introduces a 'product safety regime' that is constructed around a set of four risk categories. It imposes requirements for market entrance and certification of high-risk AI systems through a mandatory CE-marking procedure. This pre-market conformity regime also applies to machine learning training, testing, and validation datasets. Thus, according to Mauritz Kop,[39] the draft AI Act combines a risk-based approach (based on the pyramid of criticality) with a modern, layered enforcement mechanism. This means that as risk increases, stricter rules apply.

Regarding the definition of 'biometric data' in the law enforcement area, the proposed AI Act makes a reference to the Law Enforcement Directive.[40] However, the draft Act provides separate definitions for 'remote biometric identification system', '"real-time" remote biometric identification system', '"post" remote biometric identification system', and so on., with a specific regime being applicable to these categories. For example, the draft Act states that it is prohibited to use the '"real-time" remote biometric identification systems' in publicly accessible spaces for the purpose of law enforcement, unless and in as far as such use is strictly necessary for one of the following objectives:

---

[39] Mauritz Kop, 'EU Artificial Intelligence Act: The European approach to AI' (2021) (2) *Transatlantic Antitrust and IPR Developments*, Stanford Law School, https://law.stanford.edu/publications/eu-artificial-intelligence-act-the-european-approach-to-ai.

[40] Proposal for a Regulation of the European Parliament and of the Council Laying Down Harmonised Rules on Artificial Intelligence (Artificial Intelligence Act) and Amending Certain Union Legislative Acts (Com/2021/206 Final), Recital 7.

212   *Eglė Kavoliūnaitė-Ragauskienė*

(1) the targeted search for specific potential victims of crime, including missing children;
(2) the prevention of a specific, substantial, and imminent threat to the life or physical safety of individuals or of a terrorist attack;
(3) the detection, localisation, identification, or prosecution of a perpetrator or suspect of a criminal offence.[41]

As stated in the Explanatory Memorandum to the proposed Artificial Intelligence Act, the choice of a regulation as a legal instrument is justified by the need for a uniform application of the new rules, such as definition of AI, the prohibition of certain harmful AI-enabled practices and the classification of certain AI systems. The direct applicability of a Regulation, in accordance with Article 288 TFEU, should reduce legal fragmentation and facilitate the development of a single market for lawful, safe, and trustworthy AI systems. It is expected to introduce a set of harmonised core requirements regarding 'high-risk' AI systems and construct obligations for providers and users of those systems – improving the protection of fundamental rights and providing legal certainty for operators and consumers alike. At the same time, the provisions of the regulation must not be too prescriptive and should instead leave room for different levels of member state to take action regarding elements that do not undermine the objectives of the initiative, in particular the internal organisation of the market surveillance system and the uptake of measures to foster innovation.[42]

To summarise, the adopted Artificial Intelligence Act should bring more precision to the types of FRT used in law enforcement activities, and apply more controls to its use. However, the issue of transparency of FRT usage and making information available to the public or academics may still remain restricted as it is now, unless rising social pressures force such a practice to change.

14.6 CONCLUSIONS

There is quite a significant gap between the regulatory rules, which set requirements for FRT from a data protection perspective, and rules regulating the activities of separate law enforcement institutions and law enforcement activities. This may be because the usage of personal data, including facial images and their processing, was established in the specific laws regulating law enforcement much earlier than 2016, when the general data protection framework was established. Therefore, the Lithuanian legal framework clearly demonstrates that there are separate rules allowing the collection and processing of personal data (i.e., biometric data) in law enforcement activities, as well as separate rules that are more general and require

---

[41] Proposal for the Artificial Intelligence Act, Art. 5(1)(d).
[42] Explanatory Memorandum to the Proposal for the Artificial Intelligence Act (COM(2021) 206 final), para. 2.4.

a specific protective regime to be applied for the collection and processing of personal, including biometric, data.

Notwithstanding the fact that in theory the standards of data protection in general seem to be sufficient to protect against the rapid progression of technologies processing personal (and biometric) data and the evident threats to privacy and other human rights they pose, it still seems that the specific requirements on processing of personal data, especially processing biometric data, are not yet fully included in the practices of law enforcement in Lithuania. Moreover, it may be seen that the practices used in the development and usage of the Register of Habitoscopic Data do not comply with the regulatory requirements, in particular with the rules regulating the establishment, structure, and use of habitoscopic data. Rules on processing and sharing biometric data contained in this Register are not sufficient to ensure its proper protection, as required in data protection laws and EU documents.

Regarding the public attitudes to the regulation and usage of FRT in law enforcement in Lithuania, it may be noticed that neither society nor NGOs working in the field of human rights show any particular interest in analysing or restricting the usage of FRT in law enforcement institutions. On the contrary, media sources indicate that society at large is satisfied with the fact that the number of surveillance cameras in public places is increasing, and feels that it is a good and acceptable development that the possibility particular persons in public spaces can be recognised is increasing, as this brings the feeling of safety and order.

Although the adopted EU Artificial Intelligence Act should bring some discipline and clarity to the national regulation of FRT systems as well, as the reasons for using FRT, there are still doubts as to whether the transparency of FRT usage will be increased if societal and organisational attention and interest regarding FRT remains at the same level.

15

An Overview of Facial Recognition Technology Regulation in the United States

Mailyn Fidler and Justin (Gus) Hurwitz

15.1 INTRODUCTION

The United States generally takes a light-touch approach to regulation, and notably so in the technology sector. This approach applies equally to facial recognition technology (FRT). But while the US regulatory touch may be light, this does not mean that it is either simple or non-existent. This chapter chronicles regulation of FRT in the United States at federal, state, and local levels, and considers potential regulatory issues on the horizon.

Every chapter in this volume discusses FRT, so the reader is assumed to have more than passing familiarity with its salient technological capabilities and limitations. Very briefly, for purposes of our analysis, FRT is a tool by which computers can identify individuals by an image of their face, generally using sophisticated algorithms that compare visual characteristics of an image to vast databases of other faces. We emphasise the role of image-based analysis, because there are other FRTs that may use other indicators. For instance, specialised systems may use infra-red cameras to recognise the structure of blood vessels underneath the skin and use these to identify individuals. This is certainly a form of FRT, but because high-resolution infra-red imaging is not a pervasive technology (yet?), technologies such as this are not currently a focus of this debate. Similarly, research into FRT benefits adjacent fields, such as autofocus technologies that dramatically improve the quality of devices such as cameras. Because such technologies are not used for identification purposes, they generally are not directly implicated by the discussion in this chapter. However, restrictions on the use of one application of FRT could well affect the development or use of other applications of related technology.[1]

FRT presents unique challenges as an identification technology. The simple explanation for this is that faces are pervasive. Humans present them publicly every time we are outside. We cannot meaningfully obstruct them, for both practical and social

---

[1] While not discussed at length in this chapter, there are other potentially problematic uses of FRT beyond identification. For instance, firms are developing technologies that purport to use characteristics of facial expressions during interviews to help assess the suitability of candidates for jobs.

Overview of FRT Regulation in the United States

reasons – and, it bears note that FRTs are increasingly able to identify individuals based even upon obstructed images of their faces. And like all biometric markers, individuals cannot alter the appearance of their faces in the same way that they can, for instance, change a password or have multiple email addresses. Taken together, this makes faces both uniquely pervasive and uniquely persistent as identification tokens.

There is a wide range of potential use cases for FRT, ranging from contextually positive, to neutral, to potentially problematic. For instance, at the possibly innocuous end of the spectrum, FRT can be used to facilitate consumer convenience features, such as information kiosks that recognise individuals and automatically present relevant information to them. Or FRT could facilitate contactless payment or check-out features. Social media platforms can use FRT to automatically identify individuals in posted images. This information could be used for tracking purposes, or to learn information about those individuals that could be used for advertisement targeting. It could also be used to alert individuals when others post recognisable images of them, potentially giving them an opportunity to take privacy-protecting steps in response.

Perhaps the most potentially concerning class of FRT use cases stems from the widespread use of surveillance cameras in public settings – all of which can, in principle, incorporate FRT systems. In this setting, FRT can be used expansively by both private and public actors. For instance, venues such as shopping malls can use FRT-enabled security systems.[2] FRT can be used to help law enforcement identify or track fugitives or other wanted individuals in public places – or to help search for missing persons. In the most extreme setting, FRT effectively eliminates any sense of privacy or anonymity that individuals may have when in public spaces. Where before the advent of FRT there was 'anonymity in crowds', today there is none.

This chapter proceeds in four parts. US law presents a complex set of regulatory tools and institutions – institutions that are often overlapping and often competing with one another. Section 15.1 provides a brief overview of this myriad of institutions. Sections 15.2 and 15.3 then bifurcate the discussion along two sets of institutions: federal and state-level regulatory efforts. Section 15.2 looks at recent federal efforts relating to FRT; Section 15.3 looks at recent state-level efforts. Section 15.4 offers some observations on issues that are on the horizon for the regulation of FRT technology in the United States.

15.2 SETTING THE STAGE: TECHNOLOGY REGULATION IN THE UNITED STATES

US law does not present a single, unified, legal system. The United States is a federation of more than fifty states and territories, each with unique constitutions and legal

---

[2] Joel Schipper, 'Jefferson Mall adds new security system with facial recognition' (2 August 2022), *WDRB*, www.wdrb.com/news/jefferson-mall-adds-new-security-system-with-facial-recognition/article_66714a42-128b-11ed-b95c-7fc634889bf9.html.

environments. The federal government has its own Constitution and enacts its own laws, which sometimes displace, sometimes co-exist with, and other times are secondary to state law. Beyond that, most 'law' in the United States actually comes in the form of regulations enacted by federal or state agencies. And in many settings – perhaps most notably those relating to the technology sector and privacy-related concerns – US law relies extensively on self-regulation and sectoral regulation.

Before turning to any specific US regulatory approaches to FRT, this chapter presents a brief overview of these interrelated regulatory institutions.

The starting point for understanding the US legal approach to FRT – as well as many related issues, such as privacy issues generally – is to understand US law's emphasis on protecting individual autonomy from intrusion from the government. That is, US law is largely premised on negative rights, or rights to be free from interference from the government. This stands in stark contrast to many other legal systems that are premised on positive rights, or guarantees that the government provide or protect individual liberties.

Thus, for example, the US tradition of privacy law is largely anchored in the First and Fourth Amendments.[3] Beyond those found in these amendments, Americans have limited fundamental privacy rights against the government. These amendments protect the freedom of speech and limit the government's ability to encroach upon individuals' other rights without due process of law. And the privacy rights facilitated by these amendments look very different from those anchored in other concepts, such as a right to dignity or self-determination.[4] The First Amendment guarantees that individuals cannot be compelled by the government to speak, including potentially by disclosing information about themselves. And similarly, the Fourth Amendment prohibits the government from searching and seizing individuals' property – again preventing compelled disclosure of information to the government – absent obtaining a specific warrant from a federal court subject to due process of law. Critically, both of these amendments only run against the government. Neither prohibits private entities from compelling speech or disclosure of information, such as a condition of service. And neither prevents others from sharing or disclosing facts known about others, absent specific indicia of harm.[5]

These principles give rise to a defining doctrine of US privacy law: the third-party doctrine. This doctrine says simply that one has no reasonable expectation of privacy in information disclosed or publicised to a third party. If a user shares information

---

[3] James Whitman, 'The two Western cultures of privacy: Dignity versus liberty' (2003–2004) 113 *Yale Law Journal* 1151.

[4] Ibid.

[5] Such 'indicia of harm' include, for instance, the so-called privacy torts. These are state-level (not federal offences) that typically include intrusion upon seclusion, disclosure of private information, false light, and appropriation of likeness. To be actionable, however, these torts generally require demonstration of concrete harm, such as monetary loss or conduct amounting to trespass. At federal level, statutes such as the Wiretap Act and Stored Communications Act create liability for specific conduct that is akin to a violation of privacy.

Overview of FRT Regulation in the United States

with another private entity, such as an online service, that entity is largely (though not entirely) free to do with that information as it pleases, and the Fourth Amendment provides the user with no protection against government efforts to obtain that information. And if an individual shares their information publicly, that information may be used generally. This includes merely being seen in public – with few exceptions, under US law an individual may have their public activities tracked, documented, and shared by other individuals and private entities. The Fourth Amendment may prohibit the government from tracking individuals in this way, but does not reach other private entities – indeed, government actors may even be able to acquire information about an individual from third parties, even where the government could not have created that information itself.

There is some limited ability for the government to impose narrowing laws. For instance, it can write laws that constrain its own conduct. Laws such as the Wiretap and Stored Communications Acts were adopted principally to limit the conduct of law enforcement agencies that might have otherwise been considered permissible under the Fourth Amendment. In other cases, most notably where concrete and particular harms are identifiable from information disclosure, the government may be able to proscribe such disclosures. This most often happens in heavily regulated industries that transact in sensitive information, such as health and financial information. For instance, the Stored Communications Act prohibits electronic communications services from disclosing the contents of users' communications except under specific circumstances. Even then, however, the First Amendment limits the extent of such regulations. For instance, a law that prohibited the exchange of consumer data for marketing or promoting prescription drugs has been found to violate the First Amendment rights of pharmaceutical research companies and manufacturers who may have reason to use that data.[6]

The discussion so far has focussed primarily on the federal government as a regulator. The federal government may regulate by writing laws (which happens through Congress); it also relies extensively on federal agencies to promulgate and enforce regulations. In the United States, these regulators are generally sector-specific. For instance, the Federal Aviation Administration regulates the airline industry; the Federal Communications Commission regulates communications industry; and the Department of Health and Human Services regulates the healthcare sector. Regulators such as the Federal Trade Commission have more general regulatory authority – but the courts and Congress have generally been sceptical of efforts by such generalist regulators to use their authority to regulate pervasive or cross-industry practices.

In addition to the federal government, the states play an important role in regulating these issues. For instance, every state recognises various 'privacy torts'.

---

[6] *Sorrell v. IMS Health* (2011) 564 U.S. 552; see also *Zauderer v. Office of Disc. Counsel* (1985) 471 U.S. 626 (providing other protections for commercial speech).

These cover harms such as intrusion upon seclusion, disclosure of private information, presenting someone in a false light, and appropriation of likeness. This means, among other things, that enforcement generally occurs in the courts of the state where a given injury occurred. There may also be substantive differences in these laws between the states, including both whether specific causes of action are even recognised and the damages available for violating them. Each state also has its own constitution and legal system – there are sometimes important differences between these constitutions, both between the states and between the states and the federal Constitution. For instance, the federal Constitution has more onerous standing requirements than many state constitutions, which means that federal courts may not be able to recognise certain types of harms as allowing judicial remedies, whereas state-level courts may be able to adjudicate those same claims.

More recently, many states have adopted specific statutes that may relate to FRTs. Illinois's Biometric Information Privacy Act (BIPA), discussed in Section 15.4, for instance, directly affects the use of FRT and has caused firms such as Facebook to alter the services they offer to individuals located in that state. State-level laws create a complex set of implementation issues, including compliance costs and difficulties, especially where the specific requirements of a law may not be clear at the time it is enacted and the need (at times) to comply with contradictory requirements between state laws. The relationship between state and federal law can also be uncertain. In many cases, the existence of a related federal law will pre-empt state laws – it can even be the case that the non-existence of a federal law or regulation can prevent the adoption of a state law. While these issues are foundational to the operation of any legal system, as modern technology has increasingly brought state-level regulations into tension with those of other states and the federal government, there has been a surprising amount of debate in the United States as to how they ought to play out.

Extra-regulatory tools play a significant role in governing technologies such as FRT in US law. Such tools include mechanisms such as self-regulation and self-regulatory organisations, and executive regulatory tools such as government procurement policies. Self-regulation comes up in many contexts. Legally, it is closely related to consumer protection law: self-regulation often requires firms or industries to publicly disclose governance principles and to implement them in a binding way. A failure to do so might be the basis for liability based upon unfair or deceptive practices claims. Self-regulation can also be based upon the threat of legislation or even mere investigation: Congressional hearings into a firm's or industry's business practices can be disruptive or costly.

The use of procurement policies as a regulatory tool draws from the government's role as a large purchaser of goods and services, including of technology products and services. Government entities can decide which goods and services to purchase without the need for legislative or regulatory authority. For instance, the president

Overview of FRT Regulation in the United States 219

or a local government entity can often issue a policy directive that prohibits law enforcement from using certain technologies (such as FRT) or that directs how they may be used (such as for locating missing persons but not for tracking criminal suspects). Because the federal government is one of the largest purchasers of goods or services in the country (even the world), these policies have the potential to shape entire industries. A decision to use, or to not use, certain types of technology can cause private industry to invest billions of research and development dollars to develop technologies that meet those needs.

The brief discussion here offers a capsule summary of many aspects of US legal institutions that are relevant to regulation of FRT. It is far from a comprehensive introduction to US law. But for readers unfamiliar with these institutions it introduces several important idiosyncrasies and provides context for the discussion that follows – and for all readers it begins to develop themes that will be seen in the remainder of this chapter.

15.3 FEDERAL REGULATION OF FACIAL RECOGNITION TECHNOLOGY

Federal FRT regulation is still nascent in the United States. Administrative agencies have played the biggest role so far, approaching the issue through standard-setting and existing consumer protection regulation. For instance, since 2017, the National Institute of Technology and Standards (NIST), a non-regulatory agency under the auspices of the Department of Commerce, has developed standards for absolute and comparative accuracy of facial recognition algorithms and publishes results for software available through commercial vendors.[7] And these federal standards inform state approaches. For instance, Virginia allows its police to use only facial recognition software that performs well according to NIST standards.[8]

The Federal Trade Commission, the US consumer protection agency, published a set of 'best practices' regarding the use of FRT in 2012.[9] Publications such as these 'best practices' may inform future Commission activity, but do not constitute legally binding rules. More recently, the Commission has enforced general consumer protection principles against at least one software company for misleading consumers about when and how facial recognition software would be used on photo and videos uploaded to the app. In 2021, the Commission settled with a photo app company called Everalbum for allegedly only using facial recognition

---

[7] Patrick Grother, Mei Ngan, Kayee Hanaoka, Joyce Yang, and Austin Hom, 'Ongoing face recognition vendor test (FRVT)' (28 July 2022), National Institute of Standards and Technology, https://pages.nist .gov/frvt/reports/11/frvt_11_report.pdf.

[8] 117th Congress American Data Privacy and Protection Act 2022.

[9] Federal Trade Commission, 'Facing facts: Best practices for common uses of facial recognition technologies' (22 October 2012), www.ftc.gov/sites/default/files/documents/reports/facing-facts-best-practices-common-uses-facial-recognition-technologies/121022facialtechrpt.pdf.

after affirmative consent from users, when, in reality, the company automatically activated the feature.[10]

The US Congress has begun debating legislation that would regulate both the US government's own use of federal regulation technology, as well as private use of regulation technology. But the fates of each of these bills is far from certain. In June 2021, Senator Markey proposed a bill that would regulate the federal government's own use of facial recognition.[11] The bill, which was not enacted into law but was reintroduced again in 2023, would prohibit any federal agency from using FRT, or information obtained from any such technology, without specific approval from Congress.

Congress also commissioned a study of the federal government's use of FRT by the Government Accountability Office, which was published in August 2021.[12] Most of the agencies used some form of facial recognition to help ensure the digital security of agency devices. Six reported using the tool for law enforcement purposes and five for security purposes, including live monitoring of locations.

The Internal Revenue Service (IRS), the United States' taxation authority, came under bipartisan scrutiny in 2022 for using FRT to verify the identities of taxpayers online. Lawmakers criticised the agency's use of the tool as intrusive and requiring taxpayers to sacrifice privacy for data security. Advocates criticised the tool's potential for bias.[13] The IRS eventually reversed its plans and now offers an identity verification tool that does not involve facial recognition software. But even after this controversy, other federal agencies, including the US Patent and Trademark Office, are still moving forward with plans to use the same software.[14]

The US Congress has recently turned serious attention to a potential federal privacy regulation bill that would cover many contexts, including facial recognition.[15] The bill's political future is uncertain, but the proposed language would place restrictions on the purposes for which companies could collect certain data, including facial recognition data, requires privacy policies, requires consent from consumers,

---

[10] Federal Trade Commission, 'FTC finalizes settlement with photo app developer related to misuse of facial recognition technology' (27 May 2021), www.ftc.gov/news-events/news/press-releases/2021/05/ftc-finalizes-settlement-photo-app-developer-related-misuse-facial-recognition-technology.

[11] 117th Congress Facial Recognition and Biometric Technology Moratorium Act of 2021, S.2052. This bill was not enacted into law during the 117th Congress. On March 7, 2023, the bill was re-introduced for consideration in the 118th Congress. 118th Congress Facial Recognition and Biometric Technology Moratorium Act of 2023, S.681.

[12] US Government Accountability Office, 'Facial recognition technology: Current and planned uses by federal agencies' (24 August 2021), www.gao.gov/products/gao-21-526.

[13] ACLU, 'Coalition letter on government use of facial recognition identify verification services' (14 February 2022), www.aclu.org/letter/coalition-letter-government-use-of-facial-recognition-identify-verification-services.

[14] Alessandro Mascellino, 'USPTO to start verifying identities, including with biometrics, for trademark submission' (1 July 2022), BiometricUpdate.com, www.biometricupdate.com/202207/uspto-to-start-verifying-identities-including-with-biometrics-for-trademark-submission.

[15] 117th Congress American Data Privacy and Protection Act 2022.

Overview of FRT Regulation in the United States

and prohibits forms of algorithmic bias. Again, this bill would apply to FRT, but also to much wider categories of data. Similarly, the Federal Trade Commission (FTC) has recently announced a potential proposed rulemaking relating to 'Commercial Surveillance and Data Security' in which the Commission is considering, among many other issues, 'limiting commercial surveillance practices that use or facilitate the use of facial recognition, fingerprinting, or other biometric technologies'.[16] As with legislative proposals, the future of this potential rulemaking is uncertain.

15.4 REGULATING FACIAL RECOGNITION TECHNOLOGY IN THE UNITED STATES

States and localities have a primary advantage over the federal government when regulating new technologies: They can usually get regulations on the books faster. And, indeed, states and localities have taken an interest in regulating FRTs, but these non-federal approaches have been varied and fluid. FRT has many uses, so regulatory approaches target a similarly broad span of conduct. Some states regulate government or law enforcement use of FRT.[17] Some only regulate a sub-set of government use, such as banning use of facial recognition on drivers' licences or on police body cameras.[18] Other states regulate the technology only as applied to vulnerable populations, although the efficacy of the laws varies.[19] Yet other states regulate commercial applications.[20]

[16] Federal Trade Commission, 'FTC explores rules cracking down on commercial surveillance and lax data security practices' (11 August 2022), www.ftc.gov/news-events/news/press-releases/2022/08/ftc-explores-rules-cracking-down-commercial-surveillance-lax-data-security-practices.

[17] Washington, Oregon, California, Colorado, and Alabama all have limited government actor or police use. Up to date information about state regulation of facial recognition technology can be found at www.banfacialrecognition.com/map/.

[18] Oregon's regulation only encompasses the technology applied to drivers licenses. California's applies to police body cameras. See City of Portland, Oregon, 'City Council approves ordinances banning use of face recognition technologies by City of Portland bureaus and by private entities in public spaces' (9 September 2020), Portland.gov, www.portland.gov/smart-city-pdx/news/2020/9/9/city-council-approves-ordinances-banning-use-face-recognition#:~:text=The%20second%20ordinance%20will%20go,and%20visitors%2C%20first%20and%20foremost; Jeffrey Dastin, 'California legislature bars facial recognition for police body cameras' (12 September 2019), *Reuters*, www.reuters.com/article/us-california-facial-recognition/california-legislature-bars-facial-recognition-for-police-body-cameras-idUSKCN1VX2ZP.

[19] New York's regulation bans use of the technology in schools. Colorado's regulation includes a moratorium on new facial recognition technologies in schools for a period of time. *See* Chris Burt, 'New York school districts plan facial recognition security despite ban' (29 June 2022), BiometricUpdate.com, www.biometricupdate.com/202206/new-york-school-districts-plan-facial-recognition-security-despite-ban; Rachel Sandler, 'New York issues first-in-nation moratorium on facial recognition in schools' (22 December 2020), *Forbes*, www.forbes.com/sites/rachelsandler/2020/12/22/new-york-issues-first-in-nation-moratorium-on-facial-recognition-in-schools/; Linn F. Freedman, 'Colorado law restricts use of facial recognition technology by government agencies' (2022) XII *National Law Review* 12.

[20] Illinois and Texas both require informed consent before private actors can deploy facial recognition technology. *See also* 740 Illinois Compiled Statutes 14 and what follows (2008); Texas Business & Commerce Code Annotated s 503.001 (West 2017).

Illinois's BIPA (2008) was one of the first state regulations of commercial use of FRT, although the bill encompasses more than just facial recognition. Before a private entity collects biometric information, the law requires (1) notice to the consumer, (2) informed consent from the consumer, (3) written policies about retention and destruction, and (4) limits retention of and profit-making from that information.[21] Suing under BIPA, consumers reached a landmark $650 million settlement against Facebook for using FRT on photos uploaded to the site without consumer consent.[22] In another major lawsuit, plaintiffs sued Clearview AI, a company that provided facial recognition software to law enforcement agencies and sector companies, under BIPA. Clearview attempted to argue that its activities – selecting and curating facial images – were protected under the First Amendment in the same way a search engine's results might be.[23] But the suit settled, and the terms of the settlement prohibit Clearview AI from selling its database to most private companies.[24]

Other states have comprehensive privacy laws that cover facial recognition data. California's comprehensive privacy law, the California Consumer Privacy Act, for example, applies to facial recognition data, requiring companies to conform to certain obligations, including giving the consumer notice, access, and the right to have the data deleted.[25] Texas and Virginia also have some of their own state privacy laws that apply to biometric information.

State laws that allow consumers to sue companies face two possible hurdles as federal regulation catches up. The first is pre-emption, which is when a new federal law essentially is substituted for a state law on the same topic. Pre-emption could happen if federal legislation regulating FRT is passed. But the most recently proposed federal privacy legislation, the American Data Privacy and Protection Act, would *not* pre-empt state laws that solely cover FRTs.[26] BIPA would also remain un-pre-empted in a special carve-out.

State facial recognition laws that end up challenged in federal court – which could happen when a state resident sues a company that is based in another state – face a standing problem. In US law, standing refers to one's legal ability to bring a suit. To

---

[21] Jason Binimow, 'State statutes regulating collection or disclosure of consumer biometric or genetic information' (originally published 2019), Volume 41 of the 7th series of American Law Reports, Article 4 Section 2, Annotation *2.

[22] Taylor Hatmaker, 'Facebook will pay $650 million to settle class action suit centered on Illinois privacy law' (1 March 2021), TechCrunch, https://techcrunch.com/2021/03/01/facebook-illinois-class-action-bipa/.

[23] Jameel Jaffer and Ramya Krishnan, 'Clearview AI's first amendment theory threatens privacy – And free speech, too' (17 November 2020), *Slate*, https://slate.com/technology/2020/11/clearview-ai-first-amendment-illinois-lawsuit.html.

[24] Cyrus Farivar, 'Clearview AI settles facial recognition suit with ACLU, will alter some practices' (9 May 2022), *Forbes*, www.forbes.com/sites/cyrusfarivar/2022/05/09/clearview-ai-facial-recognition-suit-with-aclu/; *American Civil Liberties Union, et al., v. Clearview AI, inc.* (case documents available at www.aclu.org/cases/aclu-v-clearview-ai) (citation pending).

[25] California Civil Code s 1798.100 and what follows.

[26] 117th Congress American Data Privacy and Protection Act 2022.

Overview of FRT Regulation in the United States

have standing, a person must typically have suffered a concrete injury. Under BIPA and other state FRT laws, an injury might be defined as use of biometric data without consent. Federal courts have split on whether such an injury is concrete enough to satisfy the federal requirements for standing.[27]

State regulation of police or other government actors within its own borders will not face pre-emption or standing problems. Vermont's law regulating police use of FRT, as one of the most comprehensive such laws, provides an example at one end of the spectrum of regulation. Vermont's law is straightforward: With one exception (child sexual exploitation), until otherwise approved by the legislature, police may not use FRT or information derived from such technology.[28] But Vermont is an outlier: At the other end of the spectrum, some states, such as Oregon, only regulate certain police or government use of FRT. For example, Oregon's law prevents FRT from being used in conjunction with police body cameras.[29]

State regulation of this technology continues to be fluid. Many state and local regulations have taken the form of moratoriums with sunset provisions, merely delaying an ultimate decision about regulation until a future date. Others have already added exceptions to their bans, as in the case of Vermont. The Vermont legislature added an exception to its ban on police use of FRT in all circumstances.[30] Now, police can use the technology in cases involving sexual exploitation of children.[31] And Virginia repealed its de facto ban on police use of the technology a little more than a year after the ban was passed.[32] As of July 2022, police in Virginia can use facial recognition software in certain investigatory circumstances, with 'reasonable suspicion', and only if the software achieves an accuracy score of at least 98 per cent (measuring true positives) on NIST metrics, across all demographic groups.[33] The new Virginia law demonstrates the interplay between state and federal regulation: A state law uses a federal standard to guide the technology's use within its borders.

States, cities, and other localities have also enacted regulations on FRT use within their borders. These efforts are part of a broader trend in localities regulating the use of law enforcement technology. Advocates argue that the benefits of such governance include expanded democratic control over technology, improved responsiveness to changing technology, and more timely governance than post-hoc

---

[27] Carmen Sobczak, 'BIPA and Article III standing: Are notice and consent more than "bare procedural" rights?' (2020) 35 *Berkeley Technical Law Journal* 1391.

[28] 2020 Vermont Acts and Resolves 799 s 14.

[29] 2019 Oregon Revised Statutes s 133.741.

[30] ACLU, 'ACLU of Vermont statement on the enactment of S.124, the nation's strongest statewide ban on law enforcement use of facial recognition technology' (8 October 2020), www.acluvt.org/en/news/aclu-vermont-statement-enactment-s124-nations-strongest-statewide-ban-law-enforcement-use.

[31] 2020 Vermont Acts and Resolves 799.

[32] Denise Lavoie, 'Virginia lawmakers ban police use of facial recognition' (29 March 2021), *APNews*, https://apnews.com/article/technology-legislature-police-law-enforcement-agencies-legislation-033d77787d4e28559f08e5e31a5cb8f7.

[33] 2020 Vermont Acts and Resolves 799.

224   *Mailyn Fidler and Justin (Gus) Hurwitz*

rules developed through challenges brought through criminal litigation.[34] At least sixteen localities throughout the United States had passed facial-recognition specific regulations as of July 2022, with others having comprehensive police surveillance regulations that also apply to facial recognition.[35]

Both states and localities can regulate technology such as facial recognition in ways and at speeds that the federal government cannot. And experimentation with regulation of such technology at state and local level demonstrates ways in which these governance units are the laboratories of democracy. At the same time, the impact of these laws is limited to the boundaries of states and localities, affecting fewer people than federal regulation would. And states and local governments have their own types of problems with interest capture, raising concerns that, for instance, large companies might be able to outgun local privacy advocates. Local and state regulations are also much more easily reversible than certain federal regulations, as we have already seen with facial recognition regulation in some states and cities.

15.5 ISSUES ON THE HORIZON

Prediction is an always-fraught, if often necessary, endeavour. When it comes to predicting the future of FRT, and regulation of FRT, in the United States, it is more fraught than ever. US legal and political landscapes today are tempestuous, perhaps nowhere more so than where they relate to technology. There has been growing concern about technology in recent years on both the political left and the political right – albeit animated by very different concerns. At the same time, recent judicial decisions have made the prospects of regulation less, not more, likely. A number of issues relating to FRT that are on the horizon are identified and discussed here.

We start with topics that are most likely to be discussed but that also seem least likely to actually translate into action: Federal legislation or regulation intended to broadly limit or even prohibit the use of FRT.[36] Such legislation is unlikely to come to pass in the United States without a strong bipartisan coalition supporting

---

[34] See, e.g., Mailyn Fidler, 'Local police surveillance and the administrative Fourth Amendment' (2020) 36 *Santa Clara High Technology Law Journal* 481; Barry Friedman and Maria Ponomarenko, 'Democratic policing' (2015) 90 *NYU Law Review* 103; Vincent Sutherland, 'The master's tools and a mission: Using community control and oversight laws to resist and abolish police surveillance technologies' (2023) 70 (2) *UCLA Law Review*.

[35] See www.banfacialrecognition.com/map/ for an updated list of facial recognition local regulations; see also Mailyn Fidler, 'Fourteen places have passed local surveillance laws. See how they're doing' (3 September 2020), Lawfare, www.lawfareblog.com/fourteen-places-have-passed-local-surveillance-laws-heres-how-theyre-doing.

[36] For examples of calls for such regulations, see, Evan Selinger and Woodrow Hartzog, 'The inconsentability of facial surveillance' (2019) 66 *Loyola Law Review* 101, 102; Woodrow Hartzog and Evan Selinger, 'Facial recognition is the perfect tool for oppression' (2 August 2018), *Medium*, https://medium.com/s/story/facial-recognition-is-the-perfect-tool-for-oppression-bc2a08fofe66&gt – this proposes an outright ban on the use of facial recognition technology; Lindsey Barrett, 'Ban facial recognition technologies for children-and for everyone else' (2020) 26 *Boston University Journal of Science & Technology Law* 223.

its adoption. Given the potential for abuses of FRT by the government and the American tradition of scepticism of government power, an outside observer might think this coalition would readily manifest. But there is strong countervailing support for law enforcement and 'law and order' policies. Narratives about the use of FRT to find missing children and track dangerous criminals – whether substantively valid or not – are likely to have great valence in policy discussions and make it unlikely that a necessary coalition will be able to form.

The dynamics are somewhat different when it comes to the potential for administrative regulation of FRT. Regulatory agencies enjoy some insulation from the political process: Congress has already delegated authority to agencies that may empower them to adopt regulations. The political question is therefore more limited to whether an agency's leadership is interested in adopting given regulations. In the case of the current FTC, for instance, it is overwhelmingly clear that the agency is interested in adopting rules that could address the use of technologies such as FRT: as discussed previously, the Commission has recently issued an Advance Notice of Proposed Rulemaking relating to Commercial Surveillance and Data Security practices, which includes some consideration of rules that could limit, or at least affect, the use of FRT in the United States.

However, while the FTC may have the political will to adopt such regulations, it is less clear whether the courts will hold that it has the legal authority to do so. Recent trends in US administrative law have been hostile to expansive claims of authority by federal agencies, especially when adopting regulations that would affect entire industries or areas of commerce.[37] It does seem likely that the FTC would be able to adopt narrow rules that prescribe specific, and likely modest, requirements governing the use of FRT; it seems less likely, however, that the courts would uphold any broad regulatory moves that FTC makes, especially were they so broad as to proscribe the use of FRT or similar technologies.

Looking beyond the borders of the United States, questions will likely arise about whether US law can be harmonised with, or otherwise show comity for, FRT regimes adopted in other countries. This will most likely come up in the context of European regulations. The relationship between US and European regulations is likely to follow much the same trajectory as we have seen in the context of privacy regulations – most notably the challenges to the Safe Harbor and Privacy Shield in the *Schrems* litigation. To the extent that European regulations are based in European conceptions of fundamental rights, those regulations are likely to conflict with US regulations; and conversely, US regulations based in the First and Fourth Amendments are likely to conflict with European regulations.

The examples here are all likely to dominate discussion about FRT, but also seem unlikely to prove viable pathways for such regulation. This does not mean, however, that FRT regulation is unlikely. Indeed, as discussed in Sections 15.2 and 15.3, we are

---

[37] *See West Virginia* v. EPA, [2022] 597 U.S. (*Law Reports* citation pending).

already seeing FRT regulation at federal and state level. And these are also where we are likely to see substantive debates over the scope, impacts, and implementation of such regulations. Such regulations, and debates, are likely to focus on government use of FRT, government access to information collected through private FRT systems, specific uses of FRT or FRT-related practices, and generally issues arising from the relationship between competing states' laws and the federal regulations.

We are likely to continue to see governmental entities at federal, state, and local level consider whether, and under what circumstances, to use FRT. It is unlikely that there will be significant uniformity in approaches adopted. While most of these efforts will result from legislatures acting to limit the scope of their executive's authority – for instance, by prohibiting the use of FRT by law enforcement, school systems, or other public entities – it is also conceivable that some states could find their hands forced. State constitutions embody myriad conceptions of privacy. It is certainly possible that use of FRT by governmental entities may be deemed to violate constitutional privacy protections in some states, and it would not be surprising to see litigation pushing theories such as this in coming years.

To take an example, a federal judge in Ohio recently held that a public school's use of proctoring software that uses a student's computer's video camera to 'scan' the room in which they are taking an exam may constitute a search of private property in violation of the Fourth Amendment.[38] Similar claims could potentially be levelled at FRT systems: if courts hold that they enable pervasive tracking of individuals on an automated basis, they might be deemed to violate a reasonable expectation of privacy. Litigation challenging the constitutionality of such systems is at least possible, and probably likely, at both the state and federal level. Such restrictions would be unlikely to apply on government property or in government facilities, but could easily apply in private facilities or even in public places.

Government access to private FRT systems or data, discussed earlier, will also continue to be an issue in coming years. Here we are already seeing moves to limit government access to these systems, including requirements for judicial oversight of the processes by and circumstances in which law enforcement requests these materials. Of all efforts to regulate FRT in the United States, this is likely the least controversial and the most likely to continue to develop apace.

Limitations on government access often operate in practice by forbidding private entities from disclosing information to law enforcement. These regulations might not directly prohibit government use of information unlawfully disclosed to law enforcement (although, increasingly, they do). In this sense, they illustrate a general approach to regulating the private use of FRT: Most regulation will not prohibit the general development or use of FRTs; rather, restrictions on private entities will likely focus on specific use cases (e.g., disclosure of information generated by an

---

[38] *Ogletree v. Cleveland State University*, ___ F.Supp.3d ___, 2022 WL 17826730 (N.D. Ohio, December 20, 2022).

Overview of FRT Regulation in the United States

FRT to law enforcement). One can speculate on a range of use cases for FRT that could be subject to regulation. For instance, the use of FRT to help evaluate job candidates could conceivably be regulated – depending upon the circumstance, such uses could even already run afoul of existing anti-discrimination laws.

A final set of issues on the horizon relate to the interplay between potential FRT regulations at the state and federal level. Importantly, these issues may arise in a range of contexts adjacent to FRT regulations. For instance, state-level privacy regulations that require disclosure of information collected about individuals, or minimisation of such information, would easily affect the technological and business practices of firms using FRT. If multiple states adopt conflicting FRT-related regulations there will be complex questions about how those regulations are applied in practice. And if the federal government also adopts other regulations – or if it deliberately decides not to adopt such regulations – there will be complex questions over whether the federal approaches to FRT pre-empt state-level regulations. On balance, this is all to say that regulation of FRT in the United States, to the extent that there are efforts to adopt such regulations, will remain fraught and unsettled for many years to come.

15.6 CONCLUSION

This chapter has considered the state of FRT regulation in the United States. The United States is not a monolith. It is a federation comprising a central federal authority along with more than fifty states and territories and hundreds of localities – all of which have legislative, executive, and administrative regulatory apparatuses. But they are also governed by the federal Constitution and share common foundational values. These values tend to limit the extent to which FRT can be regulated as a matter of law, as well as carrying a general disposition towards light-touch regulations.

This is not to say that FRT is, or will remain, entirely unregulated in the United States. For instance, the same disposition against government interference in private matters has already begun to result in regulations restricting the use of FRT by government actors. We are likely to see more of these regulations, including restrictions on private parties sharing access to their FRT systems with state actors (much in the same way that laws such as the Stored Communications Act prevent electronic communications services from sharing the content of communications with law enforcement without a court-issued warrant).

Outside limited circumstances, however, more expansive regulation of FRT in the United States is unlikely in the foreseeable future. While Congress and the Federal Trade Commission are both currently considering privacy regulations that might bear upon FRT to some extent, it is uncertain whether these efforts will be successful. Even if they are, those regulations will almost certainly face serious challenges under contemporary understandings of the United States Constitution, so will be subject to extensive and lengthy litigation. The US approach to FRT regulation is ultimately governed by broader US conceptions about privacy and regulation generally, which remain narrower than other jurisdictions and contested.

16

Regulating Facial Recognition in Brazil

Legal and Policy Perspectives

Luca Belli, Walter Britto Gaspar, and Nicolo Zingales

16.1 INTRODUCTION

Facial recognition technology (FRT) has been in use by the Brazilian public administration for various purposes since at least 2011. It has seen an uptick in the 2018–2019 period, with noteworthy implementations in Rio de Janeiro and São Paulo, among others.[1] Nonetheless, there is no general legislation or sectoral regulation on the use of FRT – thus leaving unregulated both its general implementation and specific uses, such as for public security, public transportation systems, or identification.[2]

This chapter aims at identifying vulnerabilities and opportunities posed by the use of FRT in Brazil, focussing on the current legislative and regulatory landscape. Thus, it shall attempt to describe the evolving legislative framework and assess its adequacy to deal with the risks to fundamental rights posed by such technologies.

To do so, we assume the reader's prior knowledge of the basic functioning of facial recognition. This allows us to dive deeper into the literature concerning the adoption of FRT in Brazil (in Section 16.1), prior to reviewing the existing legislation (Section 16.2) relating to its deployment, especially in the context of law enforcement. A final section (Section 16.3) concludes with a brief analysis of this normative framework and puts forward a few suggestions on how to improve the national normative framework.

16.2 IMPLEMENTATIONS OF FRT IN BRAZIL

Information on the implementation of FRTs in Brazil is scattered. States, municipalities, and the federal government have all implemented projects utilising the

---

[1] Instituto Igarapé, 'Reconhecimento facial no Brasil' (2021), https://igarape.org.br/infografico-reconhecimento-facial-no-brasil/; Jonas Valente, 'Tecnologias de reconhecimento facial são usadas em 37 cidades no país' (19 September 2019), *Agência Brasil*, https://agenciabrasil.ebc.com.br/geral/noticia/2019-09/tecnologias-de-reconhecimento-facial-sao-usadas-em-37-cidades-no-pais.

[2] FRA, 'Facial recognition technology: Fundamental rights considerations in the context of law enforcement' (2019), European Union Agency for Fundamental Rights, https://fra.europa.eu/sites/default/files/fra_uploads/fra-2019-facial-recognition-technology-focus-paper.pdf; Lucas Introna and David Wood, 'Picturing algorithmic surveillance: The politics of facial recognition systems' (2004) 2 *Surveillance & Society* 177.

technology, frequently without prior notice or consultation with civil society, which has hampered transparency and accountability. FRT is frequently introduced in the context of 'Smart City' programmes aiming at enhancing urban safety, in the absence of specific regulation and with no guidance from the National Data Protection Authority (ANPD) on how data protection impact assessments must be performed.[3] Alongside this, there are private implementations of FRT, which are even less transparent since there is no disclosure obligation of any kind.

Among several attempts at mapping FRT implementations in Brazil. the most recent one is Venturini and Faray,[4] which, drawing on access to information requests, search engines, and interviews with key actors, identifies six projects where facial recognition was being implemented. One is the emotion recognition contract for advertisement display purposes between Via Quatro, a private operator managing one of the subway lines at the city of São Paulo, and AdMobilize, an artificial intelligence (AI) analytics company headquartered in the United States.[5] Given the lack of notice and information over this contract; Idec, a civil society organisation acting in consumer rights issues, obtained a blocking injunction pursuant to a civil public action to uphold the rights of the users of the São Paulo subway system, where it argued that there was no consent for the collection and use of biometric data, no information on the functioning of the technology, the data processing, and its purposes, or the possibility to exercise data subject rights. Another project involved the subway administrator, Companhia do Metropolitano de São Paulo,[6] with the aim of installing FRT cameras for subway security in stations.[7]

Two other projects involved surveillance of public spaces: one in the city of Campina Grande, in the state of Paraíba, and the other in Itacoatiara, in the state of Amazonas. The former involves FRT-enabled cameras running Facewatch installed

---

[3] Jess Reia and Luca Belli, 'Smart cities no Brasil: regulação, tecnologia e direitos' (2021), http://bibliotecadigital.fgv.br:80/dspace/handle/10438/31403; Luca Belli, 'BRICS countries to build digital sovereignty' in Luca Belli (ed.), *CyberBRICS: Cybersecurity Regulations in the BRICS Countries* (Springer International Publishing, 2021), https://doi.org/10.1007/978-3-030-56405-6_7; Luca Belli, 'Como implementar a LGPD por meio da Avaliação de Impacto Sobre Privacidade e Ética de Dados (AIPED)' in Laura Schertel Mendes, Danilo Doneda, Ingo Wolfgang Sarlet, Otavio Luiz Rodrigues Jr. and Bruno Bioni (eds.), *Tratado de Proteção de Dados Pessoais* (Forense, 2021).

[4] Jamila Venturini and Vladimir Garay, 'Reconhecimento Facial Na América Latina: Tendências Na Implementação de Uma Tecnologia Perversa' (2021), Fundación Karisma, https://estudio.reconocimientofacial.info/.

[5] Via Quatro informed in a press announcement that the technology would be implemented, without giving further details. Later news revealed that this was done through a partnership with LG and the pharmaceutical company Hyperapharma consisting in the projecting of their ads on digital screens of the subway equipped with cameras that would read and register the emotions in response to the ads.

[6] This was an 'empresa de economia mista' – a mixed controllership company in which the state is the controlling shareholder, but the company is legally structured as a private entity.

[7] Both Via Quatro and Cia. do Metropolitano de São Paulo's intent were halted by civil public actions moved by civil society organisations, the state's prosecutor office, and public defender's office. Via Quatro's implementation was grounded to a halt by judicial decree, but the case against Metropolitano de São Paulo is still ongoing (although an interim decision suspended the use of FRT).

during the city's São João festival, beginning in 2019. The cameras were still being utilised in 2022, when they aided in the arrest of twenty-five people during that year's festival and were expanded to two other cities in the same state (João Pessoa and Patos) via a command-and-control centre, totalling 1,600 cameras.[8] In Itacoatiara, a command centre was also created, with sixteen face recognition cameras for public security purposes.[9]

Finally, the authors highlight the use of FRT by the Federal Data Processing Service (SERPRO), a public company, to confirm the identity of driver's licence holders; and by SERPRO and the Social Service's information technology company (DATAPREV) to confirm identity and provide proof of living for social security beneficiaries.

A paper focussed on FRT application in public security and police work reports on the use of these technologies in the states of Bahia, Rio de Janeiro, Santa Catarina, and Paraíba from March to October 2019.[10] Although the specifics (contracting parties, public procurement format, etc.) are not disclosed, the article contains insightful information on the efficacy of such systems, which led to 151 arrests in total. Particularly, out of forty-two cases where information on race was available, 90.5 per cent of suspects were black and 9.5 per cent were white.[11] The research also analyses one specific case where FRT was applied for four days during the Carnival at Feira de Santana, a city in the state of Bahia, with an efficacy rate of less than 4 per cent.[12]

A more recent work by Nunes and colleagues goes into more detail about FRT in Rio de Janeiro.[13] The researchers scrutinise a pilot-project involving the deployment of FRT in Copacabana, during Carnival 2019, which was later expanded to two more areas of the city. The two-phase FRT programme for public security was managed by the State Military Police Office (SEPM) in a partnership with Oi, one of

---

[8] Governo de Paraíba, João Azevêdo Inaugura Centro Integrado de Comando e Controle e Sertão Ganha Equipamento Referência Para a Segurança Pública Do Nordeste. Governo Da Paraíba' (2022), https://paraiba.pb.gov.br/noticias/joao-azevedo-inaugura-centro-integrado-de-comando-e-controle-e-sertao-ganha-equipamento-referencia-para-a-seguranca-publica-do-nordeste; Portal Correio, 'Recon hecimento facial pemite a prisão de 25 procurados da Justiça no São João de Campina Grande' (11 July 2022), https://portalcorreio.com.br/reconhecimento-facial-pemite-a-prisao-de-25-procurados-da-justica-no-sao-joao-de-campina-grande/. It is not clear whether the 1,600 cameras in use in 2022 are a continuation of the 2019 implementation of Facewatch, since public announcements found on the state government's website merely mention the use of 'facial recognition', without specifying contract-ors and technology used.

[9] Portal de Amazônia, 'Itacoatiara Terá Centro Integrado de Câmeras Com Reconhecimento Facial e de Placas de Veículos' (6 April 2021), https://deamazonia.com.br/?q=278-conteudo-196736-itacoatiara-tera-centro-integrado-de-cameras-com-reconhecimento-facial-e-de-placas-de-veiculos.

[10] Pablo Nunes, 'Novas Ferramentas, Velhas Práticas: Reconhecimento Facial e Policiamento No Brasil' in Rede de Observatórios da Segurança & CESeC (eds.), *Retratos da Violência: Cinco meses de moni-toramento, análises e descobertas* (Rede de Observatórios da Segurança/CESeC, 2019), pp. 67–70.

[11] Ibid., p. 69.

[12] Ibid., p. 68.

[13] Pablo Nunes, Mariah Rafaela Silva, and Samuel R. de Oliveira, 'Um Rio de câmeras com olhos seletivos: Uso do reconhecimento facial pela polícia fluminense' (2022), O Panoptico, https://opanoptico.com.br/Caso/um-rio-de-cameras-com-olhos-seletivos-uso-do-reconhecimento-facial-pela-policia-fluminense/.

the major telecommunications operators in Brazil. Firstly, thirty-four FRT-enabled cameras were installed in Copacabana during a ten-day period, and coordinated by four military policemen trained by Oi and Huawei.[14] This programme was extended for two more months in the same year in additional locations in the city, increasing the number of cameras to ninety-five.

The database against which matches were checked was fed by information from the state's Civil Police Office (Sepol), the Department of Motor Vehicles (Detran), and the missing and wanted persons database. SEPM indicated that the data was encrypted, and information regarding persons identified via facial recognition was stored and made available to public security organs and criminal justice for purposes of planning, investigation, and enforcement, while false positives were immediately discarded by the system operator at the monitoring site.[15]

During the first phase, 2,993,692 facial images were captured, with 2,465 face correlations being established between those and the database records. This amounts to a 0.082 per cent match rate. There are no specific numbers for the second phase alone, but in total, from March to October 2019, sixty-three people were arrested, two missing persons were located, and five vehicles were recovered thanks to the use of FRT.[16]

Another study by Instituto Igarapé identifies forty-seven use cases of FRT in Brazilian cities from 2011 to 2019, spanning sixteen states out of the twenty-seven federal units composing the Brazilian federation.[17] Most instances (twenty-one) were related to public transportation – fraud prevention in free passes. These were followed by public security (thirteen cases), education (five cases), and border control (four cases).[18] Critically, the researchers report that 'many of the publicly announced cases focus mainly on the expected efficiency and implementation and less so on informing results'.[19] This is a perception shared by Nunes and colleagues when analysing the aforementioned case of Rio de Janeiro, pointing to a lack of metrics enabling performance reviews and stressing several instances where clarifications are needed to evaluate the projects' objectives and results.

Traditionally, Brazilian municipalities have adopted poor data governance practices, with sensitivity to personal data protection only kicking in after the applicability of sanctions in the General Data Protection Law (LGPD) in August 2021.[20] From

---

[14] Although Oi was the contracting party, the technology utilised was developed and provided by Huawei.

[15] Nunes, Silva, and Oliveira, 'Um Rio de cameras', p. 11.

[16] Instituto Igarapé, 'Videomonitoramento Webreport' (2020), https://igarape.org.br/videomonitoramento-webreport/; Nunes, Silva, and de Oliveira, 'Um Rio de cameras'.

[17] Instituto Igarapé, 'Reconhecimento facial no Brasil'.

[18] Ibid.

[19] Ibid.

[20] Luca Belli and Danilo Doneda, 'Municipal data governance: An analysis of Brazilian and European practices/Governança de Dados Municipal: Uma Análise Das Práticas Brasileiras e Européias' (2020) 12 Revista de Direito da Cidade 1588. For a non-official translation of the LGPD,

this perspective, a central concern regarding FRT use is the possible re-purposing of the personal data that has been collected, notably the sharing of such information with the government. For instance, in the case of FRT usage to prevent abuse of gratuity programmes in public transportation, it was revealed that the processed data may also be shared with the security forces 'when requested'.[21] Similar concerns apply when FRT is used to monitor student attendance, such as a case in the municipality of Itumbiara, in the state of Goiás. Questioned by researchers, the municipal education office made assurances that the data were stored in the same device it was captured on and a prior Data Protection Impact Assessment had been done, although the assessment was not shared publicly or with the researchers.[22]

Despite existing assurances from public bodies responsible for FRT implementation, the risk of surveillance creep remains significant – not only involving a possible transferring of biometric data to third parties, but also the receiving of such data from third parties. In July 2021, for instance, the governor of Bahia announced the expansion of a FRT project from Feira de Santana to seventy-six other cities in the state, for a total of 4,095 cameras, on a R\$ 665 million partnership with a conglomerate formed by Oi and the security tech company Avantia. In making the announcement, the governor also revealed an ambition to have private security cameras connected to the system, allowing for 'banking agencies, shopping malls and condominiums [...] to connect their cameras and deliver the movements and faces of passers-by to authorities'.[23]

16.3 CURRENT LEGISLATION, REGULATION, AND GOVERNANCE

There is currently no specific law regarding FRTs in Brazil, whether for public or private ends, and whether in security, transportation, or any other area. Furthermore, there is no specific law or regulation framing the usage of AI systems in Brazil, although legislative efforts are being made. There is, however, a set of laws that regulate specific areas of FRT and can be used to build the basis for a regulatory framework; they are briefly explained in this section.

---

see Luca Belli, Laila Lorenzon, Luã Fergus and Walter B. Gaspar, 'The Brazilian General Data Protection Law (LGPD) – Unofficial English version' (22 January 2020), CyberBRICS, https://cyberbrics.info/brazilian-general-data-protection-law-lgpd-unofficial-english-version/.

[21] Leonardo Zvarick, 'Reconhecimento Facial Bloqueia 331 Mil Bilhetes Únicos Em SP – 12/06/2019' (12 June 2019), São Paulo Agora, https://agora.folha.uol.com.br/sao-paulo/2019/06/reconhecimento-facial-bloqueia-331-mil-bilhetes-unicos-em-sp.shtml.

[22] Bárbara Simão, Blenda Santos, Carolina Reis, Eduarda Costa, Elora Fernandes, Enrico Roberto, Felipe Rocha and Rafaela de Alcântara, 'Cidades Inteligentes e Dados Pessoais: Recomendações e boas práticas' (2022), Internet Lab, ARTICLE 19, LAPIN, p. 47.

[23] Cíntia Falcão, 'A Bahia está virando um laboratório de reconhecimento facial' (2021), The Intercept Brasil, https://theintercept.com/2021/09/20/rui-costa-esta-transformando-a-bahia-em-um-laboratorio-de-vigilancia-com-reconhecimento-facial/.

16.3.1 *General Data Protection Law (LGPD)*

A first important port of call is the LGPD. Four key elements for FRT purposes are:

(1) its characterisation of biometric data, such as facial images, as 'sensitive personal data' (Art. 5°, II), which means that its processing can be grounded only on a more limited range of legal bases (Art. 11°);

(2) the overarching principles of data processing, which set the fundamental elements of all personal data processing, including those involved in FRT (Art. 6°);

(3) the right to revision regarding automated decision-making based on personal data that affect the data subject's interests (Art. 20 and Art. 20. §1); and

(4) the limited scope of the LGPD when it comes to security, prevention, and repression of criminal activities, and the obligation to perform data protection impact assessment in such cases (Art. 4. §3.).

The first point refers to the fact that, being categorised as sensitive, the codified data of every individual's facial print, used in face recognition to identify matches, must be based on explicit and informed consent of the data subject or else be 'indispensable' to achieve one of seven legal bases as set in Article 11. One can imagine some of these alternative legal bases being in principle suitable to justify FRT for public interest purposes. For instance, 'prevention of fraud' can justify one-to-one authentication of an individual who needs to access a secure electronic system (an example being biometric authentication for one's own bank account). Moreover, 'compliance with legal or regulatory obligations' allows data controllers to conduct FRT operations when this is imposed as a legal or regulatory obligation; and 'execution of public policies' allows the shared use of information between public entities or between public and private entities, upon prior authorisation, for the execution by the public administration of public policies.

This latter provision is a peculiarity of the Brazilian framework, allowing the sharing of datasets between government departments, executive agencies, and private entities who have been involved in the execution of public policies. However, this can only be done under terms and conditions that have been previously defined in legislation or equivalent legal sources (ordinances, resolutions, regulations, etc.), which provide a mechanism to ensure transparency and accountability of such processing.

The third relevant aspect of the LGPD concerns its principles, which construct concrete obligations for the data controllers and processors. Good faith (duty to maintain an honest and trustworthy conduct in the data processing relationship) opens the set of principles contained in Article 6 of the law,[24] followed by principles similar to those found in other data protection frameworks – for example, purpose

---

[24] Good faith (*boa fé*) is divided in Brazilian legal doctrine into subjective and objective manifestations. In the case of its use in Art. 6 of LGPD, as well as in Art. 422 of the Brazilian Civil Code, it is meant in its objective form, that is, a duty to behave according to the legitimate expectations of one another in a legal relationship. Bioni (2019) comments on this point connecting the objective good faith

limitation, data minimisation, security. Of particular interest for FRT are the principles of non-discrimination and responsibility and accountability, in conjunction with the transparency principle. Since LGPD principles must inform and shape the whole design and implementation of data processing, this means that controllers must be able to demonstrate that specific measures have been taken to mitigate risks, such as biased and unfair processing, and have been communicated in a clear and intelligible manner.

Owing to the invasive nature of FRT, the correct implementation of the LGPD principles requires the performance of periodic data protection impact assessments. This is particularly relevant when FRT is deployed for security purposes by public organs and law enforcement agencies, as only auditable technologies can be legitimately used by the state bodies without undermining constitutional guarantees. Unfortunately, this is far from being the case. Furthermore, a sound implementation of the transparency principle is key in the case of FRT. This not only demands an analysis and audit of FRT's impact, but also requires that the information resulting from such analysis be transparently communicated in an accessible language.

The second key element of the LGPD that is relevant for FRT concerns automated decision-making. According to LGPD, these decisions should be structured in a way that allows for revision,[25] which, logically, also demands that the data subject be informed they are subjected to automated decision-making.[26] A hard question would be what form of communication of that information is suitable for giving notice: would this require a 'just-in-time' notification, or would consent to a generic statement in a controller's privacy policy be sufficient?

Lastly, it is important to mention that the LGPD creates a rather large exception within the data protection framework regarding any data protection processing aimed exclusively at fostering public security, national defence, the safety of the country, or crime investigation and repression (Art. 4). While this exception currently leaves the door open to a wide range of illegitimate uses from state organs, the LGPD also foresees that these exceptions 'shall be governed by a specific law, which shall contain proportional measures as strictly required to serve the public interest, subject to due process of law, general principles of protection and the rights of the data subjects set forth in this Law' (Art. 4 §1). Furthermore, paragraph 3 of the same LGPD article also provides a key element for the purposes of FRT regulation, specifying that the ANPD will issue technical opinions or recommendations regulating the exceptions

---

contained in LGPD to the concept of contextual privacy, based on the trust between parties in a data processing relationship that the information shared will not be used in manners that contradict the original context of its sharing. See B. R. Bioni, 'Proteção de dados pessoais : a função e os limites do consentimento' (Forense, 2019), http://bibliotecadigital.tse.jus.br/xmlui/handle/bdtse/5973.

[25] Not necessarily human revision, although one could argue an automated revision of automated decisions constitutes another instance of possible 'revision' under the law.

[26] This is an accessory obligation – since one cannot assert one's right if one is unaware of the fact that there is a situation that gives rise to that right. It can also be derived from the general transparency principle.

mentioned earlier and shall request a data protection impact assessment to the persons in charge of data processing for such purposes. Hence, we may assume that whenever FRT is used for safety and security reasons it is necessary to undertake a data protection impact assessment. Moreover, the ANPD has general competence to regulate how data protection impact assessments should be conducted (Art. 55-J, XIII).

16.3.2 *Additional Legislation*

In addition to LGPD, some other normative references are relevant to FRT. First of all, the Brazilian Constitution contains provisions on intimacy (Art. 5, X), secrecy of communications (Art. 5, XII), habeas data (Art. 5, LXXII), and personal data protection (Art. 5, LXXIX).

Secondly, the Brazilian Consumer Code applies to business-to-consumer relations, potentially impacting the viability of FRT deployments in consumer-facing applications, products, and services. For instance, it contains provisions on databases, anticipating many of the rights that would be afforded to data subjects by the LGPD in general (the Code precedes LGPD by more than two decades). Importantly, it establishes strict liability in consumer relations (Art. 12 and Art. 14); an obligation to maintain correct and updated data; and the right of the consumer to be informed of a new registry of their personal data (Art. 43).

Another relevant provision is Federal Decree no. 10.046/2019, which establishes guidelines for the sharing of data among the Federal Public Administration. This norm allowed the unification of fifty-one existing databases and created two new ones (including biometric and biographic data), and was criticised for laying out insufficient safeguards of compliance with the LGPD.[27] Two actions challenging the constitutionality of the Decree were filed before the Constitutional Court in 2021, due to its alleged clash with fundamental rights to privacy and data protection. In a unanimous decision, the court interpreted the Decree in conformity with the Constitution, clarifying data sharing must be conditioned to:

(1) the pursuit of legitimate, specific, and explicit purposes;
(2) the compatibility with the stated purposes;
(3) compliance with the LGPD's public sector norms;
(4) its transparency and publicity, including the control mechanisms for access to the database, insertion of new data, and the security measures enabling the imposition of liability on the relevant public servant in case of abuse;
(5) its respect for the norms established in specific legislation and case-law in the operations of data sharing and intelligence;

---

[27] Estela Aranha, 'Elaboração de parecer sobre a legalidade dos Decretos nº 10.046/2019 e 10.047/2019 em face das normas que disciplinam os direitos fundamentais à proteção de dados e à privacidade no ordenamento jurídico brasileiro' (12 February 2020), OABRJ, www.oabrj.org.br/noticias/comissao-protecao-dados-privacidade-lanca-parecer-sobre-decretos-federais-criam-grande.

236 *Luca Belli, Walter Britto Gaspar, and Nicolo Zingales*

(6) the existence of norms of civil responsibility of the state in case of illegality; and
(7) the existence of norms of responsibility for administrative impropriety of any agent acting on behalf of the state in case of intentional violation of the duty of publicity established by Article 23 of the LGPD.[28]

At the same time, the ruling found unconstitutional the part of the Decree concerning the composition of the Central Committee for Data Governance (the entity that may formulate the concrete norms and standards for data sharing under the Decree). The court gave the government sixty days to open its composition to effective participation of other democratic institutions, with minimum guarantees against undue influence on its members. In other words, the ruling consecrated the importance of both transparency and multi-stakeholder participation in the formulation of policies regarding government use of data.

Finally, Ordinance no. 793/2019 of the Ministry of Justice and Public Security is directly concerned with the use of FRT for public security purposes. This norm establishes financial incentives for security-oriented actions aimed at implementing the National Public Security and Social Defence Policy. FRT is explicitly mentioned in Article 4, §1, III, b,[29] which allows the application of funds from the National Public Security Fund (which reached more than 1 billion reais in 2021 and almost 2 billion reais in 2022) in the implementation of technologies such as video monitoring systems with facial recognition solutions, optical character recognition, and AI.[30] Although the intent to increase such applications is expressed, no safeguards in terms of transparency and accountability are described.

16.4 DISCUSSION: IS THE EXISTING FRAMEWORK ADEQUATE?

To assess if the existing (or proposed) legal framework regarding AI and FRT in Brazil is adequate for the protection of fundamental rights, it is first necessary to understand the risks associated with the application of these technologies. A brief discussion of these risks is presented here. Based on such an understanding, we then draw some necessary conclusions.

16.4.1 *The Probable Risks of FRT Deployment in Brazil*

One of the most cited and known risks is the discriminatory consequences that these technologies may have. Particularly, systems trained based on discriminatory

---

[28] Gilmar Mendes, Voto Conjunto ADI 6649 e ADPF 695.
[29] Portaria no. 793/19, de 24 outubro de 2019, Imprensa Nacional de 25 outubro (Brazil), www.in.gov.br/en/web/dou/-/portaria-n-793-de-24-de-outubro-de-2019-223853575).
[30] Portal da Transparência, 'Fundo Nacional de Segurança Pública' (n.d.), www.portaltransparencia.gov.br/orgaos/30911?ano=2022.

datasets will likely tend to reproduce the biases and discriminatory tendencies inferred from the data. Systems developed by under-representative teams may suffer from more subtle dysfunctionalities – resulting from issues such as limited selection criteria set by developers, the conceptualisation of the elements that will constitute inputs and outputs of the system, and a myopic view of the results in terms of their discriminatory impacts. Poorly designed systems and datasets might result in systems that disproportionately target these populations, and consequently, new disproportionate data being generated and fed into the system.

Possa highlights how, in a country where black individuals made up 66.7 per cent of the national prisoner population in 2019 and where in 2015 the Supreme Court declared the general state of the carceral system as an 'unconstitutional situation', adopting public security technologies that harm the presumption of innocence and present biases toward structurally discriminated peoples only reinforces that unconstitutionality.[31]

All these issues result in systems that are inept at dealing with certain aspects of the social phenomena they are built to address – in the case of FRT, systems are unable to recognise non-Caucasian, non-male faces, resulting in undue targeting of these groups, as many studies and cases have previously shown.[32] This seems also to be the case with some of the previously discussed implementations of FRT in Brazil, as anecdotal evidence suggests.[33]

Those problems are compounded by AI systems' opacity, which impairs accountability and public oversight.[34] This is further complicated by the information asymmetry between private actors who source these technologies and the public using them, or the public institutions that contract AI services. As stated by Mazzucato

---

[31] Alisson Possa, 'O reconhecimento facial como instrumento de reforço do estado de coisas inconstitucionais no Brasil' (2021) 1 *IDP Law Review* 134.

[32] João Victor Archegas and Christian Perrone, 'Don't snoop on me' (16 December 2021), Verfassungsblog: On Matters Constitutional, https://intr2dok.vifa-recht.de/receive/mir_mods_00011576; Moriah Daugherty, Katie Evans, Edward J. George, Sabrina McCubbin, Harrison Rudolph, Ilana Ullman, Sara Ainsworth, David Houck, Megan Iorio, Matthew Kahn, Eric Olson, Jaime Petenko and Kelly Singleton, 'The perpetual line-up: Unregulated police face recognition in America' (18 October 2016), Georgetown Law Center on Privacy and Technology, www.perpetuallineup.org; Karen Hao and Jonathan Stray, 'Can you make AI fairer than a judge? Play our courtroom algorithm game' (17 October 2019), *MIT Technology Review*, www.technologyreview.com/2019/10/17/75285/ai-fairer-than-judge-criminal-risk-assessment-algorithm/; Will Douglas Heaven, 'Predictive policing algorithms are racist. They need to be dismantled' (17 July 2020), *MIT Technology Review*, www.technologyreview .com/2020/07/17/1005396/predictive-policing-algorithms-racist-dismantled-machine-learning-bias-criminal-justice/; Jennifer Lynch, 'Face off: Law enforcement use of face recognition technology' (May 2019), Electronic Frontier Foundation, www.eff.org/files/2019/05/28/face-off-report.pdf

[33] Carolina Reis, Eduarda Costa Almeida, Fernando Fellows Dourado and Felipe Rocha da Silva, 'Vigilância automatizada: uso de reconhecimento facial pela Administração Pública no Brasil' (7 July 2021), LAPIN, p. 51, https://lapin.org.br/2021/07/07/vigilancia-automatizada-uso-de-reconhecimento-facial-pela-administracao-publica-no-brasil/. Nunes, 'Novas Ferramentas'.

[34] Frank Pasquale, 'Secret algorithms threaten the rule of law' (1 June 2017), *MIT Technology Review*, www.technologyreview.com/2017/06/01/151447/secret-algorithms-threaten-the-rule-of-law/.

and colleagues: 'The proprietary nature of most AI applications means the public lacks insight as well as the ability to design proper oversight. Advancing technical capabilities without matching adjustments to governance, institutional and organisational models is leading to failure in effectively evaluating the risks of AI and managing its opportunities.'[35]

On top of all this, there are issues particular to the Brazilian context. As systematically demonstrated by Reis and others, and reflected in anecdotal evidence from various other authors previously referenced, most of the FRT being implemented by the Public Administration in the country come from foreign sources, especially China, Israel, the United States, and the United Kingdom. In many instances, contracting was based on aggressive negotiation tactics directed at conquering market dominance and locking-in the contracting administrations.[36] This trend is particularly marked in Latin American countries.[37]

This raises concerns around the strategic value of technologies and the underlying personal data being collected – especially considering that data sharing terms with these private companies are not always publicly transparent.[38] One other concern is the ability of the state to incentivise the emergence of national AI and FRT capabilities, directing their development into interests aligned with national societal goals or 'missions',[39] and strengthening the national innovation system.[40]

Much has been said in public debate about the harms of algorithmic bias and the need to combat or fix it. Powles and Nissenbaum comment on how focussing on solving bias is a reflection of society's deference to technologists even in the fields of ethics, law, and the media, and how focus should not be shifted from discussions such as which systems really deserve to be built; which problems most need to be tackled; who is best placed to build them, and who decides?[41] Souza and Zanatta

---

[35] Mariana Mazzucato, Marietje Schaake, Seb Krier and Josh Entsminger, 'Governing artificial intelligence in the public interest' (28 July 2022), UCL Institute for Innovation and Public Purpose, Working Paper Series (IIPP WP 2022–12), www.ucl.ac.uk/bartlett/public-purpose/wp2022-12.

[36] Reis et al., 'Vigilância automatizada'.

[37] Gaspar Pisanu and Verónica Arroyo, 'Surveillance tech in Latin America: Made abroad, deployed at home' (9 August 2021), Access Now, www.accessnow.org/surveillance-tech-in-latin-america-made-abroad-deployed-at-home/.

[38] Nunes, Silva, and de Oliveira, 'Um Rio de câmeras'; Reis et al., 'Vigilância automatizada'; Reia and Belli, 'Smart cities no Brasil'.

[39] Mazzucato et al., 'Governing artificial intelligence'; Mariana Mazzucato and Josh Ryan-Collins, 'Putting value creation back into "public value": From market-fixing to market-shaping' (2022)25(4) *Journal of Economic Policy Reform* 345–360.

[40] Glauco Arbix, Mario Sergio Salerno, Guilherme Amaral, and Leonardo Melo Lins, 'Avanços, equívocos e instabilidade das políticas de inovação no Brasil' (2017) 36 *Novos estudos CEBRAP* 9; Chris Freeman, 'The economics of technical change' (1994) 18 *Cambridge Journal of Economics* 463; Chris Freeman, 'The "national system of innovation" in historical perspective' (1995) 19 *Cambridge Journal of Economics* 5.

[41] Julia Powles and Helen Nissenbaum, 'The seductive diversion of "solving" bias in artificial intelligence' (7 December 2018), *OneZero*, https://onezero.medium.com/the-seductive-diversion-of-solving-bias-in-artificial-intelligence-890df5e5ef53.

Regulating Facial Recognition in Brazil

add to this debate,[42] connecting the application of FRT to a broader neo-liberal tendency for the decentralisation of state functions to technology firms, and the associated push from the market in the context of 'surveillance capitalism'.[43] This 'techno-solutionism' serves as a smokescreen over the deeper-seated issues of structural racism and the surveillance state,[44] forcing public debate into the question of *how* to make FRT fair and efficient instead of *if* it is truly needed and proportional to the desired ends. An adequate regulatory framework should deal with these issues.

16.4.2 *Moving from the Existing to the Ideal FRT Framework for Brazil*

Based on the analysis conducted in the previous sections, we can argue that the current and proposed framework for FRT regulation adopts a rather lenient approach to the ex-ante regulation of risk – by leaving a measure of discretion to the control of high-risk applications by the public administration. Such choice may be detrimental in terms of compliance with the LGPD principles, especially considering the ANPD has demonstrated a remarkably timid stance regarding overseeing the implementation of LGPD by public bodies and law enforcement agencies – *de facto* leaving the correct implementation of the existing framework to the good faith and good will of the bodies that deploy FRT.

Moreover, the existing framework does not foresee a differentiated approach that customises specific obligations and safeguards based on the purposes for which FRT is implemented. As we have emphasised, the purpose for which FRT is deployed – for instance identification in the context of crime prosecution versus authentication – has a considerable impact not only on the legislation that will be applied, but also on the obligations of the data controller and the guarantees of the data subject. The complexity of this situation might be exacerbated further by the jurisdictional uncertainty over what administrative level is competent to regulate the use of FRT. Indeed, the regulation of security issues is a state issue, but data protection is an issue of exclusively federal competence.

In addition, we argue that more information needs to be pro-actively made available by public administrators and public service concessionaires on the intended FRT implementations, adopting an accountability-first stance and a transparency-by-design approach. As we have emphasised, information should be communicated in a clear and intelligible manner and should at least specify: when, where, and why FRT is used; what databases are used to train the FRT systems; what data is collected; what measures are taken to guarantee information security; with which

---

[42] M. Souza and R. Zanatta, 'The problem of automated facial recognition technologies in Brazil: Social countermovements and the new frontiers of fundamental rights' (2021) 1 *Latin American Human Rights Studies*, https://revistas.ufg.br/lahrs/article/view/69423.

[43] Shoshana Zuboff, *The Age of Surveillance Capitalism: The Fight for a Human Future at the New Frontier of Power* (Kindle) (Profile Books, 2019).

[44] Evgeny Morozov, *Big Tech: A Ascensão Dos Dados e a Morte Da Política* (Ubu Editora, 2019).

entities data are shared, if any; and what indicators will allow to evaluate the performance of the FRT deployment, such as how many investigations and criminal proceedings are carried out and how many crimes are solved based on the use of the FRT system under discussion.

Lastly, it seems necessary that the ANPD enact regulations and publish technical guidelines on specific aspects of the data processing pipeline, which are essential to make sure FRT systems are used in compliance with LGPD. In fact, as long as critical elements such as data anonymisation, algorithmic accountability and auditing, data protection impact assessments, and data security measures remain undefined, (FRT) compliance with LGPD will continue to be extraordinarily challenging.

In Brazil, the main legal reference concerning the use of FRT, owing to their intrinsic use of personal data, is the LGPD, which is enforced and detailed by the ANPD. There are, however, other concerned institutions that should be included in the discussion. One such is the Governance Committee of the Brazilian Artificial Intelligence Strategy, a multi-stakeholder body created in April 2021 and tasked with translating the strategy – which has been criticised for being overly general and more akin to a letter of intent than to an actual strategy – into concrete objectives and actions.[45] ANPD, however, only started participating in the Committee at its fourth meeting, in December 2021, and no specific progress on these matters has yet been announced.[46]

16.5 CONCLUSIONS

All in all, there are still substantial gaps in the regulation of AI and, consequently, FRT in Brazil, although a strong basis of principles is in place and there are important laws working to provide the necessary basis for the judicial protection of fundamental rights – as demonstrated by the Via Quatro case. A deeper issue with the implementation of these technologies is its scattered character – popping up in news announcements as sure techno-solutions to issues such as efficiency and public security. As discussed, this scattered nature is equally observed in the legislative

---

[45] Walter Gaspar and Yasmin Curzi de Mendonca, 'Artificial intelligence in Brazil still lacks a strategy' (2021), Report by the Center for Technology and Society at FGV Law School, https://cyberbrics .info/wp-content/uploads/2021/05/EBIA-en-2.pdf; Ronaldo Lemos, 'Estratégia de IA Brasileira é Patética' (2021), Folha de São Paulo, www1.folha.uol.com.br/colunas/ronaldolemos/2021/04/ estrategia-de-ia-brasileira-e-patetica.shtml; Eduardo Magrani, 'Estratégia Brasileira de Inteligência Artificial: Comentários Sobre a Portaria 4.617/2021 Do MCTI' (2021), https://secureservercdn .net/192.169.220.85/dxc.177.myftpupload.com/wp-content/uploads/2021/12/OPINION-Brasil-PORT-.pdf?time=1643260747; Francisco Saboya, 'Existe Mesmo Uma Estratégia Brasileira de Inteligência Artificial?' (13 April 2021), CanalMyNews, https://canalmynews.com.br/francisco-saboya/existe-mesmo-uma-estrategia-brasileira-de-inteligencia-artificial/.

[46] MCTI, 'Inteligência Artificial Estratégia – Repositório. Ministério Da Ciência, Tecnologia e Inovações – Gov.Br' (n.d.), www.gov.br/mcti/pt-br/acompanhe-o-mcti/transformacaodigital/inteligencia-artificial-estrategia-repositorio.

scenario, with federal, state, and municipal norms and proposed bills creating a cacophony that ultimately impairs advancement of a strong position on the role that these technologies should play in society.

In this context, one major institution that might play an important role is the ANPD, which was given ample ground to not only control, but also guide data processing activities in Brazil. ANPD must embrace its role as a technical agency aimed at providing market and public implementations of innovative data-based technologies with the guidelines necessary to build technological solutions that respect fundamental rights and the means to innovate within those limitations.

Another institutional actor that could play a bigger role in the future is the Governance Committee created to implement the National Artificial Intelligence Strategy. This multi-stakeholder body is seated within the Ministry for Science, Technology, and Innovation, a crucial actor in promoting the full enjoyment of the benefits that may arise from science and innovation, especially in promoting economic and social development. However, this must be guided by a strategic vision that recognises the position that Brazil occupies in the process of recovering its industrial basis and catching-up with advanced economies.

Overall, the debate on FRT in Brazil has been marked by two movements that appear contrary to each other. On the one hand, reliance on FRT as a solution to immediate issues brings about hastened implementations that do not provide the necessary degree of transparency, accountability, proportionality analysis, and sensitivity to the fundamental rights to privacy and data protection. On the other hand, as mentioned in the opening of Section 16.2, civil society has reacted with increasing degrees of rejection of these technologies, reaching a generalised sentiment for the ban of FRT in the surveillance of public spaces. In the midst of these movements, existing and proposed norms seem to tackle some of the problematic aspects of FRT use, but fall short of giving a systematic and unified answer.

17

FRT Regulation in China

Jyh-An Lee and Peng Zhou

17.1 INTRODUCTION

Facial recognition technology (FRT) applications enjoy a staggering level of penetration in China. Valuing the technology's function in facilitating social control and public security, the Chinese government has not only implemented it widely,[1] but also used it to build a national surveillance architecture together with other mechanisms, such as the social credit system.[2] When providing telecommunications, banking, and transportation and other services, an increasing number of state-owned enterprises record citizens' facial data for their FRT systems.[3] FRT-empowered applications are also commonly adopted in the private sector,[4] for functions such as online payment, residential security, and hospital checking in.[5] The rapid development and wide adoption of FRT has made China a global leader in this field. In a recent round of the 1:N section of the US National Institute of Standard and Technology's (NIST's) Face Recognition Vendor Test, where algorithm providers compete for accuracy, the Hong Kong-based industry giant SenseTime came out on top, together with another China-based service provider.[6] SenseTime, as

---

[1] See, e.g., Seungha Lee, 'Coming into focus: China's facial recognition regulations' (4 May 2020), Center for Strategic & International Studies, www.csis.org/blogs/trustee-china-hand/coming-focus-chinas-facial-recognition-regulations.

[2] Qingxiu Bu, 'The global governance on automated facial recognition (AFR): Ethical and legal opportunities and privacy challenges' (2021) 2 *Int. Cybersecurity L Rev.* 113–145, at 130.

[3] See Yan Luo and Rui Guo, 'Facial recognition in China: Current status, comparative approach and the road ahead' (2021) 25 *U. Pa. J.L. & Soc. Change* 153–179, at 160–162.

[4] See Masha Borak, 'Facial recognition is used in China for everything from refuse collection to toilet roll dispensers and its citizens are growing increasingly alarmed, survey shows' (27 January 2021), *South China Morning Post*, www.scmp.com/tech/innovation/article/3119281/facial-recognition-used-china-everything-refuse-collection-toilet.

[5] Tristan G. Brown, Alexander Statman, and Celine Sui, 'Public debate on facial recognition technologies in China' (Summer 2021), *MIT Case Studies in Social and Ethical Responsibilities of Computing*, https://doi.org/10.21428/2c646de5.37712c5c.

[6] See Chris Burt, 'Top performing developers steady in updated NIST facial recognition 1:N test results' (4 May 2022), BiometricUpdate.com, www.biometricupdate.com/202205/top-performing-developers-steady-in-updated-nist-facial-recognition-1n-test-results.

FRT *Regulation in China* 243

Asia's largest artificial intelligence (AI) software company, has 22 per cent share of China's computer-vision market.[7] Moreover, surveillance camera makers, such as Hangzhou Hikvision Digital Technology, Zhejiang Dahua Technology, and Megvii Technology, are also leaders in the industry and provide essential equipment for China's pervasive implementation of FRT.[8]

FRT has triggered serious privacy concerns in many countries, and China is of no exception. Although some commentators indicate that Chinese culture is more tolerant towards privacy violations than that of Western countries and many Chinese favour FRT because of increased security or convenience,[9] there have been extensive debates concerning the justification and proper scope of FRT adoption in the country. China has been working on developing a regulatory framework for FRT since 2020. Although this framework aimed to substantially enhance personal data protection, there have been increasing risks and challenges to protect citizens' data in the FRT environment.

This chapter first introduces China's legal framework regulating FRT and analyses the underlying problems. Although current laws and regulations have restricted the deployment of FRT under some circumstances, these restrictions may function poorly when the technology is installed by the government or when it is deployed for the purpose of protecting public security. We use two cases to illustrate this asymmetric regulatory model, which can be traced to systematic preferences that existed prior to recent legislative efforts advancing personal data protection. Based on these case studies and evaluation of relevant regulations, this chapter explains why China has developed this distinctive asymmetric regulatory model towards FRT specifically and personal data generally.

17.2 REGULATING FRT IN A FISHBOWL SOCIETY

Given China's over-arching national security drive built on a strong state-centric approach to data governance, its turn to strengthen personal information protection can be somewhat of a puzzle.[10] Heavy investment in FRT and the extensive use by the Chinese government in security applications often portray an invasively transparent 'fishbowl society' straight from Orwellian nightmares.[11] Although the move to more robust protection of personal information appears to conflict with this perception, China has provided an interesting example regarding how authoritarian

---

[7] See Daniel Ren, 'AI, machine learning tech promises US$6000 billion annually for China economy as it pervades industries, says McKinsey' (25 July 2022), *South China Morning Post*, www.scmp.com/business/banking-finance/article/3186409/ai-machine-learning-tech-promises-us600-billion-annually.

[8] Ibid.

[9] Ibid.

[10] Ngoc Son Bui and Jyh-An Lee, 'Comparative cybersecurity law in socialist Asia' (2022) 55 *Vand. J. Transnat'l L.* 631–680, at 660–662.

[11] See Jonathan Turley, 'Anonymity, obscurity, and technology: Reconsidering privacy in the age of biometrics' (2020) 100 *B.U. L. Rev.* 2179–2261, at 2185–2186.

states balance their digital surveillance and the protection of individuals' personal data. The case of FRT regulations and their enforcement is a particular case to illustrate the challenges of maintaining this balance in China.

17.2.1 *National Laws and Judicial Interpretations*

As early as 2012, the Standing Committee of the Eleventh People's Congress, which is China's top legislative authority, declared its determination to protect digital privacy and planned to legislate data protection principles, such as specific limitations to the collection of personal information and other necessary precautions to safeguard privacy.[12] The 2020 PRC Civil Code (the Civil Code) marked a major shift to the regulatory landscape for the protection of personal information, including biometric data.[13] Prior to the Civil Code, China had no laws regulating FRT. Piecemeal regulations on personal data protection were scattered mostly under laws addressing cyber-crime and cyber-security breaches.[14] The Civil Code dedicates a new chapter to Chinese privacy laws and views personal information as a basic civil right (with the first clause declaring such right in the General Provisions of the Civil Law that came in 2017, as an interim step towards the Civil Code).[15] Article 1035 of the Civil Code establishes general data protection principles, such as purpose and scope limitations as well as the requirement for informed consent by data subjects in processing personal information.[16]

Following the Civil Code, the Supreme People's Court issued the Judicial Interpretation on the Regulation of FRT (the Judicial Interpretation) in 2021.[17] The Judicial Interpretation confirms that facial data falls within the scope of biometrically identifiable information, a type of personal information, prescribed by

[12] Quanguorenmin Daibiaodahui Changwuweiyuanhui Guanyu Jiaqiang Wangluoxinxibaohu de Jueding (《全国人民代表大会常务委员会关于加强网络信息保护的决定》) [Decision of the Standing Committee of the National People's Congress on Strenghening Information Protection on Networks] (2012). Issued by the Standing Committee of the National People's Congress, on 28 December.

[13] Zhonghua Renmin Gongheguo Minfadian (《中华人民共和国民法典》) [Civil Code of the People's Republic of China (Civil Code)] (2020). Promulgated by the Standing Committee of the National People's Congress on 28 May, effective on 1 January 2021 (hereafter Civil Code), Art. 1034.

[14] See, e.g., Zhonghua Renmin Gongheguo Wangluo Anquan Fa (《中华人民共和国网络安全法》) [Cybersecurity Law of the People's Republic of China] (2016). Promulgated by the Standing Committee of the National People's Congress on 7 November, effective on 1 June 2017), Art. 41.

[15] Civil Code, Chapter 6; Zhonghua Renmin Gongheguo Minfa Zongze (《中华人民共和国民法总则》) [General Provisions of the Civil Law of the People's Republic of China] (2017). Promulgated by the Standing Committee of the National People's Congress on 15 March, effective on 1 October 2017, Art. 111.

[16] Civil Code, Art. 1035.

[17] Zuigao Renmin Fayuan Guanyu Shenli Shiyong Renlian Shibie Jishu Chuli Geren Xinxi Xiangguan Minshi Anjian Shiyong Falu Ruogan Wenti De Guiding (《最高人民法院关于审理使用人脸识别技术处理个人信息相关民事案件适用法律若干问题的规定》) [Provisions of the Supreme People's Court on Several Issues concerning the Application of Law in the Trial of Civil Cases Relating to Processing of Personal Information by Using the Facial Recognition Technology] (2021). Promulgated by the Judicial Committee of the Supreme People's Court on 8 June, effective on 1 August 2021 (hereafter FRT Judicial Interpretation).

Article 1034 of the Civil Code.[18] Article 2 of the Judicial Interpretation specifically forbids the use of the technology by 'information processors' in public spaces such as hotels, shopping malls, and airports, unless otherwise authorised by authorities.[19] As a reflection of widespread use of facial scanning for identity verification and authentication purposes on residential and commercial properties, Article 10 forbids using FRT without individual consent.[20] The Judicial Interpretation also strengthened remedies for data subjects, including monetary damages and injunctive relief.[21] According to Article 5 of the Judicial Interpretation, liability can be exempted under some circumstances, such as on public security grounds.[22]

Shortly afterwards, the Standing Committee of the National People's Congress passed the PRC Personal Information Protection Law (the PIPL), with a focus on the obligations and liabilities of 'personal information processors' (PIPs).[23] Article 33 stipulates that rules under the PIPL apply to state agencies as well.[24] Moreover, the PIPL views biometric data as a type of 'sensitive personal information',[25] and the processing of such information is subject to a higher standard of protection. PIPs have to obtain independent 'opt-in' consent from data subjects to process such information and inform the latter of the necessity of processing measures as well as the impact on their rights.[26] For individuals under the age of fourteen, such consent must be obtained from parents or statutory agents.[27] Notably, the law allows image collection and personal identification equipment in public places for the purpose of safeguarding public security.[28] Thus, this rule provided a legal basis for security cameras widely deployed by the government.

Several local governments' metropolises have since introduced regulations at provincial and municipal levels to target more narrowly defined scenarios of FRT applications, such as for identity verifications on residential properties.[29] The Municipal

---

[18] Ibid., Art. 1.
[19] Ibid., Art. 2.
[20] Ibid., Art.10.
[21] Ibid., Art. 8 and Art.9.
[22] Ibid., Art. 5.
[23] Zhonghua Renmin Gongheguo Geren Xinxi Baohufa (《中华人民共和国个人信息保护法》) [Personal Information Protection Law of the People's Republic of China (PIPL)]. Promulgated by the Standing Committee of the National People's Congress on 20 Aug 2021, effective on 1 November 2021 (hereafter PIPL).
[24] Ibid., Art. 33.
[25] Ibid., Art. 28.
[26] Ibid., Art. 29.
[27] Ibid., Art. 31.
[28] Ibid., Art. 26.
[29] See, e.g., Hangzhoushi Wuye Guanli Tiaoli (《杭州市物业管理条例》) [Hangzhou Realty Management Regulation] (Hangzhou, China) (2021). Promulgated by the Standing Committee of People's Congress in Hangzhou on 9 August, effective on 1 March 2022, Art. 50; Shanghai Shi Shuju Tiaoli (《上海市数据条例》) [Shanghai Data Regulation] (2021). Promulgated by the Standing Committee of People's Congress in Shanghai on 25 November, effective on 1 January 2022, Art. 23; Shenzhen Jingji Tequ Shuju Tiaoli (《深圳经济特区数据条例》) [Data Regulations of Shenzhen

Government of Hangzhou, for example, amended its Regulation on Realty Management in 2020, limiting the compulsory collection and verification of biometric data such as facial information on residential and commercial properties.[30]

17.2.2 *Problems Underlying the Current Regulatory Framework*

Although China has adopted many internationally recognised data protection principles in its domestic laws,[31] its laws, regulations, and practices regarding FRT and their impact on personal data protection are still controversial. While the consent of data subject is required for another party's data collection, processing, and use, all these procedures can be omitted in the name of public security. A major challenge for personal data protection, in the context of deploying FRT for security purposes, is that the concept of public security does not seem to have any limit and can be interpreted quite expansively.

Taking the hospitality industry, for example, although the Judicial Interpretation specifically forbids the deployment of FRT in places such as hotels, it allows 'laws and regulations' to override this rule for security reasons.[32] To enforce the real-name registration rules,[33] quite a few local governments have mandated hotels to verify the identity of their guests by deploying FRT systems connected to the police database and scanning their faces at check-ins.[34] Although it is not clear whether the hotels have the legal right to process the facial data of their guests, local governments might take advantage of the vague language of the PIPL and infringe on personal data by interpreting the law in a less protective way. Article 13 of the PIPL allows data processing without the data subject's consent for the purpose of 'fulfilling legal responsibility or obligation'.[35] Local governments can easily argue that requiring

---

Special Economic Zone] (2021). Promulgated by the Standing Committee of People's Congress in Shanghai on 29 June, effective on 1 January 2022, Art. 19.

[30] Ibid.

[31] See James Y. Wang, 'The best data plan is to have a game plan: Obstacles and solutions to reaching international data privacy agreements' (2022) 28 *Mich. Tech. L. Rev.* 385–419, at 401–444.

[32] See FRT Judicial Interpretation, Art. 1 and Art. 5.

[33] See Jyh-An Lee and Ching-Yi Liu, 'Real-name registration rules and the fading digital anonymity in China' (2016) 25 *Wash. Int'l L.J.* 1–34, at 11–15.

[34] In Hunan Province, for example, according to provincial-level real-name registration measures, hotels are required to deploy police systems (the Lüguanye Zhian Guanli Xinxi Xitong, or Public Security Administration Information System) at check-ins to collect facial data. Failing to comply to these measures would deny guests from staying at hotels. In Yushu City of the Qinghai Province, local police started to upgrade the system with FRT-empowered capabilities in 2019. See Hunan Sheng Luguanye Luke Zhusu Shiming Dengji Guanli Guiding (《湖南省旅馆业旅游住宿实名登记管理规定》) [Provisions on the Administration of Real-Name Registration for the Hospitality Industry in Hunan Province] (2021) Promulgated by the Provincial Public Security Department of Hunan Province on 1 December, effective on 1 January 2022, Art.4; The Paper Government Affairs, Lihaile! Yushushi Lüguan Ruzhu Jiang Kaiqi Shualian Shidai (《厉害了！玉树市旅馆入住将开启"刷脸"时代》) [Amazing! Yushu Hotels Now Use Facial Recognition to Check in Guests], *The Paper* (20 November 2019) www.thepaper.cn/newsDetail_forward_5017320.

[35] See PIPL, Art. 13.

FRT Regulation in China   247

hotels to implement FRT is to 'fulfil its legal responsibility or obligation' regarding real-name registration or sector-specific safety policies. This typical example demonstrates that many of the personal data protection mechanisms regarding FRT provided in the laws and judicial interpretation could in reality function less effectively.

Another problem is the asymmetric regulation of FRT in the public and private sectors. While government agencies ordinarily have more chances to be exempted from personal data liabilities because of public security reasons, their liability for data breach is also lighter than that of private parties. While a private party's data misuse would result in both civil and administrative liabilities,[36] Article 68 of the PIPL indicates that violation of personal data rights by the government only leads to administrative liabilities, which would rely on self-correction measures conducted by state agencies.[37] Under this asymmetric framework, it is not surprising that administrative agencies may weigh their own convenience purpose more than personal data protection and thus use FRT in an unbalanced way. The technology has also been deployed to police individuals, including for minor misbehaviour such as jaywalking or wearing pyjamas in public places.[38] It is even reported that the government has used FRT on toilet paper dispensers installed in public toilets to fight off paper thieves.[39] During the COVID-19 pandemic, FRT was deployed comprehensively to verify identities and to monitor and control virus outbreaks on a regular basis.[40]

17.3 CASE STUDIES

In recent years, several FRT-related incidents have caught wide public attention and led to lively debates on the potential harm brought by this technology to society.[41] The most noticeable two cases were both raised by law professors challenging the justification of FRT use in citizens' daily lives. Their outcomes, however, differed significantly. While one professor successfully convinced the court that enterprises

---

[36]   See FRT Judicial Interpretation, Art. 8; PIPL, Art. 66 and Art. 69.
[37]   See PRC PIPL, Art. 68. A recent case might illustrate this point. In April 2022, a member of the Big Data Authority in Henan Province was identified in a scandal linked to illicit tempering of personal information from the 'health code' mobile application to wilfully prevent people from retrieving their money from banks that are involved in financial scams. After a public outcry, people deemed directly responsible, including the person from the Big Data Authority, were given administrative and intra-party sanctions, which cited the authority of both the PRC Law on Administrative Discipline for Public Officials (2020) and the party's disciplinary regulations. See, e.g., Phoebe Zhang, 'China officials who abused health codes to stop bank protests punished' (23 June 2022), *South China Morning Post*, www.scmp .com/news/china/politics/article/3182742/china-officials-who-abused-health-codes-stop-bank-protests.
[38]   See, e.g., John Wagner Givens and Debra Lam, 'Smarter cities or Bigger Brother? How the race for smart cities could determine the future of China, democracy, and privacy' (2020) 47 *Fordham Urb. L.J.* 829–882, at 865.
[39]   Ibid., 865–866.
[40]   See, e.g., Jacques deLisle and Shen Kui, 'China's response to Covid-19' (2021) 73 *Admin. L. Rev.* 19–51, 47–48.
[41]   Brown, Statman, and Sui, 'Public debate on facial recognition technologies'.

248 — Jyh-An Lee and Peng Zhou

could not unilaterally impose FRT on its consumers, the other failed to stop its pervasive use in Beijing metro stations.

17.3.1 *The Hangzhou Safari Park*

China had its first lawsuit concerning the commercial use of FRT in 2019.[42] Bing Guo, a law professor specialising in data protection law, sued Hangzhou Safari Park (HSP) for illegally imposing FRT-based access control after he purchased the annual pass.[43] The Fuyang District People's Court in Hangzhou ruled that HSP breached its contract with Guo by unilaterally changing its entrance policy.[44] However, the court failed to find any data protection violation because the plaintiff agreed to take a photo when he purchased the pass.[45]

In the second instance, the Hangzhou Intermediate People's Court's viewpoint was more favourable to the plaintiff on HSP's use of his facial data. The court explained that biometric information concerning facial characteristics was more sensitive than most other types of personal data.[46] Therefore, although there was no clear standard in the law regulating FRT at that time, the court held that HSP's use of this technology should be subject to more scrutiny.[47] Based on such understanding, the court ruled on 9 April 2021 that HSP was liable for using the plaintiff's facial data in the FRT systems without his consent.[48]

Some might believe that the political atmosphere was also favourable for Guo. While the Hangzhou Intermediate People's Court was hearing the case, the National People's Congress passed the Civil Code on 28 May 2020, with personal information protection as one of its salient points. China Central Television, the nation's largest state broadcaster, collaborated with China's Supreme People's Court and showcased this case as one of the ten benchmark cases in 2021.[49] Official publications by China's judiciary likewise prized the case as a sign of a progressive, more benevolent legal system.[50]

---

[42] Ibid.

[43] See Guobing Su Hangzhou Yesheng Dongwushijie Youxian Gongsi Fuwu Hetong Jiufen An (郭兵诉杭州野生动物世界有限公司服务合同纠纷案) [*Guo Bing v. Hangzhou Safari Park Co., Ltd.*], Hangzhou Fuyang District People's Court Case No. (2019) Zhe 0111 Minchu 6971, 20 November 2020.

[44] Ibid.

[45] Ibid.

[46] Guobing Su Hangzhou Yesheng Dongwushijie Youxian Gongsi Fuwu Hetong Jiufen An (郭兵诉杭州野生动物世界有限公司服务合同纠纷案) [*Guo Bing v. Hangzhou Safari Park Co., Ltd.*], Hangzhou Interm. People's Ct. of Zhejiang Province Case No. (2020) Zhe 01 Minzhong 10940, 9 April 2021.

[47] Ibid.

[48] Ibid.

[49] See, e.g., *China Daily*, 'Xin Shidai Tuidong Fazhi Jincheng 2021 Niandu Shida Anjian Jiexiao' (《"新时代推动法治进程2021年度十大案件"揭晓》) [Revealing ten cases of the year 2021 for the progress of the rule of law in the new era] (22 January 2022), https://cn.chinadaily.com.cn/a/202201/22/WS61ebd6caa3107be497a036f7.html.

[50] See, e.g., China Court, 'Renlian Shibie Jiufen Diyi An: Geren Xinxi Sifa Baohu De Dianfan' (《人脸识别第一案：个人信息司法保护的典范》) [The first court case involving facial recognition

FRT Regulation in China

Nevertheless, Guo himself was not satisfied with the judgment. He argued that the use of FRT by HSP was illegal per se,[51] but this viewpoint was not accepted by the court. Given the pervasive FRT in China, agreeing with Guo could be a step too far.

17.3.2 *The Beijing Metro Station*

In January 2022, Tsinghua law professor Dongyan Lao posted a long essay about China's social and legal problems on Weibo – the Chinese equivalent of Twitter.[52] One thing Lao lamented was her failed attempt to prevent the use of FRT in Beijing's subway stations.[53]

When the Beijing Subway Limited Company proposed to implement FRT in its 'real-name-based passenger' system, Lao was among the first against it.[54] In 2019, the Beijing's Rail Transit Control Centre, which is the administrative body responsible for underground transport in Beijing, announced the plan of enhancing subway station security by building an FRT-based railway passenger classification system.[55] The Centre explained that this system would not only protect public security of the Beijing subway, but also promote traffic efficiency.[56] The system was based on an AI-enabled facial image database, which could push security alerts automatically to personnel on site and drastically lessen their workloads.[57]

Shortly after the announcement, Lao openly expressed concerns regarding the over-intrusiveness of FRT in public venues and questioned the justification of this decision.[58] While China did not have any legislation regulating the FRT at that time, Lao argued that the rail transit agency had no authority to make such a

---

technology: A judicial epitome for personal information protection] (8 March 2022), www.chinacourt .org/article/detail/2022/03/id/6562816.shtml.

[51] See, e.g., Ye Yuan, 'A professor, a zoo, and the future of facial recognition in China' (26 April 2021), *Sixth Tone*, www.sixthtone.com/news/1007300/a-professor%2C-a-zoo%2C-and-the-future-of-facial-recognition-in-china.

[52] See David Cowhig, '2022: Chinese law prof's lament and encouragement' (29 January 2022), David Cowhig's Translation Blog, https://gaodawei.wordpress.com/2022/01/29/2022-chinese-law-profs-lament-and-encouragement/.

[53] Ibid.

[54] See Jeffrey Ding, 'ChinAI #77: A strong argument against facial recognition in the Beijing subway' (10 December 2019), *ChinAI Newsletter*, https://chinai.substack.com/p/chinai-77-a-strong-argument-against.

[55] Masha Borak, 'Beijing's subway system will use facial recognition to single out people for different security measures' (1 November 2019), *South China Morning Post*, www.scmp.com/abacus/tech/article/3035661/beijings-subway-system-will-use-facial-recognition-single-out-people.

[56] See Jeffrey Ding's translation of Lao's post at Ding, ChinAI #77.

[57] See *Beijing News*, 'Beijing Ditie Youwang Yingyong Renlian Shibie Jishu' (《北京地铁安检有望应用人脸识别技术》) [Beijing Metro security checks set to adopt facial recognition technology] (30 October 2019), http://epaper.bjnews.com.cn/html/2019-10/30/content_769638.htm?div=0.

[58] See Jeffrey Ding's blog: Ding, ChinAI #77

decision without conducting a public hearing.[59] In addition, Lao indicated that the system treated all passengers as potential criminals and therefore violated the presumption of innocence doctrine, which is fundamental to any modern criminal law system.[60] Shortly after this criticism, Lao's Weibo account was suspended and her posts were no longer available.[61]

To Lao's dismay, although the Centre postponed the plan of implementing FRT for nearly two years, it started to introduce the system in several stations in 2022.[62] The Centre compromised by adopting the FRT-based system on a voluntary basis. Passengers could get an express pass by completing real-name registration and uploading their facial data.[63] Beijing municipal government explained that the facial data was also linked to vaccination and testing results for the purpose of pandemic control. The Beijing municipal government announced in May 2022 that the system would be further linked to China's 'health code' – the mobile application used by Chinese people for mandatory checks on location data as well as COVID-19 testing reports.[64] Linking facial data to other types of sensitive personal information such as one's records of geo-location, could construe a form of highly aggregated data profiling. Information that does not seem to pose immediate harm might be less innocuous once a person's social relationships and patterns of behaviour are revealed through an extended period of data collection and aggregation. This aggregation problem can lead to highly intrusive portrayals of an individual's intimate life details, posing a unique threat to one's privacy. Lao's case reveals that the use of FRT for public security purposes can be easily justified by the authority and that challenging the government's use of FRT can face unsurmountable difficulties.

17.4 FRT IN THE SURVEILLANCE STATE

Although the Civil Code and PIPL have advanced personal data protection in China, Sections 17.2 and 17.3 have revealed that FRT used by the public sector has not been subject to much limitation. The government can always justify such use

---

[59] Ibid. for Ding's translation.

[60] Ibid.

[61] See, e.g., Stella Chen, 'Weibo chairman backs Chinese censor's crackdown and promises "ecologically sound" cyberspace' (25 September 2022), *South China Morning Post*, www.scmp.com/news/china/politics/article/3193605/weibo-chairman-backs-chinese-censors-crackdown-and-promises.

[62] See Cowhig's translation of Lao's essay: Cowhig, 'Chinese law prof's lament'.

[63] See *Southern Metropolis Daily*, 'Beijing Ditie Youjian Shualian Anjian, Yin Yinsi Xielu Danyou Zhuanjia: Yingxian Zhengqiu Yijian' (《北京地铁又见刷脸安检，引隐私泄露担忧 专家：应先征求意见》) [Beijing Metro resorts to facial recognition for security checks, causing concerns for data leaks. Experts: should consult the public's opinion] (29 December 2021), *Southern Metropolis Daily*, https://m.mp.oeeee.com/a/BAAFRD00002021122963889 3.html.

[64] See, e.g., Coco Feng, 'Coronavirus: Beijing, fighting Omicron, adds identity info to transport passes to speed up checks of Covid-19 status' (18 May 2022), *South China Morning Post*, www.scmp.com/tech/article/3178195/coronavirus-beijing-fighting-omicron-adds-identity-info-transport-passes-speed.

for the purpose of public security. This asymmetric regulatory model is rooted in China's unique political economy and regulatory philosophy.

First, the asymmetric regulatory model has been hugely influenced by China's unique human rights values. The fundamentals of China's human rights are different from those of the Western world. In the Western world, human rights were designed to protect individuals from state power from the beginning.[65] However, China has viewed human rights as derived from the state, which reigns supreme over the individual.[66] Consequently, China's approach to human rights has been largely state-centric and emphasises individual responsibilities over individual rights.[67] Privacy is no exception. China's data protection philosophy is built on the view that data collection and analysis should be actively cultivated to boost state capacity to achieve a wide range of social governance objectives.[68] Although the law provides citizens with considerable protection for their data privacy, it also creates numerous opportunities for the government to infringe upon citizens' privacy. This understanding well explains why the public security interest, which is usually represented by the government, is always superior to personal data rights.

Second, Chinese law's tolerance of FRT is closely related to its real-name registration policy. While anonymity is an important instrument to promote citizens' free speech and to protect them against government retribution in many countries,[69] the Chinese government has strictly enforced a nationwide 'real-name registration' policy to maintain social and political stability by eliminating digital anonymity.[70] Under this policy, Chinese authorities have required users to register their real identities with internet and telecommunications service providers when using their services through various authentication mechanisms for easy traceability since the early 2000s.[71] The wide adoption of FRT has been a natural development to streamline the enforcement of the real-name registration policy because this technology has become the most efficient and effective identity verification technique.[72] Mobile users, for example, are required to register through facial scanning when buying new SIM cards.[73]

---

[65] Jyh-An Lee, 'Hacking into China's cybersecurity law' (2018) 53 *Wake Forest L. Rev.* 57–104, at 99–100.

[66] Ibid., 100.

[67] Ibid.

[68] William Chaskes, 'The three laws: The Chinese Communist Party throws down the data regulation gauntlet' (2022) 79 *Wash. & Lee L. Rev* 1169–1224, at 1182–1184.

[69] Christopher Slobogin, 'Public privacy: Camera surveillance of public places and the right to anonymity' (2002) 72 *Miss. L.J.* 213–315, at 240–243.

[70] See Lee and Liu, 'Real-name registration rules', pp. 11–15.

[71] Ibid.

[72] Elizabeth A. Rowe, 'Regulating facial recognition technology in the private sector' (2020) 24 *Stan. Tech. L. Rev.* 1–54, at 23–24.

[73] See Lily Kuo, 'China brings in mandatory facial recognition for mobile phone users' (2 December 2019), *The Guardian*, www.theguardian.com/world/2019/dec/02/china-brings-in-mandatory-facial-recognition-for-mobile-phone-users.

Third, China is an unparalleled surveillance state extensively using digital technologies to maintain its regime. Personal data, including facial data, is a key resource for the Chinese government to implement its ambitious national plans towards an algorithmically governed socialist state.[74] The collection and processing of facial data has become increasingly essential for the government to build an effective surveillance system and to carry out economic plans, such as the ambitious 'smart city' initiative.[75] According to a recent report analysing more than 100,000 government bidding documents from China, one FRT-based project in Fujian Province alone could produce more than 2.5 billion images to be stored by the police in the cloud at any given time.[76] Given the extensive integration of FRT in public infrastructures, it is unlikely that the Chinese judiciary and government would easily declare such use illegal or unjustified. Similarly, it will be too costly for the legislators to roll back FRT deployment prescribed by other branches of the authorities.[77]

17.5 CONCLUSION

With the enactment of the Civil Code and PIPL, China has substantially enhanced its personal data protection. According to these two laws and the Judicial Interpretation on FRT, facial data is defined as sensitive personal information, and the deployment of FRT is more restrictive. The case of *HSP* represents the country's determination to prevent the over-use of facial data in the private sector. However, China still faces serious challenges regarding FRT-related personal data protection under its asymmetric regulatory framework. While the use of FRT is increasingly regulated in the country, the regulatory restrictions can be invariably lifted for the reason of public security. Government agencies have invariably claimed this regulatory exemption for its massive FRT deployment. Moreover, the liability for the government's abuse or misuse of personal data is quite insignificant compared with that that for private parties. This asymmetric framework has resulted from China's unique human rights philosophy, the endeavour to enforce a real-name registration policy, and, more importantly, its determination to sustain a digital surveillance state.

---

[74] Ira S. Rubinstein, Gregory T. Nojeim, and Ronald D. Lee, 'Systematic government access to personal data: a comparative analysis' (2014) 4(2) *International Data Privacy Law* 96–119, at 98, https://doi .org/10.1093/idpl/ipu004; Kevin Werbach, 'Orwell that ends well? Social credit as regulation for the algorithmic age' 2022 (4) *U. Ill. L. Rev*, 1417–1475, at 1427–1431.

[75] Givens and Lam, 'Smarter cities or Bigger Brother?', 851–858.

[76] Isabelle Qian, Muyi Xiao, Paul Mozur, and Alexander Cardia, 'Four takeaways from a *Times* investigation into China's expanding surveillance state' (21 June 2022), *New York Times*, www.nytimes .com/2022/06/21/world/asia/china-surveillance-investigation.html.

[77] See Luo and Guo, 'Facial recognition in China', 178.

18

Principled Regulation of Facial Recognition Technology

A View from Australia and New Zealand

Nessa Lynch and Liz Campbell

18.1 INTRODUCTION

Scholarly treatment of facial recognition technology (FRT) has focussed on human rights impacts,[1] with frequent calls for the prohibition of the technology.[2] While acknowledging the potentially detrimental and discriminatory uses that FRT use by the state has, this chapter seeks to advance discussion on what principled regulation of FRT might look like. It should be possible to prohibit or regulate unacceptable usage while retaining less hazardous uses.[3] In this chapter, we reflect on the principled use and regulation of FRT in the public sector, with a focus on Australia and Aotearoa New Zealand. We draw on our experiences as researchers in this area and from our professional involvement in oversight and regulatory mechanisms in these jurisdictions and elsewhere. Both countries have seen significant growth in the use of FRT, but regulation remains patchwork. In comparison with other jurisdictions, human rights protections and avenues for individual citizens to complain and seek redress remain insufficient in Australia and New Zealand.

A note on scope and terminology. In this chapter we concentrate on FRT use by the state or public sector – by which we mean government, police, and security use. Regulation of private sector use is a wider issue that is outside the scope of this chapter.

---

[1] Joe Purshouse and Liz Campbell, 'Privacy, crime control and police use of automated facial recognition technology' (2019) 3 *Criminal Law Review* 188–204.

[2] Lindsey Barret, 'Ban facial recognition technologies for children-and for everyone else' (2020) 26 *BUJ Sci. & Tech. L.* 223–286

[3] Nessa Lynch, 'Beyond the ban – Principled regulation of facial recognition technology' in Kelly Pendergast and Anna Pendergast (eds.), *More Zeros and Ones: Digital Technology, Maintenance and Equity in Aotearoa New Zealand* (Bridget Williams Books, 2022), pp. 121–182.

18.2 CONTEXT

18.2.1 *What Is FRT?*

FRT is a term used to describe a range of technologies involving processing of a person's facial image.[4] A facial image is a biometric that means a biological measurement or characteristic that can be used to identify an individual person. Though it may be collected from a distance, in public, and without the person's knowledge or consent, it remains an intrusion on the individual's privacy.[5] FRT may enhance and speed up existing human capabilities (such as finding an individual person in video footage) or create new capabilities (such as purporting to detect emotional states of people in crowds).

18.2.2 *Contemporary Usage in the Public Sector in Australia and New Zealand Jurisdictions*

FRT is a fast-growing technology, and it has many uses and potential uses in the public sector. In previous joint work we have canvassed the many usages of FRT across various sectors in New Zealand,[6] and discussed uses and potential uses in policing internationally and in New Zealand.[7] It is not possible here to review these uses in detail, but the main use-cases will be discussed briefly now.

First, the use of FRT is established in border security and immigration – the Smart Gate system widely in use at the Australian and New Zealand borders. The Australian Electronic Travel Authority may now be obtained by means of an app, using FRT. These use-cases are in the 'verification' category principally – comparing an individual's biometric template with another, but 'identification' (one to many) use-cases are also apparent.[8] Biometric data (including facial images) may be used to make or guide decisions.[9] Detection of identity fraud is the principal use-case.

Second, there is security usage by central government, local government, and policing authorities in camera networks in public spaces. For instance, police and councils in Perth and Melbourne use FRT to identify particular individuals,[10]

---

[4] Nessa Lynch and Andrew Chen, 'Facial recognition technology – Considerations for use in policing' (December 2021), New Zealand Police.

[5] Purshouse and Campbell, 'Privacy, crime control and police use'.

[6] Nessa Lynch, Liz Campbell, Joe Purshouse, and Marcin Betkier, 'Facial recognition technology in New Zealand: Towards a legal and ethical framework' (December 2020), The Law Foundation of New Zealand.

[7] Lynch and Chen, 'Facial recognition technology'.

[8] For example, in passport fraud detection. See Lynch et al., 'Facial recognition technology in New Zealand'.

[9] Immigration Act 2009 (NZ) s. 30.

[10] City of Melbourne, 'Safe city cameras' (n.d.), www.melbourne.vic.gov.au/community/safety-emergency/pages/safe-city-cameras.aspx; Elias Visontay, 'Councils tracking our faces on the sly' (29 August 2019), *The Australian*, www.theaustralian.com.au/nation/councils-tracking-our-faces-on-the-sly/news-story/eea2b51fa82b076796ad7e294e111d3e.

and Adelaide is proposing to use FRT through its closed-circuit television (CCTV) network.[11]

Thirdly, FRT technology may be used in policing. In Lynch and Chen's independent review of New Zealand Police's use and potential use of FRT, it was found that current or imminent planned use of FRT by New Zealand Police was limited and relatively low risk, including authentication for access to devices such as iPhones, identity matching, and retrospective analysis of lawfully acquired footage in limited situations. There was no evidence that the police are using or formally planning the use of live automated FRT. By contrast, police forces across Australia use live FRT as a means of preventing and investigating crime.[12] Facial images may also be submitted manually by a specified list of law enforcement, anti-corruption, and security agencies to the federal Identity Matching Services for a 'Face Identification Service matching request'. This does not connect to live video feeds, such as CCTV, and is not available to private sector or local government authorities.[13]

Fourthly, digital identity face recognition can be used to access certain government services online.[14] For instance, in Australia, signing into the MyGov account to access government services can be through FRT.

18.2.3 *A Spectrum of Impact on Individual and Collective Rights*

The variety of use-cases for FRT means a spectrum of impact on individual and societal rights and interests. As we expand on through case-studies, FRT can impact rights and interests such as privacy (both individual and collective), freedom of association, lawful protest, freedom from discrimination, and fair trial rights.[15]

As discussed earlier, it is vital to note that FRT has a range of use cases, ranging from consensual one-on-one identity verification (e.g., at the border) to widespread and intrusive live biometric tracking in public spaces. FRT technologies can have many legitimate and socially acceptable uses, including speed and scale improvements in processing evidential footage, identity matching, security and entry

---

[11] Erik Tlozek, 'SA Police could use Adelaide City facial recognition technology, despite being asked not to' (20 June 2022), *ABC News*, www.abc.net.au/news/2022-06-20/sa-police-could-use-adelaide-city-facial-recognition-technology/101166064

[12] See NT Police, Fire and Emergency Services, 'Success for Northern Territory Police at IAwards' (20 June 2016), Media release, https://pfes.nt.gov.au/newsroom/2016/success-northern-territory-police-iawards; NSW Government, 'NSW Police Force and facial recognition' (2022) www.police.nsw.gov .au/crime/terrorism/terrorism_categories/facial_recognition.

[13] Australian Government, 'ID match' (2022), www.idmatch.gov.au.

[14] Judy Skatssoon, '600k MyGov accounts now connected to digital ID' (24 October 2021), *Government News*, www.governmentnews.com.au/600k-mygov-accounts-now-connected-to-digital-id/

[15] Bethan Davies, Martin Innes, and Andrew Dawson, 'An evaluation of South Wales Police's use of automated facial recognition' (September 2018), Report, Universities' Police Science Institute and Crime & Security Research Institute, Cardiff University; Suzanne Shale, Deborah Bowman, Priyah Singh, and Leif Wenar, 'London Policing Ethics Panel: Final report on live facial recognition' (May 2019), London Policing Ethics Panel, London.

controls, and digital identity.[16] Factors such as who is operating the system, what the purposes are, whether there is independent authorisation or oversight, whether the person has consented to the collection and processing of their facial image, and whether the benefits are proportionate to the impacts are all relevant in considering the appropriate uses of FRT.[17]

18.2.4 Case Studies of Human Rights Impact

As an example of the rights and interests engaged by live automated FRT (AFR) in the context of a largely unregulated environment, there has been a legal challenge to police use in Wales. AFR is being deployed by police forces across England and Wales, with the Metropolitan Police and South Wales Police (SWP) among others trialling AFR for both live surveillance and identity verification.[18] As in Australia and New Zealand, the Westminster Parliament has not introduced any specific laws relating to AFR, but rather the police maintain that common law and human rights principles, the Data Protection Act 2018, and the Surveillance Camera Code of Practice provide a valid legal basis.

In the first ever legal challenge to the use of AFR, a Mr Bridges (described as a civil liberties campaigner) challenged the legality of SWP's general use and two particular deployments of AFR on the grounds that these were contrary to the Human Rights Act 1998, Data Protection legislation, and that the decision to implement was not taken in accordance with the Equality Act 2010.[19] The Divisional Court rejected this application.

On appeal, the Court of Appeal ruled that the Divisional Court erred in its finding that the measures were 'in accordance with the law'. The court engaged in a holistic analysis of whether the framework governing the SWP's use of live AFR was reasonably accessible and predictable in its application,[20] and sufficient to guard against 'overbroad discretion resulting in arbitrary, and thus disproportionate, interference with Convention rights'.[21] While the Court of Appeal rejected that statutory authorisation was needed, it accepted that AFR requires more safeguards than for overt photography.[22] The legal framework gave too much discretion to individual officers to determine who was on the watchlist, and where AFR could be deployed.[23]

---

[16] Lynch and Chen, 'Facial recognition technology'.

[17] Lynch et al., 'Facial recognition technology in New Zealand'; Lynch and Chen, 'Facial recognition technology'.

[18] Gareth Corfield, 'Tech firm used by Met and MoD forced to delete billions of Facebook photos' (23 May 2022), *The Telegraph*; Home Office UK, 'Police transformation fund: Successful bids 2016 to 2017' (4 September 2017), www.gov.uk/government/publications/police-transformation-fund-successful-bids-2016-to-2017

[19] *R (Bridges) v. The Chief Constable of South Wales* [2019] EWHC 2341 (Admin).

[20] Here, *R (Catt) v. Association of Chief Police Officers* [2015] UKSC 9 at [11]–[14] per Lord Sumption was cited with approval.

[21] *Beghal v. Director of Public Prosecutions* [2016] AC 88 at [31] and [32] per Lord Hughes.

[22] *R (Bridges) v. The Chief Constable of South Wales*, [85]–[90].

[23] Ibid., [96].

Principled Regulation of FRT

Moreover, the Court of Appeal held that the SWP never had due regard to the need to eliminate discrimination on the basis of sex and race.[24]

That said, the Appeal Court held that the SWP's use of AFR was a proportionate interference with the European Court of Human Rights Article 8 right to privacy and family life, and as such was 'necessary' and 'in pursuit of a legitimate aim' under Article 8(2).

South Wales Police indicated that it would not appeal the Court of Appeal's decision: 'There is nothing in the Court of Appeal judgment that fundamentally undermines the use of facial recognition to protect the public. This judgment will only strengthen the work which is already underway to ensure that the operational policies we have in place can withstand robust legal challenge and public scrutiny.'[25]

In this region, a key illustration of the impacts on privacy concerns is the use by Australian police of Clearview AI's facial recognition software.[26] Though there has not been a legal challenge in the courts here, the Office of the Australian Information Commissioner (OAIC) has investigated and made findings as to the use of this software. Clearview AI's technology operates by harvesting images from publicly available web sources and offering its technologies to government and law enforcement agencies.[27] From October 2019 until March 2020, Clearview AI offered free trials to the Australian Federal Police, Victoria Police, Queensland Police Service, and South Australia Police.[28] This revelation about its use was despite initial police denials.[29]

In November 2021, following a joint investigation with the United Kingdom's Information Commissioner's Office, the OAIC found that Clearview AI breached Australia's privacy laws through its practice of harvesting biometric information from the web and disclosing it though a facial recognition tool. In a summary

---

[24] Ibid., [199]. See Joy Buolamwini and Timnit Gebru, 'Gender shades: intersectional accuracy disparities in commercial gender classification' *Conference on Fairness, Accountability, and Transparency*, New York (February 2018); Joy Buolamwini, 'Response: Racial and gender bias in Amazon Rekognition – Commercial AI system for analyzing faces' (25 January 2019), *Medium*, https://medium.com/@Joy.Buolamwini/response-racial-and-gender-bias-in-amazon-rekognition-commercial-ai-system-for-analyzing-faces-a289222eeced.

[25] South Wales Police, 'Response to the Court of Appeal judgment on the use of facial recognition technology', South Wales Police, Media release (11 August 2020), www.south-wales.police.uk/en/newsroom/response-to-the-court-of-appeal-judgment-on-the-use-of-facial-recognition-technology/

[26] Stephanie Palmer-Derrien, 'Aussie entrepreneur launches "disturbing and unethical" facial recognition tech in Silicon Valley' (22 January 2020), *Smart Company*, www.smartcompany.com.au/startupsmart/news/aussie-clearview-ai/.

[27] Hannah Ryan, 'Australian Police have run hundreds of searches on Clearview AI's facial recognition tool' (28 February 2020), *BuzzFeed News*, www.buzzfeed.com/hannahryan/clearview-ai-australia-police.

[28] *Commissioner Initiated Investigation into Clearview AI, Inc. (Privacy)* [2021] AICmr 54 (14 October 2021) [8].

[29] Jake Goldenfein, 'Australian police are using the Clearview AI facial recognition system with no accountability' (4 March 2020), *The Conversation*, https://theconversation.com/australian-police-are-using-the-clearview-ai-facial-recognition-system-with-no-accountability-132667.

258 Nessa Lynch and Liz Campbell

released with the OAIC's formal determination, the OAIC found that Clearview AI breached the Privacy Act 1988 (Cth) by:

- collecting Australians' sensitive information without consent;
- collecting personal information by unfair means;
- not taking reasonable steps to notify individuals of the collection of personal information;
- not taking reasonable steps to ensure that personal information it disclosed was accurate, having regard to the purpose of disclosure;
- not taking reasonable steps to implement practices, procedures, and systems to ensure compliance with the Australian Privacy Principles.[30]

Following the investigation, Clearview AI blocked all requests for user accounts from Australia, and there is no evidence of Australian users of the technology since March 2020.[31] Further, the OAIC required that all scraped images and related content be destroyed as they breached the Privacy Act.[32] Subsequently, the OAIC determined that the Australian Federal Police failed to comply with its privacy obligations in using the Clearview AI facial recognition tool, and instructed the AFP to review and improve its practices, procedures, systems, and training in relation to privacy assessments.[33]

18.3 OPTIONS FOR PRINCIPLED REGULATION

Despite the considerable impact on individual and collective rights and interests, there is no discrete law governing the use of FRT in either Australia or New Zealand. Patently, FRT can be subject to existing legislative regimes such as privacy and search and surveillance, but unlike other forms of biometrics, such as fingerprints and DNA, the collection and processing of facial images remains largely unregulated.

In this section we canvass various options for principled regulation of FRT, at state and international level, with different degrees of specificity and latitude. These include proposals for domestic legislation, a case study of cross-national regulation, state-level principles, and self-governance.

18.3.1 Domestic Legislation

We favour the introduction of specific and tailored legislative provisions with an associated code of conduct to regulate the use of FRT by public entities. In March

---

[30] Office of the Australian Information Commission (OAIC), 'Clearview AI breached Australians' privacy', OAIC Media Release (2 November 2021), www.oaic.gov.au/updates/news-and-media/clearview-ai-breached-australians-privacy. See further, *Commissioner Initiated Investigation into Clearview AI, Inc.*
[31] *Commissioner Initiated Investigation into Clearview AI, Inc.*, at [239].
[32] Ibid., at [242].
[33] Office of the Australian Information Commissioner (OAIC), 'AFP ordered to strengthen privacy governance' (16 December 2021), www.oaic.gov.au/updates/news-and-media/afp-ordered-to-strengthen-privacy-governance.

Principled Regulation of FRT

2021, the Australian Human Rights Commission (AHRC) released its report *Human Rights and Technology*, which assesses the impact of FRT and biometric technology and makes the case for regulation.[34] The report recognises the potential human rights impacts arising from the use of these technologies, including most obviously to the right to privacy.[35] To guard against this, the AHRC recommends that commonwealth, state, and territory governments should:

> Introduce legislation that regulates the use of facial recognition and other biometric technology. The legislation should:
>
> (a) expressly protect human rights
> (b) apply to the use of this technology in decision making that has a legal, or similarly significant, effect for individuals, or where there is a high risk to human rights, such as in policing and law enforcement
> (c) be developed through in-depth consultation with the community, industry and expert bodies such as the Australian Human Rights Commission and the Office of the Australian Information Commissioner.[36]

Until such reforms can be enacted, the AHRC recommends a moratorium on the use of facial recognition and biometric technologies that would fit within para. (a) above.[37]

In September 2022, the newly formed Human Technology Institute based at the University of Technology Sydney released a report.[38] This proposes reform to existing regulation around FRT and outlines a Model Law 'to foster innovation and enable the responsible use of FRT, while protecting against the risks posed to human rights'.[39] While the report recognises that FRT can be used consistently with international human rights law, 'FRT necessarily also engages, and often limits or restricts, a range of human rights'.[40]

Reform to existing law dealing indirectly with FRT in Australia is needed because of the rapid development and deployment of FRT which can extract, store, and process a vast amount of information. Australia has existing laws that apply to the deployment and use of FRT, including privacy laws that regulate the handling of biometric information, but 'on the whole, these existing laws are inadequate in addressing many of the risks associated with FRT'.[41]

---

[34] Australian Human Rights Commission (AHRC), 'Human rights and technology' (March 2021), Final report, p. 9.
[35] Ibid., pp. 114–116.
[36] Ibid., p. 116.
[37] Ibid.
[38] Nicholas Davis, Lauren Perry, and Edward Santow, 'Facial recognition technology: Towards a model law' (September 2022), Report, Human Technology Institute, University of Technology Sydney, September. One of the report's authors, Professor Edward Santow, is the former Australian Human Rights Commissioner and worked on the AHRC's report just discussed.
[39] Ibid., p. 7.
[40] Ibid.
[41] Ibid., p. 8.

The report sets out the following purposes of the Model Law:

- Uphold human rights
- Apply a risk-based approach
- Support compliance
- Transparency in the use of FRT
- Effective oversight and regulation
- Accountability and redress
- Jurisdictional compatibility.[42]

The human rights risks of FRT are discussed in Section 31–2, including infringements on the right to privacy and intrusion into private life. Other concerns are raised in relation to rights to equality and non-discrimination, and here the report authors note the *Bridges* case and the acknowledged discriminatory impact of FRT through inherently discriminatory algorithms. The potential of FRT to interfere with the right not to be subject to arbitrary arrest or detention and the rights to equality before the law and to a fair trial are also considered.

The Model Law includes specific legal requirements for the deployment of FRT, including compliance with specific technical standards,[43] and specific privacy law requirements.[44] Importantly, the Model Law also contemplates assigning regulatory oversight to a body that has human rights expertise, specifically expertise in privacy rights. The report suggests that potential regulators could be the OAIC or the AHRC, but notes that whatever regulatory body is given regulatory responsibility it must be provided with necessary financial and other resources to fulfil its role adequately in a sustainable long-term way.[45]

The risks of a legislative gap are clear. Indeed, ClubsNSW (the representative body for registered clubs in New South Wales, NSW) announced its intention to proceed with the roll-out of FRT in all NSW pubs and clubs (it is already being used at about a hundred licensed venues) after the NSW government announced that it would not proceed with law reform on the regulation of FRT.[46]

18.3.2 *State-Level Principles and Guidance*

In the absence of legislation, many jurisdictions worldwide have established state level principles and guidance to regulate algorithm and data driven technologies such as FRT. New Zealand is the first country to establish standards for algorithm

---

[42] Ibid., p. 13.
[43] Ibid., p. 65.
[44] Ibid., pp. 67–68.
[45] Ibid., p. 80.
[46] Tasmin Rose, 'Clubs likely to proceed with facial recognition after NSW Government shelves reform bill' (2 November 2022), *The Guardian Australia*, www.theguardian.com/australia-news/2022/nov/02/clubs-likely-to-proceed-with-facial-recognition-after-nsw-government-shelves-reform-bill.

Principled Regulation of FRT 261

usage by government and public sector agencies.[47] The Algorithm Charter sets principles for public sector agencies using algorithms to make or guide decisions to which agencies can commit publicly. The term 'algorithm' is undefined, with a focus on the impact of the decision made using the algorithm rather than the complexity of the algorithm itself.

The Algorithm Charter requires transparency in algorithm use, respect for the Treaty partnership (with the Indigenous people of Aotearoa New Zealand), a focus on people, use of data that is fit for purpose, safeguarding privacy, human rights and ethics, and retention of oversight by human operators.[48] Also in New Zealand, the Government Chief Data Steward and the Privacy Commissioner have jointly issued guidelines for public sector use of data and analytics, with similar emphasis on transparency, societal benefit, retaining human oversight, and focussing on people:[49]

Principles and guidance of this nature are useful in setting high level expectations and entrenching fundamental values, but lack any regulatory enforcement mechanism. Unlike legislation, they cannot be used to respond to individual breaches of rights or provide an objective mechanism for redress.

18.3.3 *Cross-National Standards*

The Artificial Intelligence Act (AI Act) is a nearly-finalised European Union law that will introduce a common regulatory and legal framework for AI across all sectors (excluding the military) and all types of AI.[50] This is important because, like the General Data Protection Regulation (GDPR), the AI Act will have extra-territorial effect and immense influence on national laws, given the extent of the EU market. Technology suppliers are likely to align product design with these regulations even in non-EU countries. It seeks to so do through 'a balanced and proportionate horizontal regulatory approach to AI that is limited to the minimum necessary requirements to address the risks and problems linked to AI, without unduly constraining or hindering technological development or otherwise disproportionately increasing the cost of placing AI solutions on the market'.[51]

AI is defined in the proposed AI Act in a two-stage model. First, it is defined in Article 3 somewhat generally by reference to the concept 'artificial intelligence system', which is 'software that is developed with one or more of the techniques and

---

[47] Charlotte Graham-McLay, 'New Zealand claims world first in setting standards for government use of algorithms' (28 July 2020), *The Guardian*, www.theguardian.com/world/2020/jul/28/new-zealand-claims-world-first-in-setting-standards-for-government-use-of-algorithms.

[48] Algorithm Charter for Aotearoa New Zealand (2020), https://data.govt.nz/toolkit/data-ethics/government-algorithm-transparency-and-accountability/algorithm-charter/.

[49] Privacy Commissioner and the Government Chief Data Steward, 'Principles for the safe and effective use of data and analytics' (16 May 2018), www.privacy.org.nz/publications/guidance-resources/principles-for-the-safe-and-effective-use-of-data-and-analytics-guidance/

[50] Proposal for Artificial Intelligence Act (European Commission, 2021/0106 (COD)).

[51] Ibid.

approaches listed in Annex I and can, for a given set of human-defined objectives, generate outputs such as content, predictions, recommendations or decisions influencing the environments they interact with'. Annex I lists the techniques as:

- machine learning approaches, including learning supervised, unsupervised, and by reinforcement, using a wide variety of methods, including deep learning;
- approaches based on logic and knowledge, namely knowledge representation, inductive (logic) programming, knowledge bases, inferences and deduction engines, reasoning systems (symbolic), and expert systems; and
- statistical approaches, Bayes estimation, research and optimisation methods.

Regulation of AI technologies under the proposed Act are based on a risk assessment model. This model is complex. Article 5(1)(d) bans 'real-time remote biometric identification systems in publicly accessible spaces for law-enforcement purposes (and so would cover a *Bridges*-type scenario). However, the ban does not cover FRT used by law-enforcement that is not real-time, or that is used by other public or private entities but equally pose a threat to fundamental human rights.[52] Nevertheless, the majority of FRT is classified as a high-risk AI (save for emotional recognition systems), which is a classification updated in accordance with technological advances and takes into account not only the technology itself, but also the use to which that technology may be put.[53]

In a similar way to the GDPR, the proposed AI Act has a presumption prohibiting high-risk AI systems unless their use is subject to various requirements including a control and monitoring procedure and requirements to report serious incidents and malfunctions of these high-risk AI systems (Art. 6, Annex III). Conversely, those systems designated as being low-risk may be used without being subject to these requirements (Art. 52(2)).

A concern about the proposed AI Act in the EU is 'its silence on the right to take legal action against suppliers or users of AI systems for non-compliance with its rules'.[54] Other concerns have been raised about the potential for conflicts between bodies and institutions set up to regulate AI under the proposed law.[55] Concerns have also been raised about the broadness of the definition of AI in the proposed law, such that it does not account for combinations of algorithms and data and potentially covers software not generally considered AI.[56] These are fair criticisms.

Notwithstanding these concerns about the proposed AI Act, it has been argued that the AI Act will have international significance. Indeed, Dan Svantesson argues that the Act will first have an impact in Australia in the same way that the GDPR impacts cross-border data flows, with the likelihood being that it will become the

---

[52] Vera Lúca Raposo, 'Ex machina: Preliminary critical assessment of the European Draft Act on Artificial Intelligence' (2022) 30 *International Journal of Law and Information Technology* 88, 95.

[53] Ibid., p. 96.

[54] Ibid., p. 103.

[55] Ibid., p. 107.

[56] Ibid., p. 91.

Principled Regulation of FRT
263

default international setting for dealing with AI given the size of the EU market.[57] Second, and perhaps more substantially, the AI Act may also apply indirectly to Australian actors who operate within the EU market, such as by providing AI systems.[58] Also important is the ability of the AI Act to be utilised in law reform in Australia and New Zealand as the basis for progressing towards an regional approach to the regulation of AI.[59]

At the time of writing, the AI Act has been voted on in the EU Parliament, and lawmakers are now conducting the negotiation to finalise the provisions of the new legislation, which could include revising definitions, revising the list of prohibited systems and the parameters of obligations on suppliers.[60]

On 12 May 2022, the European Data Protection Board adopted Guidelines 05/2022 on the use of FRT in the area of law enforcement (Guidelines 05/2022).[61] The Guidelines recognise that FRT 'may be used to automatically recognise individuals based on his/her face' and is 'often based on artificial intelligence such as machine learning technologies'.[62] For law enforcement agencies, Guidelines 05/2022 recognise that such technologies promise 'solutions to relatively new challenges such as investigations of big data, but also to known problems, in particular with regard to under-staffing and observation and search measures'.[63] The Guidelines recognise that the application of such technology by law enforcement agencies engages a number of human rights, including the right to respect for private and family life under Article 8 of the European Convention on Human Rights.[64] More broadly, the application of FRT by law enforcement will – and to some extend already does – have significant implications for individuals and groups of people, including minorities. The application of FRT is considerably prone to interfere with fundamental rights beyond the right to protection of personal data.[65]

Turning to the technology, the Guidelines differentiate FRT from biometric technology because the former technology can fulfil two distinct functions, namely: (1) the identification of a person in order to verify who that person claims to be (one-to-one verification); and (2) identification of a person among a group of individuals, in a specific area, image or database (one-to-many identification).[66] It is the unique

---

[57] Dan Svantesson, 'The European Union Artificial Intelligence Act: Potential implications for Australia' (2022) 47 *Alternative Law Journal* 4, 6.

[58] Ibid., pp. 6–8.

[59] Ibid., pp. 8–9.

[60] Tambiama Madiega, *Briefing: Artificial Intelligence Act* (2nd ed., European Parliamentary Research Service, 2023).

[61] Guidelines on the Use of Facial Recognition Technology in the Area of Law Enforcement, Guidelines No 05/2022 (European Data Protection Board, European Union, adopted 12 May 2022) (Guidelines 05/2022).

[62] Ibid., p. 6.

[63] Ibid., p. 6.

[64] Ibid., p. 2.

[65] Ibid.

[66] Ibid., p. 7.

functions to which FRT can be put and the potential consequences of its use that justify special regulation.

The Guidelines next summarise the applicable legal framework as a guide 'for consideration when assessing future legislative and administrative measures as well as implementing existing legislation on a case-by-case basis that involve FRT'.[67]

The remainder of the Guidelines contains a number of annexes; these include Annex II (practical guidance for managing FRT projects in law enforcement agencies) and Annex III (practical examples). These form a potential starting point for the development of law enforcement agency guidelines, including of the kind contemplated by the English and Welsh Court of Appeal in *Bridges*.

18.3.4 *Self-Governance*

In the absence of legislative or robust state-level regulation, some state actors have moved to establish self-regulation. In New Zealand, trials of a FRT application (Clearview AI) by a section of New Zealand Police in 2020 sparked a review of the use of technology, owing to the adverse publicity generated and also the lack of any firm legislative or regulatory regime to govern its use.

Initial Guidelines for the trial of emerging technology were published in September 2020, and the Police Manual Chapter was published in July 2022.[68] New Zealand Police are now required to seek advice from senior management even when responding to an offer from a technology company and even when the new technology would only be explored in a non-operational test setting. Approval for any trial must go through a formal governance and risk assurance process. Submissions for approval are expected to consider ethical and legal considerations, including public expectations and legal obligations surrounding the right to privacy.

However, there is no reference in the guidelines to the principles of human rights (such as the right to be free from discrimination, freedom of expression, the right to peacefully protest).

In April 2023, New Zealand Police publicly released a stocktake list of technology capabilities. This is an extensive list that details all instances of technology capabilities – from routine business procedures to state-of-the-art technologies.[69]

Further, an independent review of FRT (carried out by one of the present authors with a co-author) investigated and reported on use and potential use of FRT within New Zealand Police and made ten recommendations, which were accepted by the

---

[67] Ibid., p. 11.

[68] New Zealand Police, 'Trial or adoption of new policing technology – Police Manual chapter' (July 2022), www.police.govt.nz/about-us/publication/trial-or-adoption-new-policing-technology-police-manual-chapter.

[69] New Zealand Police, 'NZ Police technology capabilities list' (April 2023), www.police.govt.nz/sites/default/files/publications/technology-capabilites-list.pdf.

leadership.[70] This included a commitment to continue to pause any consideration of live automated FRT, ensure continuous governance and oversight of deployment of FRT, implement guidelines for access to a third party system, embed a culture of ethical use of data in the organisation, and implement a system for ongoing horizon scanning.

Again, in the absence of a state level regulatory mechanism, New Zealand Police has established an expert panel (composed of experts with expertise in technology, governance, assurance, criminal law, and Te Ao Māori). This panel's role is 'to provide advice and oversight from an ethical and policy perspective of emergent technologies'.[71]

In another example of self-regulation, Scotland has a moratorium on live AFR in policing. While Police Scotland's strategy document *Policing 2026* included a proposal to introduce AFR,[72] a Scottish parliamentary committee was critical of this owing to its discriminatory implications, lack of justification for its need, and its radical departure from the principle of policing by consent.[73] Police Scotland responded that the force was not using live FRT currently and that it would ensure safeguards were in place prior to doing so; it was agreed that the impact of its use should be fully understood before it was introduced.[74]

These decisions by police organisations to self-regulate the use of technology are probably driven as much by perceptions of social licence and public attitudes as principle. It demonstrates again that state-level regulation is required to provide an objective and transparent standard, with mechanisms for redress.

18.3.5 A Robust Regulator

Any regulation of FRT must be accompanied by a robust regulator.

A case study of a regulator in a comparable jurisdiction is the Biometrics Commissioner role in Scotland, who has established a Code of Practice for biometric data use (encompassing facial images) in policing. Scottish law defines biometric data as 'information about an individual's physical, biological, physiological or behavioural characteristics which is capable of being used, on its own or in combination with other information … to establish the identity of an individual'.[75]

---

[70] Lynch and Chen, 'Facial recognition technology'.

[71] New Zealand Police, 'Advisory panel on emergent technologies' (2022) www.police.govt.nz/about-us/programmes-and-initiatives/police-use-emergent-technologies/advisory-panel-emergent.

[72] Police Scotland and Scottish Police Authority, 'Policing 2026: Our 10-year strategy for policing in Scotland' (2017), Report.

[73] Justice Sub-Committee on Policing, 'Facial recognition: How policing in Scotland makes use of this technology' (11 February 2020), SP Paper 678, 1st Report, 2020 (Session 5).

[74] Letter from Assistant Chief Constable Duncan Sloan to Justice Sub-Committee Convener (8 April 2020).

[75] Scottish Biometrics Commissioner Act 2020, s 23(1) and (2).

The purposes of the Scottish Biometrics Commissioner are to review law, policy, and practice relating to collection, retention, use, and disposal of biometric data by Police Scotland, keep the public informed and aware of powers and duties related to biometric data (e.g., how the powers are used and monitored, and how the public can challenge exercise of these powers), and monitor the impact of the Code of Practice and raise awareness of the Code.

As another example, the AHRC report cited earlier argues that the rise of AI technology (including FRT) provides an important moment to develop standards and apply regulation in a way that supports innovation while also addressing risk of human rights harm.[76] To this end, the AHRC recommends the establishment of an AI Safety Commission in Australia 'to support regulators, policy makers, government and business [to] apply laws and other standards in respect of AI-informed decision making'.[77]

18.4 CONCLUSION

While biometric technologies such as FRT have become more prevalent and more complex, and are being utilised in increasingly diverse situations, legislation, regulation, and frameworks to guide ethical use are less well developed.

This chapter has demonstrated how state agencies, particularly in policing and security services in New Zealand and Australia, have a broad discretion as to their use of FRT.

We suggest that FRT should be used only when predicated upon explicit statutory authorisation and following appropriate ethical review.[78]

Principled regulations should comprise a national statutory framework with a concomitant code of practice. Moreover, we recommend independent approval and oversight of the proportionality and necessity of operations. Jurisdictions should have a robust regulator, with the Scottish Biometrics Commissioner being a good example.

---

[76] AHRC, 'Human rights and technology', p. 127.
[77] Ibid.
[78] Cf. Biometrics and Forensics Ethics Group, 'Ethical issues arising from the police use of live facial recognition technology' (February 2019), where the pilot project had begun already.

19

Morocco's Governance of Cities and Borders

AI-Enhanced Surveillance, Facial Recognition, and Human Rights

Sylvia I. Bergh, Issam Cherrat, Francesco Colin, Katharina Natter, and Ben Wagner

19.1 INTRODUCTION[*]

Owing to advances around artificial intelligence (AI), such as computer vision and facial recognition, digital surveillance technologies are becoming cheaper and easier to use as everyday tools of governance worldwide.[1] Typically developed by companies and governments in the Global North and tested in the Global South or on the 'periphery' of powerful actors,[2] they are becoming key tools of governance in both democratic and authoritarian contexts.[3] As the AI Global Surveillance Index

---

[*] We are grateful to the former Centre of Expertise on Global Governance at The Hague University of Applied Sciences and the Institute of Security and Global Affairs at Leiden University for the seed grant that made this research possible.

[1] Louise Eley and Ben Rampton, 'Everyday surveillance, Goffman, and unfocused interaction' (2020) 18 *Surveillance & Society* 199–215, https://ojs.library.queensu.ca/index.php/surveillance-and-society/article/view/13346; David Lyon, *Theorizing Surveillance: The Panopticon and Beyond* (William Publishing, 2006); David Lyon, *Surveillance Society: Monitoring Everyday Life* (Open University Press, 2001); Rocco Bellanova, Kristina Irion, Katja Lindskov Jacobsen, Francesco Ragazzi, Rune Saugmann, Lucy Suchman, Jesus Benito-Picazo, Enrique Domínguez, Esteban J. Palomo, and Ezequiel López-Rubio, 'Toward a critique of algorithmic violence' (2021) 15 *International Political Sociology* 121–150. https://academic.oup.com/ips/article/15/1/121/6170592; Jesus Benito-Picazo et al., 'Deep learning-based video surveillance system managed by low cost hardware and panoramic cameras' (2020) 27 *Integrated Computer-Aided Engineering* 373–387, www.medra.org/servlet/aliasResolver?alias=iospress&doi=10.32 33/ICA-200632; Eley and Rampton, 'Everyday surveillance'; Francesco Ragazzi, 'Security Vision: The algorithmic security politics of computer vision' (2021), www.securityvision.io/.

[2] Jozef Andraško, Matúš Mesarčík, and Ondrej Hamul'ák, 'The regulatory intersections between artificial intelligence, data protection and cyber security: Challenges and opportunities for the EU Legal Framework' (2021) 36 *AI & SOCIETY* 623–636, https://link.springer.com/10.1007/s00146-020-01125-5; Steve Gold, 'Military biometrics on the frontline' (2010) 2010(10) *Biometric Technology Today* 7–9, https://linkinghub.elsevier.com/retrieve/pii/S0969476510702071; Josh Chin and Clément Bürge, 'Twelve days in Xinjiang: How China's surveillance state overwhelms daily life' (20 December 2017), *Wall Street Journal*, www.wsj.com/articles/twelve-days-in-xinjiang-how-chinas-surveillance-state-overwhelms-daily-life-1513700355.

[3] Taylor C. Boas, 'Weaving the authoritarian web: The control of internet use in nondemocratic regimes' in John Zysman and Abraham Newman (eds.), *How Revolutionary Was the Digital*

268   *Bergh, Cherrat, Colin, Natter, and Wagner*

shows,[4] countries with authoritarian systems and low levels of political rights are investing particularly heavily in AI surveillance techniques such as advanced analytic systems, facial recognition cameras, and sophisticated monitoring capabilities.[5]

AI surveillance offers governments two major capabilities. First, it allows regimes to automate many tracking and monitoring functions formerly delegated to human operators. This brings cost efficiencies, decreases reliance on security forces, and over-rides potential principal–agent loyalty problems.[6] Second, as AI systems never tire or fatigue, AI technology can cast a much wider surveillance net than traditional control methods. As Feldstein points out, 'this creates a substantial "chilling effect" even without resorting to physical violence as citizens never know if an automated bot is monitoring their text messages, reading their social media posts, or geotracking their movements around town'.[7]

Some scholars have observed the radical interdependence of the global AI development ecosystem, as only a few countries can afford to build their own local AI ecosystems.[8] For example, China is a major supplier of AI surveillance, with Huawei

---

    Revolution? National Responses, Market Transitions, and Global Technology (Stanford University Press, 2006), pp. 373–390; Bert Hoffmann, 'Civil society in the digital age: How the internet changes state–society relations in authoritarian regimes. The case of Cuba' in Francesco Cavatorta (ed.), *Civil Society Activism under Authoritarian Rule: A Comparative Perspective* (Routledge, 2012), pp. 219–244; Lydia Khalil, 'Digital authoritarianism, China and COVID' (2 November 2020), Lowy Institute, www.lowyinstitute.org/publications/digital-authoritarianism-china-covid; Justin Sherman, 'Digital authoritarianism and implications for US national security' (2021) 6(1) *The Cyber Defense Review* 107–118, www.jstor.org/stable/2699411; Ben Wagner, 'Whose politics? Whose rights? Transparency, capture and dual-use export controls' (2021) 31 *Security and Human Rights* 35–46, https://brill.com/view/journals/shrs/31/1-4/article-p35_35.xml.

[4]   Steven Feldstein, 'The global expansion of AI surveillance' (17 September 2019), Carnegie Endowment for International Peace, Paper, https://carnegieendowment.org/2019/09/17/global-expansion-of-ai-surveillance-pub-79847.

[5]   See ibid., pp. 18–19, for details on the technologies themselves. Suffice it to state here that facial recognition 'is a biometric technology that uses cameras – both video or still images – to match stored or live footage of individuals with images from a database. [...] They can scan distinctive facial features in order to create detailed biometric maps of individuals without obtaining consent. Often facial recognition surveillance cameras are mobile and concealable.' However, advanced video surveillance and facial recognition cameras could not function without cloud computing capabilities. If video surveillance is the 'eyes' then cloud services are the 'brains' that connect cameras and hardware to the cloud computing models via 5G networks. However, as cloud computing in isolation is not inherently oriented toward surveillance, these secondary technologies are categorised as 'enabling technologies': ibid., p. 21.

[6]   Ibid.

[7]   Ibid., p. 13.

[8]   Roxana Akhmetova and Erin Harris, 'Politics of technology: The use of artificial intelligence by US and Canadian immigration agencies and their impacts on human rights' in Emre E. Korkmaz (ed.), *Digital Identity, Virtual Borders and Social Media* (Edward Elgar Publishing, 2021), pp. 52–72, www.elgaronline.com/view/edcoll/9781789909142/9781789909142.00008.xml; Ausma Bernot, 'Transnational state-corporate symbiosis of public security: China's exports of surveillance technologies' (2021) 10(2) *International Journal for Crime, Justice and Social Democracy* 159–173, www.crimejusticejournal.com/article/view/1908; Peter Dauvergne, 'The globalization of artificial intelligence: Consequences for the politics of environmentalism' (2021) 18 *Globalizations* 285–299. www.tandfonline.com/doi/full/10.1080/14747731.2020.1785670; Orabile Mudongo, 'Africa's expansion of AI surveillance – Regional gaps and key trends' (26 February 2021), Briefing Paper, Africa Portal, www.africaportal.org/publications/africas-expansion-ai-surveillance-regional-gaps-and-key-trends/; Ben

alone providing technology to at least fifty countries. France, Germany, Japan, and the United States are also major players in this sector.[9] As a consequence, the governance challenges around AI-enhanced technologies are inherently trans-national.

Indeed, the rise of AI accentuates several existing challenges for human rights law around (digital) technology. For example, such technology obscures the identity of the violator and makes violations themselves more invisible. This makes it much harder for citizens to hold duty bearers accountable.[10] It is also becoming much less clear whom citizens should try to hold to account in the first place. The current framework for addressing human rights harms inflicted by business entities is built on the distinction between public authority exercised by the state (which gives rise to a binding obligation to respect and protect rights) and private authority exercised by a company (which gives rise to a moral responsibility to respect rights). However, the distinction between the public and private spheres is becoming increasingly blurred, and as a result, it is less clear how human rights law is applicable.[11] Instead, citizens must rely on states to take seriously their duty to protect individuals from harms by non-state actors, such as requiring private companies to institutionalise the practice of technology risk and impact assessments.[12] It is clear that this is a formidable challenge in liberal democratic countries, let alone in authoritarian ones such as Morocco.

In this chapter, we focus on the role played by AI-enhanced surveillance tools in Morocco's governance of cities and borders. We ask to what extent AI technologies are deployed in Morocco, and how they could reshape existing modes of public governance. We address these questions in two areas: urban surveillance and the control of migration at the Moroccan–Spanish border. We focus on the use of facial recognition technologies (FRT) in AI-enhanced cameras in particular, but we also address other technologies and other uses of AI, following a pragmatic approach that investigated where it was possible to access data. Indeed, AI surveillance is not a stand-alone instrument of repression, but complements existing forms of repression. As Feldstein observes, 'it forms part of a suite of digital repression tools – information and communications technologies used to surveil, intimidate, coerce, and harass opponents in order to inflict a penalty on a target and deter specific activities or beliefs that challenge the state'.[13]

Wagner, 'After the Arab spring: New paths for human rights and the internet in European foreign policy' (July 2012), Briefing Paper, European Parliament: Directorate-General for External Policies, European Union, www.europarl.europa.eu/RegData/etudes/note/join/2012/457102/EXPO-DROI_NT%282012%29457102_EN.pdf; Ben Wagner, 'Push-button-autocracy in Tunisia: Analysing the role of internet infrastructure, institutions and international markets in creating a Tunisian censorship regime' (2012) 36(6) *Telecommunications Policy* 484–492, https://linkinghub.elsevier.com/retrieve/pii/S0308596112000675.

[9] Feldstein, 'The global expansion of AI surveillance', p. 8.

[10] Molly K. Land and Jay D. Aronson, 'Human rights and technology: New challenges for justice and accountability' (2020) 16(1) *Annual Review of Law and Social Science* 223–240, www.annualreviews.org/doi/10.1146/annurev-lawsocsci-060220-081955.

[11] Ibid., p. 226.

[12] Ibid., pp. 226, 235.

[13] Feldstein, 'The global expansion of AI surveillance', p. 16.

The chapter is structured as follows. First, we outline the legal framework and governance context around Morocco's use of AI technologies for urban and border surveillance. We then discuss our methodological approach, including some of the key limitations we faced during the research, before sharing our findings with respect to the use of FRT in the governance of cities and borders, respectively. Subsequently, we discuss AI-enhanced surveillance as an intrinsically transnational challenge in which private interests of economic gain and public interests of national security collide with citizens' human rights across the Global North/Global South divide. We also reflect on the challenges and opportunities of monitoring human rights in the face of increasing deployment of AI-enhanced technologies in authoritarian governance.

19.2 THE LEGAL FRAMEWORK AND GOVERNANCE CONTEXT IN MOROCCO

The Moroccan governance system has been described as 'an entrenched neo-authoritarian system'.[14] Over the past decades, the monarchy has repeatedly weakened the political opposition by co-opting major parties into government. Human rights violations, lack of press freedom, and the harassment of human rights non-governmental organisations (NGOs) persist. However, while these deficiencies have attracted the attention of human rights organisations and press freedom watchdogs, they have not been properly taken up by inter-governmental actors. Quite the contrary: in the wider regional context, Morocco's political stability has been viewed as an asset and is likely to become even more valuable (to the EU and United States), further insulating the regime from critiques of its civil and human rights records.[15]

At the same time, Morocco is one of the highest performers in e-governance in Africa.[16] Morocco has more than 27 million internet users, or 75 per cent of its population,[17] and ranks high in the UN's 2016 E-Government Survey in terms of e-participation, e-consultation and online service delivery as well as in its E-Government Development Index, a composite indicator used to measure the willingness and capacity of national administrations to use information and communications technologies to deliver public services. Indeed, Morocco's new development model focusses on consolidating technological added value, and public administrations are increasingly making use of algorithms in online public services.[18] The combination of authoritarian rule and advanced use of e-government

---

[14] Bertelsmann Stiftung, 'BTI 2022 country report – Morocco' (2022), p. 38.
[15] Ibid.
[16] Privacy International, 'State of privacy Morocco' (26 January 2019), https://privacyinternational.org/state-privacy/1007/state-privacy-morocco.
[17] Mounir Bensalah, 'Toward an ethical code of AI and human rights in Morocco' (2021) 1(2) *Arribat – International Journal of Human Rights* 187–203.
[18] Ibid.

makes Morocco a particularly interesting case to study the role of AI in technologies in public governance.

At first glance, Morocco's legal framework around privacy seems robust. The constitution contains an explicit protection of the right to privacy (Art. 24), there is a data protection law (Law n° 09-08, promulgated in February 2009), and a data protection agency, the *Commission nationale de contrôle de la protection des données à caractère personnel* (CNDP). In addition, Morocco is a signatory of a number of treaties with privacy implications, including the Council of Europe's *Convention for the Protection of Individuals with Regard to Automatic Processing of Personal Data* and its additional Protocols.[19] Furthermore, in 2018, Morocco joined the Open Government Partnership, an inter-governmental organisation promoting government transparency and citizen participation, and in 2021 it submitted its second two-year action plan, including twenty-two commitments that span a wide range of participatory, accountable, and transparent governance areas.[20] Since 2010, the security sector has also been put on a clearer legal footing: private security was regulated, state security services were given statutes and mandated to better respect human rights, thanks in no small measure to the efforts of human rights organisations.[21]

Yet, as Hagmann[22] points out, some laws still lack implementation decrees. In addition, clientelist and political interests continue to influence whether and how penal provisions are implemented, human rights abuses investigated and reprimanded, or demonstrations and NGOs authorised and banned. Indeed, Privacy International notes that 'there remains vast grey areas regarding the discretionary powers offered to judges and intelligence agencies' when it comes to rules around legitimate breaches of individual privacy.[23] This situation is worsened by the fact that the judiciary is not independent and that public scrutiny and democratic oversight over the work of intelligence services is lacking. In addition, the law on the protection of personal data (09–08) does not cover those data collected in the interest of national defence or the interior or exterior security of the state.[24]

Against the backdrop of this legal framework, technological tools are already integrated in everyday authoritarian governance and surveillance, especially at urban level. Traditionally based on a wide network of informants (car guards, local shop owners, informal vendors and beggars, etc.), mass surveillance is evolving through

---

[19] Privacy International, 'State of privacy Morocco'.

[20] See www.opengovpartnership.org/members/morocco/.

[21] Jonas Hagmann, 'Globalizing control research: The politics of urban security in and beyond the Alaouite kingdom of Morocco' (2021) 6(4) *Journal of Global Security Studies* 1–23, https://academic.oup.com/jogss/article/doi/10.1093/jogss/ogab004/6208882; Privacy International, 'State of privacy Morocco'.

[22] Hagmann, 'Globalizing control research'.

[23] Privacy International, 'State of privacy Morocco'.

[24] Anaïs Lefébure and Mehdi Mahmoud, 'De la "smart" à la "safe" city, au détriment de nos vies privées?' (2 July 2021), *Tel Quel*, https://telquel.ma/2021/07/02/de-la-smart-a-la-safe-city-au-detriment-de-nos-vies-privees_1727757.

the use of technology. Phone tapping is common for listening to conversations, and more refined tools for surveillance have also been employed. For example, during the regional and local elections of September 2015, 30,000 mobile phone lines of candidates and regional or provincial party officials, in addition to local government officials and others, were reportedly tapped at the request of the Ministry of Interior.[25] Another example is the Moroccan government's use, at least since October 2017, of Pegasus spyware produced by the Israeli firm NSO Group, to surveil and attack human rights defenders.[26] The general impression is that these technologies have allowed the bringing about of a more 'surgical' approach to the repression of dissent, one that systematically targets key figures,[27] instead of the population as a whole.

Israeli companies are not the only provider of surveillance technology to Moroccan authorities. In 2015, there was a leak confirming that Morocco had bought the technology of Italian spyware company Hacking Team.[28] In June 2017, an investigation by BBC Arabic and the Danish newspaper *Dagbladet* revealed that UK defence firm BAE Systems had sold mass surveillance technologies – called Evident – through its Danish subsidiary ETI to six Middle Eastern governments, including Morocco.[29] There are also concerns that the European Neighbourhood Instrument may have been used to fund the training of Moroccan authorities in 'telephone tapping and video recordings' and 'special investigation techniques for electronic surveillance'.[30] More recently, there have been plausible but unconfirmed reports that the Moroccan police used COVID-19 mobile passport application check-ins to

[25] Privacy International, 'State of privacy Morocco'.
[26] Amnesty International, 'Morocco: Human rights defenders targeted with NSO Group's spyware' (10 October 2019), www.amnesty.org/en/latest/research/2019/10/morocco-human-rights-defenders-targeted-with-nso-groups-spyware/; Bill Marczak, John Scott-Railton, Sarah McKune, Bahr Abdul Razzak, and Ron Deibert, 'HIDE AND SEEK: Tracking NSO Group's Pegasus spyware to operations in 45 countries' (18 September 2018), The Citizen Lab, https://citizenlab.ca/2018/09/hide-and-seek-tracking-nso-groups-pegasus-spyware-to-operations-in-45-countries/; Bethan McKernan, 'Emmanuel Macron "pushes for Israeli inquiry" into NSO spyware concerns' (25 July 2021), *The Guardian*, www.theguardian.com/world/2021/jul/25/emmanuel-macron-pushes-for-israeli-inquiry-into-nso-spyware-concerns. 'Once installed on a phone, the [Pegasus] software can extract all of the data that is already on the device, such as text messages, contacts, GPS location, email and browser history. It can additionally create new data by using the phone's microphone and camera to record the user's surroundings and ambient sounds.' N. Hopkins and D. Sabbagh, 'WhatsApp spyware attack was attempt to hack human rights data, says lawyer' (14 May 2019), *The Guardian*, www.theguardian.com/technology/2019/may/14/whatsapp-spyware-vulnerability-targeted-lawyer-says-attempt-was-desperate, cited in Land and Aronson, 'Human rights and technology', p. 228.
[27] Such as Mâati Monjib, Hicham Mansouri, Taoufik Bouachrine, Souleiman Raissouni, and Omar Radi, *Marruecos y el cambio de ciclo: en busca de un nuevo pacto social y de nuevas legitimidades*, ed. Alfonso Casani and Beatriz Tomé-Alonso (Fundacionalternativas, 2021), p. 11, https://.org/wp-content/uploads/2022/07/115f8026034f62907a4d1382c8788886.pdf.
[28] Privacy International, 'Eight things we know so far from the Hacking Team hack' (9 July 2015), https://privacyinternational.org/news-analysis/1395/eight-things-we-know-so-far-hacking-team-hack.
[29] Privacy International, 'State of privacy Morocco'.
[30] Parliamentary question dated 19 November 2019 (E-003890/2019/rev.1) to the Commission, Rule 138, Pierfrancesco Majorino (S&D), www.europarl.europa.eu/doceo/document/E-9-2019-003890_EN.html.

Morocco's Governance of Cities and Borders 273

track the movements of citizens and identify those who disobeyed the rules of the state of emergency linked to COVID-19 measures.[31]

In terms of surveillance in public spaces, protests still see a heavy deployment of security forces. Violence and arrests of demonstrators are still common and recent research shows how the strategic use of violence to clamp down on protest events can serve as a tool for regime survival.[32] However, whether and to what extent AI-enhanced technologies are used to respond to and control these events remains unclear. So far, most information on the use of AI-enhanced surveillance of public spaces has come from news reporting on the business arrangements and calls for tenders – either leaked or public – concerning the development of these technologies. This includes a series of articles detailing the deployment of video-surveillance technologies in Al Hoceïma, Agadir, Casablanca, Marrakech, and Meknes.[33] In July 2022, the weekly magazine *TelQuel* also published an interview with a high-level police officer about the potential improvement achieved by the use of drones and AI in Casablanca, which is the only example of a public statement by a government official on the matter.[34]

With regard to border control, AI-enhanced technologies have been introduced by countries around the world not only to deter or stop irregular migration by surveilling borders, but also to serve as systems for tracking, controlling, and accelerating cross-border mobility more generally. In Morocco, for instance, this has resulted in the mounting of facial recognition cameras or procurement of thermal imaging cameras at its borders with the two Spanish enclave cities Ceuta and Melilla, largely funded by the EU.[35] These borders are regularly mediatised as the main entry points for Sub-Saharan African migrants into Spain (and thus the EU), but they also experience a high daily flow of visitors and cross-border workers throughout the year.

---

[31] Antónia do Carmo Barriga, Ana Filipa Martins, Maria João Simões, and Délcio Faustino, 'The COVID-19 pandemic: Yet another catalyst for governmental mass surveillance?' (2020) 2(1) *Social Sciences & Humanities Open* 1–5, https://linkinghub.elsevier.com/retrieve/pii/S2590291120300851.

[32] Chantal E. Berman, 'Policing the organizational threat in Morocco: Protest and public violence in liberal autocracies' (2021) 65(3) *American Journal of Political Science* 733–754.

[33] *TelQuel* dedicated an entire issue to the use of high-tech surveillance in Moroccan cities, available at the following link: https://telquel.ma/sommaire/securite-nos-villes-sous-haute-surveillance; Kenza Filali, 'Le Maroc parmi les importateurs de materies d'espionnage Britannique' (11 March 2018), Le Desk, https://ledesk.ma/encontinu/le-maroc-parmi-les-importateurs-de-materiel-despionnage-britannique/; Kenza Filali, 'El Mahdi El Majidi s'allie au Francais Cerbair specialiste des solutions anti-drones' (9 June 2021), Le Desk, https://ledesk.ma/enoff/el-mahdi-el-majidi-sallie-au-francais-cerbair-specialiste-des-solutions-anti-drones/; *Africa Intelligence*, 'National police to expand all-seeing eye on Casablanca' (21 April 2021), www.africaintelligence.com/north-africa/2021/04/21/national-police-to-expand-all-seeing-eye-on-casablanca,109659676-art.

[34] Yassine Majdi, 'Fathi Hassan (DGSN): Nous planchons sur le recours aux drones et a l'intelligence artificielle' (July 2022), *Tel Quel*, https://telquel.ma/sponsors/fathi-hassan-dgsn-nous-planchons-sur-le-recours-aux-drones-et-a-lintelligence-artificielle_1774312.

[35] *Africa Intelligence*, 'Spain and EU to supply border surveillance equipment to Morocco' (14 June 2022), www.africaintelligence.com/north-africa/2022/06/14/spain-and-eu-to-supply-border-surveillance-equipment-to-morocco,109791869-art.

For Spain, controlling and preventing irregular migration into Ceuta and Melilla has been a hot topic since the 1990s, while Morocco considers Ceuta and Melilla as cities colonised by Spain, and they are therefore a regular cause of diplomatic crisis between the Moroccan and Spanish governments.[36] Spanish media regularly accuse Morocco of attempts to put pressure on Spain by not effectively controlling borders, while Morocco invokes its unwillingness to play a gendarme role and calls for an integrated and participative approach to deal with the issue, including financial support from the EU.[37]

Managing the Spanish–Moroccan border is certainly big business given the considerable budgets allocated by the EU to 'fight' irregular migration and to 'protect' Ceuta and Melilla.[38] For example, Indra Sistemas, a Spanish information technology and defence systems company, received at least 26.6 million euros across forty public contracts (twenty-eight without public tender), mostly from the Spanish Ministries of the Interior and Defence, for migratory control tasks including: the maintenance of the Integrated External Surveillance System (SIVE) of the Civil Guard, the installation of radars on the southern border and facial recognition at border posts, or the integration of the new 'intelligent borders' system.[39] The French technology giant Atos also obtained at least twenty-six contracts from the Spanish Ministry of the Interior from 2014 to 2019, totalling more than 18.7 million euros, in order to repair and supply equipment for the SIVE. Similarly, from 2014 to 2019, the Government of Spain awarded French company Thales at least eleven migration control contracts (3.8 million euros in total), most of them to supply night vision systems and their respective maintenance services.[40] The most recent deal over 4.8 million euros on the procurement of thermal surveillance cameras for the Moroccan Ministry of Interior has been concluded between the Spanish defence equipment company Etel 88 and the Spanish development agency FIIAPP.[41]

In co-operation with mostly European tech companies, both Moroccan cities as well as Morocco's northern border with Spain have thus seen the increasing

---

[36] K. Natter, 'The formation of Morocco's policy towards irregular migration (2000–2007): Political rationale and policy processes' (2014) 52 *International Migration* 15–28, https://doi.org/10.1111/imig.12114; R. Andersson. 'Hardwiring the frontier? The politics of security technology in Europe's "fight against illegal migration"'. (2016) 47(1) *Security Dialogue* 22–39, https://doi.org/10.1177/0967010615606044.

[37] Público, 'Diez multinacionales se embolsan el 65% del dinero que España destina a frenar la migración' (1 July 2020), El control de la migración, un oscuro negocio, https://temas.publico.es/control-migracion-oscuro-negocio/2020/07/01/diez-multinacionales-se-embolsan-el-65-del-dinero-que-espana-destina-a-frenar-la-migracion/.

[38] R. Andersson, *Illegality, Inc.: Clandestine Migration and the Business of Bordering Europe* (University of California Press, 2014); El Confidencial and Fundación PorCausa, 'Fronteras SA: la industria del control migratorio' (n.d.), www.elconfidencial.com/espana/2022-07-15/fronteras-industria-control-migratorio_3460287/.

[39] Público, 'Interior Implantará Un Sistema de Reconocimiento Facial En La Frontera de Melilla' (27 July 2015), www.publico.es/politica/interior-implantara-sistema-reconocimiento-facial.html.

[40] Fundación Por Causa, 'Industria Del Control Migratorio 2: Quién Se Lleva El Dinero?' (2020), https://porcausa.org/somos-lo-que-hacemos/industria-del-control-migratorio/

[41] *Africa Intelligence*, 'Spain and EU to supply border surveillance equipment'.

Morocco's Governance of Cities and Borders

deployment of and reliance on AI-enhanced technologies as governance tools. While Morocco's legal framework around privacy and data protection has also been upgraded over the last decade, its limited implementation and the vast leverage of security and legal actors in interpreting the law, however, raise a host of challenges on the intersection between AI technologies and human rights. In the next section, we outline how we methodologically approached our research on urban and border surveillance, as well as some of the key limitations we faced.

19.3 METHODOLOGY

Francesco Colin and Issam Cherrat conducted the fieldwork for the urban and border surveillance cases, respectively, during the period March to August 2022. The fieldwork relied on extensive desk reviews, including various published and unpublished publications on the use of technology in urban and border governance, academic studies, grey literature from NGOs and state institutions, as well as the available press in French and English.

The other main component of the fieldwork was a set of nine semi-structured interviews on urban surveillance and twenty interviews on border surveillance with key stakeholders. Given the scarcity of information on the topic of the research, as well as the difficulty in accessing knowledgeable actors, we relied on snowball sampling. The interviewees included scholars, journalists, public officials, police officers, and civil society actors. Great care was taken during the research process to ensure the safety and anonymity of the interviewees and researchers. All interviewees were informed orally about the scope of the research and gave their consent prior to the interviews. Only two interviewees in the urban use case granted their permission to be recorded, while all of them asked to be quoted anonymously in the research outputs. Six interviewees contacted for the case study on border governance declined to have their interview mentioned in the study.

The study was severely limited by the broader security context in which the research was carried out. The sensitive nature of the topic – related to matters of national security and territorial integrity – as well as its relatively novel application in the Moroccan context made it complicated to access information and interviewees. All data revolving around surveillance practices is perceived to be the exclusive competence of Morocco's security apparatus, and thus represents a subject on which one simply cannot ask too many questions. The limited information on the use of these technologies was extracted from calls for tender (CFT), to the extent that they were in the public domain. Such documents are accessible only when they get leaked by the press or in the case of privileged sources. In addition, many of these calls were still ongoing (or had been re-issued) at the time of writing. Finally, it was not possible to acquire first-hand information on the actual functioning of these technologies. Our attempts to establish direct contact with the staff of the

276   *Bergh, Cherrat, Colin, Natter, and Wagner*

intelligence services have been unsuccessful, and none of the interviewees had a direct knowledge of how these technologies are employed on the ground.

In addition to the issue of access, the overall general climate of repression (and associated fears of reprisals for speaking out) limited the fieldwork on both urban and border surveillance. Despite the precautions taken by the researchers, such as the exclusive use of secure platforms for communication, interviewees measured their words carefully when speaking about surveillance technologies. Representatives of private companies engaged in the deployment of these technologies were unwilling to participate in the research, saying that they did not want to jeopardise the relationship with the General Directorate for National Security (DGSN), the national police force, in the event of future tenders. In the case of border controls, several stakeholders refused to be interviewed once they learned about the topic, and access to information from government institutions was denied.

19.4 AI-ENHANCED TECHNOLOGIES IN MOROCCAN CITIES

Across Moroccan cities, pilot experiences with AI-enhanced technologies are being developed for a plethora of applications – such as traffic management, monitoring of air quality, and energy efficiency, but also irrigation and waste collection.[42] However, generally speaking, in Morocco 'there is still very little actual AI in smart cities'.[43] As we noted earlier, most of the available data on the procurement of AI-enhanced technology such as facial recognition cameras is based on CFT documents, but information on its actual deployment, functioning, and use is extremely scarce.

Based on the desk review, it was possible to develop Table 19.1, which provides a schematic summary of the technology deployed in the urban context in Morocco.

Although Table 19.1 shows an impressive deployment of technology, especially for the city of Casablanca, these numbers still pale in comparison with other countries: while in Casablanca there are 'only' 0.74 cameras per 1,000 people, in the ten most surveilled cities of the world this ratio ranges from 62.52 to 8.77 cameras.[44] Moreover, although the absolute lack of transparency surrounding these projects does not allow us to trace a clear timeline, we know that the deployment of high-tech surveillance technology has accelerated after the 2011 bombing at the Café Argana in Marrakech – as the attacked area was supposed to be covered by video surveillance, but apparently cameras were not working.[45] Furthermore, Table 19.1 shows that the current wave

---

[42] Interviewee 8, 18 July 2022. Due to security and ethical concerns, it is not possible to provide further details about interviewees.

[43] Interviewee 3, 10 June 2022.

[44] This data is available at: www.comparitech.com/vpn-privacy/the-worlds-most-surveilled-cities/.

[45] Interviewee 6, 29 June 2022. See also France Media Agency, 'À Marrakech, 38 caméras sur la place Jamaa el Fna' (4 May 2012), *La Presse*, www.lapresse.ca/voyage/destinations/afrique/maroc/201205/04/01-4522102-a-marrakech-38-cameras-sur-la-place-jamaa-el-fna.php.

Morocco's Governance of Cities and Borders

TABLE 19.1 *Review of video-surveillance technologies in Moroccan cities*[a]

City	Technology deployment	Main stakeholders involved
Al Hoceïma	Existing installation: no cameras installed. Future projects: 60 cameras in 'strategic areas' of the city.	Tender managed by the *Agence pour la promotion et développement du Nord* (SDL).
Agadir	Existing installation: no cameras installed. Future projects: 220 video-surveillance cameras to be installed and a new HQ to manage them.	Tender launched by the *Agadir Souss Massa Aménagement* (SDL). It has been awarded to *TPF Ingénierie* (France). The separate tender for the HQ has yet to be awarded.
Casablanca	Existing installation: 60 cameras deployed in 2015; 500 cameras deployed in 2016; 150 cameras deployed in 2017. Future projects: 577 new cameras currently under CFT; 2 drones; new HQ to control operations.	Tender co-ordinated by *CasaTransport* (SDL), on behalf of the DGSN. The companies *Tactys* and *CeRyX* (France) developed the technical elements, and the tender has been unsuccessful in early 2022.
Fez	Existing installation: exact number unclear, sources report 'a hundred cameras in the main arteries of the city'[b] Future projects: no information on future projects.	Project co-ordinated by the DGSN. Cameras installed by *Sphinx Electric* (Morocco) in 2018.
Marrakech	Existing installation: no information available. Future projects: 223 new cameras in the old medina and a new data centre to be installed in Jamaâ el Fna square.	Tender co-ordinated by Al Omrane, which has been awarded to *Sphinx Electric* (Morocco) in February 2022.
Meknes	Existing installation: no cameras installed. Future projects: new video surveillance system (2021).	Project launched by the municipality.
Rabat	Existing installation: no information available. Future projects: video-surveillance of the forest ring road surrounding the city ('*Ceinture verte*').	Tenders are managed by *Rabat Région Aménagement*. The new project has yet to be launched officially.
Tangier	Existing installation: 200 cameras installed. Future projects: no information on future projects.	Project co-ordinated by the DGSN. Cameras deployed by *Cires Technology* (France).

[a] Last updated: 19 August 2022.
[b] Anaïs Lefébure and Mehdi Mahmoud, 'Casablanca, Marrakech, Dakhla ... Nos villes sous haute surveillance?' (2 July 2021), *Tel Quel*, https://telquel.ma/2021/07/02/casablanca-marrakech-dakhla-nos-villes-bientot-sous-haute-surveillance_1727723.
Source: Compilation by Francesco Colin from multiple sources.

of projects represents an extension of past deployments in some cities (Casablanca, Marrakech, Rabat) and the creation of new installations in others (Al Hoceïma, Agadir, Menkes). In any case, interviewees generally agree that these projects only represent the beginning, rather than the end, of such endeavours.[46]

However, there is no information available on the concrete way in which AI is employed in the analysis of images captured through these cameras. As one interviewee put it, 'we know there is a computer at the central police station in Rabat, but god knows what goes on there'.[47] CFT documents provide some useful information here: the CFT for the expansion of the surveillance system in the city of Casablanca runs to 389 pages and outlines the type of technology that needs to be provided, as well as its potential. It specifies that the cameras must be able to perform facial recognition tasks, that is, to be able to identify a target against a picture or a recorded photo, either in real time and on recorded footage (p.12 CFT's Annex).[48] The CFT for the new video surveillance project in the city of Al Hoceïma provides more details in terms of cameras' (desired) capabilities: to compare the data collected via video surveillance against existing databases of pictures, to easily add pictures to databases based on live video feed, and to search for a specific person through an image added to the system.[49] The capacity to identify a target on the basis of an image is the central function of face recognition systems in these contexts.[50] However, the role of central security agents on the ground is still substantial: they would need to perform dynamic search functions (based on video metadata and on visual inputs), compile reports based on different data types and sources, and ensure co-ordination with police intervention on the ground.

In line with discursive shifts in the global surveillance trade,[51] the massive investment by Moroccan cities in AI-enhanced surveillance technology is presented as a shift from the 'smart' to the 'safe' city. Official discourse stresses the physical security purposes of the systems, such as catching accidents and thefts on camera. However, a small but increasing number of Moroccan civil society actors are raising concerns about the consequences of mass transmission of personal data to government entities in terms of privacy and individual liberties.[52] In addition, our study found that

---

[46] Interviewee 2, 31 May 2022; interviewee 5, 24 June 2022; interviewee 8, 18 July 2022.

[47] Interviewee 5, 24 June 2022.

[48] Casa Transports SA, 'Cahier Des Clauses Techniques Particulières (CCTP) – Préstations de Réalisation de La 2ème Phase Du Poste Central de La Gestion de La Circulation et de La Vidéoprotection de Casablanca' (2021) [unpublished].

[49] The system deployed in Al Hoceïma also needs to allow the future integration of other 'intelligent analytics', such as intrusion detection, people's count, gatherings, etc. (p. 43).

[50] Interviewee 8, 18 July 2022.

[51] Privacy International, 'From smart cities to safe cities: Normalising the police state?' (15 August 2018), https://privacyinternational.org/long-read/2231/smart-cities-safe-cities-normalising-police-state.

[52] Lefébure and Mahmoud, 'De la "smart" à la "safe" city'; Lefébure and Mahmoud, 'Casablanca, Marrakech, Dakhla'; see also Hagmann, 'Globalizing control research', for a case study of the surveillance system in place in Marrakech. Interviewee 9, 22 July 2022.

the legal framework attributes all control of local security issues to the local representatives of the Ministry of the Interior, rather than to elected local governments, limiting public oversight and accountability.

19.5 AI-ENHANCED TECHNOLOGIES AT MOROCCAN BORDERS

Unlike the unclear situation with regard to urban surveillance, it is known that the borders between Morocco and the two Spanish enclaves Ceuta and Melilla are progressively being transformed into 'smart' borders through the increasing deployment of AI-enhanced cameras and FRT. Yet, border control management is surrounded by secrecy in Morocco. Topics related to national security are treated with suspicion, and only fragmentary pieces of information are leaked to the press. It is almost impossible to know which firm or company has won a tender to install cameras or such equipment on the borders between Morocco and Spain, including the use of FRT cameras in its airports.[53] In the words of an interviewee who did not want to be listed, 'as a police officer, we do not ask about these things, I guess we do not have the right even, we are simply trained to use new technologies when they are deployed'. Therefore, for this section on the use of FRT at the Moroccan–Spanish border, we are relying on information from the Spanish side.

According to the Spanish Minister of Interior's declaration in March 2022, Spain has modernised its entire technological systems at the border posts in Beni Enzar, Melilla, and in El Tarajal, Ceuta.[54] This modernisation consists of the implementation of a fast-track system for cross-border workers, the installation of fifty-two posts for greater agility in the passage of people, and sixteen registration kiosks featuring the control and collection of biometric data. Furthermore, currently up to thirty-five cameras equipped with facial recognition systems are being installed between the entry and exit points of the borders of Ceuta and Melilla. The project is based on an entry control system with FRT, in which, in addition to the thirty-five cameras, there are four micro-domes,[55] and a software platform to host the Live Face Identification System for the control of the closed-circuit television system. It is implemented by the company *Gunnebo Iberia*, a subsidiary of the Swedish world leader in security products, and *Thales Spain*, a subsidiary of the technological multi-national dedicated to the development of information systems for the aerospace, defence, and security markets.

Overall, the use of AI-enhanced cameras at the Ceuta and Melilla borders aims to shorten border control processing, enhance security at the crossings, and increase control over people and goods entering and exiting the border. The main problem at

---

[53] Ayoub Khattabi, 'La reconnaissance faciale bientôt à l'aéroport de Rabat-Salé' (4 August 2022), le360, https://fr.le360.ma/economie/la-reconnaissance-faciale-bientot-a-laeroport-de-rabat-sale-264740.

[54] Senado, 'Diario de Sesiones Senado 22 Marzo 2022' (2022), www.senado.es/legis14/publicaciones/pdf/senado/ds/DS_P_14_83.PDF.

[55] Wide-angle dome cameras with a small form factor (i.e., building them as small as possible).

the Tarajal entry gate (Ceuta), for example, was that the poor existing infrastructures made it impossible to control the waiting line and to systematically track who enters and leaves through this passage. The poor infrastructure allowed for the smuggling of illegal goods and made it difficult to track whether minors entered Ceuta irregularly. The main objective of the deployment of new technologies is thus to monitor the number of people who enter and leave and to detect the number of people who do not return after a period of time. The technology used allows for flexible mobile facial scanning, that is, the inspection of people inside cars, trucks, buses, and on motorcycles or bicycles.[56] It will also allow the implementation of 'black lists' during the passage of border control, showing personal information of the individual transiting through the border if they are registered on such a list. Deploying this technology, it is expected that some 40,000 facial readings per day can be carried out in Ceuta and 85,000 in Melilla.

Civil society actors have already drawn attention to the risks inherent to the use of those technologies at the Ceuta and Melilla borders: more than forty Spanish organisations and associations signed a statement rejecting the 'smart borders' project.[57] They emphasised that the project's ambition to 'exercise greater security control through the use of artificial intelligence, by collecting biometrics, such as facial recognition, fingerprints, [...] poses a risk of violating human rights'.[58] They particularly highlighted that 'the collection of biometric data for people who do not have a European passport is not in accordance with the principle of proportionality'.[59] Indeed, as another civil society association highlighted, the Spanish–Moroccan borders risk being turned 'into a laboratory for security practices'. They argue that with regards to the right to data privacy, 'this will not happen at other borders such as Barajas-Madrid airport and will not happen with European citizens, but will happen at the borders where migrants cross in a state of extreme poverty, and it will happen with populations suffering from racism'.[60]

In terms of migration control, the deployment of FRT at the Moroccan–Spanish border is probably effective in controlling regular migration, for instance by facilitating and speeding up the circulation of individuals and cars, but less so when it comes to attempts at irregular migration. While it will inevitably make it harder for those migrants who need to reach Spanish territory in order to claim their rights to protection, that is, asylum seekers and unaccompanied minors, FRTs cannot

---

[56] Fundación por Causa, 'Industria Del Control Migratorio 2: Quién Se Lleva El Dinero?'.
[57] Amal Kennin, 'Munẓmāt Isbānya Tantqad Mašrwaʿ "Ālḥudwd Ālḏakya" Fy Sbta Wa Mlylya [Spanish organizations criticize the "smart borders" project in Ceuta and Melilla]' (14 January 2022), Hespress, www.hespress.com/930243-الذ-الحدود-مشروع-تنتقد-إسبانية-منظمات.html.
[58] Ibid.
[59] Ibid.
[60] Mohammad Okba, 'Paula Guerra Cáceres: "La Inteligencia Artificial Es Una Amenaza Para Los Migrantes y Es Una Forma de Control Migratorio"' [Paula Guerra Cáceres: Artificial intelligence is a menace for migrants and a form of migratory control] (14 June 2022), Bayana, https://baynana.es/es/paula-guerra-caceres-la-inteligencia-artificial-es-una-amenaza-para-los-migrantes-y-es-una-forma-de-control-migratorio/.

predict when migrants will attempt to pass the fences of Ceuta and Melilla and are ineffective when thousands gather and decide to climb the fence simultaneously, such as the 2022 attempts in Melilla that caused the death of thirty-seven migrants.[61] Moreover, migrants adapt their border crossing strategies according to the technologies in place, for example in Fnideq,[62] where irregular migrants reach Ceuta's shore by swimming when it is foggy and cameras cannot detect them. Lastly, the installation of 'smart borders' in the north of Morocco has (once again) redirected irregular migrants towards the longer, more costly and deadly migratory routes in the south of Morocco, where one can reach the (Spanish) Canary Islands through a perilous journey by boat.[63]

Despite Spain's massive investment in these technologies, it remains unclear what the actual effects and outcomes of FRT used are on Moroccan–Spanish border dynamics since no official reports have been released yet. The impression from the field is that the new 'smart' border has slightly improved the quality of daily tasks, but that border crossings are still overwhelmed during periods of intense flux (during summer and national holidays). Furthermore, irregular migration dynamics seem to not have been affected by the use of new technologies, as migrants have adapted their strategies to cross the border.

19.6 DISCUSSION

Despite the rapidly increasing use of FRT in Moroccan urban and border surveillance, public debate around these issues is still lacking in Morocco. In both cases, authorities justify the use of AI-enhanced technologies by the will to improve users' experience and security.[64] Between the high sensitivity of the data that is captured through these technologies and the generalised opacity with which it is treated, there are grounds to be concerned for the respect of citizens' right to privacy.

From the two cases analysed, two cross-cutting issues emerge. The first one is the involvement of external actors, such as international donors, multi-national companies and foreign states, which makes AI-enhanced surveillance an inherently transnational issue. External actors play a key role in the development and financing of FRTs, in their installation on the ground, but also in the (limited) monitoring of human rights protection frameworks. International donors provide funding for urban and border surveillance projects for instance, but they could also play a more active role in enforcing mechanisms for transparency in using such surveillance

---

[61] Aurélie Collas and Sandrine Morel, 'Au Maroc, Dans l'enclave de Melilla, Une Tentative d'entrée de Migrants Tourne Au Drame' (27 June 2022), *Le Monde*, www.lemonde.fr/afrique/article/2022/06/27/a-melilla-une-tentative-d-entree-de-migrants-tourne-au-drame_6132174_3212.html.

[62] A Moroccan city neighbouring Ceuta.

[63] Andersson, *Illegality, Inc.*; El Confidencial and Fundación PorCausa, 'Fronteras SA: la industria del control migratorio'.

[64] Khattabi, 'La reconnaissance faciale'.

infrastructures. Yet, this is not always the case. For Casablanca's first video surveillance projects (2015 and 2017), part of the funding came from a World Bank loan through a project to improve urban transportation. Although the World Bank raised concerns about the use of its funds, and demanded an audit that concluded the video surveillance system was not eligible for funding in the framework of their project, the project was still financed.[65] Recently, the World Bank even approved an increase of 100 million dollars (in addition to the already committed 200 million dollars) to finance further development projects by the city of Casablanca.[66]

Similarly, the EU is extensively funding border control and surveillance technologies in Morocco, with little transparency concerning their use and few requirements in terms of associated human rights protection. For instance, the Moroccan DGSN acquired spying software from the Swedish firm MSAB and the US company *Oxygen Forensic* with funding from the Africa Emergency Fund, set up by the EU in 2015 for its 'fight against irregular migration'.[67] While this technology transfer project was implemented in the context of migration co-operation, the EU has no effective mechanism in place to prevent the misuse of such technologies for other repressive activities. More generally, although the EU has timidly tried to regulate the export of high-risk surveillance,[68] it faces resistance from Members States.[69] Additional rules were put in place in the revision of the EU's Export Control Framework under EU Regulation 2021/821. But although export controls in the EU are becoming increasingly strict, EU Member States still often find ways to export these technologies that are deemed relevant for reasons of national security.[70]

The second cross-cutting issue that emerges from the analysis is that Morocco's existing legal framework through which these projects are launched and implemented provides important obstacles to any kind of public oversight. Most of the tenders that accompany the development of these projects are circulated behind

---

[65] Interviewee 6, 29 June 2022.

[66] World Bank, 'World Bank supports additional financing for the Casablanca Municipal Support Program-for-results', World Bank, Press Release (22 June 2022), www.worldbank.org/en/news/press-release/2022/06/22/world-bank-supports-additional-financing-for-the-casablanca-municipal-support-program-for-results.

[67] Lorenzo D'Agostino, Zach Campbell, and Maximilian Popp, 'Wie die EU Marokkos Überwachungsapparat aufrüstet' [How the EU is arming Morocco's surveillance apparatus] (25 July 2022), Der Spiegel, www.spiegel.de/ausland/marokko-wie-die-eu-rabats-ueberwachungsapparat-aufruestet-a-d3f4c00e-4d39-41ba-be6c-e4f4ba650351.

[68] See Ot L. van Daalen, Joris V.J. van Hoboken, and Melinda Rucz, 'Export control of cybersurveillance items in the new dual-use regulation: The challenges of applying human rights logic to export control' (2022) 48 *Computer Law & Security Review* 105789; European Parliament, 'Draft Report by the Committee of Inquiry to investigate the use of Pegasus and equivalent surveillance spyware' (2022), www.sophieintveld.eu/nl/pega-draft-report.

[69] See Sabrina Winter, 'Spähsoftware für Autokraten – Wie die Europäische Union ihre Kontrollen aufweichte – und Deutschland half' (5 October 2023), FragDenStaat, https://fragdenstaat.de/blog/2023/10/05/wie-die-europaische-union-ihre-kontrollen-aufweichte-und-deutschland-half/.

[70] Wagner, 'Whose politics? Whose rights?'.

closed doors and not made public. Occasional leaks to the press are the main way in which these projects come to public knowledge. However, when tenders are unsuccessful, Moroccan law authorises the contracting authority to proceed through 'over-the-counter' contracts – which do not require any kind of publicity.[71] In other words, the companies that will implement these projects are selected directly by the contracting authority without a public tendering process, raising important questions in terms of transparency of the use of public funds. This will be the case for the 720 million Moroccan Dirhams project that will set up the new video surveillance system in the city of Casablanca.[72] Some interviewees also noted that when these tenders escape public scrutiny, they tend to be attributed to companies that have close ties to the regime.[73]

While the leaked CFTs provide some insights into which cameras are installed and how many, they leave Moroccan citizens and civil society in the dark as to how they will actually be used. Companies deploying these technologies argue that they have no control over their end-use. For instance, a source working for Huawei in Morocco highlighted: 'if Huawei sells video surveillance products, it does not have access to what the final clients do with them, and does not participate in their installation'.[74] Similarly, European companies seem impervious to ethical concerns for the eventual misuse of the technology provided. In the framework of these projects, they 'do what they are asked to without too much resistance'.[75]

Other state institutions that should monitor the ethical implications of the use of AI-enabled surveillance technologies are not raising any concerns either. In its position paper on the digital transition, the Moroccan *Conseil Économique, Social et Environmental* defines AI development as a 'national priority', but it does not touch upon the use of AI in urban video surveillance. Similarly, the *Conseil National des Droits Humains* recently organised an international colloquium to discuss ethical implications of uses of AI, but it dealt with this topic from a purely academic perspective and avoided raising the issue of FRT-based surveillance by state authorities.[76] Lastly, while raising the issue of the storage and analysis of personal data through facial recognition by private actors, the *Commission nationale de contrôle de la protection des données à caractère personnel* seemed untroubled by the use of the same technologies by security services and the exponential increase in the collection of personal data. In short, video surveillance is treated as the sole prerogative of the security apparatus, and so far public monitoring actors have avoided to engage directly with the topic. It seems that, implicitly and explicitly, public security should not be the public's concern.

---

[71] Interviewee 6, 29 June 2022.
[72] Equivalent to roughly 69 million euros.
[73] Interviewee 5, 24 June 2022; interviewee 6, 29 June 2022.
[74] Lefébure and Mahmoud, 'Casablanca, Marrakech, Dakhla'.
[75] Interviewee 6, 29 June 2022.
[76] A press release of the event is available at http://cndh.org.ma/an/taxonomy/term/447.

19.7 CONCLUSION

Our analysis shows that the umbrella argument of public security is applied not only to the use of AI-enhanced technologies in Moroccan urban spaces and at the Moroccan-Spanish border, but also to their deployment, oversight, and monitoring. As a result, the information on whether (and eventually how) high-tech surveillance technology is used is confidential, national security agencies are seemingly exempt from the monitoring of other state institutions, and independent actors are expected to trust that these institutions are acting in citizens' best interest. This makes effective public oversight impossible, and amplifies the potential for it to be used for 'surgical' repression.

The lack of oversight is also nurtured by the absence of a public debate – and ostensibly of public interest – on the matter. An exemplary anecdote is that among the inhabitants of Casablanca, many think that the cameras around the city do not work, and are put there only to bring about an improvement in public behaviour.[77] Kindling a public discussion on the securitisation of public spaces through high-tech surveillance was one of the ambitions of the *TelQuel* issue of July 2021, but so far this debate is still lacking.[78] On the contrary, interviewees perceived Moroccans as being quite ill-informed about related issues of personal data protection.[79]

However, if the future plans inventoried in this chapter are indeed implemented, Morocco is rapidly advancing towards the implementation of AI-enabled technologies in urban and border surveillance, including FRT. It is clear that state institutions plan to use these technologies extensively, and the lack of (trans)national institutional oversight and public debate on the matter should raise concerns about the extent to which such implementation will affect citizens' rights. Until the topic is picked up in public debate and diplomatic relations and reforms in the way this technologies are purchased and governed, Moroccan authorities will continue to conduct widespread AI-enabled surveillance without any oversight or accountability.[80]

---

[77] Interviewee 8, 18 July 2022.

[78] 'Vidéosurveillance: au doigt et à l'œil' (2 July 2021), *TelQuel*, https://telquel.ma/2021/07/02/videosurveillance-au-doigt-et-a-loeil_1727702.

[79] Interviewee 2, 31 May 2022; interviewee 5, 24 June 2022; interviewee 8, 18 July 2022.

[80] Interviewee 8, 18 July 2022.

For EU product safety concerns, contact us at Calle de José Abascal, 56–1°,
28003 Madrid, Spain or eugpsr@cambridge.org.

www.ingramcontent.com/pod-product-compliance
Ingram Content Group UK Ltd.
Pitfield, Milton Keynes, MK11 3LW, UK
UKHW020405060825
461487UK00009B/811